THE FUTURE OF LOVE

Essays in Political Theology

JOHN MILBANK

scm press

For my Mother
Jean Milbank

© John Milbank 2009

First published in the UK in 2009 by SCM Press
Editorial office 13–17 Long Lane
London, EC1A 9PN

SCM Press is an imprint of Hymns Ancient and Modern
(a registered charity)
St Mary's Works, St Mary's Plain,
Norwich, NR3 3BH

www.scm-canterburypress.co.uk

British Library Cataloguing in Publication data

A catalogue record for this book is available
from the British Library

978-0-334-04326-3

Printed in the UK by CPI William Clowes Beccles NR34 7TL

CONTENTS

Contents

PREFACE

September 2008—The Politics of Paradox

The following book contains eighteen essays that have been written over roughly the past twenty-five years. Together they constitute a fragmentary political theology, written from a British perspective, but one that opens itself out to Continental and North American intellectual influences, as well as to global concerns.

It was once said to me, by the late Texan theologian John Clayton, in Lancaster, that he had finally worked out what was "weird" about me: "Most of us, John, are trying to combine German theology with Anglo-Saxon philosophy. A few trendy people go for Continental philosophy as well. But you're doing the opposite—with utter perversity you're trying to combine *British* theology (of all things!) with Continental philosophy—and what is worse, with *French* stuff!"

This is by no means altogether true. But it contains a grain of truth. I have been consistently interested in the "minority report" of British intellectual history that resists reductive empiricism and utility in the name of what Coleridge called "the old, spiritual, Platonic England" as well as in the name of a more radical empiricism, open to the arrival of the strange and the unexpected. This is not simplistically linked to an "anti-science" stance. In the late seventeenth century there was much fashionable discussion about the Scottish Highlands phenomenon of "second sight." But the skeptics and the scoffers here were the "wits," who were equally disdainful of the curious new things being revealed by natural philosophical "experiment." The Royal Society, by contrast, remained rather agnostic, and took so seriously the initial interest of Robert Boyle in this phenomenon that the far north of Britain became for it, for a while, as Michael Hunter puts it, "an occult laboratory."[1] Of course this was to confuse what may be experienced with what can be reliably measured and repeated—but the instance does reveal a non-dogmatic dimension to the British empirical temperament that is not confined to an induction to conclusions from "atomic" items of sensory information. In the case of the nineteenth-century "sages" Coleridge, Newman, and Ruskin, whose perspectives figure strongly in what follows, one sees a particular insular blending of "the empirical" with "the Platonic."

And though I have said that they represent "a minority report," it is nonetheless the case that Anglicanism itself, from Hooker onwards, remained closer in its "Toryism" and "metaphysical bent" to this report on English and British culture than the "mainline" Whig-utilitarian tradition, that was in reality of course the voice of aristocratic and bourgeois dissent, usurping the theoretically official consensus. Yet the "minority report," which tries to articulate this consensus, is also, as the voices of William Cobbett, William Wordsworth, or John Clare reveal, the deepest tradition of the British populace and its various regional expressions.

My main concern, though, is with how this diffuse cultural current, at once theological *and* philosophical, as well as literary, has informed political thought and practice. Here I engage with a tradition of British political reflection, largely Anglo-Catholic and Catholic, which has a great deal in common with that of Catholic Social Teaching on the continent, and which, like that tradition, has been in continuous debate with secular socialism and Hegelianism-Marxism. I try to carry forward the thinking of both traditions in response to the circumstances of recent times and to "postmodern" philosophies. The scope of my theopolitical analyses extends to matters of culture and cultural pluralism, government, economics, history, ecclesiology, and pedagogy.

Mostly I have let the original versions of these essays stand, only revising in order to remove anachronisms and what now seem irrelevancies or outright mistakes. The essays are arranged thematically rather than chronologically, but it will be clear to the reader that sometimes my thought has shifted or evolved over the years. However, I have deliberately eliminated all that I would now renounce, and so as they now stand I

1. See *The Occult Laboratory* edited by Michael Hunter. This volume contains several original texts, including Robert Boyle's *An Interview with Lord Tarbat, 3 October 1678* and the Scottish Minister Robert Kirk's later extraordinary neoplatonic defence of second sight and fairy belief, *The Secret Commonwealth*.

regard these essays as consistent with each other. As I revised them though, I was struck by the degree to which—collectively or sometimes individually—they appear to combine opposite tendencies. There is both subtlety and robustness here, just as there is both radicalism and conservatism. Only the "middle" of an anaemic liberalism is consistently and relentlessly refused. I suspect that there will be many readers who will like the "subtle and radical" on the one hand, but not the "robust and conservative" on the other, while there will be many others with exactly the reverse set of discriminations. However, for my own part, I consider that I am only understood and agreed with when the reader is prepared to endorse a "subtle robustness" which is a "robust subtlety," and a "radical conservatism" which is a "conservative radicalism."

This paradoxicality I believe, makes my political theology greatly relevant to the global juncture at which we now stand.

As Phillip Blond has suggested, there are now three crucial global forces in the world: Capitalist rationality, Islam, and Christianity. And of the latter two, the global reach and universalism of Christianity is far more serious and far more likely to prevail in the long term. This means that the anomaly pointed out almost a century ago by Hilaire Belloc is likely to pose its cultural contradiction ever more strongly upon the world stage. This is the manifest gap between the teachings of Christianity that still undergird Western morality on the one hand and the theory and practice of capitalism on the other.[2]

I believe, along with Radical Orthodoxy in general, that only the Church has the theoretical and practical power to challenge the global hegemony of capital and to create a viable politico-economic alternative. I stand thereby in a long tradition of Anglican and Catholic Christian socialism, which has always insisted on the necessity of the "Christian" component for the "Socialist" one. In that sense I have always stood proudly amongst those who see themselves as "conservative theologically, radical politically."

But over the years I have become more aware of the potential for smugness and inertia in that perspective. One can gently challenge it in three ways. First, there is a dimension that I have already hinted at. Can Christians really, fundamentally, categorize themselves as either left or right? Surely, as André de Muralt has argued, both the ideas of "the rule of

2. See for this and some of what follows, Hilaire Belloc, *The Servile State*.

One," of the sovereign center, and of the "rule of the Many," of individuals either in contracted dispersion or collective unity, are equally "nominalist"—both genealogically and ontologically?[3] For both deny primary real relation, the real universal that is "the common good," and the role of "the few," whether that of the guiding virtuous elite, or of the mediating institutions of civil society. But "right" and "left" define themselves variously in terms of either "the One" or the "the Many," both nominalistically construed.

Today, of course, what we really have is two versions of a "left" celebration of the "Many" either as individuals or as a democratically voting mass. For reasons still not yet sufficiently accounted for by historians and social theorists, we have a "liberal right" stressing economic negative liberty and a "liberal left," stressing cultural and sexual negative liberty. In reality, of course, the two liberalisms are triumphing both at once and in secretly collusive harmony. So perhaps what still sustains party conflict is alternating anxieties amongst the populace about the inevitable insecurities generated by now economic and now cultural "freedom" in different temporal phases.

It follows that the very division of left and right assumes a nominalist social ontology that of course I would reject. And it is also critically important to remind oneself that this division only postdates the French revolution. This has created a curious historical delusion from which almost no one is really free. For we suppose that the premodern is somehow allied with "the right," just as barbarous journalists frequently imagine that the divine right of kings was a medieval theory, when it was in reality an early modern one. But pre-nominalist modernity was neither left nor right, neither "progressivist" nor "reactionary"—it was simply "other" to most of our assumed sociopolitical categories.

There is a further point to be made here. When the French revolutionaries invented "left" and "right," they arguably took us back to paganism and indeed they often explicitly supposed that they were doing so. For characteristically, the ancient Greeks lined up philosophies of the spirit and of "ideal forms" with aristocracy and philosophies of matter with democracy. It is as if they assumed that the latter was always a matter of LCD and not of HCF. But as I have already suggested, the Christian revolution cuts right across this categorization. Instead of siding with "the

---

3. Muralt, *L'Unité de la Philosophie Politique.*

noble" over against "the base," or inversely with "the base" over against "the noble," it paradoxically democratizes the noble: hence Paul addresses his interlocutors as "all kings." Yet at the same time, if there is now a new possibility of the spread of virtue (virtue being redefined as the more generally possible attitudes of love and trust, immune to the instance of "moral luck" as usually understood), there is still a political place for the superior role of the more virtuous and of those appointed to be the "guardians" of virtue, the virtuosos of *charisma*.

But unlike those paradigms of virtue hitherto, "the heroes," these Christian "pastors" (who are "shepherds" like Plato's guardians) will frequently remain both mocked and invisible, since they may lack the glamour of obvious "honor," and may need to retain a hidden "outlaw" status in order both to escape the need to appease the masses, upon whose adulation manifest power depends, and to directly execute a summary justice that the procedures of inevitably inflexible law might foil. This is the theme brilliantly explored in Christopher Nolan's Batman film, *The Dark Knight*, with its explicit Platonic resonances concerning the noble lie and so forth. But the film leaves us with the Platonic *aporia* of a division between the ignoble hero-ruler (a J. F. Kennedy figure) whom the people must *believe* to be noble if they are to have any ideals and the genuinely noble outlaw-guardian who must pursue virtue in uncorrupted secrecy (thereby passing the test of Gyges's ring).

The only dimension that can in part resolve this aporetic tension is the Christian one of sacramental ordination and anointed monarchy. The ideal symbolic dimension of the pastoral role implicitly corrects, with its equitable outlawry, any abuse of legal authority—it also to an extent permits the enactment of such equity to the degree that awe at sacred charisma can override the blandishments of popular concession to which mere democracy must remain prone. And yet—save for the example of Lear on the heath in the storm, or Walter Scott's Richard the Lionheart in Sherwood Forest—the bishop-as-apostle rather than the monarch surpasses even this possibility of visible purity by stepping, like Paul, in and out of visibility, in alternation of command and vagabondage. Thus likewise there is still a monarch at the summit of the *ecclesia*—but it is the crucified, resurrected, ascended, and so apparently absent Jesus, who died as a king but had nowhere on earth to lay his head, and it is this pattern that is followed by the Church hierarchy which mediates his authority.

The politic-ecclesial pattern suggested by the NT therefore remains classically democratic/aristocratic/monarchic. Following the norms of antique political thought, this has often in Christian history implied that one or the other stress should dominate according to the prevalence or otherwise of virtue. One could nonetheless validly say that the ultimate bias of Christianity is democratic, because its aim is that all should love and trust, all should become virtuous. In this sense it has a populist bias "to the left." But this is not exactly "the modern left," because Christianity (unlike Bush and Blair) sees no automatic merit in democracy in all circumstances, nor any validity in the notion that the will of the majority should always prevail. Its reasons for favouring democracy are rather that the entire truth of Christianity exists in harmonious dispersal amongst the body of Christ (eschatologically the entire human race and the entire cosmos) and that agreement in the truth requires ideally a free consensus.

The post-revolutionary "left," however, tends to revive a pagan sense of democracy as LCD: it links democracy to naturalistic materialism and to a sophistic individualism. I constantly contrast this with John Ruskin's genuinely Christian and explicitly at once "Tory" and "communist" desire to extend norms of nobility, of self-regulation of standards of behaviour, work, outcomes, and protection of members from the "liberal" professions also to mercantile and artisanal pursuits.

It is mainly for this reason that "a Christian left" is not really situated within the same spectrum as the secular left—for it both aspires to democratize excellence and to grant an educative and political role to the exponents of excellence in order to balance out the verdict of the many. But this requirement does not compromise democracy—rather it enables it. For democracy is not an infinite regress—no one finally votes on *the dominant options presented to people*, and if these are not the work of disciplined elites, educated towards virtue as well as knowledge, then they will be the work of propagandists, of a corrupted elite, as now prevails.

The second reason for questioning an over-glib "conservative in theology/radical in politics" equation is that one has to integrate one's politics with one's ecclesiology. The Lamennaisian combination of hierarchy in metaphysical truth, democracy in pragmatic politics, will not quite do. Of course it is by no means entirely false: in Church affairs what matters is truth, not opinion, and so hierarchy must prevail. In secular affairs, though, a second-best pragmatic peace may usually be the priority, and therefore consensus must prevail at the cost otherwise of unacceptable violence and outright inhumanity.

Yet in the end there can be, for Christianity, no such absolute contrast. The earthly city is valid insofar as it serves the heavenly, and from the outset Christianity has modified the role of the political ruler in a "pastoral" direction (sometimes for ill as well as good). He becomes more a kind of ecclesial pastor of material affairs—which always have an implication for our salvation.

Here we need to balance Western with Eastern Christian perspectives: the "monarch" may be properly subordinate to "the priest," and his dealing in law and coercive violence is now (uniquely by Christianity) desacralized because of its ambivalence—and yet the "kingly" role remains Christological insofar as it foreshadows the integrity of the resurrected body, when the material will fully shine with the glory of the spiritual. In the end Christ's priesthood fades, and his kingship remains. Perhaps, therefore, something authentically "Byzantine" has shone out in the Anglican stress upon the "incarnational" aspect of sociopolitical transformation—even if this has often been perverted by support for the modern absolutely sovereign and disciplinary state.

The sense that the secular arm is "within" as well as "outside" the Church accords then with the need also for secular hierarchy, for the reasons that I have explained. But inversely, one can argue that we need more participatory (*not* formally representative) democracy inside the Church. This is because, as Newman pointed out, the "correctness" of doctrine must finally be tested in practice by the assent of all. For Christian truth abides more fundamentally in the entirety of liturgical and pastoral life than it does in abstract reflection.

Political theory and ecclesiology must finally then be of one piece. Both involve a classical mixture of democracy, aristocracy, and kingship, even if the Christian *demos* is paradoxically anointed and Christian "kingship" is paradoxically kenotic.

The third reason for questioning a facile Christian leftism is circumstantial. In the face of the ever-increasing triumph of capitalism in our times, secular socialism has all but vanished and the left increasingly understands itself as liberal, and frequently, in addition, as atheist and anti-religious. The minority who have continued seriously to question the free market have increasingly begun to realise that in some measure an opposition to this can only be "conservative"—and indeed I argue below (in an essay that dates from the 1980s) that originally in France socialism itself was somewhat "counter-enlightenment" in character. This is because only what is "sacred," what possesses a value that reason cannot fully fathom—that which, therefore, is validated only by modes of usually religious tradition—is truly immune from commodification. Equally, a non-nominalist politics, stressing the role of "the Few" both in the mode of mediating associations and of virtuous elites, must perforce appeal back to the Middle Ages and seek to re-commence what Belloc referred to as its unfinished project of freeing people from antique slavery by assuring the widest possible distribution of land and capital which will allow both individual creativity and collective sharing and conviviality. (The latter being something which Belloc's overly modern liberal perspective—despite everything—failed properly to emphasise. It is for this reason that one can correct his "distributism" with the articulation of a "distributist socialism").

It is also the case that a secular liberal left is unable metaphysically to validate even its own liberalism, because its abandonment of any belief in the spiritual reality of "mind" or "soul" leaves it with only a sham belief in either freedom or ideals worth struggling for. Inevitably it plays more and more lip service to "scientific" diagnoses of human behaviour and more and more favors a utilitarian state-plus-market control of human beings designed to facilitate their maximally efficient collective functioning. The danger of the current financial crisis is that the Keynesian measures to which we should properly for the moment return (and may *have* to return) will mutate into a new blending of market monopoly and state oligarchy, merely further politicizing the power of the very rich.

In the long term, to exit the Hayekian/Keynesian cycles which capitalism objectively imposes (as Marxists have correctly understood—see chapter 5 below), we require the more stable dynamism of a genuinely collectivist (and so socialist) distributist/corporatist economy. This would be built upon a socially-judged recognition of the inherent relative value of natural and produced things and the inherent relative needs and deserts of all human beings as all workers as well as consumers. Of course, only the general embrace of a realist metaphysics of transcendence can render this possible. The way forward therefore, has to be thoroughly "paradoxical."

With the above provisos, I stand on the whole within that tradition of non-statist Christian Socialism which regards modern statism as involving the support of the very rich, a guarantee of their finances, and an enabling additional support through "welfare" of their dispossessed workforce. However, one needs also to recognize a wider family resemblance with many variants of Christian social teaching which characteristically stress subsidiarity (the distribution of money and power to appropriate levels, not necessarily the lowest) and the break-up of central sovereignty through the operation of intermediary associations. These theories can appear as relatively more "left" or "right," yet all in reality question the left/right distinction in its secular form. In relation to the latter, Christians must pursue a politics of seeming paradox from apparently "opposite" vantage points. Thus some within Radical Orthodoxy may follow Phillip Blond in his espousal of a new British form of "Red Toryism." Others, currently the majority, will follow my own brand of "Blue Socialism"—socialism with a Burkean tinge, now common to many of the more reflective on the left, including some within the centre-left (anti New Labour) British Labour party "Compass Group."[4]

But these differences may not be what matters. In either case the debate is about how one would bring about an "initially" just distribution that would render reactive state "re-distribution" mostly redundant and how this would be sustained. These debates concern the role of nuclear and extended families, of co-operatives, of trade guilds, of mutual banks, housing associations and credit unions, and of the law in setting firewalls between business practices, defining the acceptable limits of usury and interest, and the principles that must govern the fair setting of wages and prices. Above all perhaps they concern how we can turn all people into owners and joint-owners, abolishing the chasm between the mass who only earn or receive welfare and so are dependent and the minority who own in excess.

This abolition will then allow a more genuine, multi-stepped and educationally dynamic hierarchy of virtue to operate. For in the economic sphere also there needs to be a mixture of the democratic and the paternalistically guided: some enterprises are adapted to the cooperative, others require more hierarchical corporations. But the corporation based upon Christian principles must, like the units of "feudalism" (though that is a mis-description) in the Middle Ages, combine political and economic functions, since the engineered indifference of these to each other is not a

4. Outside the United States, of course, red is always the color of the Left, blue of the Right.

division of spheres preserving liberty, but rather an abuse which permits both "the purely economic" and the "purely political" to enjoy a nihilistic sway. For defined in purity apart from each other they both cease to involve moral concern and oversight and instead come to have an exclusive regard for the positive power of money as such or the positive power of law as such. By contrast, exchange for the social good must also be "political" in character, while legislation for the social good has to have regard to the economic in all its aspects.

This mention of a "corporatist" aspect is bound of course to raise charges of fascism, as are those paradoxical titles that seem to invoke a crossover of left and right. But this is ahistorical—the Christian Democratic parties at the end of WWII for a short time (before they succumbed to the lure of liberalism) sought to recapture from fascism principles of Catholic social teaching which it had perverted. For fascism involves a secular cult of state, race, or military power that really lines up with modern political nominalism: it is bound in reality (as experience has always proved) increasingly to eradicate the role of the few and so both to exalt the One at the sovereign centre and to disguise through *ersatz* paternalistic pretense the market manipulation of the Many at the margins.

It should be added here that it is possibly only *religion* that can provide the element of tacit binding ethos that prevents both distributism and corporatism from drifting back towards the twin dominance of the state and monopoly capitalism. More specifically, one needs the *Church* as an organisation in continuous excess of the state to coordinate, without suppressing, the diverse activities of intermediate associations. (Lack of this, as William Cavanaugh has argued, has often led to the perversion of Christian Democratic projects in Latin America.[5]) And when one asks, as one must, how one is initially to bring a radical distribution about, then the answer can only be through the construction of a new mass cultural ethos which will empower a new sort of elite who will win self-respect for their social generosity rather than their wealth (this will then be their "self-interest") and so will be able to ensure that governments will encourage through new legislation, tax structures, and regulation of banking the emergence of a radical distribution. But perhaps it is only the Church that has the capacity to inspire and coordinate such a switch in ethos.

This ethos would be radically Catholic rather than radically Protestant. An aspect of the deadlock in British and American politics today is

5. Cavanaugh, *Torture and Eucharist.*

the way in which the hinterland of the left's assumptions remain deter-minatively Protestant. Indeed its subjectivism, emotionalism, restrictive puritanism, iconoclasm, and opposition to high culture owe more in the end to the Reformation than they do to the Enlightenment. These atti-tudes are all powerless to resist capitalism and bureaucracy, because both are profoundly promoted by the mainstream Protestant legacy. Even the radical Protestant legacy is in the end unable to think beyond individu-alism, sectarian isolation, and collectivism—which is but individualism dialectically inverted or else writ large. Anabaptism also is usually mired in the social metaphysics of the *via moderna,* or else its anti-metaphysical perpetuation—though one can allow that certain British dissenting radi-cals, like William Blake (as Peter Ackroyd has suggested) were strangely echoing, in a newly creative way, the suppressed British Catholic past.

By contrast, it is only a "Catholic center" more extreme than either of the extremes, because it points metacritically to a different plane, which can think and act its way out of our current heretical, immoral, and neo-pagan political morass.

ACKNOWLEDGMENTS

The following chapters of this book appeared in an earlier form in various journals and books. The author and publisher gratefully acknowledge permission to reprint from these publications:

1. "Divine Logos and Human Communication: A Recuperation of Coleridge" was orginally published in *Neue-Zeitschrift für Systematische Theologie und Religionphilosophie* 29, no. 1 (January, 1987) 56–73.

2. "Religion, Culture, and Anarchy: The Attack on the Arnoldian Vision" was originally published as "Religion, Culture and Anarchy," *New Blackfriars* 69, no. 820 (October, 1988) 436–45.

4. "Were the 'Christian Socialists' Socialists?" was originally published in *Papers of the Nineteenth Century Theology Working Group*, American Academy of Religion, vol. 14 (1989) 86–95.

5. "The Body by Love Possessed: Christianity and Late Capitalism in Britain" was originally published in *Modern Theology* 3, no. 1 (October, 1986) 35–65.

6. "On Baseless Suspicion: Christianity and the Crisis of Socialism" was originally published in *New Blackfriars* 69, no. 812 (January, 1988) 4–19.

7. "Enclaves, or Where is the Church" was originally published in *New Blackfriars* 73, no. 861 (April, 1991) 341–52.

8. "On Theological Transgression" was originally published in *Arachne* 2, no. 1 (1995) 145–76.

9. "The Invocation of Clio" was originally published as "The Invocation of Clio: A Response," *Journal of Religious Ethics* 33, no. 1 (March 2005) 3–44.

10. "Sovereignty, Empire, Capital, and Terror" was originally published in *South Atlantic Quarterly* 101, no. 2 (Spring 2002) 304–24.

11. "Liberality versus Liberalism" was originally published in *Religion and Political Thought*, ed. Michael Hoelzl and Graham War (London: Continuum, 2006) 225–36.

12. "Stale Expressions: The Management-Shaped Church" was originally published in *Studies in Christian Ethics* 21, no. 1 (April 2008) 117–28.

13. "The End of Dialogue" was originally published in *Christian Uniqueness Reconsidered*, ed. Gavin D'Costa (Maryknoll: Orbis, 1990) 174–92.

14. "The Conflict of the Faculties" was originally published in *Zutrauen zur Theologie*, ed. A-K. Finke and J. Zehner (Berlin: Wichern, 2000) 381–93.

15. "Faith, Reason, and Imagination: The Study of Theology and Philosophy in the Twenty-First Century" was originally published as "Faith, Reason and Imagination: The Study of Theology and Philosophy in the 21st Century" in *Transversalités* 101, no. 1 (Jan–March 2007) 69–86.

16. "'Postmodern Critical Augustinianism': A Short *Summa* in Forty-Two Responses to Unasked Questions" was originally published in *Modern Theology* 7, no. 3 (April 1991) 225–37.

17. "The Transcendality of the Gift: A Summary in Answer to Twelve Questions" was originally published as "The Gift and the Given" in "Problematising Global Knowledge", ed. Mike Featherstone et al., special issue, *Theory, Culture and Society* 23, nos. 2–3 (March–May 2006) 444–48.

18. "The Future of Love: A Reading of Pope Benedict's Encyclical Deus Caritas Est" was originally published in *Communio* 33, no. 3 (2006) 368–74.

PART I

Theology and English Culture

1

DIVINE *LOGOS* AND HUMAN COMMUNICATION

A Recuperation of Coleridge

Coleridge's writings can be interpreted as a series of fragmentary notes for his great unwritten work *On the Communicative Logos*. As this title indicates, Coleridge sought a single doctrine embracing both a meta-physical theology and a theory of language and literature. Yet in addition to this, "communication" was for Coleridge also a political matter. So if the development of this central theme is to be adequately understood, one must trace the constant interweaving of political concerns with aesthetic-cultural and philosophical-cum-religious ones. Coleridge's work constitutes—at least in its aspiration—a sort of theological-political-poetic *tractatus*.

In this chapter I shall argue that if one resists abstraction from this complexity, then Coleridge's intellectual development must be divided into three integrated phases. The first phase is here represented especially by the *Lectures on Revealed Religion*, the second by *The Friend*, and the third by the *Lay Sermons*. In the early phase I shall outline Coleridge's biblically based political radicalism, and in the middle period the lapse into political conservatism that coincides with his conversion to Kantian idealism. The late phase I describe as that of the "imperfectly emergent" Coleridge, and here I trace the resurgence of a political biblicism in an altered form, which remains of relevance to contemporary theology.

The Circles of the Lake

In his early poem *Religious Musings*, when he is giving an account of the development of human civilizations, Coleridge writes:

> O'er waken'd realms Philosophers and Bards
> Spread in concentric circles; they whose souls
> Conscious of their high dignities from God
> Brook not wealth's rivalry.[1]

One might almost say that these lines indicate the most constant structure of Coleridge's entire thought. There is a class of inspired people who can be variously considered as poets, prophets, philosophers, or legislators; a class which existed most perfectly in antiquity in the times of a precise coincidence of all these roles, but a class whose function must be constantly revived if true human culture is to continue. These philosopher-poets "spread in concentric circles" because they are able to mediate continuities both in space and time. They establish a process of communication, of human interchange, which represents a constant counterpoise to the economic exchanges of the marketplace.

The image of the concentric circles occurs again in *The Lectures on Revealed Religion*. Coleridge compares the processes of human cultural and moral development to "the expanding circles of a lake."[2] Here the immediate context is his defense of privileged familial and friendly affections against William Godwin's demand for an indifferent rational benevolence. In accordance with his own associationist psychology, the early Coleridge stresses that morality is a matter of social instincts that can only grow from the imaginative ties to particular places and persons arising in childhood. It is the empirical contingency of the route towards a general ethical concern that allows both the early Coleridge and the early Wordsworth to insist on the fundamental moral role of poetry and the imagination. As Hans Aarsleff has argued, one has here to see the positive role of the Lockean tradition as mediated by thinkers like Condillac in the evolution of the Romantic outlook.[3] Locke's "way of ideas" had already led him to argue that there were radical differences between various human cultures because they were based on a series of contingent and arbitrary

1. Coleridge, *Poetical Works*, 61.
2. Coleridge, *Lectures on Revealed Religion*, 162.
3. Aarsleff, "Woodsworth, Language and Romanticism."

associations, able to persist only because of the uniquely conserving role of language.

The drawback of the Lockean analysis from the point of view of a Coleridgean aesthetics would be that that while it indicated a pre-eminent role for linguistic creativity in relation to cultural idiosyncrasies, it could not show that this creativity was linked to a growth in real knowledge. By contrast, Hartley's necessitarianism at first provided a far more beguiling model for Coleridge the poet, for here it was argued that a succession of purely empirical associations, unregulated by any pre-given rational norm, was nonetheless part of a providentially guided process leading to the highest possible knowledge.

Coleridge applied the theories of Hartley and his follower Priestley to the narratives of the Bible, and thereby tried to see "the expanding circles of the lake" in terms of the cultural becoming of the human race, and not just the development of the individual. However, this biblical engagement also caused him to *modify* the necessitarian perspective, well before his engagement with idealism. The series of influences to which primitive human beings are subject is now seen in terms of a primary divine language to which human beings are capable of a free response, but on which they depend for their future growth. Coleridge probably takes over from Warburton the notion that all the "irrational" features of the Old Testament—miracles, prophecies, and sacrifices, which were so ridiculed by the deists—are really evidence of the divine providential wisdom in accommodating himself to primitive intellects which are only able to think by means of a "real language" of concrete symbols, taken from nature.

The Hebrews were thought by Coleridge to share this language with other primitive peoples. It is linked to a predominance of greed, fear, superstition, and envy. However, with the Hebrews, these aspects are muted because of their political constitution that has been directly instituted by God. The law of Jubilee, the law of tithes, and the distribution of the land place limits on the role of material accumulation. The injunctions against idols ensure that there are no arbitrary and bloodthirsty gods who require propitiation, and this, thinks Coleridge, is *politically* significant. He takes his notions of the ideal character of the Hebrew theocracy from Moses Lowman,[4] but places especial stress on the role of the Levites and the Nabim, the priestly and prophetic classes who are sustained by the contribution of tithes.

4. Lowman, *On the Civil Government of the Hebrews.*

For Coleridge, the great contrast between the Hebrews and other peoples is that, whereas in the latter case the prophetic class arose later, as an outcome of the achievements of *civilization*, in Israel they were from the beginning the initiators, and thus Israel was always a *culture*. Here Coleridge's emphasis, both in the early and middle periods of his writings, is always frankly Platonic—the initiators are first and foremost *prisci philosophici* rather than *priscae poetae*.

Within Israel the priestly and prophetic classes are considered to have played two important functions. First of all they were the recipients of surplus wealth and therefore functioned as a kind of safety valve preventing the growth of usury or inequitable accumulation.

Secondly, they were instituted by God as a providential substitute for the lack of writing among ancient peoples. Their role was to ensure continuity, to preserve the records. In this function as historians they were also, naturally, the legislators. And also poets, in so far as imagistic discourse was the language of primitive humanity, and peculiarly well-adapted to mnemonic tasks. Prophecy is understood by Coleridge to be in direct continuity with this legal "provision for the future," though at this stage Coleridge still thinks of prophecy in characteristically eighteenth-century "dogmatic-rationalist" terms as purely a matter of a providential provision of "evidence of Christianity" for later peoples.

This clerical class exists then, to uphold the Hebrew theocracy, which means, precisely, to guard against the growth of a market economy, for the early Coleridge identified original sin with private property that led to possessiveness, and he insisted (because of this associationist stance) on precisely that order of causation. Nevertheless this picture was not a statically utopian one. The Hebrew theocracy existed to educate people out of the need for private property and for coercive law altogether. The full possibility of a society based upon the sharing of goods, and on perfect collective agreement, was finally proclaimed, according to Coleridge, by Jesus. It was this ideal which the young Coleridge sought to realize firstly in his "Pantisocracy," and secondly in his domestic rural retreats.

Two things must now be said about Coleridge's early politics to conclude this section. First, as has been shown by Kelvin Everest and David Aers, his desire for retirement was not an escape from politics.[5] To understand this one must realize that his "Christian Socialist" vision was much

5. See Everest, *Coleridge's Secret Ministry*, esp. 69–97, and Aers, "Coleridge and the Egg."

more radical than that of even his revolutionary contemporaries. There was no working-class movement with which Coleridge could have identified, because at this time what movements there were were dominated by a Painite version of capitalist ideology. Coleridge considered that the "spirit of trade" had corrupted the language and culture of every class, and that in consequence the only hope consisted in the educative work that might be done by those still in touch with positive values. The latter were seen as derivable only from a tradition that, though imperfectly developed, had at least not been totally overlain by the spirit of mere utilitarian calculation and self-interest, a spirit which Coleridge saw as affecting language itself, the most basic medium of social existence.

Thus to characterize Coleridge's approach to politics at this stage as simply "idealist" begs too many questions concerning the structurally fundamental character of communication. His vision only becomes culpably idealist when, in his middle period, he opts, not for the overcoming of the market, but for a dualist co-existence of the wealth-seeking market on the one hand, and truth-seeking literary communication on the other.

The second thing to be said is that Coleridge's early radicalism is totally inseparable from his dissenting Christianity. His "socialist" perspective did not and could not have emerged from the inheritance of the Enlightenment, but is culled from the "underground" survival of the ideas of the Levellers and the Diggers. The debate with Godwin shows this up acutely. William Godwin's thought accommodated liberty and equality, but not, in a sense, fraternity. His anarchism remained in the tradition of possessive individualism. Property is to be equally divided, but not shared, and the claims of a "common good" cannot normally override individual right. So, for example, promises cannot be considered binding because this usurps the atomistic individual's persistent "possession" of his own volition, his right to change his mind at any time. Similarly, marriage is considered an infringement of one's self-ownership, one's property rights in one's own person. And in Godwin there is no passage from associationism to developmentalism; the rational and objectively benevolent individual must show no special favor to those with whom he happens to be closely associated.

Against all this, Coleridge claimed, like the seventeenth-century English radicals, that the earth belongs to its Creator, God, and that people only have rights over it in so far as they use it creatively for the common good. From his radical dissenting account of divine "accommodation" he asserts that ideal communities do not spring from an introspective grasp of rational principles, but from the slow growth of human affections from the more immediate to the more general, a growth in which the starting point can never, in fact, be lost sight of. Promises are seen as vital in ensuring social continuity in future time, and marital fidelity is declared to be the necessary beginning of a wider faithfulness.

In the early Coleridge, then, collectivism is only enabled by cultural identity that derives from a particular tradition, which must be linguistic-religious in character. Any atavistic dangers in this form of thought are, at this stage, obviated by the eschewing of nationalism, the political state, and all forms of violent coercion.

The Politics of The Friend

In this section I want to argue that Coleridge's conversion to an establishment viewpoint belongs more to his adoption of Kantianism (which is encountered during his sojourn in Göttingen in 1799) than to his progress towards Christian orthodoxy, which was less marked in his middle years. Although I am here identifying a perspective that emerges in Coleridge's "second period," it is not a perspective that he ever perfectly surmounted.

There are several misapprehensions regarding Coleridge's relation to German idealism. In particular, it is not true, as still sometimes seems to be implied, that a stress on the epistemologically fundamental character of creativity could grow only out of Kant's subjectivism. It has already been seen how there is a partial grasp of this within the empiricist tradition. But the thesis that a specifically linguistic creativity is indispensable for all knowledge, and even its prime character, emerged in its most radical form among those who were the heirs of Baroque rhetoric: Vico in Italy, Young and Lowth in England, and finally Hamann in Germany as their proto-Romantic successor. The rationalist tradition, by contrast, was from its beginning in Descartes an effort to contain the theme of finite creativity as it had developed in the Renaissance. So we find a constant attempt in this tradition, as with the occasionalists, to reserve finite causality and true knowledge of nature and history to God alone.

Yet the paradoxical effect of the Cartesian attempt to, as it were, draw up unambiguous spheres of human and divine causal influence, is to make human creativity demiurgically absolute within a purely "internal" realm of knowledge and perception, and in the rational construction of ethical laws for spiritual beings. This essential structure fully persists in all the Kantian critiques.

In so far as some of the Romantics are heirs of the rationalists and idealists, they also make creativity an "inward" process: they regard the real, outward, linguistic creation as simply the "expression" of a prior inward act of the imagination, itself expressive of the dynamically rational being of the autonomous subject. Thus in both Shelley and the Coleridge of the middle period the concrete processes of art and even those of the imagination are always finally subordinated to the workings of the rational spirit. This is surely a less radical vision of creativity than that contained for example in Vico, for whom the primary field of creation is quite specifically language, and thereby history itself. Likewise, in Hamann and Herder, who define their thought *over against* Kant, one finds an explicit refutation of linguistic instrumentalism. This is missing in Coleridge at this stage, because while he insists in "Cratylist" fashion that language exists in a natural relation to thought, he still in his middle period thinks of rational ideas as enjoying a pre-linguistic primacy.

In this perspective one can see the influence of Kant upon Coleridge's poetics as largely a negative one. Creativity becomes, as it were, exiled within, and its connection with the making of history is lost to view. Particularly damaging is Coleridge's adoption of a scheme/content dualism, whereby mental contents are exactly allocated: either to a mass of atomistic information on the one hand, or to a set of *a priori*, organizing categories on the other. In this perspective everything "external" is essentially passive with respect to a creative action upon it, while on the other hand formation always yields primacy to categorial form. The image-making work of the imagination has to take all its stimulus from within itself, and finally from the reason which informs it.

It is for this reason that in *The Friend* the aesthetic dimension temporarily recedes in Coleridge's consideration of politics. There is no real room for an essential work of the imagination in the face of a dualism of schematizing "reason" over against generalizing "understanding." Coleridge certainly appreciates the Kantian thesis that schemes and principles are only intuited in their making possible of empirical observation and calculation, but it is precisely the once-and-for-all immediacy of this relation that dispenses with the primacy of the constant mediation performed by the imagination.

The dualism is compounded on the moral plane where Coleridge has now accepted Kant's view of ethics as a matter of private, inward assent to absolute duties. In contrast to this, the public sphere of politics is seen by Coleridge as a series of material contingencies. The embracing of Kant, curiously enough, allows Coleridge also to embrace a very English view of politics in which principles are thought of as a private affair, guiding politicians in the background, while the details of state affairs are largely to be governed by considerations of prudential expediency. The division of Church and state is conceived on the same lines, so that Coleridge can say that ecclesiastical persuasion and state coercion are "two polar forces of one and the same power."[6]

Despite Coleridge's attack on a utilitarian calculation of consequences, he accepts that ideals should only be applied in so far as "circumstances" permit. On the one hand, one must have a "distinct notion of the desirable ENDS, in the complete accomplishment of which would consist the perfection of such a thing, or its ideal excellence"; on the other hand, this must be supplemented by a "calm and kindly mode of feeling" that notes "the circumstances which prevent these ends from being all perfectly realised in the particular thing which we are to examine."[7] Moral ends are to be conceived privately and in abstraction from social practice, while politics is characterized by the inhibition of ideal realization. When Coleridge embraces Burke's stress on political prudence, it is quite clear that this has the non-Aristotelian meaning of the empirical judgment of contingent facts. An example of the prudential adaptation to circumstance for Coleridge is the British attack on the Danish fleet in Copenhagen Harbor without prior declaration of war. This was justified, he thinks, because enemy acts meant that a *de facto* state of war already existed, and a declaration would have robbed the action of the advantage of surprise. This is seen as an application of a "principle" (of prior declaration) to a particular situation.

Thus in ethics and politics Coleridge's Kantian idealism maintained a collusive co-existence with a "circumstantialism" that could serve the same establishment purposes as the utilitarianism he so indignantly rejected.

6. Coleridge, *The Friend*, 94–95.
7. Ibid., 249.

Going beyond Kant

The necessary prelude to the politics of the third, "imperfectly emergent" Coleridge, was a growing critique of Kant, often implicit, sometimes explicit. Although he never perfectly or consistently articulates this, there is, in the later writings, a constant moving beyond Kant's scheme/content dualism.

Donald MacKinnon claimed that Coleridge did not grasp the difference between the pre-critical Kant and the Kant of the *Critique of Pure Reason*.[8] In fact, as Stephen Prickett later pointed out, Coleridge makes it clear that he well understands the vital distinction between purest schematism and actually constitutive metaphysical ideas.[9] However, he evidently wishes to plead for the latter. If, as is arguable, Kant's denial of the possibility of transcendent metaphysics in the sphere of speculative reason collapses once the scheme/content dualism is overcome, then any indications of such an overcoming in Coleridge may tend to legitimate his metaphysical project.

There are several such signs. In the first place, in the *Biographia Literaria*, despite Coleridge's rude remarks about the Scottish common-sense philosophy, there are points in his own argument where he appears to be actually echoing the opinions of Thomas Reid. There is the characteristically Reidian attack on empiricism as substituting for our direct and unmediated knowledge of reality a series of unverifiable fictions about the transmission to us from objects of subtle bits of matter that somehow turn into ideas, and from which the mind "deduces" the existence of an external world. Like Reid, Coleridge thinks that this empiricism ultimately leads to idealism and skepticism, which he rejects. Coleridge's notion of "outness" (taken from Berkeley, but shorn of immaterialism), which he speaks of as given to "common sense," and as an unmediated presence of being to knowledge, seems somewhat akin to Reid's "simple realism,"

---

8. MacKinnon, "Coleridge and Kant." MacKinnon is right to protest at the unqualified language of "immediate rational intuition of transcendence" and of supposed speculative certainties, like the Newtonian system, in Coleridge, for example in certain passages of *Aids to Reflection*. However, the later Coleridge supplies an account of the complementary necessity for discursive mediation in religious apprehension that depends precisely on breaking with Kant's residual too immediate intuitionism. In the *Opus Maximum*, Coleridge speaks of "a pure sensuous *intuition* of God—or—we know God by the *sense* as distinguished from the *senses*" (Coleridge, *Opus Maximum*, 275).

9. Prickett, *Romanticism and Religion*, 22.

which was based on the rejection of knowledge as "representation," or on what Richard Rorty calls the idea of the mind as a "mirror of nature."[10] For Reid and Coleridge the mind has no need to "copy"; its apprehension is inscrutable and direct.

But Reid—much more radically—believed that philosophy had no need to obey the imperative of an economy of first principles. In the *Biographia* Coleridge explicitly rejects this view and endeavors to reduce the givenness of both self-consciousness and "outness" to a single subjective principle. Here he appears to pass beyond the Reidian perspective to the absolute idealist notion of a subject constituting itself as object. The surpassing of Kantian phenomenalism seems then to be much more in line with the Romantic return to Spinozistic perspectives than with any tendency to realism.

However, both these ways of going beyond Kant are indicated by Coleridge. There is a definite ambiguity, and this ambiguity is coterminous with Coleridge's confessed hesitancy between pantheism and orthodox creationism. In the *Biographia* he rather awkwardly draws back from absolute idealist conclusions. He concedes the impossibility of disentangling the subjective from the objective contribution to knowledge and so of making an unambiguous beginning with the subject. Later he posits self-consciousness as something which in its immediacy involves a relation to an irreducibly other object. Furthermore, Coleridge explains that the starting with the subject as a single principle belongs to transcendental philosophy, but that this has to be supplemented by physical science that adopts the opposite procedure. Both approaches have then to be included in the ultimate science of metaphysical theology. Here indeed, in the supposition of a creative God, all objectivity has to be seen as totally derived from an absolute subject; "science" permits the causal induction back to a power infinitely transcending our capacities, "transcendental philosophy" provides the analogy of a subjective origin of reality. However, it is implied by Coleridge's Trinitarian vision that constant Paternal "attention" to the constructed or communicated objectivity that is within God the Logos remains indispensable to the divine reality. In God alone subjectivity and "outness" are finally co-extensive, and yet the differential relation

10. See Rorty, *Philosophy and the Mirror of Nature*, and Reid, *Essays on the Intellectual Powers*, esp. 100 and 133. For Coleridge's critique of knowledge as "copying," see Coleridge, *Biographia Literaria*, 70–71 and 140–41. On "outness," see Barfield, *What Coleridge Thought*, 59–69.

remains irreducible. Although Coleridge's understanding of the Trinity is too confined by the psychological analogy, and he does not consistently attain to a grasp of "three persons," nevertheless his relative orthodoxy here marks a difference with idealism. He does not succumb (like Hegel) to the Gnostic myth of a self-actuating spirit that objectifies itself, and thereby finds itself in estranged form, only to return, with this gain, back to an abstract, rational, self-presence.

Thus Coleridge's version of "metaphysical ascent" is not simply of an increasing subjective *reductio*, or emergence of subjective presence through the resolution of contradictions. And just as finite objectivity is not for him a moment in a process of divine becoming, so also "outness" cannot be transcended or fully resumed by the human spirit. And "outness" implies some limited apprehension of things in themselves; there is no epistemological agnosticism in Coleridge, and so he is as far from Kant as he is from Hegel. His phenomena are not equivalent to Kantian phenomena, but are identical with *natura naturata*, with nature in herself, as she occupies fixed forms. When the primary imagination does its work it actually reaches outwards and operates in sympathy with *natura naturans*, the plastic power in nature. Thus Coleridge denies that what presents itself to us is a mere "sensible manifold," and wonders whether Kant can *really* mean to posit for the *materiale* of our sensations a matter without form.[11]

If doubts remain about this realist strand in Coleridge's outlook, then one might appeal to his invoking of the scholastic principle of intentionality, after reading Duns Scotus in the Durham cathedral library. This notion, he claims, exposes a sophistry in Kant's distinction of the phenomena from "things in themselves," because it shows that bound up in our certainty about what we mean, is a certainty that we are thereby referring to a world with independent reality, although it is impossible to further explicate this certainty in empiricist fashion.[12]

---

11. Coleridge, *Biographia Literaria*, 77.

12. Coleridge, *Philosophical Lectures*, 439. Coleridge wants to convert Kantian categories into scholastic universals: ". . . the Critical Philosophy by no means supplies a satisfying answer to the objections of D. Scotus respecting the mere subjectivity of genera and species. How can that be denied to be true, the contrary of which would destroy all meaning and intelligible purpose of that ('the Subjective Understanding') by which the truth is to be denied? . . ."

A second element that allows Coleridge to overcome the scheme/content dualism of Kant is the pre-Cartesian and pre-empiricist inheritance of English philosophy. So far we have been concerned with a "realism" that stresses the objectivity of nature and the non-mediated character of the insertion of mind within the natural world; there is nothing, for Coleridge, "between" thought and being. Now we are concerned with a "pragmatism" that seeks to do justice to the modern concern with human creativity, and that regards the mind as existing and developing through a series of mediations—not of thought with being but of being with being in so far as reality is purposively and operatively dealt with and grasped as a linguistic network of signs. This is the area of human participation in the communicative *Logos*, which—beyond our grasp—constitutes the totality of being.

In explicating this "pragmatism" Coleridge cleverly conflates the views of Francis Bacon and the seventeenth-century English Platonists, although he is right in thinking that they have something in common that separates them both from Locke's post-Cartesian empiricism. In Coleridge's writings the clear *a priori* categories of Kant fade into the English Platonist notion of an indeterminate mental *anticipatio* of later concrete discovery.[13] Coleridge fuses this with the Baconian, non-empiricist understanding of the experiment. Experiments, for Coleridge as for Bacon, are not essentially for the testing of hypotheses; rather the labor of the experiment is itself knowledge: "Lord Bacon, equally with ourselves demands . . . some self-consistent anticipation, the ground of the *prudens quaestio* . . . with him therefore as with us, an idea is an experiment proposed, an experiment is an idea realised."[14]

The pragmatist overcoming of scheme/content dualism permits Coleridge to move towards a more radical view of human creativity in which the synthesis achieved by the imagination is no longer assignable as either purely *a priori*, or purely *a posteriori*. In this perspective however, the imagination/fancy distinction in its philosophical form is a hindrance, because it is clearly based on scheme/content dualism. What now matters is the view that imagination mediates between reason and understanding,

13. See, for example, Culverwell, *An Elegant and Learned Discourse*, xxii–xxxv. Culverwell eschews the fixed "inscription" of innate ideas in favor of *Prolepsis, Praesuptiones* or *Anticipationes Animi* which are "seeds of light," "Common and Fountain-Notions," "first risings," "bubbling endeavours," 54–55.

14. Coleridge, *Treatise on Method*, 42.

and in such a fashion that the "resistance" it receives from external objects has no merely negative value, but can actually act as a suggestive spur to new creative synthesis. Likewise the later Coleridge makes remarks that show that he is able to take a non-instrumentalist view of language. In the first of the *Lay Sermons*, *The Statesman's Manual*, Coleridge interprets Ezekiel's chariot vision—"withersoever the Spirit was to go, the wheels went, and thither was their spirit to go also . . ."—in terms of the belonging together of language and thought. Words are not merely the vehicle of the intellect but its "wings," and "The truths and the symbols which represent them move in conjunction and form the living chariot that bears up (for *us*) the throne of the Divine Humanity."[15] The words in brackets indicate how language in fact "outruns" thought and is thus "typical," and prophetic.

From here one can go on to say that it is also Coleridge's overcoming of the scheme/content dualism which permits him to give religion rather than philosophy the central mediating role in his later writings. Religion is understood as the collective work of the imagination—as, according to Appendix C of *The Statemean's Manual*, the participation in the creative power of God that generates human culture and human history.[16] Thus the social dimension is here regained. And it is religion, with its reliance on concrete symbols, which alone permits attainment of the metaphysical perspective which ideally, in God, is at once the "Science of Being" and the "Being and life of all genuine Science." But the human lack is now apparently on the concrete side; true religion "elevateth knowing into being."[17]

Only from this perspective should one seek to understand why Coleridge regarded his metaphysical speculations as objective despite Kant.

In particular one must note that, once it is supposed that our thought works in an indeterminately creative fashion such that it is not possible to isolate a determinate *a priori* contribution, then it also becomes less easy to classify as absolutely diverse the necessary categorial intuitions of pure reason, and its world-transcending speculations.

15. Coleridge, "Statesman's Manual," 29. On "winged words," see *Aids to Reflection*, author's preface. Here also Ezekiel is cited; words embody a living *energia*; they are not, as for Horne Tooke, empirical atoms.

16. Coleridge, "Statesman's Manual," 59–70 and 89–93, esp. 91. Note here that it is the religious command of creative communication that makes love, for Coleridge, a peculiarly religious virtue.

17. Ibid., 93.

These "metacritical" considerations apply especially to Kant's view that we can only make sense of "being" in so far as we encounter determinate phenomenal existence. Kant is only able to confine being to the area of empirically synthetic propositions, because he maintains the Leibnizian framework that modally privileges possibility over actuality. Thus he assumes that the mind can penetrate to an area of pure concepts, pure possibilities, as yet untainted (as language must inevitably be) by the actual.[18] There then arises a radical disjunction between categories that may be assigned a sensibly intuited content, and categories whose *entirely formal* transcendent aspiration must restrict them to the purest schematism. In this metaphysics God is not only first thought of as possibly existing, he is first thought of as primarily, in himself, possibility; it is not seen as equally feasible to move towards transcendence from the side of realized being. And in this way metaphysics is metaphysically forbidden.

For Coleridge, inversely, metaphysics pursues equally the fully possible and the fully actual. But it is only religion that attains the metaphysical perspective, because religion is none other than the primary primitive language by which human beings inhabit the world, and in which constructions of meaning that tie our spiritual existence to concrete forms are in indissoluble connection with the normative projections of transcendence. The indeterminacy and symbolic character of religious meanings are seen by Coleridge to be in continuity with the "prophetic" character of language itself, and both are seen to determine the metaphysical, not as an aberration, but as the inescapable context and character of human existence. Thus the later Coleridge makes no distinction between metaphysics and the theological explication of the biblical tradition. He also declares that, "True natural philosophy is comprised in the study of the science and language of symbols"[19] and associates this with the universal primitive belief in divination, in "antecedent signs of future events." For Coleridge, this, in its non-superstitious "prophetic" form, is to do with *sunesis,* with "going along with," or attachment to "long continued assent, as a presumption of truth."[20] The mode of faith is no longer extraordinary; it is the mode of a necessary metaphysics because it is the mode of language itself.

18. See Findlay, *Kant and the Transcendental Object,* 253–55 and 350f.

19. Coleridge, "Statesman's Manual," 79. And see note 25, below.

20. Coleridge, *The Friend,* 427–28. (Note that despite my three-stage division there is a continuous development towards the final stage of Coleridge's thought).

This is not, of course, at all to suggest that because Coleridge wishes to reinstate speculative metaphysics (in a peculiar way) he at all fails to share in the Kantian desire to connect religious metaphysics with ethics. It is rather that Coleridge extends the scope of practical reason, in connection with a consideration of language. Here he is anticipated (and certainly influenced) by Berkeley, who in *Alciphron* argues that signs stand sometimes not for clear ideas in the mind but for things imperfectly known or for actions to be done. Thus Berkeley already connects signs both with indeterminacy and with the guidance of action, as is shown in his view of the doctrine of the Trinity as *both* a regulative pattern for our conduct, and the symbolic basis for a metaphysics of Creation.[21]

Besides subordinating philosophy to religion, the later Coleridge also identifies religion with Christianity. He explicates this by saying that religion posits a transcendent reason as the coincidence of "Unity" and "Omneity" in "Totality." By this Coleridge implies that the Trinitarian God is thought of as a unity including in the *Logos* the plenitude of all that is. Inversely, religion in its practice works by symbols, because it posits the unity of the all as present in every particular. Other religions are thought by Coleridge to betray the Trinitarian vision and to forego this intensity of practice because they either "lose the ONE in the striving after the infinite," resulting in atheism or polytheism, or lose "the INFINITE in the striving after the ONE" resulting in "anthropomorphic monotheism."[22] True religion is now thought of by Coleridge as an historical practice and logic revealed especially in the Bible, which depends entirely upon contingent processes of linguistic creativity, and yet by remaining within this poetic logic and exercising it in especially "sublime" fashion explicates the most genuine metaphysics.

The Science of Realities

Within the terms of his emergent metaphysical and linguistic theology which celebrated religion as the prime communicative mode of culture, and God as perfectly communicative being, the later Coleridge evolved his mature political outlook. He returns in a new form to a biblical and historical perspective and to prophecy as the prime political category. In

21. Berkeley, *Alciphron, or the Minute Philosohper,* 286–308.

22. "Statesman's Manual," 60. This also seems to echo Berkely. See *Alciphron,* 300.

theoretical terms the significance of this is that he thereby transcends the dualism which contrasted "ideals" with "circumstances," and thinks instead of a progressive realization of simultaneously concrete and teleological "ideas" that are projected forwards from the past and experimentally realized in present practice. But it is the Bible which is held to contain the logic of true cultural becoming. Coleridge here makes large and mysterious claims to the effect that the Bible alone contains the "true political science" and the "true political economy."[23] We can only understand these claims if we have some inkling of what he means by the assertion that the Bible contains an encyclopedic "science of realities."

Coleridge talks of this in *The Statesman's Manual* where he declares: "The Bible alone contains a science of *realities*, and therefore each of its elements is at the same time a living GERM, in which the present involves the future, and in the finite the infinite exists potentially."[24] Here he wishes to explain that the Bible's genuinely prophetic nature consists in its symbolic character, and that the symbolic reference to the transcendent is inseparable from the indeterminacy of symbolic meaning which moves the cultural process forwards. In his final published work, *On the Constitution of Church and State*, in a passage with very Warburtonian echoes, Coleridge links theology with writing, and so with conservation and projection of cultural norms. In ancient times, he says, "under the name of theology and divinity were contained the interpretation of languages, the conservation and tradition of past events; the momentous epochs and revolutions of the race and nation; the continuation of the records, logic, ethics, and the determination of ethical science, in application to all the rights and duties of men in their various relations social and civil; and lastly the ground of knowledge, the *prima scientia* as it was named—PHILOSOPHY, or the doctrine and discipline of ideas."[25] But it is important to realize that the symbolic writing-activity of these early poet-theologians comprises not just recording, but the actual constitution of social norms and so of historical happenings themselves. The point here is not that the Bible is a poetic record of real events, but rather that it is an account of primitive events which had to take place poetically, that is to say were instantiated in poetic writing. Coleridge has grasped the

---

23. Coleridge, "Statesman's Manual," i, 49, and 128.

24. Coleridge, "Statesman's Manual," 49. But I doubt if David Aers would say this today.

25. Coleridge, *On the Constitution*, 46–47.

inner-textual character of all culture and so is able to interpret the Bible as the "remains" of past human time, rather than as the "evidence" of such a time. History and writing are at root identical: "the sacred history becomes prophetic," "the sacred prophecies become historical."[26] Here alone for Coleridge lies the possibility of any sort of verification. This can only consist in the possibility of future application and development of the inherited historical logic.

It is then not possible to say, following Aers, Cook, and Punter, that what begins for Coleridge as a demand for a concrete science of the historical is replaced with a concern for "the historical structure of metaphor."[27] Coleridge's point is surely that the specific concreteness of history consists in nothing other than this structure of metaphor; that this is the site of social structure also. He is here, if anything, not pre-, but post-Marxist.

Nevertheless, there does appear to be a tension in Coleridge's notion of the Bible as the source of science. On the one hand, it is clear that the claim is to do with our reliance on symbolic structures of meaning. Yet on the other hand, just like Vico, he compares this historical knowledge to the certainty we have in geometry, and contrasts it with our uncertainty concerning the knowledge of nature. We know geometry as science because we make it, says Coleridge, following Jacobi, following Vico.[28] It is a kind of knowledge in which the idea has precedence over being, and therefore is like the creative knowledge possessed by God. However, the Bible as a *book* is compared to this sort of antecedent idea, and clearly the understanding of idea-as-text must modify the conception of creative knowledge as genuine science.

For now the idea is no longer genuinely antecedent to the "work" of which it is the model. Model now only commences as product, and the scientific grasp of "first principles" can only mean a knowledge of aesthetic completeness, although even here it is the "original product"—the Bible—which defines for us what such completeness should be like. The Bible is for Coleridge the source of principles and method, because it is already a series of realizations. As a set of achieved "experiments" it is a kind of Baconian *organon*, "the perfect instrument, the only adequate organ of humanity."[29]

26. Coleridge, "Statesman's Manual," 29.

27. See Aers, Cook, and Punter, *Romanticism and Ideology*, chap. 5.

28. Coleridge, "Statesman's Manual," 16, 43.

29. Coleridge, *Confessions of an Inquiring Spirit*, 69–70.

There is an implicit anti-foundationalism in Coleridge's placing of textuality at the origin. Yet he cleverly converts this into the claim that the Bible is *the text*, containing the "*possibility*—of every position to which there exists any correspondence in reality."[30] This claim depends upon the "self-consciousness" of the Bible; it attains to foundational status because it is fully aware of the *impossibility* of any absolute starting point and rather understands itself as the moving response of faith to the mysterious presence of God. For Coleridge, as Jean-Pierre Mileur points out, it is this movement of faith in the enunciation of the word "God" which accounts for all textuality, all culture.[31] Thus the Bible alone is able to "explain" its own textual being and the being of all subsequent texts that it has generated.

The Bible, then, is an irreplaceable store of archetypes; it predefines the true norms and goals of all our cultural processes, including political and economic ones. While these archetypes are irreducibly tied to particular constructions of motive in particular past times and places, nevertheless they have for the person of (necessary) faith a full Platonic value: "The imperative and oracular form of the inspired Scripture is the form of reason itself in all things purely rational and moral."[32] The Bible is the only adequate counter to the current ethics of economic expediency, because it shows that a concern with ultimate ends, and non-negotiable preferences, is the most fundamental stratum of human intercourse, and generative of human reality.

Thus the "science of realities" is also an ethics which does not seek to prescind from history. In a famous passage, Coleridge avers that he seeks the *moral copula* which would "take from history its accidentality, and from science its fatalism."[33] Within the moral perspective, all our historical actions, including the construction of language, can be seen as belonging to the context of choice or refusal of God. In other words, history possesses the *structure* of *personal* being.

---

30. Coleridge, "Statesman's Manual," 18.

31. Mileur, *Vision and Revision*, 99.

32. Coleridge, "Statesman's Manual," 18.

33. See Coleridge, *Table-Talk and Omniana*, 157.

Political Indeterminism

The politics of the later Coleridge transcend the earlier admixture of Kantian idealism and Burkean prudentialism. This can be seen in three specific ways.

In the first place, the later Coleridge moves beyond an individualist understanding of Christianity. He has a very clear concept of the Church as a society existing in its own right, and not simply as a spiritual aid to the real national society, the State. The ambiguous relation between the middle Coleridge and the imperfectly emergent Coleridge is nowhere more clearly seen than in the ingenious scheme in *On the Constitution of Church and State*, whereby Coleridge argues that the national Church is not *necessarily* the Christian Church at all; the Christian Church just happens to fill this necessary clerical, prophetic role within the political order. What most commentators fail to see is that it is *only* in the latter respect that the Christian Church stands in an organic relation to the State, whereas the Christian Church *as such* stands in a critical relation to all States. Despite what is usually said, Hartley Coleridge was quite right to note that Coleridge's version of the Christian Church's relation to the state was still in line with Warburton's idea of a Church-state contract.[34]

Secondly, Coleridge renews his critique of Capitalism, though from a conservative standpoint. Although he finds a place for the so-called "interests of progress," he strongly suggests that all wealth-producing and technologically innovative processes be brought under a paternalist surveillance. The role of the market is to be reduced to the minimum. One cannot say that he is merely, like Burke (in his first phase), giving an organicist legitimacy to certain capitalist activities that remained more in the control of the traditional classes.

In the third place, Coleridge's political appeal to his "science of realities" causes him to insist on the temporal dimension of politics against those empiricists and rationalists who saw it in essentially spatial terms. His *apologia* for the role of the secular prophets, the clerisy, or the learned class pivots on this point, because it is this group which should be particularly aware of the location of politics in time. No recommendations of democracy, Coleridge suggests, can ever displace the need for a consideration of education as the most primary political dimension. Liberal democratic considerations are here inadequate, because education depends not

34. H. N. Coleridge's preface in Coleridge, *On the Constitution*, 197–98.

simply on free agreement, but on the constant inheritance of patterns of life and thought that are not, in the first place, chosen.

In accord with his understanding of the symbolic logic of human evolution, Coleridge develops a sort of doctrine of political indeterminism, which insists, against all rationalist politics, on the essential political value of the latent and obscure. He writes: "A Democratic Republic and an Absolute Monarchy agree in this; that in both alike the Nation or People delegates its whole power. Nothing is left obscure, nothing is suffered to remain in the idea, unevolved as an existing, yet indeterminate right." The notion of sovereign power, notes Coleridge, too often involves the idea that our entire will has been alienated from us: it is as if "the whole will of the body politic is in act at every moment."[35] Instead of this, Coleridge proposes, political delegation must be thought of as a trust, in which authority is not only answerable to the declared will of electors, but must be attuned to their latent will, so that "non-formalised" interests can also play their part in politics. Coleridge wishes to supplement any version of "present" constitutionalism with the constant appeal to past wisdom, and a laying down of patterns for the future that will not totally pre-empt the capacities of future peoples to appropriate the past legacy in a new way. Instead of political technology, Coleridge wants political culture. The political word must be prophetic deed and therefore must be rooted in the true prophetic tradition.

These insights did indeed give pause to later Victorian liberalism. In *On Representative Government* J. S. Mill actually gives a "Coleridgean" account of the prophets as the equivalent of the "free press" in Israel.[36] And he makes important use of Coleridge's distinction between actual and latent powers, in support of a contention that democracy must be a matter of direct participation and not merely formal constitutionalism.

The Contemporaneity of Coleridge

We have seen that Coleridge's thought moved from Unitarian Christian Socialism, through an idealist justification of liberalism, to a critique of liberalism on Christian Trinitarian grounds. One can interpret this as an

35. Coleridge, *On the Constitution*, 96.
36. Mill, *Three Essays*, 177.

astonishing trajectory across three major types of "political theology" within English tradition.

Beyond this, Coleridge can in fact be seen as standing at the commencement of modern English theology. His significance now, I would claim, is not so much that he "anticipates" many of our contemporary concerns, but rather that he stands alongside us on the margins of still unresolved problems. I want to point, in conclusion, to two particular matters which emerge from this chapter.

First of all it is notable that what one might anachronistically call the "narratological" elements in Coleridge part company with epistemology only to re-embrace metaphysics. Is Coleridge here simply deluding himself? It might seem so, in that the real essence of his implicit critique of Kant is that the possibility of human meaning is tied not to *a priori* categories, but to contingent, historical, linguistic constructions. How can this pragmatism be compatible with a transcendent metaphysical realism?

One should note here that the confinement of metaphysics to a regulative function depends upon the establishment of the world as a closed structure, and this in turn upon showing the essential and sufficient internal self-reference of the world. Kant achieves this through his scheme/content dualism. But for Coleridge the real world for human beings is first constituted and apprehended as the language of God, as the religious text in which normal, finite categories only exist in the tension with what is infinite and normative. The theological question is not, historically, a secondary one, and thus it is *history* which denies that theology can be grounded in a word of God confronting an otherwise godless, or merely transcendentally aspiring world.

In the second place, there is the continuing question of whether one may synthesize the politics of the first and final Coleridge. Just as Coleridge rejects the closed world of epistemology, so he "deconstructs" secular political autonomy. The clear message of *The Statesman's Manual* is that there are no empirical political facts, but that the politics of Coleridge's time is still situated (mostly to its condemnation) within the text of the Bible. History can only exhibit recognizable novelty and difference in so far as it remains repetition, a *mimesis* of the original text. All a genuinely resistant politics can do is to re-activate, self-consciously, the judgments and promises of this prophetic narration.

In our own times, a resistant politics has, up to now, been failing. It often seems as if apparent opposition to liberal capitalism must always turn out to be only liberalism after all. This may be because it lacks at once absolute metaphysical grounding and positive ethical content. In either case this can be traced to a failure to understand tradition as a vital critical resource. To move beyond liberalism one requires something like Coleridge's account of the primacy for politics of the dimension of time. And Coleridge still dares theology to have the courage to say that this political-cultural time is prophetic time, the time of the Bible. In what other way, after the advent of historical understanding, could theology make the claim to be theology?

2

RELIGION, CULTURE, AND ANARCHY

The Attack on the Arnoldian Vision

In the early 1990s, when it still existed, the Department of Religious Studies at Newcastle University ran into controversy, because of its acceptance of a bequest which endowed a post in theology on condition that its holder be a practicing Christian. To some commentators this case appeared as an ominous harbinger of what was to come: university departments, starved of public funds, were increasingly forced to turn to private means, sometimes under conditions which threaten the upholding of academic objectivity. There was, however, a possibly irony in the Newcastle case, an irony which should cause us to ponder more deeply the pros and cons involved: the professorial research fellow at Newcastle had a brief to reflect, theologically, on the situation in the inner cities, so although the appointment had been made against the background of governmental withdrawal of financial support from the universities, the results of the new professor's research were much more likely to be a critical embarrassment to the government than the usual more abstruse, more detached and "scholarly" products of research in religious studies.

Of course, pointing up the irony is not to resolve the argument. However, the reflection that the irony can invite is the following: does the critical function of an academic community in relation to the wider society *really* proceed from its detachment, its initial non-commitment to social, cultural, or ideological formations? And as a corollary to this: is the bland, politically unthreatening character of an academic department like the usual religious studies department *really* a reflection of its intellectual innocence, or is the notion of scholarly neutrality itself a mask which conceals the function of a realm of humanistic and cultural studies within an overall economy of public power? Below I shall try to explore these questions, but in the quite specific context of the Thatcherite upheaval, which totally re-arranged a historically received equilibrium, a particular disposition of the interactions between politics, religion, education, and culture.

In this inherited disposition of social fields a consensus was at work which one is tempted to describe as a *secular* consensus about the rational character of the public realm: a consensus that this public sphere should be expanded precisely because it *is* rational, concerned with our common humanity. This consensus built the post-war new towns, new schools with lots of plate glass and generous imitations of the playing fields of Eton; it secured and extended state-funded education; it encouraged public transport; it achieved universal health provision for all. However, I want to argue that this consensus, although making claims to common rationality, was *not* simply a secular consensus; on the contrary, it was, at least in its origins, a quasi-religious consensus. And in sweeping this consensus away, Thatcherism, although it eventually raised the specter of market and bureaucratic dominance by religiously fundamentalist forces, or by new forms of fascism, was nonetheless, objectively and in itself, at one with the forces of secularization. It was a hyper-modern, rather than a post-modern, phenomenon.

The old consensus can conveniently be dubbed "Arnoldian." In his work *Culture and Anarchy*, the Victorian poet and prophet Matthew Arnold both advocated and foreshadowed a new era in public life that would leave behind the individualism and "philistinism" nurtured by nonconformist Christianity, and encourage a more positive, "Germanic" view of the state as the guardian of common standards and common aspirations. Arnold self-consciously saw himself as the representative of the apparently "lost cause" of Oxford, the great romantic but vanishing tide of resistance to the gradual disestablishment of the Church of England, and the growing institutional pluralism in education, and the banishment of "sweetness and light"—i.e., the pursuit of beauty and truth—by purely economic, pragmatic values. Arnold insisted that the "cause" was only apparently "lost," and conjectured that the new, anti-liberal democratic movements arising amongst the working class would prove more receptive to the "values of Oxford" than middle-class nonconformity.[1] Here he correctly anticipated the conjuncture in which the Labour movement would gradually embrace his own project for a new cultural establishment acting as a counter-ballast to the forces of the marketplace, which Arnold described as essentially "anarchic" in their operations and implications (and which invite, so Arnold feared, real physical anarchy on the part of a frustrated "populace" whose appeal to "self-interest" society will no longer have the right to gainsay).

For Arnold, as for the Oxford Movement before him, the decline in reality and influence of the Church-establishment meant that a vacuum had arisen in the heart of the state; no longer was there any accepted public doctrine, no longer did political unity center on a shared concept of human flourishing, or a common notion of what sort of character is to be nurtured in British subjects. Yet, under the influence of his father's continentally-tinged idealism, which ran deeper within him than the influence of Newman, Arnold did not despair. He conceived public education as a new, all-inclusive, established "broad church," not just preserving a commitment to the moral fervor of biblical religion, but supplementing this with the "sweetness and light" of the Hellenic inheritance. It is important to realize that when Arnold rhapsodizes over "right reason," he is not thinking merely of a detached theoretical inquiry: culture, he contends, extends beyond mere *curiositas*; it is, rather, concerned with the practical development of "perfection" in the individual human character.[2] "Right reason" concerns a process of moral discernment which develops only gradually, and which is indissociable from certain qualities of aesthetic sensibility. Although the person of culture exhibits an ethical *finesse* inaccessible for the philistine disparager of beauty who relies for his morality on revealed, fixed commandments, this finely attuned sensibility nonetheless registers an objective, natural law, instilled into things from a transcendent source. Hence when Arnold advocates more attention to reason and less to revelation, this is only apparently a secularizing move: more precisely, Arnold is the advocate for a new, more classically tinged religiosity which looks to the "inwardness" of reason for the deliverance of a new, transcendentally sanctioned, public consensus. Arnold is above all against the dominance of instrumental rationality, or mere "machinery" as he calls it: in Victorian England, he argues, all that can be publicly agreed upon is that there

1. Arnold, *Culture and Anarchy*, 63.
2. Ibid., 43–45.

should be *more* health, *more* industry and *more* freedom, but the "right reason" instilled through true culture is to answer the questions, What are health, industry, and freedom *for*? In other words, in the full classical and medieval sense, what are the true ends of humankind?

Arnold's transcendentalism or "Platonism," or whatever one wishes to call it, is admittedly vague: moreover, it is already tinged with aestheticism; Arnold the *flaneur*, the dandy, implies that, could the naked world of "jealousy of the establishment, disputes, tea-meetings, openings of chapels, sermons"[3] (one may well think of Grantham) only be clothed with more style, more grace, then a lighter, more delicate, yet finer existence would ensue. Bloomsbury is in sight as much as Leavis, and one can take both as manifestations of an Arnoldian era in which the expansion of the British state went hand in hand with the lingering presence of idealistic philosophy, the assumption that values were objective and accessible either to reason or emotional "intuition", and the belief that true education was concerned with the nurturing of such values. Of course, the increase in the scope of state institutions had much to do with economic exigencies, and the need for capitalism to compromise with the new aspirations of the mass of the population. Nevertheless, the character of this response did not lie "ready to hand" in material circumstances, and the confident progress of the state in the fields of planning, education, and health owed something, in Britain, to the idealist vision of the state as guardian of the highest and the best. The dandy's modest gestures towards transcendence persist in the careful attention given to the appearances of the public realm: the garden cities, the national parks, the National Trust; the characteristic motifs adopted by the Royal Mail, by British Railways, by London Transport, whose repetition once gave unobtrusive harmony and uniform character to the entire country. At the same time, the vision of Arnold, Britain's first national inspector of government schools and the eldest son of the pioneer in the modern generation of Britain's "public schools," survived in the ethos of the grammar school; in the emergence of the university study of English; in the creation of public service broadcasting; in the 1906 and 1944 Education Acts, which provided for a non-denominational study of the Bible as "religious literature" without mediation by particular doctrinal creed; and, finally, in the setting up of new universities offering (under the initial aegis of the two ancient university foundations) the full panoply of humanistic studies.

3. Ibid., 58.

Over all these institutions, unnoticed, there hovered an ecclesiastical pall, its "Hebraic" presence nonetheless warmed by "Hellenic" sweetness and light, fraying to aestheticizing dissipation at the edges.

It was with all this that Thatcher had no patience: not for her the delicate qualms and flutterings of a refined sensibility; not for her that Oxford "reserve" in the face of modernity, which to the perplexed undergraduate from Grantham seemed to mix an addiction to triviality with elusive claims to transcendence. Thatcher realized, as Arnold and his descendants did not, that to ask what are health, industry, and freedom *for* is a superfluous luxury in a capitalist system: this system works best when freedom, production, and wealth—which hitherto had always appeared to be only a means—are themselves treated as ends. Now, finally, the logic of a public philosophy of "do as you please" was to be carried through with a remorselessness undreamt of by Arnold's nonconformists (who had certainly not reached quite the stage of individualist decadence which he attributes to them). Public guardianship of aesthetic and moral values now had no place because this notion cannot be subject to the arbitrations of the principle of the sovereignty of individual choice. Hence public service broadcasting should be dismantled: in place of a guardianship of quality, one must hand it over to the operations of market preference on the one hand, and often priggish government judgments of national security and private moral health on the other (Blair in sight). Hence, also, there can be no important place in education for the humanities, or for philosophy, because a government confined to the upholding of a market economy and the interests of national security no longer requires men and women possessing Aristotelian *phronesis*, or a finely attuned sense of what is just and appropriate, what is due to whom and on what occasion. Thatcherism carried the process of secularization further because it removed ethics from the public realm, in refusing to recognize any common goals beyond the maximization of wealth and individual freedom. (So when Edward Heath compared attacking higher education to Henry VIII's dissolution of the monasteries, he had it exactly right.)

This extrusion of ethics *might* appear to be belied by the puritanical bent within Thatcherism. What, however, one had here was really a tendency to reduce morality to disciplined self-control, permitting a better economic functioning on the part of the individual, along with a preference for further reducing this purely "private" morality to a set of simple prescriptions which minimizes the amount of time one needs to spend in moral anguishing and liberates one's energies for the essentially amoral tasks of so-called "enterprise." It is not that the Thatcherites *deliberately* reduced morality to what is economically functional, but rather that their preferred virtues, which supposedly give evidence of our "spiritual" status—discipline, self-reliance, literal truthfulness, preparedness to take risks—are all more to do with motivations than with ends, and therefore imply no public, substantive goals, but only the formal regulations of the marketplace and bureaucratic control. This diagnosis simply extends Arnold's interpretation of the moralism of nineteenth-century noncon-formity, but one needs, I think, to note that *this* part of Thatcherite ideol-ogy existed alongside, and was soon overtaken by, a much more purely hedonistic celebration of capitalist culture which it itself helped to nur-ture. Even the contemporary successors of the nonconformists, the neo-evangelicals of our day, embrace an increasingly *ersatz* religion which is not so much to do with disciplining for the market as with an elevation of the processes of economic risk and reward to the status of religious significance in themselves, as the safeguards of "spiritual" freedom and evidence of divine grace and favor.

Thatcherism aimed, admittedly, to eschew aesthetic decadence, the loitering of the *flaneur* with intent not merely to work, not merely to choose, but also to gaze: this, perhaps, was the secret reason for its apparent homophobia. Yet in the banishing of all concern with public style, with the appearance of the common surfaces of things, which is the level at which we interact, the only level at which we really, concretely exist, it was Thatcherism itself which was truly decadent. Instead of rest-ing content with the succession of surfaces, this credo suggested that we should perversely pursue merely the means of our own public engage-ment—namely our own subjectivity or freedom—and merely the aggre-gate of concrete surface objects, namely wealth, in the abstract. And yet, however often we may point out this decadence (and this can degenerate into obsession) it seems that our public institutions have been themselves too mired in the same degeneracy for them to be able to mount a prin-cipled resistance. This is, perhaps, for two reasons: firstly, the Arnoldian vision was in decline long before Thatcher; secondly, the Arnoldian vision was always a deficient one.

The Arnoldian vision was in decline long before Thatcher: the classi-cist-idealist tradition in English philosophy already gave way in the inter-war years to a renewed empiricism which eventually could not sustain notions of objective goodness and beauty. Philosophy and, considerably later, literary, historical, and social studies began to confine themselves to the supposedly detached classification of positions, theories, and social and textual structures. Analytic philosophy's most ambitious claim in its English heyday was to be able to resolve conceptual confusions between "matters of fact" and "matters of value," and so to confine ethical and aesthetic matters to a non-discussable realm of personal choice and preference. The "brilliantined positivists" of the 1950s who still stalked the provincial universities of the 1980s, were, for all their grayness, in a sense portents of our recent market hedonism. For they helped to *banish* from universities serious areas of public discourse—about politics, about moral issues. The Arnoldian illusion of a rational viewpoint above the "interests" of the various classes still survived in this period, but it had now lost its Platonic grounding, so that transcendence no longer consisted in the attainment of a higher standpoint of virtue and aesthetic appreciation, but simply in the cold gaze of truth upon the many varieties of non-rational preference. In too many disciplines—in philosophy, English, history, sociology—the illusion had been fostered that in a university one discovers special privileged words which re-express, re-describe, or re-interpret the varieties of social discourse in a way which renders them immune to the ordinary preferences, prejudices, and practical purposes of such discourse. As with Arnold, culture was still to stand in judgment, but now this was a cold judgment whose claim was to position and define, yet not to advise. Once the universities had refused the old humanist rationale for the relevance of liberal studies to the political realm, it is not wholly surprising that their political masters should have eventually judged these studies to be a superfluous luxury or at least as undeserving of public money. Of course *later* there comes a qualified revival of moral and political philosophy, later some philosophers again recognize that there is no reason to see judgments of value as any more subjective or imposed than our other judgments. The Owl of Minerva has taken its flight; but it's medium of transport remains, as ever, belatedness.

The universities, then, had already claimed an agnostic transcendence of such merely human questions as: What is industry for? What is freedom for? So they could hardly complain about Thatcherism (and its mutation into Blairism), which is, as it were, ordinary language philosophy in action. The louder Thatcher insisted that commitment to freedom of choice is *all* we have in common, the more our secularized society knew this to be really true in present practice, and thus one saw desperate expedients arising, like the attempt to ground socialism in the principle of maximization of choice alone. This attempt ignored the way in which over-concentration on libertarian goals on the left in the 1960s in fact helped to pave the way for the libertarian right—such that Mick Jagger has to join the brilliantine boys in the dock as a forerunner to Thatcherism. The transition is a logical process, because, if one maintains freedom of choice and expression as the ultimate principle, then it remains the case that the market is the most efficient, most minimally violent way of mediating diverse choices. One may say that there should also be a real, substantive equality of opportunity to choose, and that this entails an equality of provision of resources for choice, including educational resources. But in selecting which educational resources to provide for people, one is molding their capacities, developing certain skills rather than others and so one has already started to choose *for* them—because there is no skill not partially defined by the end it has in view. To choose publicly a certain provision of means for freedom is also to decide publicly the ends of true freedom. (Reflections like these still made sense to thinkers like R. H. Tawney, but are largely incomprehensible to modern Labour party pundits, who tend to water down what is meant by "positive freedom" to equality of opportunity alone.)

In this sense, then, the Arnoldian point of view remains valid: one can only resist the philosophy of "do as you please," of unfettered market freedom, one can only add equality to freedom, if one is open, beyond libertarianism, to the idea of public goods, to the view that we should publicly encourage certain aesthetic appearances, certain kinds of human character rather than others. It is not an accident that socialism flourished in an era when the "lost cause" had a final fling before the shades of secular night fell upon us all.[4] And yet, as I have pointed out, Arnold's new establishment, his "new church"—the universities, the BBC, the Christian churches themselves—have singularly failed to develop a culture of shared values. And this is not really surprising.

For the Arnoldian vision was always a deficient one: it fell into the Hegelian trap of supposing that the modern state could really be the equivalent of the antique city-state and support a *paideia*, meaning an educational process which is the nurture of its citizens in human flourish-

---

4. For the argument that some aspects of socialism are "anti-modernist" in character, see chapter 6 in this volume, "On Baseless Suspicion."

ing, understood as participation in political processes. There were two things wrong with this. First of all, the modern state is essentially alien to the notion of participation; it is born out of the perceived need for there to be a centre of absolute sovereign power in the face of irresolvable religious and moral conflict. Hence Arnoldian education may have helped to train bureaucrats and schoolmasters, but it has not helped to train citizens, nor to elevate the working-class *en masse*, and this appears scarcely surprising when one notes that Arnold himself held in disdain both local government and corporate associations not directly subordinate to the state.[5] The second thing wrong with Arnold's vision is this: the growth of a consensus about values which supports *paideia* only occurs in the context of a *tradition*, and in a real sense the modern state does not situate itself in a tradition—its paradigm is the United States of America, which claims to accept as citizens people from each and every tradition with favor given to none. But, going much further back, one could even claim that the writers of the New Testament, and the Church Fathers, already helped to separate *paideia* from the *polis* by promoting a new community of primal allegiance and primary nurture—the Church—outside the political state. In a way the modern attempt to re-establish a state monopoly on education begins to look, historically, like a strange anomalous attempt to revert to antiquity. Because the *polis* cannot really be reproduced, the Blairite attempt to impose an "Arnoldian" common curriculum in fact reinforced precisely the "philistine" conjunction of merely aggregate public goals with a private morality reduced to self-control or "freedom through strength." But earlier Arnoldian programs—like Leavisite English studies—themselves already sustained the modern *political* fiction of a "culture" detached from community, and accessible to a properly purged intuitive sensibility.

In the modern world, the communities that might support genuine notions of the common good, and common standards of character and beauty, do not inhabit the political level. And yet it may be that it is only these communities, which are often religious in character, which are able—for the logically clear reasons I have tried to point out—to go beyond the *rationale* of right-wing libertarianism and sustain a critique of this new political hegemony.

5. Arnold, *Culture and Anarcy*, 62.

And this returns me, via the question of religion and community, to the question of religious studies in the university. Reading through Ninian Smart's inaugural address as Professor of Religious Studies in the University of Lancaster—given in the *Annus Mirabilis*, 1968—one gets the impression that, on the whole, his agenda fitted into the retreat from the Arnoldian vision I have already described.[6] Envisaging a kind of *Literae Humaniores* on a world scale, Smart wanted an external, objective description of religious traditions, plus a certain scope for these traditions to "express" themselves theologically, leaving the place of honor for analytic philosophy to get conceptually clear, though not to judge, what the different traditions were trying to say. And, on the whole, religious studies has tended to be dominated by too condescending an attitude to religious traditions, treating their intellectual explorations as mere "expressions" of a faith with which the outsider can supposedly empathize and resonate, rather than as exercises in reason undertaken according to their own diverse notions of rational criteria. On the other hand, at its very worst, religious studies has maintained the Arnoldian vision in the shape of searching for an ultimate object of religious reference, or an essential religious experience, or a universal religious culture of which the particular religious traditions would be themselves mere "expressions." Both tendencies, especially in their implications for religious education in schools, cannot be held to be finally unrelated to an exaggerated respect for the political state as the community of primary loyalty.

But if, today, we now recognize, unlike Arnold, the importance of participation, and of communities below the level of the state, then we should realize that our difficult, perhaps impossible, quest for some measure of moral and aesthetic consensus between different traditions, cannot be won by trying to *bypass* those traditions. On the contrary, we must help to give these traditions, when they are serious, substantive and of long-standing, a voice in the public conversation. And this means that within religious studies departments of universities we must abandon the claim to a spurious perspective of final judgment on all traditions, and instead encourage the development of their different intellectual perspectives according to their own lights, and, where possible or sensible or necessary, bring them into dialogue. One should note that whereas the claim to represent a purely academic, rational culture, unbound by tradition, is *necessarily* "ideological" and self-deluding, it is at least *possible*

6. See Smart, "Principles and Meaning."

for a tradition to become clearer about its own social insertion, because real traditions always include a self-awareness of their own supportive communities.

But this more positive attitude to traditions, if embraced in academic life, might imply, in certain circumstances, that the holding of certain beliefs sometimes helps to qualify one for the holding of a certain job. For, as Alasdair MacIntyre has pointed out, it is only a modern prejudice to suppose that personal commitments are irrelevant to certain rational tasks.[7] Beyond the level of formal logic there is no single "reason" without presuppositions, there are only many different, complexly overlapping, traditions of reason. So to suggest, in *some* circumstances, that one requires for a post a Christian, a Jew, or a Buddhist, or a Nietzschean atheist would not be so much to ask for a person with a particular "inner" attitude as for someone with a certain irreplaceable intellectual training, a certain facility, a certain linguistic competence. By contrast, the preference since the eighteenth century for a single "neutral" inquiry in philosophy and the humanities may have much to do with the academic community's all too intimate relationship with the sovereign state, a relationship surreptitiously confirmed precisely at the point where academics claim to stand aloof to public issues. But today, unless the many "traditions of reason"—the local, rather than the metropolitan logics—are represented in universities, these institutions may once again fail to make a contribution to the vital public debates of our time.

7. MacIntyre, *Whose Justice*, 99 passim.

3

WHAT IS LIVING AND WHAT IS DEAD IN NEWMAN'S *GRAMMAR OF ASSENT*

One can read Newman's *Essay in Aid of a Grammar of Assent* as in one respect a thoroughgoing critique of English culture, which is compared unfavorably to the culture of Catholic Europe. At the heart of this comparison stands a contrast between a predilection for the abstract and verbal on the one hand, and a foregrounding of the visual or imagistic on the other. And yet, in arguing for the superiority of the latter emphasis, Newman draws on the resources of British intellectual tradition—on empiricist philosophy and the British proto-romantic and romantic exploration of the role of the imagination. In both cases, though, he turns these traditions against themselves: a radicalized empiricism is deployed to defend the miraculous, mysterious, and transcendent, while the Coleridgean understanding of the imagination is newly seen to require a displacing of the primacy of the merely literary in favour of the pictorial, the devotional, the lyrical, hymnic, and liturgical.

If one were to argue, as one well might, that the British traditions of empiricism, scientific experiment, and imaginative vision linked with mysticism have strong pre-Reformation roots, then it could be suggested that the coherence of Newman's cultural mission lies in a demand that the British genius further realize itself by returning to its Catholic origins. And this is something which I personally would wish to endorse.

However, I shall argue in what follows that the *Essay* is a seriously inconsistent treatise. It is not possible to read it always as building to an *apologia* for the Catholic faith rooted in a radical empiricism and an insistence on the primacy of the visual imagination. In the latter emphases lie the book's continued interest, yet disappointingly it frequently lapses into an *apologia* based upon a more conventional empiricism in which, surprisingly, the abstract and the notional reassert their dominant sway. This is the strand in Newman's thought which one might describe as "all too British" or perhaps even "all too English." And it is here that one can situate the central paradox of Newman's intellectual biography—namely the redeployment of quintessentially Anglican empiricist arguments, derived in large part from Bishop Butler, in order to assert the claims of the Church of Rome. This particular mode of apologetics has—as many others, particularly David Nicholls and Fergus Kerr, have argued—the unfortunate result of engendering an overly rationalistic, yet equally overly fideistic, voluntaristic, and authoritarian account of the role of the Papacy.[1]

Here I must hasten to say that the question of whether Anglicans should become Catholics, and of the validity of Papal claims, are not at all at present the issue for me. Rather, it is the *mode* of Newman's assertion of the Catholic case that is in question, along with the depth of his grasp of a Catholic ecclesiology. So I am going to argue that the *Essay* points the way to a profound and interesting apologetic and yet confuses this with a superficial and dangerous one.

Newman's Radical Empiricism

Broadly speaking, the more interesting approach is, I think, articulated in the first four chapters of the *Essay*, and then in chapter 9 on the illative sense. This claim implies that the more implicitly theological Newman becomes, the more he retreats to a more wooden and traditional empiricism: reasons for this I shall indicate later.

In the first four chapters, Newman adumbrates his crucial distinction between real and notional assent. However, in a prior move, "assent to terms" is seen as far more fundamental than assent to proofs or to inferences.[2] Arguments about logical consistency may be interminable, but they are in principle publicly resolvable, since they concern consistency with formal procedures under agreed rules. This is less clearly the case with our apprehension of first terms, which is required in order that an argument be actually *about* anything whatsoever. Here Newman re-

1. Kerr and Nicholls, *John Henry Newman: Reason, Rhetoric, and Romanticism.*

2. Newman, *Grammar of Assent*, chapter 2, 32–35.

peats in his own manner the antique insistence on the primacy of *topica* over *dispositio* in both rhetoric and dialectics. Outside the realm of the apodeictic or the tautologically analytical, argument is subordinated to a desire either to persuade someone to do something—in rhetoric—or else, in dialectics, to get someone actually and immediately to see the truth for themselves. Argument and inference can here only perform the role of a midwife.

So with "assent to terms" Newman is concerned with our theoretical assent to "what is the case" prior to argument and with our assent to more complex states of affairs in instances where following a chain of logical links allows us to grasp a series of causes and relations: his example is our final intuitive grasp that John is "great-uncle-in-law to Richard" once we have apprehended that John is Richard's wife's father's aunt's husband.[3] The latter apprehension is deemed by Newman to be "notional," but the former "real." Yet this example shows, I think, how for Newman the two forms of assent are always involved in the thinking process and are mutually complementary.

One can try to grasp what he means here by contrast with a Hobbesian, Lockean, or Humean philosophy. In that mode of empiricism, the raw "givens" of understanding are atomistic items of sensory information combined, at least in Locke's case, with certain *a priori* norms of reasoning. This tradition sustained a nominalist suspicion of abstract terms, because the latter might tend to sediment false inferences or generalizations from the basic givens, and to hypostasize generalizations as real universals, having a supposedly "thingy" consistency.

Now the concealed contradiction of such a philosophy is that empiricism ought to be agnostic as to what may exist and should always wait on the deliverances of experience. However, if one has decided that all that is incontrovertibly given are isolatable items of sensory experience, whose arising in our mind can be explained according to the laws of motion, then one has foreclosed the question of what may be encountered, in terms of an entirely dogmatic ontology. Empiricism is reductionist not when it disputes metaphysics, but rather when it embraces it in a particularly virulent form by asserting that all that can be, or at least all that can be known, is that whose genesis can be broken down into the *combinatorium* of isolated units—which, one might propose, if they

---

3. *Grammar of Assent*, chapter 3, 36.

are to be uncontaminated by any scholastic notion of intrinsic form or substance, must in the end fractalize away into atoms of nothingness.

Yet the empirical impulse *as such* does not encourage such reductionism. Thus other manifestations of this impulse in British culture have encouraged an openness to the extraordinary, the unclassifiable, and the irreducibly prolix, as well as to the recognition (in contrast to Cartesian physics) of mysterious and yet clearly operating forces in nature like gravity and electricity. In the case of Thomas Reid and the Scottish commonsense tradition, empiricism was somewhat disconnected from sensory atomism, and linked rather with a recognition that we are originally confronted with complex realities and have no warrant for supposing that the mind (as opposed to the brain) builds up such pictures from multiple initially discrete elements.[4] Reid rightly insisted that the process by which sensations lead us to acknowledge certain features of the external world, such as space, motion, extension, and color is actually "unfathomable." He argued in consequence that these mysterious inferences "common" to our sensing must operate by a kind of interpretation of natural signs according to regular rules established by God. In this way he suggested that only a theistic metaphysic overcomes skepticism as to the existence of an external world, and that our trust in our senses is very akin to the trust we accord to the testifying words of other people. In both these two respects Newman's reflections echo those of Reid (whatever the case may be as to the question of influence).

---

4. Reid, *An Inquiry into the Human Mind on the Principles of Common Sense*. See, for example, chapter 5, sections VI–VII, 67; chapter 6, section VI, 90; section XXIII, 189. One is struck by the fact that Reid failed to see that the linguistic and pragmatist dimensions of his epistemology are already present in Berkeley; this is because he too easily accepted, or perhaps helped to foster, the standard idealist reading of the Bishop of Cloyne's notions. In point of fact both thinkers later strongly influenced American philosophy, especially C. S. Pierce—and for similar reasons. For both these philosophers from the Celtic margins rejected the metropolitan barbarism of English and Edinburgh empiricism. See Milbank, "The Linguistic Turn as a Theological Turn," especially 97–105. One can mention also that, without a scholastic notion of "form" as common to material things and to knowledge, Reid's doctrine sounds too near to one of pre-established harmony and has to remain agnostic as to the finite causal aspects of human understanding. Yet, on the other hand, if Aquinas's *species* as the mode that intelligible "form" takes in our mind is not a "picture" of a material object (and it is not) then the Aberdonian's reflection that our sensations and ideas are "signs" joins up with Aquinas's view that the form in our mind evolves into an "inner word" which mysteriously conveys back to us the presence of the material thing that we know.

And Newman, like Reid, and perhaps still more emphatically, insists that thought primarily considers complex—even inexhaustibly complex—phenomena. Like Reid again, he suggests that in this respect thought always remains close to the joint operation of the senses and paradigmatically to the sense of sight. Even the ability of thought to abstract away from the immediate present has always as its accompanying vehicle the operation of the imagination.[5] We remember first of all vivid objects; on this basis we imagine other concrete instances, and only on that foundation do we arrive at the abstractly general.

It follows that Newman's empiricist suspicion of abstract terms is not at all like that of Hobbes, Locke, and Hume—if anything it is more like that of Wittgenstein. For Newman is not advocating a nominalist priority of the individual thing as pure atom. Rather, in a fashion comparable to Gerard Manley Hopkins's reinterpretation of the Scotist *haeccitas,* he is insisting that the concrete individual case is always more complex, pregnant, and mysterious than any term abstracted from it. In a sense though, this position, as later with Wittgenstein, *does* involve following the line of nominalist suspicion to the very end, even if this end undermines the very contrast of nominalism with realism. For one crucial part of Newman's case seems to be that the most innocent seeming atomic terms are *themselves* contaminated by abstraction and universality. Thus he notes that counting seven items is only true if one has already perceived or decided that there are seven items that are denumerable—or as we would now say, seven things that fall within the same mathematical set. Newman mentions that one can count seven or more species of animals, but no species of angels whatsoever—and that "God" cannot be counted as an item at all.[6] The implication of these statements is that the classical empiricist program desires ontology to correspond to simple arithmetic, whereas, to the contrary, the latter could only apply after one has made certain ar-

5. *Grammar of Assent,* 37–43, 41: "And by means of these particular and personal experiences, thus impressed upon us, we attain an apprehension of what such things are at other times when we have not experience of them; an apprehension of sights and sounds, of colours and forms, of places and persons, of mental acts and states, parallel to our actual experiences such that, when we meet with definite propositions expressive of theory our apprehension cannot be called abstract and rational."

6. Ibid., 75–76. "Unless numeration is to issue in nonsense, it must be conducted on conditions. This being the case there are, for what we know, collections of beings to whom the notion of number cannot be attached, except catachrestically, because, taken individually, no positive point of real agreement can be found between them, by which to call them."

bitrary incisions in the real, whose character may well by "catachrestic" as Newman the rhetorician puts it. If classical empiricism is to hold, then it must remain inescapably Cartesian, in so far as the only paradigm for the accumulation to the complex from the simple must be an arithmetic or a geometric one. In the case of his allusions to the geometric field, Newman again shows a dim glimmering of the revolutionary developments of his own century, happening far away from Oxford; for example he points out that the statement that two straight parallel lines do not enclose a space is not a statement about reality, but only about a formal system abstracted from reality.[7] Yet classical empiricism, which is in the end but a variant of Cartesianism, would seem to require that physical reality be Euclidean.

Therefore, where classical empiricism would wish to isolate basic given elements such as space, efficient cause, appetite, will, and so forth, Newman sees only abstracted and conventional notions to which words have been affixed. He even suggests that alternative valid lenses through which we view physical process will necessarily entail incompatible implications, yet still be equally legitimate or even required—this sounds like a premonition of a "quantum" perspective.[8] Where Locke and Hume thought universals were "only words," Newman insists that concepts for individual items are also "only words" and, moreover, that as incorporated into grammar they can only make sense if they already compare and relate different items. To say "this is a stone" is already to deploy the words "this" and "stone" as universal categories, as Hegel had insisted.[9] Newman's reflections here exceed in their critical rigour the conclusions not only of Locke but also of William of Ockham, who had considered that all concepts and signs are only "true" if traceable back to an original intuition of an irreducibly singular presence.[10]

---

7. Ibid., 59: "I have defined a straight line in my own way at my own pleasure; the question is not one of facts at all, but of the consistency with each other of definitions and their logical consequences."

8. Ibid.: "Notions are but aspects of things; the free deductions from one of these aspects necessarily contradict the free deductions from another."

9. Hegel, *Phenomenology of Spirit*, A.II, 67–79.

10. See Alférì, *Guillaume d'Ockham*, 265–99, 362–402, 453–54. Whether or not Ockham's position is a realist (as opposed to idealist) one, or admits of a skeptical reading, saving the invocation of the divine guarantee of the truth of our intuitions, remains a matter of scholarly dispute. In the case of our thoughts of God, for Ockham, our predications are not backed up by any intuition, yet the intention of our naming of God is grounded in a faith in his absolute unknown singularity whose unlimited power

Newman's perspective here could perhaps be construed as an ultra-nominalism which discovers that the artifice of universalizing is involved in all predication and is unavoidable (since the raw particulars that would provide genuine foundations are unavailable) even though it must be viewed with extreme suspicion. This would entail outright skepticism. His swerving away from such an extreme is linked to the fact that he did not regard "notional assent" as simply secondary and inferior to "real assent." For while he certainly viewed abstract notions with some suspicion, as tending to provide merely a "thin" account of reality, he never takes the nominalist step of claiming that abstractions are only generalizations from many particulars or else must be taken as if they were such (in the case of an ultra-nominalism which has concluded that the legitimating data are always already contaminated by abstraction). To the contrary, he time and again declares that abstract notions select certain *aspects* of concrete reality—hence one aspect of physical space is indeed Euclidean. He clearly did not think that these aspects were arbitrary pragmatic ploys in a Nietzschean fashion, because he declares that *real* assent to an envisaged or imagined state of affairs is always "fertile in aspects."[11] Indeed it is this term "aspect"—which so remarkably seems to anticipate Husserl (as well as Heidegger and Wittgenstein)—that provides the crucial mediating link between real and notional assent.[12] If a notional term picks out an aspect and real assent goes on discerning further and further aspects of a complex circumstance, then, just because real assent does not grasp all aspects at once, it must always already to some degree be involved in notional abstraction. The ontological concomitant of this gnoseology would be that, for Newman, as earlier for Berkeley, a concrete thing is composed

---

and will is, indeed, the ultimate ontological basis for a created reality composed only of singular existences, in principle infinitely re-arrangeable, except for the requirement of non-contradiction.

11. *Grammar of Assent*, 47: ". . . real apprehension has the precedence, as being the scope and end and the test of notional; and the fuller is the mind's hold upon things or what it considers such, the more fertile it is in its aspects of them, and the more practical in its definitions."; 66: "the doctrines [of the British national religion] are not so much facts, as stereotyped aspects of facts and it is afraid, so to say, of walking round them."; 77: "Our notions of things are never simply commensurate with the things themselves; they are aspects of them. . . ."; 87: "inference, unlike apprehension, is necessarily concerned with surfaces and aspects."; 291: "This is what is meant by originality in thinking; it is the discovery of an aspect of a subject matter, simpler it may be and more . . . intelligible than any hitherto taken."

12. See Mulhall, *On Being in the World: Wittgenstein and Heidegger on Seeing Aspects*.

of many abstract elements, rather as a word is made up of the letters of the alphabet.[13] One can suppose that, for Newman, in a created universe the likeness and interrelation between things is not a kind of accidental and secondary upshot, but rather reflects the original architectectonic of the divine wisdom.

Newman's position then in the first four chapters is less nominalist than authentically realist in the best medieval sense, whether of Aquinas or of Scotus. Universals, or aspects as notions, are real only in our minds, but this mental reality is rooted in, and allowed to exist by, the formal synthetic complexity of substantially existing things. In a more modern mode, however, Newman adds that the rich discernment of universal relevance in a particular situation is not disabled but rather encouraged by an increased concentration on this very specificity. Here it is always the *imagination* which is able to hold together the many facets of a situation and to extend by analogy this synthesis to other real or possible instances. Conversely, the act of notional abstraction does not attain to genuine productive universality, but rather to a kind of phantom concreteness—it tends to produce a technologically manageable world where a simplified particularity can be easily produced in substitution for the rich original organic world that suggests to us ever-new universal lessons.

Newman is here certainly indebted (by whatever routes) to Coleridge and Wordsworth, and through this indebtedness tends to qualify an Aristotelian account of abstract universals with a Platonic or neoplatonic account of productive and concrete universals. This can be seen in the way in which he understands real and notional assent to be complementary and mutually corrective. When aspects are apprehended as abstracted terms, one achieves a "broad but shallow" grasp of reality. When, on the other hand, aspects are grasped visually and imaginatively, as manifested in a single instance—like greenness, height, light, circularity, dependence, growth, seasonality, teleology, and beauty in one oak tree—then one gains a "deep but narrow-minded" apprehension of things.

Neither intellectual strategy is adequate on its own and Newman argues for their complementarity by making some psychological and sociological observations. The inventors, discoverers, leaders, and scientific geniuses of the world often do badly at school, he declares, precisely because they tend to see something new in a single intuition, but are bad

13. See Milbank, "The Linguistic Turn as a Theological Turn."

at orderly arrangement and generalization. Yet the latter capacities are not simply humdrum things to be sneered at, precisely because the full truth of the aspects of a particular thing concerns its regular relations to other things. The intuitive genius may ignore what generally holds, and as a result go wildly astray in his conclusions because he is locked in "one small circle of knowledge." And to some degree, knowing what generally holds can only be accomplished as a collective task down the generations. Thus the individual imagination, if it is to operate with genuine insight, requires a balancing by abstracting reason, common sense and cultural tradition. Depth may indeed be linked to obsession and even (here Newman agrees with Coleridge) to obscurity, but it requires to be linked with the relative superficiality and yet breadth of a clearer and more regular reasoning.[14] Romanticism seems to modulate into a proto-modernism at this point.

I have been arguing that the key to Newman's account of assent and the relation of real to notional assent is the concept of "aspect." But why, a critic could ask here, can one not simply reduce notional aspects to observed states of affairs? Such a reduction would be equivalent to the Fregean extreme extension of the program of classical empiricism— beyond even Ockham, the aspects or "qualities" of things do not really inhere in things because there are no qualities and no substances, only accidental *congeries* of atomic circumstances. If, in this way, there are no aspects or qualities, but only states of affairs, then it follows, as Frege tended to suggest, that analytical logic can fulfil all the tasks of philosophy.[15] Once one views the world with a demystified gaze, there can be no arguments concerning what is the case, or at least what is deemed to be the case, since this is simply a matter for empirical scientific investigation. Philosophy now only impinges on the real in terms of the category of reference and thus can be reduced to a logical function: A is B if and only if it is the case that A is B; B need never be seen as an intrinsic aspect of a thing without which it would not exist at all (or at least not in the same fashion), in such a way that would require from philosophy the articulation of an extra-logical ontology.

By insisting, to the contrary, that assent to the real and to basic terms is an inherently *problematic* matter, Newman refused in advance this Fregean position and therefore the entire program of analytic phi-

14. *An Essay in Aid of a Grammar of Assent*, 47, 76–80.

15. See C. O. Hill, *Rethinking Identity and Metaphysics: On the Foundations of Analytic Philosophy*.

losophy in the strict sense. He would have seen its logical discriminations as important but ultimately trivial, since he asserts that the question of apprehension lies both before and after that of logic or inference. And the real ground for this assertion lies in his view that we apprehend reality primarily in terms of bundles of aspects that hold together beyond mere arbitrary synthesis. In the twentieth century Husserl, Heidegger, and Wittgenstein have provided better justifications for this assertion, which all amount to the point that we do not first see raw items or combinations of such items, but rather first apprehend something as shown in something else which in some sense belongs to it and yet not exclusively. We originally apprehend a river as flowing and sparkling and making music, for example. But Newman already insisted that our primary perception of things is moral, aesthetic, and pragmatic as well as detachedly observational. He correctly reasoned, in consequence, that any bracketing out of moral and aesthetic responses as ontologically irrelevant is an arbitrary decision.

It is therefore arguable that Newman already offered something like a phenomenology: intuition has primacy over discourse and presents us with all the serious, grown-up philosophical problematics. However, his insistence on the surplus of real over notional assent would prevent any sort of Husserlian idealist confinement of phenomenological conclusions. And just because that is for Newman impossible—because it is assumed that what is presented to us remains irreducible to how we experience its presentation on pain of surrendering its otherness and reality—he can also retain, unlike Husserl, yet without skeptical despair, an awareness that nothing apprehended is *sheerly given*, but is always interpreted, acted upon, decided upon by us creatively and imaginatively. Newman notes how the experience of 60° Fahrenheit is never sensorially neutral, yet may be subjectively one of either heat or chill; how some people do not distinguish red or green; how some see a curve as convex that others see as concave; likewise, how the same upright letters can seem to different children to lean one way or the other.[16] We always see *as*—with a qualitative supplement that is always already bent by our responses. Hence Newman offers in effect a phenomenology which is also a hermeneutics and a pragmatics and therefore he avoids a Husserlian foundationalism as much as a Fregean one.

16. *An Essay in Aid of a Grammar of Assent*, 291–92.

By starting to develop a radical empiricism, Newman draws on deeper insular resources against the more superficial, philistine ones. However, he is convinced that the development must point the British back to the continent and to Rome. Why should this be the case? Interestingly, Newman isolates two aspects of British culture—the literary and the scientific—which from Matthew Arnold through to C. P. Snow came to be regarded as antagonistic rivals. Yet Newman appears, beyond Arnoldean insight, to hint at a deep underlying kinship between the two. *Both,* he seems to suggest, are somehow abstractive and notional, for both tend to substitute regular systems—numerical, experimental, or grammatical—for reality, and live only within those systems and their endless possibility for manipulation. Science is comforting because it offers us a regular control; literature is consoling because it secures a world where humane ideas can fictionally hold or can be abstractly perfected by the rearrangement of a system of signs.[17]

Against this twin complicity of technology and literary humanism—offering us both material comfort and a smug sense of self-revelation—Newman suggests that the mass of the population cannot be moved to act for the better by such bloodless machines. Rather, people will only fundamentally assent with their whole being to images and dramas that are at once concretely real and yet imbued with the imaginatively enhanced. Here Newman's strategy is at its most daringly post-secular: Christianity may have lost its hegemony forever he concedes, yet this must leave a problematic cultural vacuum. Cultures are *not* formed either by "science"—by facts drained of value—*nor* by "literature"—by values drained of factuality. For Newman, presumably, the secular literary/scientific split was not inevitable, but rather the result of a religious development—Protestantism—which had already encouraged the loss of the integration of fact and value in image, theater, and narrative. Crucial here to Newman's entire cultural strategy was his youthful recognition that the magisterial Reformation has rendered belief incredible precisely by insisting that the age of miracles is closed, such that in consequence the sacred drama and radically empirical possibility of the irruption of the *exceptional event* is a thing of the past.[18] Once the deep sacred past had been claimed by evolution, it became doubly crucial, as Newman realized, to claim the present also for the continuation of sacred drama or the

17. Ibid., 88-89.

18. Newman, *Two Essays on Biblical and Ecclesiastical Miracles.*

"scenic" as he terms it. (Indeed, Robert Bruce Mullin has shown that the shift towards the holiness and charismatic movements within the Protestant churches was the fruit of a similar neo-Catholic transformation.)[19]

Likewise, for Newman, the religious manifestation of the British literary obsession as biblicism offers no vivid epiphanies but only a vague sense of the providential, which itself will be eroded by biblical criticism, if the literal authority of the sacred word is all that we can rely upon. Instead, Newman suggests that we need to see that the biblical histories concern a personal apprehension of the intertwining of the mythical with the historical which the canons of written history will tend to reject, since they concern only thinned-out aspects of events which all can recognize without benefit of subjective inspiration.

In these respects one can see Newman as carrying forwards strands of the Oxford Movement which were not simply conservative or reactionary but post-secular and critically counter-cultural. Frequently, he insists that intellectual understanding is not the pursuit of a method, nor an act of technical manipulation, but the ineffable judging or creative response of a living mind. In the face of modern physical reductionism, his metacritical response is to insist on the mysterious manifestations of the psychic as constituting our primary reality and as undergirding the unpredictable drama of human history. This psychic excess over any technical medium Newman also seems to extend to an excess of thinking over language. Here, arguably, he breaks with the romantic sense (as mediated to Britain by Carlyle) that we are always trapped within a shadowy world of signs within which the subject can only ironically and negatively assert himself. However, just as Newman denies that real aspects are purely available in isolation from notional ones, so also he is not necessarily saying that there are any concepts independent of verbal mediation. Rather, he is perhaps suggesting, in a fashion that recalls Kierkegaard, that if language discloses the real this can only be affirmed by an entirely subjective judgment which enacts the intrinsic but incomprehensible bond that exists between the psychic and the ontological. This bond is for Newman more manifest in the iconic and sacramental taken along with language than it is by language alone, since the imagistic directly conjoins the conceptual and the semiotic with the plenitude of the concretely real.[20]

19. See Mullin, *Miracles and the Modern Religious Imagination*.

20. *Grammar of Assent*, 87: "Belief is concerned with 'things concrete' 'which variously excite the mind from their moral and imaginative properties.'" 90: "It is well to

For this reason statues, pictures, totems, and processions stand at the center of culture as much as narratives and recitals. But for Newman, British culture has lost this vital dimension, and hence has become increasingly incapable of such real passionate religious commitment as remains possible in the south of Europe. Perhaps he would not have been surprised by the way in which, during the first decade of the twenty-first century a new irruption of the religious in world affairs has coincided with the re-direction of the course of events by singular incidents whose visual impact, albeit of a negative order, moves more than any arguments or demonstrations—the Twin Towers dissolving in flames, terrorists torturing hostages on video, David Kelly on his last walk in the Oxfordshire countryside.

In the end, Newman's work in the first four chapters of the *Essay* and in the chapter on the illative sense shows a deep kinship with that of other genuine counter-enlightenment, rather than merely conservative, thinkers like Vico, Jacobi, and Hamann.[21] Like them, as his frequent mathematical examples tend to show, he resists above all the algebraicization of the real in both a literal and an extended sense. In supposedly grasping the real, science must inevitably substitute its own system of signifying equivalents of the real for the real itself—just as geometry, says Newman, can be algebraicized, even though algebra will not let us know that there is no real fourth dimension and will merely mention certain things like the square root of minus A, which it cannot intuit, whereas the intuition of an equivalent spatial phenomenon is possible for geometry.[22] In a fashion somewhat akin to the reflections of the later Husserl, Newman fears that the reduction of science to repeatable procedure will lose the original intuitions on which it is based, and that this will further disguise the fact that this intuition was but one of many possible intuitions, all inevitably abstracting from a real plenitude. If, by contrast, the sciences remember that they begin with a compelling icon and a commitment in

---

freshen our impressions and convictions from physics, but to create them we must go elsewhere." 91: "to act you must assume, and that assumption is faith." (One should note here that it is in fact arguable that Carlyle, in *Sartor Resartus*, was exploring this conjunction as a kind of tension when he ironically takes 'clothes', which are altogether material and yet utterly ornamental and signifying, to be the paradigm for culture.)

21. See Milbank, "Knowledge: The Theological Critique of Philosophy in Hamann and Jacobi."

22. *Grammar of Assent*, 57.

excess of *given* warrants—since warrants are never sufficient to justify commitment—then the analogous reasonableness of religious vision and commitment may come into view. Evidential warrants never demand assent in any human field for Newman, for one can always suspend one's certainty as to the referential bearing of any formal system, as well as withhold one's psychological commitment to it. From this perspective, religious assent is not exceptional and aberrant but rather normative—for it is given precisely where the real is deemed to coincide with human passions and interests. This arises in the case of dramatic events and their representations which exemplify in concrete form the compellingly attractive and uplifting.

All Too English, All Too Anglican?

And yet . . . when Newman turns more directly to the religious case, he seems partially to forget the radical character of his critique of modern intellectual norms and to fall back upon specifically modern modes of religious apologetic. He rejects, indeed, Paleyian arguments from design in nature, since such inferences, being too complex, can support no true assent to an immediate apparition. Yet he endorses Butlerian or Manselian or quasi-Kantian moral proofs for God's existence whose inherent structure is really in no better case. In the early part of the book Newman seems to insist on the concrete co-belonging of the true, the good, and the beautiful; yet in his treatment of the ethical he rejects the moral-sense tradition dating back to Shaftesbury which sustained a link between goodness and aesthetic harmony and thereby preserved an irreducibly social dimension to morality, which does not prise questions of conscience apart from those of appropriate social roles. Following instead the purer stoicism of Bishop Butler, Newman views the moral response as proceeding from the entirely inner voice of conscience that prescribes a non-negotiable duty and is concerned with persons not things—he concomitantly (but questionably) denies that we can have any true passions for the latter. This approach tends to divorce practical recognition of the good from the interpretation of theoretical states of affairs and from judgment about what will promote social harmony. Where the latter, more classical approach is taken, one's vision of reality, including transcendence, will tend to be inseparable from one's understanding of what ought to be done. But for Newman at times, our sense of the beautiful and of empirical truth is self-contained and does not point beyond the circle of immanence. This leaves the inner voice of conscience alone as that which points us towards God, now divorced from a wider "reading" of the world, while the voice of conscience of itself "vaguely reaches forwards to God." Newman also resorts to more extrincisist arguments for which the fact of conscience supports a strongly probabilistic *inference* as to God's existence, such that the latter alone can explain why we should be subject to an inward moral imperative.[23]

Despite his insistence on the primacy of revelation for all real religion, Newman offers here a weak natural theology based upon the supposedly universal human recognition of "conscience," even though he acknowledges that Plato and Aristotle knew nothing of conscience, but only acknowledged "moral sense." Of course, after Nietzsche, all such arguments seem absurd—but it would have been open to Newman in his own terms to see that the modern deontological system of conscience is

23. For the integration of the true, good and beautiful, see ibid., 87: "Belief . . . being concerned with things concrete, not abstract, which variously excite the mind from their moral and imaginative properties, has for its objects, not only what is true, but inclusively what is beautiful, useful, admirable, heroic. . ." For the question of moral proof of God, see 97–98: the first principle of such a proof "which I assume and shall not attempt to prove . . . is . . . that we have by nature a conscience." For the separation of the moral and the aesthetic, see 99: ". . . taste and conscience part company: for the sense of beautifulness, as indeed the Moral Sense, has no special relations to persons, but contemplates objects in themselves; conscience, on the other hand, is concerned with persons primarily, and with actions mainly as viewed in their doers, or rather with self alone and one's own actions, and with others only indirectly and as if in association with self. And further, taste is its own evidence . . . but conscience does not repose on itself, but vaguely reaches forward to something higher than itself . . ." Here not just the aesthetic is subordinated, but also a "lower," more aesthetic, social, and situated aspect of morality. Newman sounds much more "Kantian" than "Hegelian" here. See also 100–101 for the denigration of objects. For Newman's "extrinsicism," see 101: "These feelings [of conscience] in us are such as require for their exciting cause an intelligent being . . . conscience . . . sheds upon us a deep peace, which there is no sensible, no earthly object to elicit. . . . If the cause of these emotions does not belong to the visible world, the object to which his perception is directed must be supernatural and divine." Here any extrinsic argument confirms the pictures of an all-seeing and retributive judge which conscience naturally (we are told) tends to elicit. Newman sounds at this point far more like Pelagius than Augustine—failing to argue like the latter, that our deeper, more primordial relation to God and the Good is that of a lover to the beloved (see also 311). Newman proceeds (102) to compare the inference from conscience to God to that from images of the external world to its reality, which works in animals more by instinct than by ratiocination. This "Reidian" as well as Butlerian analogy would be more convincing if one were to remove the sundering of moral from intellectual and aesthetic apprehension.

simply one limited and perhaps dubious notional system. Instead, at the end of the book, he offers an un-Catholic and wholly Kantian account of punishment as the formal enactment of intrinsic desert entirely detached from questions of the teleological flourishing of the offender, his victims, and the community.

There is supposed to be a parallel between conscience and the illative sense as the faculty which issues in real assent. This then requires, as Newman suggests, that the operation of conscience involve something like Aristotelian *phronesis*—yet such an exercise of moral craft, or of a tacit and impresentable sense of what should be done in particular circumstances, involves a constant reading of the world and *not* simply a listening to an inner voice.[24] There seems to be an inconsistency here, whereas Newman also more coherently approximated the illative sense to an Aristotelian or Thomist exercise of *intellectual* virtue which must be alert to practical goodness as well as to theoretical truth. More clarity on the role of *phronesis* however emerges when it turns out that, for Newman, it is associated not just with practical reasoning, but also with the governing of assents to inferences, whereas the illative sense concerns assent to terms, whether real or notional.[25]

In so far as *phronesis* governs inferences, it is clearly to do with judgments as to the probable rather than the certain. Here though, Newman seems un-alert to the radical distinction between a pre-modern sense of the probable as involving a kind of ineffable intuition which approximates to an unreachable truth, and a modern sense of the probable as concerning a *calculable* approximation to certainty—the modern sense was encouraged by the development of calculus, but in the nineteenth century enjoyed new applications to physics, biology, and sociology.[26]

This confusion emerges in Newman's contestation of the Lockean claim that assent must keep pace with the strength of inference. The contestation contains several strands. First, Newman denies that, as a matter of fact, this is psychologically true—assent can lag behind or exceed inference. In the second place, Newman sees this psychological reserve as epistemologically justifiable—inference is never complete and its real applicability never entirely certain, while practical exigencies nevertheless

24. Ibid., 277.

25. Ibid., 278.

26. See Hacking, *Emergence of Probability.* Lepew and Weber, "Genetic Darwinism and the Probability Revolution."

demand that we also commit ourselves in excess of evidential warrant. We reason in broken syllogisms—enthymemes where the middle term is loosely analogical, not univocal—scarcely ever perfect ones. In the third place, Newman points out that our most basic real assents to our own existence, our having had parents, the roundness of the globe and the physical insularity of Britain and so forth, do not correspond to evidence or inference but rather concern the sorts of assumed and all-encompassing facts that are the traditional province of ontology.[27]

All these responses to Locke are entirely cogent and unseat his "manly" reasoning which Newman supposedly admired. Yet this is not so clear when Newman turns from the question of foundational "assents" to that of "inferences." All too woodenly "male" is Newman's Butlerian extension of the range of Lockean "convergent probabilities" as legitimating a full act of "complex assent"—that is, a certain conviction concerning something not immediately given, such as a physical reality which we "simply" assent to, yet nevertheless reasonably justified in terms of a supposition that it is immediately given elsewhere and to someone else, or in potential to ourselves in another time and place. For in this case real assent is not really taking that "leap" which alone affirms the binding of the psychological with the ontological, but rather is simply affirming a sure train of inference as so nearly certain that it can be taken as truly such. Hence Newman's invocation of Butler's claim that we can affirm a somewhat uncertain event as real, if denial of its reality would tend to render incoherent a chain of preceding or consequent and incomprehensible events, seems to have little to do either with Aristotelian *phronesis* or with the real assents of the illative sense. The same applies to his statement that "a proof is the limit of convergent probabilities."[28]

The essential modernity of Newman's version of probability is also shown in his endorsement of the modern legal admission of circumstantial evidence as opposed to confession and testimony—and his failure to see that this frequently issues in miscarriages of justice. Nevertheless, there is a real confusion here, and Newman fully sustains *phronesis* as regards

---

27. *Grammar of Assent*, 136–56. On Enthymemes, see 153.

28. Ibid., 254. In general for "Informal inference," see 230–60. And see 253 for Newman's telling affirmation that his notion of informal inference is like the method of proof in Newtonian science, where likeliness becomes truth in the way a polygon infinitely tends towards a circle.

inferences, when he writes that sometimes "the reasons of [a person's] conviction are too delicate, too intricate" to be objectively traced. Thus they are "in part invisible; invisible except to those who from circumstances have an intellectual perception of what does not appear to the many. They are personal to the individual."[29]

Given this stark tension in the work, one can legitimately ask just how important for Newman is modern probabilism in the sphere of religion? To answer this final question one must consider briefly Newman's reflections in the *Essay* on the nature of the Christian doctrine of God. The attributes of God and the conception of the three persons of the Trinity, all taken one by one, can, Newman declares, be the object of a real religious, devotional, and imaginative assent. However, this is less clear in the case of the unity of the divine attributes, or the thought of the Trinity taken as whole. Here, Newman rightly says, there can be no total proof of the co-belonging of the divine attributes and so of the divine simplicity, nor can there be any adequate imagination of the divine three-in-one.

In this instance a predominantly notional, and so theological rather than religious conception, preserves an *apophasis* in relation to God. Yet while Newman seems to affirm that there must be some glimmer of intuition as to the divine simplicity, he explicitly denies this in the case of the divine Trinity. This doctrine is entirely notional and cannot be the object of any act of real imaginative assent, even dimly and remotely. Here Newman, knowing little of the traditional doctrine of the divine names (for all his earlier interest in allegory), seems to lack the concepts necessary to think a remote participatory insight into the unknown, or an obscure seeing of the invisible.[30]

Now, given Newman's general insistence on the necessity of real apprehension for any affirmation of ontological truth, this appears to render

---

29. Ibid., 259–60. On circumstantial evidence, see 256–58.

30. Ibid., 30. Here Newman rightly says that the unity of the divine attributes cannot finally be "proved," except in relation to a certain remote intuition of the divine simplicity; for the doctrine of God and the Trinity, see 95–123. With regard to the dogma if the Trinity, Newman says at 115 that ". . . the question is whether a real assent to the mystery, as such, is possible; and I say it is not possible, because although we can image the separate propositions, we cannot image them together." Again at 116 "we see Him [God] at best only in shadows, but we cannot even bring those shadows together, for they flit to and fro, and are never present to us at once." At 112 he wonders if the doctrine of the Trinity can in any way be "really apprehended" and at 115 he suggests that this can only be the case implicitly, via submission to the Word of God in the Church.

the depths of Christian doctrine unreachable by the ordinary religious imagination. As Newman often suggests, this must in consequence (including the doctrine of the Trinity) be believed primarily on grounds of submission to ecclesiastical authority. In consequence, for Newman, the overwhelmingly important act of real assent in the religious sphere is to the authority and infallibility of the Catholic Church.[31] But this surely seems crass—real assent to such authority should rather be seen as indissociable from a certain intuitive insight into the compelling truth of all that the Church teaches, just as acceptance of infallibility cannot be divorced from recognition of the presence of the Holy Spirit in the Eucharist and in every Christian congregation. One cannot deny that Newman at his best pointed towards such a perspective, and that his attraction to Catholicism concerned precisely what he saw as its greater sense of divine teaching as working gradually and organically through the developing collective insight of human beings into symbolic mysteries. Nevertheless, it seems ironically true that he better presented such a vision in his Anglican phase, dominated by his "Alexandrianism."[32] In the *Grammar*, by contrast, he too much presents real assent to Catholic authority as a kind of isolated starting point and independent foundation.

Here his original evangelical anxiety over the waning authority of the Bible leads him to abandon his sophisticated validation of the cultural primacy of tradition, the visual, the imaginative, and the active, in favor of a substitution of a foundationalist Papalism for a foundationalist Biblicism. As with a now-crude conception of science, so with a now-crude conception of religion: one begins with a few certainties and from then on it is a matter of a combination of probabilistic inference combined with unquestioning submission to intrinsic authority. It is here telling that Newman assumes the absolute truth of the Newtonian account of motion on grounds of cumulative probable evidence, whereas his suspicion of absolute schemes might have led him to suggest the relativization of a theory based upon the postulation of an ideal counter-factuality.[33]

31. Ibid., 131: "that the church is the infallible oracle of the truth is the fundamental doctrine of the Catholic religion." But of course it isn't and there is no simple 'fundamental' doctrine. See also 129.

32. See Rowan Williams, "Newman's *Arians* and the Question of Method in Doctrinal History."

33. *Grammar of Assent*, 345.

Supposedly, recognition of the Roman Church is a matter of real assent: one is overwhelmed by its sheer consistent thereness. Certainly this is linked for Newman with the necessary role of testimony for true affirmation in all of human life and hence also with the way in which assessment of personal character is bound up with the acceptance of truth. Nevertheless, his almost exclusive focus on our inward relation to God and on intimate friendship means that he provides no very convincing account of how the truth of Catholic doctrine is bound up with a new and attractive mode of corporate being. Nor does he manage, in the manner of Augustine, to link our reliance on testimony to our obscure anticipation of the full presence of that which we seek to know. Given these *lacunae* it is not surprising that, in the *Apologia,* Newman offers also a series of probabilistic arguments for Papal authority: that it is likely that God would have established it, that it could not have survived without supernatural aid, etc. He even appears to suggest in the *Grammar* that the variation of subjective judgment requires an absolute personified and supernaturally sanctioned barometer. But such a view reduces the instance of variation in subjective judgment to the arbitrary, rather than allowing it to be variously disclosive of the real. At this point Newman's subtle philosophical explorations collapse into a simple apologetic alliance of skepticism with fideism.[34]

Some British people might suppose here that Newman is succumbing to a continental Baroque authoritarianism. Yet the irony is that he is rather too much sustains a third English cultural bias that complements the literary and the scientific. This is the *politicization* of religion consequent on the Reformation, which, while it positively sustained the sense of the Church as a real society, also tended to subordinate the entirety of religion and theology to questions of a regular legal government of spiritual realities: one sees this in Hooker, in Butler, and in F. D. Maurice. In Butler it takes its most debased form of discernment of supposed analogies between the system of nature on the one hand and the system of religion on the other. Nature is seen as on the whole rewarding virtue and

---

34. Ibid., 324, 328, 336, and 344–45. At 345 Newman *does* speak of Christianity's elevation of women, protection of the poor, destruction of slavery, encouragement of culture. But he needed to give a more elaborated account of these themes in terms of their links with the nature of the Church as the true society and the Christian vision of God and his relation to the Creator. His follower, W. G. Ward, for all his ultramontanism, was much stronger at this point; Newman, *Apologia pro Vita sua.*

punishing vice, while the necessary sufferings of some for the benefit of others—clearly on the model of political economy—is seen as parallel to the Christian doctrine of vicarious atonement.[35] Despite his disparagement of the British obsession with an abstract and general doctrine of providence, Newman at the end of the *Grammar* endorses this parallel in a way that aligns him with his pro-capitalist market evangelical contemporaries rather than with those High-Church Anglicans who stressed the priority of incarnation over atonement and concomitantly the need for a social epiphany in the present that did not sacrifice some human beings to others, nor the present to the future.[36]

Newman's Catholic understanding of salvation might seem radically to distance him from the evangelical supporters of political liberalism. Yet, to the contrary, his Tridentine tendency to see justification as finally a matter of individual merit independently responsive to grace, only perfects the idea that vicarious suffering is finally educative for the individual who receives its benefits but must responsibly claim them on behalf of his own self-directed destiny.[37]

So if, in the end, Newman discovers that the real location of spiritual government lies on the Continent and in the shape of the Catholic Church, he has made this discovery in terms of an all too English projection that after all does not consistently break with Lockean empiricism nor with a necessarily related Lockean liberalism.[38] In the face of radical uncertainty and the arbitrariness of individual wills, the individual must be directly confronted with an unquestionable authority which is at once an undeniable fact and also something to be accepted on the grounds of probabilistic reasoning.

Was Newman therefore simply overwhelmed by his own inherited habits of mind, combined with a fear of an irreversible decline of Christianity? To a degree one must answer yes. But more profoundly, one

35. *Grammar of Assent*, 316: "I will but add, that, since all human suffering is in its last resolution the punishment of sin, and punishment implies a Judge and a rule of justice, he who undergoes the punishment of another in his stead may be said in a certain sense to satisfy the claims of justice towards that other in his own person." Butler, *Analogy of Religion*, part II, chapter 5, 184–204.

36. Hilton, *Age of Atonement*. This is a too little known book, whose new relevance to our own time is obvious.

37. Newman, *Lectures on the Doctrine of Justification*. And see David Nicholls's astute assessment, in Kerr and Nicholls, *John Henry Newman*.

38. See Kenny, *Political Thought of John Henry Newman*.

can conclude that he did not sustain and extend his remarkable adumbration of a radical empiricism because he did not sufficiently realise (unlike, by contrast, Coleridge) that such a view requires an elaboration of its implicit metaphysical assumptions. Thus at the heart of Newman's refusal of algebraicization lies the claim that the mind, not logical processes, concepts, nor words is the real seat of comprehension. This then allows him to say that the mind may rationally decide or judge something in an ineffable way that cannot be fully explicated, without thereby lapsing into arbitrariness or unreason. But such a view assumes that intelligence and the soul are ontological realities which are the prime sites of the truth of Being and hence in some way intrinsically linked to Being as such. Aristotle, Plotinus, and Proclus provided, in differing ways, such accounts of the soul and its relation to reality, and Coleridge had known that in insisting on the primacy of the imagination and of concrete apprehension he was ultimately indebted to the Proclean tradition.[39] Newman, by contrast, was still more of a philosophical amateur. This is shown most noticeably at the start of the chapter on the illative sense. Here he refuses after all to endorse the idea that a certainty in excess of evidence and inference concerns "intuition" or something like a recognition of "intellectual forms," and insists that he is concerned only with the practical operation of assent, not with its metaphysical possibility. Yet without some account of the latter, there is no reason why we should not account for our mental operation in terms of naturalistic vagaries.

Newman, as his correspondence reveals, remained troubled by the lack of a "test" to distinguish a commitment to the vivid yet illusory from the vividness of truth. Nicholas Lash incisively comments here that it is just as well that Newman never devised such tests, for this would obscure Newman's profounder point, that, to cite Lash, "such security . . . is, in the last analysis, received as a gift."[40] A gift, in its surprising rightness and acceptability, has to be its own guarantee, and if Newman says that only mind as mind, beyond method, techniques, and criteria can recognize the truth, then this is tantamount to saying that it is, precisely and literally, the faculty for receiving and recognizing spiritual gifts. Truth as gift is its own warrant; it must be self-authenticating. But if it is received by mind as that which is properly at home in mind and yet also as something that

39. See Trouillard, *Mystagogie de Proclus*, 44–53.

40. Nicholas Lash, "Introduction" to Newman, *Grammar of Assent*, 19.

derives at times from non-cognitive and non-reflective being, then there must be some common medium between this non-cognitive being on the one hand, and mind on the other, through which truth can be transferred and sustained.

Newman himself suggests as much in his concept of "aspects" that may be both real and notional and are thereby transferable from things to mind. And does he not sometimes say that such aspects are "intuited," and should one not think of aspects as being qualities of intelligible forms? Without such a scholastic notion, how can the concrete thing be any more than a random bundle of disparate elements? By failing to endorse the intuition of intellectual form, Newman becomes himself prey to the suspicion that real assent is but an animal and arbitrary habit which requires an authoritarian regulation if anarchy is not to ensue. In the end, therefore, his thought is inconsistently poised between a radical empiricism that could re-invigorate ancient realism and an all too modern positivism, not without kinship with the positivism of those exceedingly modern Catholic traditionalists Joseph de Maistre, Donoso Cortes, and Carl Schmitt.

The irony is that he embraced too much of an inauthentically Catholic post-Tridentine Catholicism, just because he remained too influenced by the modernizing currents of British empiricism, and, just like Edward Pusey (as Peter Nockles has rightly argued) also insufficiently attentive to the deeper currents of Anglican thought—one thinks of Ralph Cudworth, the Caroline divines, the non-jurors, the Aberdeen Circle, Robert Lowth, John Wesley, George Berkeley, and Coleridge himself—who retained links to a pre-Tridentine Catholicism, while also elaborating critiques of a reductive empiricism linked to that peculiarly British blend of the empirical and the Platonic.[41]

---

41. Nockles, *Oxford Movement in Context*. In his earlier works on Arianism, however, Newman had echoed Cudworth against his eighteenth-century German commentator Mosheim, implicitly defending the former's view that the spirit of mystical pagan philosophy was by no means entirely antagonistic to Christian theology and also Cudworth's prodigious insight that there is in Plato himself a "Trinity" closer to the that of the Christian Trinity than the subordinationist triads of the Neo-Platonists. Even though, as Rowan Williams says, this led Newman into the "opposite error" to that of Mosheim— namely blaming Antioch not Alexandria for Arianism—this does not—as Williams also rightly indicates—at all negate the importance of the perspectives which Newman derived from Cudworth. See Rowan Williams, "Newman's *Arians* and the Question of Method in Doctrinal History," and Newman, *Arians of the Fourth Century*, 44.

But at his best, Newman was also a most remarkable heir of this more authentic Britishness and *beyond* his forebears rightly saw that it could only attain its fulfilment by returning to its continental and Catholic roots.

PART II

Theology and British Politics

4

WERE THE
"CHRISTIAN SOCIALISTS"
SOCIALISTS?

Were the "Christian Socialists," extant between 1848 and 1854, really socialist at all? Was John Ruskin, that somewhat kindred spirit? Like most commentators, Edward Norman in his book, *The Victorian Christian Socialists*, seemed to think on the whole not, according to the application of most normally accepted criteria.[1] He was prepared to concede that the Guild of St. Matthew, operating from 1880 onwards, had a genuinely socialist outlook, but even here he felt that the earlier heritage held its members back from a whole-hearted participation in radical politics.

In this chapter I propose to put some queries against this consensus. It seems possible to me that a great deal of the historiography of Victorian Christian socialism, particularly since the Second World War, has been skewed by an understanding of socialism deriving from later historical perspectives. After the impact of mass industrialization in the late nineteenth century, the mobilization of working-class votes by political parties, and the beginnings of state welfare, it became natural to associate socialism with collectivism, populism, full suffrage, trade unionism, and state intervention, if not also with revolution and complete state planning of industry. Now it is true that the Victorian Christian socialists viewed all these things with various degrees of distaste, and, noting this, Norman goes on to suggest that this distaste indicates the degree of their remoteness from the working-class and genuine socialist movements of their own time.

1. Norman, *Victorian Christian Socialists*.

It is this latter verdict, however, which is much more doubtful. For precisely the same refusals can frequently be found—though not necessarily altogether in the same person—among the French socialists of the first half of the nineteenth century who, apart from the Owenites (virtually dispersed by 1848), were the only possible reference points by which Maurice, Kingsley, and Ludlow could understand what socialism entailed.

One can list the characteristics that are supposed to detract from the Christian socialists' socialism in the following way:

1. They were apolitical, disliked political organization and state intervention.

2. They ignored trade unions and political movements of the workers.

3. They indulged in ruralist and medievalist fantasies.

4. They opposed democracy and human rights in favor of paternalist schemes of education.

5. Their attitudes to women and the family were traditional.

8. They attempted to Christianize and moralize an essentially secular creed.

7. Many of their economic proposals were romantic and unrealistic.

8. They were essentially unoriginal transposers of Tory radical notions already articulated by Carlyle and others.

Taking these charges one by one, I hope to show that, in every case what is taken as a mere eccentricity of the Christian socialists in fact exhibits, at the very least, a kinship with the mainstream of socialism as it was constituted up to the mid-nineteenth century.

1. *The Christian socialists were apolitical.* This issue is in many ways the most fundamental one of all. Quite simply, nothing so clearly authenticates their socialism as their apoliticality. Only the insular perspectives of some British historians cause them to miss this point. And yet, in Britain itself, Robert Owen had thought that little was to be gained from political agitation in the short run, and favored a concentration on the setting up of new cooperative villages. Meanwhile in France, the sanguinary course of the 1789 revolution engendered a disgust with politics, and both St. Simon and Fourier, in very different ways, advocated "social" action as an alternative to political action, which was held to have

revealed its limitations. Fourier wished to concentrate on the creation of local, ideal communities, while St. Simon believed that the development of industrial organization would produce a new, more scientific, more harmonious mode of polity, which would eventually replace the existing state apparatus. The English Christian socialists had, of course, no sympathy with this aspect of St. Simonianism, but, on the other hand, they promoted cooperative programs which had something in common with those of Owen and Fourier, though much more with those of another French socialist, Philippe Buchez.[2] Their concentration on the formation of associations for production rather than on industrial or political agitation was precisely in line with a very strong current within French socialism, and not necessarily a sign of their caution, or lack of fundamental desire to change society.

2. *They were "out of touch" with workers' movements.* Like most other socialists of the time, John Malcolm Ludlow and his associates were unfamiliar with the story according to which the proletariat were to become the center of consciousness for socialist change, simply because this story had not yet been fully circulated, and the proletariat, of whom so much was therein prophesied, did not yet exist in overwhelming numbers. On the contrary, Ludlow took it for granted that workers would have to be educated in socialist ideas, and he feared that otherwise, like the chartists, they would come to make a fetish out of universal suffrage in much the same way as medieval peasants imagined that, could they but speak to the king, all the evils of domination within his kingdom would fall away.

Ludlow's French experience was important here. Along with the French socialists themselves, he perceived that universal suffrage in the revolution, and the general granting of "rights," had done little to alleviate poverty, misery, or conditions of abject social dependence. Even trade unionism was to be viewed as a merely reactive demand for guarantees from superiors which really guaranteed nothing in the long run. From this perspective, Ludlow's most important exemplar was Philippe-Joseph-Benjamin Buchez, the historian and supporter of the 1789 revolution, who had nonetheless turned against its spirit of liberalism, and proposed instead a philosophy of duty, mutual solidarity, and common aspiration, applying not, in the first instance, to the state, but to *associations*

2. Cole, *Socialist Thought*, 179, 292.

ouvrières, or productive cooperatives which he helped to promote.[3] These small associations, voluntarily entered into, with capital jointly owned by the workers themselves, were supposed to provide more effectively for the freedom and security of the worker, while at the same time offering a context for the "positive" inculcation of discipline, virtue, and duty, where the merely "negative" revolution was held to have failed.

The case of Buchez is crucial for an assessment of the English group, because it was his model of association which they imitated, following the reports of Ludlow and an exiled Frenchman, Jules Lechevalier. What is most striking here is that in certain respects Buchez's socialism was much more marked than that of his contemporaries, if one takes as crucial for socialism a refusal of private capital, and an upholding of equality. For by comparison with Buchez, Fourier, for example, did not by any means entirely reject returns on unearned income to private individuals, while Robert Owen, and much more emphatically St. Simon, continued to believe in an authoritarian role for the patron-owner within the industrial enterprise.[4] Yet the main principle of Buchez's cooperatives was that capital belonged inalienably to the entire association, and could not be divided, even if one of the members left. This principle, conveyed to England by Ludlow, continued to be applied in the period of Guild socialism, in the early twentieth century. At the same time, Buchez was not guilty of believing that cooperative organization alone would solve all problems. Like Proudhon, he also believed in the need for state direction of an infrastructure, and an apparatus of price-control and setting of the limits within which reasonable competition between associations might occur. Ludlow appears to have adhered to roughly the same set of attitudes.

It can be concluded, then, that by taking up Buchez's notion of association, the Christian socialists were, in fact, allying themselves to the advance guard of socialist thought and practice.

3. *They were wary of democracy.* Like other socialists, and like John Stuart Mill, the Christian socialists were (very sensibly) alarmed about the possible effects of manipulation of ignorant opinion, and tended, therefore, to believe that further extension of democracy should wait upon improvement of education, or even, in the case of Ruskin, that better education should entitle one to more say in the suffrage. However

3. Cuvillier, *P.-J.-B. Buchez et les Origines*; Bruhat, "Socialisme Francais."
4. Cole, *Socialist Thought*, 177–78.

dubious such proposals may appear, it is important to emphasize that English Christian socialism resembled French socialism in wishing to link democracy with education, and in seeing the former as dangerous without the latter. In both cases socialism was perhaps as much to do with promoting excellence as equality, because it was perceived that the modern liberal state had eroded a concern with common standards—the only possible base for a public promotion of both quality and equality—and that economic pursuit of profits encouraged indifference to the nature of the goods exchanged and the production of sham goods which were unnecessary or poorly designed.

4. *They were essentially conservative romantics.* It is true that the English Christian socialists, from Maurice through to Headlam, remained obsessed with the idea of a resettlement in the countryside and the re-distribution of land. But the association of socialism with industrialism is not a "natural" one, and nor was it initially a realist one, but on the contrary, a part of St. Simon's prophetic fantasy, before industry had really got off the ground in France at all. For most socialists in the nineteenth century, and especially in France, the land question remained realistically important. First and foremost, they perceived that only the mass-appropriation of land from rural property owners, and the leaving of huge numbers of people without independent means of subsistence, had produced the conditions making wage-slavery possible. At least as late as the 1880s it still appeared possible to prevent this process going any further, and to deal with rural repression as the root cause of social injustice. In the long run, of course, this kind of concern has come to be seen as unrealistic, and yet one may still wonder, with Proudhon, whether, without a much wider distribution of property-ownership and self-subsistence, any real resistance to capitalism and bureaucracy is truly possible. There is more analytic truth in this "unrealistic" view than in Marxian theodicy, for which the long-term historical outcome will vindicate and justify the horrors of primitive accumulation which Marx himself described with unrivalled clarity.

A belief in the importance of a mainly rural future was shared, therefore, not just by the Christian socialists, but also by Fourier and Proudhon, by the authors of the chartist land plan, and, to some extent, by Robert Owen. And a "romantic" celebration of rural life is not lacking in these cases either: possession of one's own plot, rootedness in a single place, attention to the beauties of nature, these are all supposed to foster robust virtue, capacities of sympathy, and inner harmony. Perhaps the Christian socialists sometimes exaggerated urban as against rural deprivation, but this is scarcely the point. For what mattered was the identification of the countryside not just as the Eden of paradise, but also as the Eden of the original Fall: where land had been enclosed, the poor dispossessed, and the nobility had preferred the savagery of hunting to the care of animal and humankind. No one who reads Ruskin, in particular, can fail to be aware that this is his real perspective.

The essential conservative romanticism of the Christian socialists is supposed, again, to be exhibited in their invocation of the Middle Ages. But this was a vital reference point for all the socialists, whether it meant, as for St. Simon, an organic order, a united Europe under a spiritual head, or else, as for Buchez, a time when voluntary associations, under religious patronage, could flourish. Again, perspectives on the 1789 revolution are crucial here: the revolution was seen as an essentially negative work of enlightenment, sweeping away privileges, establishing rights. Yet the ensuing terror implied a serious lack, and suggested that a modern equivalent for "medieval" and "positive" notions of solidarity, of limitation of state power, of inculcation of duty and self-sacrifice must now be found. What is astonishing is that these notions, first articulated by the arch-reactionaries de Maistre and de Bonald (though indeed in an often highly cynical, and, in a sense, *ultra-enlightened* form, stressing that people will only be moved by an arational *mythos*) were rapidly accepted by liberals as well as by conservatives, and "socialism" was only born under the aura of such assumptions. So that while the socialists certainly did not want just to return to the Middle Ages, they nonetheless desired an equivalent of medieval "positivity," and this generally meant some common belief that will act as a counterweight to individualism, and some institution that will fulfill the educative functions once performed by the Church.

It would be much too hasty to conclude that English medievalism, deriving from Walter Scott and Thomas Carlyle, had precisely the same ideological structure. But it is interesting to notice that Ludlow, who disliked Carlyle, nevertheless contributed a French medievalist thematic which found a ready English response. In one of his Christian socialist tracts Ludlow writes: "I must pause here a moment to point out the way the idea—the Church idea, of universal brotherhood haunts these men [the Paris *ouvriers*] and links itself in their minds with the union of all the trades connected with building."[5] Given the Masonic influence on French radicalism, there is no reason to doubt the essential truth of this report, and it may well serve to remind us that working-class solidarity had to be constructed, and that often in the nineteenth century it was constructed with the same cultural debris to hand as the intellectuals used to envisage new forms of community. The French *ouvriers* were caught up in the same highly complex—and not merely "conservative"—gothic romance as Pugin and Ruskin in England. Pugin and Ruskin were also haunted, in their case by the idea of public beauty, of common aesthetic standards being rapidly thrust aside in favor of the calculus of a subjective desire whose changing "tastes" could become the object of a continuous public speculation. But for Ruskin as much as for the French workers, the memory of churches is not merely a memory of worship, or of *theoria*, but also of what was never really valued enough, even in the Middle Ages themselves—namely the multiple creative work of the builders, which has become for him the truest mode of religious offering. Here the medieval period stands for something lost, a certain virtue, yet also as the time where this virtue *could* be lost, and so as the time where it was insufficiently prized. The appeal of the nineteenth century back to the Middle Ages, as Ruskin divined, is an *allegoric* appeal: one invokes kings, warriors and artisans, but it is not political rule, war, or servitude which one now wants, but "kingly" and "noble"—in other words not mercenary—attitudes, in the sphere of work and trade, and artisans as "gentlemen," as heroes, and exponents of liberal arts, in such a way as had never happened before.[6]

The Christian Socialists did not, then, add a romantic gloss to socialism: on the contrary, socialism was written from the start in a neo-gothic script, and long before *News From Nowhere*, it was known what style would have to be chosen for Utopia.

5. *They had traditional attitudes toward women and the family.* Naturally the English Christian socialists upheld the sanctity of marriage and the family, but was this unsocialist, or even unfeminist, according to the standards of the time? There is a rough correlation here between individualist anarchism (like that of William Godwin) and free love on the one hand, and socialism—especially of the co-operative sort—and belief in marital (or at least sexual) fidelity. Married love and loves within

5. Ludlow, "Working Associations of Paris."

6. Ruskin, *Time and Tide by Wear and Tyne*, 166–67; *Praeterita*, 5–6; "Of Kings' Treasuries," 54–55; "Unto This Last," 150.

the family are generally seen by thinkers like Buchez as a training in fraternity, and as an inhibition of egotism. The household is not envisaged
as a "private" sphere after the manner of twentieth-century suburbia. On
the contrary, there was a general desire among the French associationists
to tie production to the household, and to approximate working relationships to familial ones by the extension of apprenticeships. (Note here that
this paternalism applies to the *educative* aspect of work. If one rejects
even this measure of parental direction, it must be in preference for the
mutual egotism of a merely contractual arrangement.) This found echoes
among the English Christian socialists, and also with Christian feminists
in Britain like Josephine Butler.

And indeed, expansion of the domestic sphere often assumed
apocalyptic overtones. Proudhon believed that when the political and the
domestic became one, then a true and desirable state of "total anarchy"
would have arrived.[7] John Ruskin likewise believed in a kind of explosive
"opening out" of the domestic sphere into the public. Like the Comteans
and Mazzini, Ruskin allied this with an enhanced role for women, exhibi-
tors of the *true* economic virtues of "household management," horribly
parodied by the "political economy" of modern times. Indeed, while
Ruskin is conservative in his apportioning to men of active, creative abili-
ties, and to women of "managing, peace-making" ones, he nonetheless
goes very far in the direction of suggesting that women are best suited for
most *governmental* tasks both at home and in the public sphere.[8]

While the Christian socialists, therefore, like most socialists of the
time, were scarcely feminists, they nonetheless turned traditional attitudes to women and the family to strangely critical ends.

6. *They merely gave a Christian gloss to socialism.* Maurice's dictum,
that the group intended to "Christianize the socialists, and socialize the
Christians," has been given rather too much credence. It is clear that for
Ludlow at least, Christian socialism already existed, in France. Again, the
figure of Buchez appears crucial: Buchez, the exponent of one of the most
authentically socialist doctrines, was at the same time a Catholic of orthodox beliefs (he was not, however, practicing, but several of his associates
became Dominican friars). This fact alone suggests that, in the French
context, Christian socialism was no "secondary" or merely responsive
phenomenon. Buchez's orthodoxy was admittedly somewhat rare, yet still

7. Edwards, *Selected Writings of Pierre-Joseph Proudhon*, 92.

8. Ruskin, "Of Queens' Gardens," 61–95.

rarer, in France, was an explicitly atheist socialism: on the contrary, the thing "lacking" in the revolutionary tradition could sometimes be called "the positive," sometimes "the harmonistic," sometimes "the sacrificial," sometimes "the social," and often "religion," that which binds people together. Buchez aspired to rewrite the encyclopedia, but had now discovered that a totalizing, universal point of view could not be that of philosophic reason: on the contrary, it had to be that of a "positive" revelation, known by faith.[9] Others, like St. Simon and Comte, proclaimed that a "positive" science, adopting the "factual" point of view of a certain stage of human social development in relation to nature, performed this function. But this science was still to do the job of religion and provide the foundation for ethics and human worship: above all it was to teach the subordination of our freedom to our position within an organic whole. And as a new religion, it also required a church, and even a papacy. In France, socialism was sometimes as much about inventing a new church, as a new social order, and certainly more than about inventing a new politics.

Bearing this in mind, two points need to be made here about Ludlow and Maurice. First of all, it too often goes unremarked that Ludlow, undoubtedly a more genuine socialist than Maurice, broke with Maurice in part because he wanted to ensure that the cooperatives were explicitly Christian. For Ludlow, as for the French socialists, the Church was to be the site of the new society, albeit in his case, as for Buchez, a transformed Christian church, and not a new scientific church. And it is Ludlow, the true radical, and not Maurice, who insists in "Masonic" fashion on the association of guild with *cultus*. Maurice, notoriously, denied the sacrament of creative labor so dear to Ludlow, and, indeed, to many of the St. Simonians. Maurice's other masonry is all about "digging," all about pointing to mystic foundations already laid, as the following quotation so clearly shows. This is his summary of early English history: "A tribe of teutons came to these shores, and drove out the effeminate Roman colony which previously occupied the land. These teutons have brought with them some noble thoughts; a reverence for family society, the idea of law, the germs of a national society. To them come a set of freemasons who say they are in fact citizens of all countries, that they are bound together in a fellowship having a strong mystical foundation."[10]

9. Cuvillier, *P.-J.-B. Buchez et les Origines*, 25, 33.

10. Maurice, *The Kingdom of Christ*, III, letter 10, 157.

This quotation leads me directly to my second point. Why was Ludlow initially attracted towards Maurice? It can be suggested that this was because there are many more resonances between the theology of the *The Kingdom of Christ* and that of French Catholic social thinkers than is usually recognized—however uncertain the question of direct influence may be. Exactly like de Bonald, Ballanche, Buchez, and an entire current of thought that, in its secular, Comtian version becomes "sociology," Maurice insists that society, law, and language are not the product of human creative powers, but were originally *revealed* to mankind, as the necessary context for the emergence of individual humanity. Inversely, it is also true that revelation is *always* revelation of a social order, because social relationship is the most fundamental kind of knowledge, which has an immediate, irresistible, and "positive" character to it. (The later Maurice makes clear his attachment to a religious "positivism," and even its partial kinship with the thought of Comte.)[11] For Maurice the first revelation was of the patriarchal family order, the second of law and the state—making "inward" and conscious the law of the family—the third of the universal family, the Church. Unlike the second revelation, this one is external and sacramental, and just like Buchez in his work on the philosophy of history, Maurice stresses that salvation and atonement is offered in and through a new set of social relationships.[12] For Buchez this was an exclusively Catholic conception, and he blames Protestant Christianity for the spirit of egoism which has led to capitalist domination. Maurice's account of the Church is also in some ways a Catholic one, and yet what distinguishes Maurice from both Buchez and Ludlow is his fatal restriction of the Church as society to very little more than church attendance. Maurice disapproved of monastic orders because they were "buildings," voluntary associations freely entered into, and his attitude to cooperatives belongs here also. He sees them as a necessity in certain restricted cases, but would rather rely upon the given "familial" structure of English oligarchic society backed up by law. So the third revelation fails, in Maurice, really to transcend the first two, and the whole trouble with his in many ways profound and moving theology is that the Church society seems only to provide spiritual energy to bolster the patriarchal family and the sovereign state. Hence precisely because of his weak *ecclesiology* he is unable to contemplate a

---

11. Maurice, *The Life of Frederick Dennison Maurice*, II, 59.

12. Cuvillier, *P.-J.-B. Buchez et les Origines*, 31.

transformed social sphere, a new heroic virtue, a new gothic building, as imagined by both Ludlow and Ruskin (both, be it noted, in some ways rather Presbyterian than Anglican in spirit). He was certainly unable to envisage cooperatives as sacred, covenantal brotherhoods.

While it can certainly be conceded that Maurice was a Tory *rather than* a socialist, in a way that is much less clear in the case of Ruskin, this is not simply because he believed in monarchy, aristocracy, the family, and paternalism. What is rather decisive is his ultimate lack of interest in the Ruskinian program of extending the associative principle, "distributing" nobility and excellence, and insisting that all aristocracy be, as for Aristotle, a matter of genuine superior skill and virtue. If he drew back from this program, then, one can suggest, this was because he feared that such reconstruction smacked of Catholic meritorious works and ultramontane longings. It is Maurice's *theology* that inhibits his socialism.

7. *They proposed unrealistic solutions.* Ludlow and his friends were concerned not just with founding Christian cooperatives, but also with the economics of an entire society based upon association. Here they tended to suggest that labor-time should become the measure of value, and that a new sort of credit-money should be invented, representing "definite" quantities of actual or potential labor, and "definite" quantities of exchangeable products.[13] The trouble with such proposals, of course, is that they tend to side-step the problem of how incommensurable products and types of labor are to be valued against each other. But the French socialists and the earlier English "Ricardian socialists" were similarly blind, and promoted similarly over-simple panaceas.[14]

8. *They were not original social thinkers.* On the whole, this is true; though not of Buchez, whose ideas they followed. An exception must be made, however, for Ruskin, who alone theoretically transcended the kind of economic solutions mentioned above, which all made the same mistake of remaining *with* political economy, however vestigially, and seeking an infallible "scientific" solution to social problems. For Ruskin declared that only *qualitatively evalued* labor can serve as a standard of exchange in a society not founded upon wealth.[15] Much more rigorously than any of the other thinkers, Ruskin propounded the view that the only alternative to a

---

13. Ludlow, "Prevailing Idolatries."

14. Cole, *Socialist Thought*, 102–20, 201–19.

15. Ruskin, "*Unto This Last*," 187. See also Spear, *Dreams of an English Eden*, 146–54.

free market society short of tyranny is one based upon commonly accept-ed standards. Yet he did more than this: he also suggested that liberalism had been able to triumph precisely because of the relative neglect of the aesthetic and of the practical arts in all preceding culture. If craft-labor is merely servile, then it can be readily mutilated and exploited; if design and architecture are matters of relative indifference, then products will become mere commodities (in Marxist terms)—instances of quantifiable "wealth"; if the beauty of nature is a mere extra, of no moral significance, then nature can be subject to spoliation. The second volume of *Modern Painters* set out the antidote to all this: an account both of perception and of imagination, in which aesthetic and moral response are intimately and intricately fused; in which both aesthetic and moral qualities are held to belong objectively and intrinsically to given nature and super-added art, because everything has its appointed and fitted way of working, its true natural end.[16] Without such a metaphysics, Ruskin divined, there can be no resistance to capitalism, because capitalism is merely the logical man-agement of the death of excellence, the death of objective and transcen-dent value. Many socialists had already discovered this truth, but only Ruskin shows clearly why real socialism is necessarily "religious."

In conclusion, it would be absurd to pretend that, on the whole, the English Christian socialists were not more conservative than the French socialists who preceded them. Yet the above considerations suggest that this difference can be exaggerated, and that there is no reason, in their historical context, to doubt their claims to the title "socialist," or to view the term as a merely rhetorical exaggeration.

16. Ruskin, *Modern Painters*, II; *The Seven Lamps of Architecture*, 366–79.

5

THE BODY BY LOVE POSSESSED

Christianity and Late Capitalism in Britain

What was the living worker's activity becomes the activity
of the machine. Thus the appropriation of labor by Capital
confronts the worker in a coarsely sensuous form; Capital
absorbs labor into itself—*als hätt' es Lieb' im Leibe*.[1]
(Karl Marx, *Grundrisse*)

For there is no work or thought or knowledge or wisdom in Sheol. . . .
(Ecclesiastes 9:9–10)

During the 1980s and 1990s and to a lesser degree during the New Labour era, Church leaders in Great Britain called into question the wisdom of the economic policies of the ruling Conservative governments. Predictably, their competence to speak concerning such matters was called into question by the governments themselves, by journalists, and also by other churchmen and women.

At one level, the challenge did not need to be taken very seriously. Church leaders have a total right to speak out of their perception of immediate distress, and are courageous if they refuse to allow a fear of technical inadequacy to deter them from making moral comment.

---

1. Marx, *Grundrisse*, 704. The last phrase, "as though its body were by love possessed" is a quotation from Goethe, *Faust*, Part 1, Act 4, "Auerbach's cellar in Leipzig."

Yet in the long run, this is not enough. The very imperative which calls forth the immediate response demands also a deepening responsibility which seeks to comprehend and to recommend. If theology is to have the right to speak in the socioeconomic domain, then it has to earn such a right. And also demonstrate that it can have such a right; for the problem is that in our society power and knowledge are so articulated that "common sense" will declare that theology can have nothing of special importance to say concerning economic relationships.

Failing such a demonstration, it is likely that, beyond the level of initial immediacy, ecclesiastical and theological commentary on socioeconomic affairs will be sucked into the vortex of ideological responses. Harsh analysts will perceive that far from it being the case that, for example, the Church of England had changed its spots, rather it was speaking out in the name of the old establishment consensus, of which it was a part, but that had now been severely qualified. And to some Christians it appears almost axiomatic that they must occupy a "middle ground" in politics, because they confuse a commitment to mediation with a commitment to "compromise."

But this may fail to recognize the initial realism of neoliberalism as a response to the crisis of the capitalist economy in Britain. Certain diagnoses of socioeconomic reality were favored because they appeared to chime in with the principle of "moderation" and suggested that we can cope with our problems within the terms of welfare capitalism. Yet in fact, these diagnoses were in themselves highly ideological.

Among these diagnoses I am thinking especially of the following: the idea that Britain underwent a process of "deindustrialization," often allied to the view that we required a cultural adjustment to a world where work will in the future often be of a more sporadic character; secondly the almost opposite notion that Britain had never readily sustained a work ethic and "enterprise culture" to the same degree as the United States and that to this was attributable many of our ills; thirdly the idea that socialism was once the voice of the oppressed and exploited, but was now the ideological creed of a subversive minority.

What follows falls into four sections. In the first I shall discuss, very roughly and schematically, how theology might establish its legitimacy in the socioeconomic domain. With these considerations in mind I shall go on to consider, in the second section, the category of "deindustrialization" and, in the third section, questions to do with cultural attitudes and technological change. In the fourth section I shall tentatively outline substantive theological conclusions.

Theology, Facts, and Values

Of course, when I mention a "demonstration of theology's right to speak," this demonstration is in the first place to ourselves, to Christians, It can only be a demonstration to non-Christians in so far as it belongs to theology as a whole; that is to say, is part of talk about God, which if it is to be such—if it is to be a *logos*—must be in some fashion convincing in itself, rather than a mere "expression" of a faith wrongly thought of as preceding a rational and linguistic reflection.

It may in fact be the case that the "demonstration to ourselves" will initially undermine the very basis on which secular society is at all likely to take ecclesiastical comment seriously. For I shall argue that theology does not stake out its rights merely on the ground of "value" and "ethical dimension," but claims a much wider comprehension. Paradoxically, it is when the Church confines itself within the former, more modest bounds, that its discourse tends to appear most blatantly ideological. So, in England, the traditional terms of Anglican establishment ensure that a certain division of intellectual labor will find a ready acceptance. This division has always been validated within Anglican thought as a marriage of empiricism with "Platonism."

On the side of empiricism, it is supposed that there can be a single, objective and non-controversial description of contemporary secular reality. On the side of "Platonism," the ethical resources of Christianity are reduced to a few seemingly relevant abstractions, which often amount to no more than moral truisms. This approach received its classic expression in the thought of William Temple, but it rests on a series of all-pervasive Anglican assumptions. Within this cast of mind the historical character of Christianity as a process of developing insight and emerging praxis is usually ignored.

In the recent past, this cast of mind characteristically re-encounters its real source of legitimacy in the context of the "meeting of experts." Church committees of inquiry, composed of theologians and social scientists, produce "recommendations" which are based on empirical analyses, and doctrinal deductions performed separately and in advance of the encounter. Where it is stressed that we must interpret the general will of God in terms of its applicability to the current situation, it is easy to see that the diagnoses of the latter must in reality take the leading role in the evolution of a "moral response."

And, in fact, the danger today is that Anglicans will find it far easier to break (apparently) with the "Platonic" fallacies than with the empiricist ones. The already dubious conception of theology as a reflection on the praxis of the believing community is, within Anglicanism, transmuted into listening to the voice of the Church of England, which in turn, through its clergy and activists, is supposed to have an "authentic" intuition of mythically "urban" settings. Likewise the "incarnationalist" rhetoric of Anglicanism can sometimes be used in such a fashion as to suggest that God's will can be derived from a mere immersion in present realities. Hence an intellectual–practical procedure that halts at the incoherent notion of "involvement" is in alliance with a Christology which suggests that atonement resulted simply from God's acceptance of the world and economic adaptation to it.

Repentance with respect to the notion of "deduction from dogmas" may thus be no true repentance at all. It is worth here recalling how, in the theology of F. D. Maurice, Anglican ideology arrived at a different equilibrium in which the "given facts" and the "given values" were actually identified as the buried but positive reality of the entire set of English socio-political relations, constituting a secret theocratic order. Rigorous examination of Maurice's theological and sociological positivism—he later, as was mentioned in chpater 4, expressed a certain preference for Comtean methodology over the developmental perspectives of Coleridge and Wordsworth[2]—reveals that the innermost secret of this order is

---

2. Maurice, *Life of Frederick Denison Maurice*, Vol II, 59: To Kingsley, February 25, 1981, "I am sure that you are right, Wordsworth's Prelude seems to me the dying utterance of the half century we have just passed through, the expression . . . of that self-building process . . . in which the Evangelicals (Protestant and Romanist) were all engaged . . . For us there must be something else intended, either the mere science Millennium of Comte, from which the good Lord deliver us, or the knowledge and life of God as the ground of all human and earthly knowledge and life." Elsewhere Maurice made the paradigmatic importance of Comte clearer. Having declared against Mansel that we must "know that we know God" Maurice goes on to say that "Auguste Comte had the wisdom to perceive and the honesty to proclaim that we are in an age of science, that . . . knowledge and science are synonymous, that whatever by its nature cannot be known, must in such an age be assumed not to be" (Maurice quoted in Brose, *Frederick Denison Maurice*, 248, 261.) See also Maurice, *Lectures on Social Morality*, 415. "As a Clergyman and a Professor

always patriarchal, familial authority, taken to be the first bond between human beings and between humanity and God.

Maurice's theology—in total contrast to that of Coleridge[3]—was thoroughly anti-historical. The human work of making history is entirely alienated to the divine side, and the widening sphere of human relations culminating in the Church is seen in terms of the providential establishment of spiritual resources for the better fulfillment of the original filial and national duties. The social, the bodily, the ideally material is for Maurice the patriarchal-political; the latter is laid down by God essentially without human mediation; developments within this order are also direct supernatural impositions, and are confirmations, not dialectical transformations of what was originally given.

Anglicans have not really fully forgotten this respect for the sacred book of English history, mystically conceived. There is a successor positivism to that of Maurice. This consists in the view that it is somehow a theologically profound task to "face up to changing economic realities" and to enquire what the Church's response must be in the face of such changes. An "incarnated" theology here often appears to be one which expects theological perspectives to emerge from a "concerned" immersion; one

---

of Moral Theology, I feel myself under an unspeakable obligation to him (Comte) . . . he has compelled us to abandon all apologies for our faith, and simply to ask ourselves what we mean by it, and what we suppose it can do for mankind." Maurice is indeed to be commended for developing the very modern idea that the sphere of knowledge is coincident with the sphere of social relationships, but he takes the latter as a given, divinely instituted order, whose meaning—like that of the incarnation—is "immediately" obvious, and almost "scientifically" demonstrable. One must conclude that Mauricean scholarship hitherto has often over-stressed his continuity with the English Romantics; it may be that this is not as great as in the case of Newman who preserves and extends the developmental perspective. For a corrective to the eulogizing of Maurice, see Rowan Williams, "Liberation Theology and the Anglican Tradition."

3. Maurice's "Platonic archeology" is essentially at variance with Coleridge's developmentalism. Both, certainly, look for political models in the Bible, but Coleridge's conception of this is much more dynamic just to the extent that he embraces allegorical readings which Maurice rejects. Moreover, even Coleridge's Erastianism is more qualified. For Maurice the Christian Church in England as such stands in an organic relation to the state; for Coleridge this is only a contingent fact, in so far as the Christian Church happens to fill the function of the "National Church," the sacred function necessary to any political order. But the universal Church stands in a contingently contractual and critical relation to all states. If one reads Maurice carefully, it is clear that the Church as society only becomes fully concrete rather than ideal through the political order of family and state. In Coleridge there is actually more suggestion of Church as ultimate social locus. Here again, the essential continuity runs from Coleridge to the Oxford Movement.

which secretly equates the "changing economy" with an evolving created order; one which imagines such changes as "happening to" all of us, and as not essentially involving contested class relations, which are really seen as part of a fundamental, given arrangement.

At this point it is relevant to note that the ideology for which "economics" was the central social and historical reality—"political economy"—arose in the eighteenth century partly out of a theological background for which a designing providence and the elaboration of a theodicy had become the main categories. "Natural Theology" was also a theology of society mechanistically considered, as the writings of Tucker, Paley, Malthus, Whately, and Chalmers amply attest.[4] So, to give a choice example, we find Malthus asking why it was that God had created a world in which hardship and suffering were necessary for the attainment of prosperity, and replying that only in a world and a history where striving was necessary would an Isaac Newton have appeared.[5] Here natural theology has not simply forgotten history and the gospel; rather it has its own version of history in which Newtonocentrism (the English conquest of nature, the English inauguration of science, technology and so prosperity) has replaced Christocentrism. It is thus no accident that

4. See especially: Malthus, *Essay on the Principle of Population*, 348–872; Paley, *Principles of Moral and Political Philosophy*; Chalmers, *Application of Christianity to the Commercial and Ordinary Affairs of Life*, and *On Political Economy in Connection with the Moral State and Moral Prospects of Society*; Whately, *Introductory Lectures on Political Economy*; Tucker, *Light of Nature Pursued*. A quotation from the latter work sums up the entire *episteme*: "Nor is his wisdom less conspicuous in the moral than the natural world; . . . the principle interests and opposite views of private persons seem to balance one another and are made to produce order by their proper commixture out of that which separately would lead to confusion" (I:496.) The importance of clerical practice of political economy is mentioned by John Maynard Keynes in his *Essays in Biography*; the economic sphere continued to be thought of as a sphere to be dealt with by moralists, even though a particular theological morality constructed it as an area from which morality was banished. One might suppose that this work being done, the clergy could retire from the area; yet today we see the *return* of this theological construction of economism in the American New Right, and even in the more "philosophical" deliverances of Frederick Hayek's successors. Keynes himself could have claimed ancestry from another cleric, George Berkeley, who in *The Querist* inaugurated a "social democratic" economic option.

5. Malthus, *Essay on the Principle of Population*, 363. The same providential enticing of spirit out of the "original sin" of "chaotic matter" (Malthus also happily combines empiricism with Platonism) favors also the Bourgeoisie: "The middle regions of society seem to be the best suited to intellectual improvement; but it is contrary to the analogy of all nature to expect that the whole of society can be a middle region . . . every piece of matter lying on a surface must have an upper and an under side . . ."

when Coleridge rejected the centrality of an abstract theodicy and a calculating providence in favor of the God who became incarnate and an understanding of history as the exchange and proliferation of linguistic meaning, he also rejected the claims of political economy to be the key social science. Coleridge realized that political economy treated certain contingent conventions as "natural elements" and that it had built into its agenda the replacement of ethics with technique. In Malthus and others the immediate preoccupation with the mutual adjustments of self-interest meant that morality might determine the whole system, but could not impinge within the system; morality was endlessly postponed.

Coleridge, it seems to me, indicates to us what it is for theology simultaneously to recover a genuine sense of its own possibility, and to demonstrate its right to speak on socio-economic matters. He does not (at his best) confine himself to a "moral perspective," but calls into question the terms in which secular analyses are made. Moreover, it is manifest to Coleridge that there is a complicity between political economy and a certain sort of theology, so that for him the issues remain in some senses always internal to theology. It is entirely appropriate, and not at all a sign of muddle, that in a work like the *Lay Sermons* Coleridge should constantly interweave discussions of the workings of biblical language with pronouncements on political economy and other social matters.[6] For Coleridge, as we saw in chapter 1, there is always a linguistic exchange that is counterpoised to, and perhaps more fundamental than, the economic exchange, and this first exchange has its ground and fulfillment in Christ, the communicative *logos* itself. Here theology has its possibility, which is simultaneously the power to interpret human history and society.

This is the example that we need to try and follow when we are faced with the question of theology's competence to speak in the economic sphere. Probably there is no "Christian economics," but one only says this against a background recognition that theology has *no* proper finite territory of its own, and yet is only able to speak of God, its specific concern, by way of all other subjects and sciences. So when one is speaking of "theology and economics" one is just as *directly* concerned with the possibility of there being a mediated word of God, as when one is speaking of "theology and Church history" or "theology and the gospels."

6. Coleridge's critique of political economy is partly anticipated by Berkeley (who certainly *tries* to re-moralize the economic sphere) and by William Law's attack on Mandeville. See chapter 1 above.

Hence theology cannot evade the question of its attitude to received economic wisdom. To do so would be to accept a fact/value dualism that is in itself the outcome of a particular, modern, "liberal scientific" approach to society. If theology accepts modern liberal economics (comprising both monetarist and Keynesian streams) at their own evaluation, then it has, in reality, already made decisions within theology itself, and has endorsed a whole series of buried affinities between the modern scientific approach to politics and economics and the fideist-nominalist-voluntarist current in theology which is inherited, through seventeenth-century writers like Hobbes and Grotius, from the late Middle Ages.

The shortest route to unraveling the problem of theology and economics is to become aware of this history. It is within voluntarist theology that the key philosophy of "possessive individualism" has its origins.[7] *Ius* (right) is first thought of as *dominium* or as power over property within a perspective that understood God's creative activity and relation to the world in terms of an arbitrary exercise of power. The notion of a scientific knowledge, whether of nature or of society, has its birth from the idea of a knowledge linked to creation, a knowledge in which human beings can participate in so far as they are makers. This *schema* has myriad versions, but in voluntarist ones it suggests a science of society that is in step with the arbitrary power exercised by property-owning persons. The amoral space of the new "political science" as found in Hobbes is the self-constituted space of human technical power. And *this* is also the space of the absolutely secular, the sphere delegated by God to a spiritually neutral human control; the first space of the secular, opened up and legitimated by *theology*.

It is also the space of "political economy." The latter takes over not only the primacy of labor (Locke's labor theory of property entitlement becomes Smith and then Ricardo's labor theory of value) but also the Suarezian-Grotian view of natural law as the actual reading-off of injunctions for human life from the fixed constitution of the natural and rational order (a concept entirely at variance with earlier Thomist tradition).[8] Thus for Smith it is seen as "natural" that there are three sources of wealth—land, labor, and capital—and three classes corresponding to them. From the point of view of theology, then, classical economics

---

7. See Tuck, *Natural Rights Theories*, esp. 24–30 on late scholasticism.

8. For a conclusive demonstration of this, see Finnis, *Natural Law and Natural Rights*.

appears as the heir of a bastardized concept of natural law and also as inheritor of the medieval-renaissance theme of the co-creativity of human beings as possessing the *imago dei*, developed in a particular and distorted form. It is in relation to this latter theme—which rises so strongly to the surface in Locke[9]—that theology especially needs to assess its attitude to economics.

For Aquinas, Adam originally possessed *dominium* because he could name things through language and creatively appropriate the natural order to human use.[10] The connection of *dominium* with a direct relation of the individual to nature, rather than simply to social convention (a connection which has profoundly to do with the theology of Creation) goes at least as far back as this. However, Aquinas did not make the voluntarist move of equating right and effective ownership. This move, by contrast, undergirded liberal contractualism and later, the labor theory of value. One can say that Adam's God-given right to dispose had a certain sort of one-sided emancipatory consequence within liberal tradition.

Yet the notion of human creative power also possessed latent emancipatory implications of a far wider kind. Something of this is indicated in the writings of the Levellers and in Locke, for whom, while possession established rights of disposition of property, disposition was naturally subject to considerations of charity, and property ownership to considerations of reasonable personal and social use. For Locke, human creation is less an arbitrary and quantifiable force and more linked to notions of stewardship and responsible improvement. So unsurprisingly those who, in the early nineteenth century, read Locke in a radical, pro-socialist sense, were also those who saw radical implications in Ricardo's labor theory of value. If labor, they argued, was the "natural" source of value, then did not profits, by rights, belong to labor?

The Ricardian socialists were still thinking in liberal natural rights terms, terms that had their antecedents in the Suarezian notion of natural law. Karl Marx's labor theory of value is not at all in continuity with

9. Here, see Tully, *Discourse an Property*. Tully shows how Locke's entire epistemology and ethics is founded on the contrast of "divine creative knowledge" with "human creative knowledge." He compares him in this respect to Vico. However, Locke is both more rationalist and more voluntarist—he does not make the full "expressivist" or "pragmatist" move which sees knowing as primordially *in* making—the move which makes Vico a genuinely post-enlightenment thinker. Yet Vico can also be seen as resuming the full, aesthetic dimensions of the *homo creator* theme.

10. See Tuck, *Natural Rights Theories*, 19, and Thomas Aquinas, *S.T.* I. Q 46.

this tradition, because it is a theory about how value is created within capitalism, and not a remnant of the "natural law" approach of political economy.[11] However, it is notable that in the latter half of the nineteenth century, the labor theory of value disappears from liberal economics (in the course of the "marginalist" revolution) not so much for purely theoretical reasons as because the radical potential of this doctrine had been all too clearly exposed to view. Marginalism meant the adoption of a new *episteme* in which political economy came to an end, and was replaced by "economics," a discipline which confined itself to a purely technical description of the operations of the market place, and no longer sought to comprehend how these were interconnected with social organization. The gain here was that the "natural law" claims were abandoned. But on the other hand, the abandonment of the labor theory of value in its "natural law" form meant that even the beginning of a possibility of insight into the *social* specificity of Capitalism was lost sight of. And in addition, marginalism preserved intact the assumptions of possessive individualism, and reinforced the notion of economics as a realm of purely technical control.

Because Marx, by contrast, rejects both these assumptions, as well as the "unholy trinity" of the natural law of political economy, he is able to show the truth concealed within the Ricardian labor theory of value. The vital move which Marx makes is to show that the assumptions about the natural sources of profit made by the political economists only echo assumptions which are really made within capitalist practice, and which sustain that practice in being. Within Capitalism, labor is the source of value, not primarily because this is an empirically demonstrable fact, but because it is through the alienation of labor, through the treatment of the mass of particular, qualitatively different labor as abstract, quantitatively generalizable labor that the reality of capitalist value—exchange value—*gets constituted in the first place.* (However, Marx failed to see that the abstraction of consumer desire is an equally original source of value within capitalist logic.) The labor theory of value is an intrinsic part of Marx's theory of alienation and reification, and not just a piece of outdated economics.

11. See Clarke, *Marx, Marginalism, and Modern Sociology*, 64–108, for the relation between Marx and Ricardo and the collapse of the labor theory of value in orthodox economics.

The dominant practice and theory in our society make it appear absurd that theology could have any feelings one way or the other about something as apparently "technical" as the labor theory of value. Yet when this is considered in the historical context I have sketchily outlined above, it seems that it might be possible to say that, from a Christian perspective, Marx's theory of value can be seen as part of an exposure of the heretical and one-sided character of the liberal version of human creativity, with its voluntarist roots and its tendency to reduce the entire activity by which we shape and appropriate our world (and in which alone our "humanity" arises) to an economy of power and uniform predictability. The corollary of this view is that if "the world" is constituted as such an unsacral, technical sphere, then the spiritual or the moral lies at the transcendental boundaries of this world, and is only known by faith, and only affirmed in private.

It may indeed appear strange to read Marx as undermining the grounds of secularization, and I shall return to this later. For now it should be added that it is in certain respects Marx who develops to the full the real emancipatory implications of a stress on human creativity. On the one hand, history, which is only the history of human labor, is to be read as the history of the estrangement of that labor, whereby this human constitution of human existence is systematically concealed and mystified in the interests of asymmetrical (class-dominated) social power. On the other hand, it is "the open book of the essential powers of man"[12] and can be re-appropriated as the entire record of human achievements and possibilities in terms of genuine, qualitatively distinct, use-values. When we have understood that humanity is specifically expressive, cultural existence, then the way is open for a much more complete self-development, a history which will not be alienating because we shall simultaneously grasp that our meaningful activity is a modification of sensuous, natural being, and that nature is only real for us in this human, meaningful form. In the *Economic and Philosophical Manuscripts*, Marx makes it clear that this will abolish a situation in which the realm of industry (the entire sphere of labor) is seen only in "an external utilitarian aspect" whereas the human essence is seen in terms of the "universal" realms of politics, art, religion, considered as extra to and outside the sphere of human

12. Marx, *Early Writings*, 354.

making.[13] The abolition removes this fact/value dualism and human relationships, human relations to nature, human values and aesthetic perceptions all appear as qualitative aspects of human natural being.

It is possible here for theology to see Marx as restoring an ontological realism, yet in a manner that is cognizant of the modern recognition of human historicity which has its real centre in the view of humanity as constituting and constituted by human language as the constant mediation between mind and nature. This linguistic center is averted to by Marx in *The German Ideology*.[14] At this point it is open to theology to recognize that Marx is appealing to a version of modernity and of the "turn to the subject" whose roots are much older than Kant, and much more in keeping with that realism which must be at the centre of any Christian philosophy. An entire, gradually developing tradition of the creativity of the *imago Dei* focused initially on the (under enhanced Proclean influence) Dionysian idea of humanity as the locus of a charitable, self-diffusing *virtus*, leads variously through Eriugena, Hildegard, Eckhart, and Salutati to Nicholas of Cusa's final inauguration of the notion of a linguistic, cultural being[15] The theological inheritance is still very strongly at work (in fact, predominant) in proto-romantic and romantic rejecters of linguistic instrumentalism and developers of "expressivism"[16] like Vico, Hamann and Coleridge. Marx presents to some degree the same sort of possibility of an expressivist historicism that is realist rather than idealist. And it is vital to note, that when he engages with Christian historicism, it is only with the idealist, Hegelian version.

What I want to suggest is that by taking these historical detours—here all too briefly outlined—it may appear that a critically orthodox

13. Ibid., 354–55.

14. Marx and Engels, *German Ideology*, 118: "Language is the immediate actuality of thought."

15. Lucio Colletti, in *Marxism and Hegel*, 234ff. makes the connection between Marxism and Renaissance) anthropology. However the latter is seen as uniformly "idealist." This is not really to understand Cusanus (on whom Colletti concentrates), nor his essential continuity with medieval anthropological reflections.

16. I am inviting confusion here. By "expressivism" I mean a view for which language is a "work of art" and not just an instrument or means of communication. I do not mean that there is an essential and "prior" natural or mental content which language merely "expresses," nor that artistry implies primarily *self*-expression. The former view is in fact precisely what Vico and Hamann reject. The situation is complex, because some Romantics certainly promote "expressivism" in the pejorative sense.

theology has many more "predispositions" than one might expect with regard to the entire matter of "productivism" and of labor theory of value as they centrally appear in political economy and in Marxism. This is a propaedeutic for what I now want to go on to say about the development of neoliberalism in Britain. In my account, I shall show some favor to Marxist analyses and even to arguments for the continued relevance of Marx's labor theory of value. Despite what I have suggested, it may still appear to many that I indulge in a quite needless association of theology and Christian values with particular social theories. Against such objections I would claim that, on the contrary, the avoidance of genuine causal analysis by theology usually commits it from the start to empiricism (and all the other, kindred assumptions which that might entail) in which it appears that our starting point is merely a series of present social phenomena. By contrast, once one has abandoned fact/value distinctions and scheme/content dualism (i.e., bondage to Kant) then there is no substantive social matter that may not be decisive for one's overall theology, and no substantive social theory that may not become part (though perhaps in transmuted form) of that theology.

Neoliberalism and De-Industrialization

In this section I shall discuss the phenomenon of "deindustrialization" as a key aspect of the emergence of neoliberal dominance.

"Deindustrialization" and "Post-Industrial Society" are terms that have been used by thinkers on the right and center of politics, rarely by thinkers on the left. This is more than a question of the use of words. Nobody disputes that a catastrophic decline of manufacturing industry occurred in the latter half of the twentieth century in Britain, nor that production has become more and more automated. But it is profoundly misleading to call these things deindustrialization. Automation is a consequence of the further extension of the industrial process. And the switch in employment of labor from manufacturing to services and intellectual production is not deindustrialization either; rather it also represents the extension of the industrial process, of the division of labor, and of capitalist rationality to ever-new spheres. Academic centers like universities are included here: they are now run according to managerialist criteria of efficiency designed to further the production of economically and socially profitable expertise.

Why then, is the term "de-industrialization" allowed? I think it is because it suggests that the replacement of one type of technology with another will of itself involve social changes, and in particular the passing of the various ills peculiar to "industrial society." The term implies an outlook for which science and technology are prime determining factors, and for which the economic sphere evolves in a way that is essentially insulated from wider social processes.

The very term "industrial society" has a very specific lineage. Preference for this usage rather than for "capitalism" stretches back to St. Simon, Comte, and Durkheim. These "sociologists" tended to regard the division of labor and consequent growth of individualism as inexorable processes. Their specifically "sociological" stress on the need for corporateness and organic solidarity (and religion) appears by contrast as the advocacy of something compensatory and conservatory. While it was true that this advocacy constituted a limited reaction against possessive individualism, this was only within the "Social" (and political) area which post-marginalist economics had now vacated, and it presumed an economic base still fundamentally conceived on the liberal model.

Thus to talk of "Post-Industrial Society" is immediately to invoke an entire perspective in which one is fatalistic about the development of technology and the economy, but looks to the "social" to preserve the essence of human life. And theology should be alarmed to note that often the sociologists themselves here discover a "role" for religion.

I now want to show what is inadequate about this perspective in both temporal and spatial terms.

Since the eighteenth century there have been at least four major technological revolutions, including the present one.[17] In each case, however, we are confronted not merely with innovations in the process of production, but with new phases in the capitalist mode of production. Each of these revolutions took place in the context of increased class struggle, and each of them involved a new attempt by Capital to counteract falling profits by increasing the amount of surplus value extracted from labor as well as from renewed primary accumlation and new awakening of consumer desires. Scientific knowledge and technological innovation have often lain around unused by industry for long periods. When they are used by capitalism it is always in the interests of making profits. It is not the case that

17. For the following account I am relying partly on the writings of Ernest Mandel. See *Late Capitalism* and *Long Waves of Capitalist Development*.

it is merely technology in itself that tends to reduce the workforce and to increase the division of labor. It is rather the case that the kind of technology that Capital is interested in, and which it encourages, is a technology that enables these things. Division of labor is achieved *in the first place* by dividing up and routinizing human tasks. As a result these tasks become tasks that can be performed by machines. Robots indeed often replace human beings in tasks where the human being is more adequately suited to the job. The reason for the replacement is that robotization decreases labor costs and the risks of industrial disputes.

These considerations all apply to recent history. Automation, or at least semi-automation, has in fact been under way since the 1950s. Its application is one factor in the post-war boom or the so-called "long wave" of capitalist expansion set off by the defeats suffered by the working class under fascism and by the growth of American neo-colonialism. This automation in fact proceeded very slowly. Many firms did not become as automated as is technically possible because beyond a certain level this would not have increased profits. After the seventies there was a massive increase in the rate of application of technology precisely because the postwar boom had come to an end and Capital had to find a new way to increase surplus value, or increase the productivity of labor, in the face of falling profits. During the period of expansion, it was able to tolerate constant inflation as a price worth paying for keeping down unemployment and reducing social discontent. But faced with falling profit an inevitable order of capitalist priorities reasserted itself. The risk of high unemployment had again to be taken. This was of course now a rather *greater risk*, because of the degree to which automation is able to dispense with human labor. However, the impetus to massive applications of automation, entailing such a risk, arose not just from technological possibility, but also from the decreasing options open for capitalist expansion in the relative absence of new worlds to explore, and the reduction of even its existing sphere through the initial success of third-world revolution.

But not merely is technology incapable of determining the conditions of its use, it is in itself partially determined by extra-technological factors. Perhaps even Marx was not aware of this, and tended to think of technology as "neutral." But a little reflection tells us that this is not so. Raymond Williams once pointed out that there was nothing in the nature of the technology of sound broadcasting that dictated that it should be used for this purpose.[18] At first it was thought of as a new sort of tele-graph or telephone. The emergence first of radio and second of television as the monopoly of a government-founded corporation, has then to be explained as an essentially social and political process.

In relation to automation, parallel considerations apply. In his classic book *Architect or Bee?*, Mike Cooley demonstrated that the very forms of automated technology that are favored accord with specifically capitalist imperatives. There is no doubt that automation, considered as a purely technical phenomenon, has the capacity vastly to expand the amount of work that can be performed by a single person. But Cooley pointed out that, in the case of intellectual labor, automation also can be used to divide and parcel up formerly individual tasks rather than to extend the scope and influence of creative work—and this has now duly occurred. Capitalism encourages the former usage, and thus the progres-sive de-skilling of even intellectual tasks. Cooley already described what was happening in the cases of engineering design, and of architecture, where professionals were increasingly reduced to shuffling about pieces of pre-ordained programs that preempt a whole series of possible choices. In addition to this, the professional worker now had to work at a pace which is more able to keep up with the prodigious calculating speed of the computer. This is not a technological, but an economic necessity.

All this means that intellectual labor began to be subject to "Taylorization," to the requirements of speed of turnover, routinization, and predictability. From a purely technological point of view, this is in fact not rational, and will lead to yet further deterioration in all designed products and in human designing skills. This realization puts into proper perspective the belief that automation brings with it a problem of "adjust-ment" and that the main need is for the education of a technically sophis-ticated populace. Capitalism is unlikely to need or desire any such thing.

Cooley's observations are also a useful corrective to those over-fundamentalist Marxists, including in this instance Ernest Mandel who believe that Capitalism is not able to sustain, without eventual collapse, the increasing subordination of labor to the productive process. The more the typical worker is scientifically educated, these Marxists have believed—as Marx seems himself to have believed[19]—the more he will be able to com-

18. Raymond Williams, *Towards 2000*, 180.

19. Marx, *Grundrisse*, 706.

prehend the irrationality of the capitalist system. This is to ignore the extent to which technological expertise, and even natural science itself, may be amenable to a division of labor which keeps workers in particular sectors of a process ignorant of, and alienated from, the workings of the whole system.

To turn now to the spatial dimensions of supposed "deindustrialization," another reason why this has to be understood in socio-economic as well as technological terms, is that there is nothing like a uniform advance of automation across the world. If automation was introduced with the simple aim of extending the possibilities of individual human labor, and of saving human labor, then perhaps the primary interest would be in supplementing lack of skills in the non-metropolitan countries. But far from that being the case, it is rather true that the older, labor-intensified industries have been largely transferred to these areas. And why? Because cheap labor in those countries ensured that the old methods of production were worth maintaining, even in an age of automation. (One should note here that the third-world economy is present here in our own country in the form of exploited Asian labor in, for example, the clothing industry). Today, information-based, automated, semi-automated, and old industry co-exist on a world scale as industry and peasant agriculture did in the past and indeed continue to do so. The latter does *not* survive because certain countries are "backward" or "underdeveloped," but because it remains in the interests of Capital that such uneven levels of development should continue to co-exist. Different levels of development can be a source of greater profitability.

Thus we see that besides the fact that automation under Capital is developed in particular directions, it is also true that full automation on a world scale is unlikely, under the same aegis, ever to arrive. There is a parallel here with the long-term relative industrial decline in Britain in the late twentieth century. We have to understand this in the context of the shifting interests of international Capital. Britain, because she was already heavily industrialized, tended to miss out on the second phase of the industrial revolution, connected especially with steel, gas, and electricity. This phase already involved far more direct supervision of industry by science, and for this reason there was government encouragement of technical education in France and Germany, but not in England. This objective, economic factor has to supplement the subjective, culturalist ones often adduced.

However, British Capital did not immediately lose out, because the empire opened out new markets, abundant supplies of raw materials, and new opportunities for investment. Ultimately Britain's economic decline in this period was to do with a long-term transference of capital from manufacturing to finance. The rise of finance of course exacerbated the north/south divisions of the country. A whole sector of the United Kingdom, concentrated in the southeast, a sector in charge of all the important political and social institutions, had little obvious short-term interest in a revival of manufacturing industry—even though this could, theoretically, have been undertaken in order to restore a more mixed economy.

This would have been desirable, because the "services sector" cannot really substitute for lost manufacturing. This term is in fact a misnomer, because it indicates so many disparate things. In so far as it refers to the infrastructure that supports manufacture (transport, etc.) then it is clear that it has only grown with manufacture itself. These services are productive (in capitalist terms) only to the degree that they are essential to the enabling of manufacture. Otherwise services have pure use-value unless they can be converted by capitalist processes into commodities, in which case they are increasingly governed by market forces. This likewise happens in the second branch of "services," namely services to individuals. But automation has also intruded here; an obvious example is the long-term replacement of domestic labor by household appliances. But, *nota bene*, with this mechanization and transition to "self-service," we get also an *extension* of the sphere of the manufacturing process. Cleaning carpets, which was once an innocent extra-market activity is now for sale, in the form of a commodity: the vacuum cleaner.

And of course this mode of objective commodification of service has also been exported, as regards production, to the Global South. Hence pure "services," which are not in reality selling products like tourism, commodified food, or culture, are parasitic upon manufacturing and finance. They cannot qualify an overbalance to the latter.

Having dealt with the temporal genesis and spatial distribution of misnamed "de-industrialization," it remains to ask about future prospects. I have already suggested that there are limits to full automation under Capitalism. However, I have not yet dealt with the possibly most important reason for this. In the *Grundrisse*, Marx wrote some remarkable passages which show that he believed that the ultimate crisis of

Capitalism comes with the furthest extension of mechanization.[20] He here predicts a future development in which direct human labor will become a less and less important factor, and in which the amount of disposable time for workers as a whole (though not for all workers) will progressively increase. This is the situation envisaged in the quotation at the beginning of this article, the "full development of Capital," which Marx says takes place "when the entire production process appears as not subsumed under the direct skillfulness of the worker, but rather as the technological application of science."[21]

For Marx this marks the absolute limit of the capitalist mode of production. The reason for this is that at this stage individual labor becomes a mere moment of a total productive process. As a result, wealth ceases to be measured by the hours of labor time, and by the amount of surplus labor that can be abstracted. Yet this exploitation of labor is the very thing which, according to Marx, holds capitalism in being (this is correct, if only partially so) and allows it to make commensurate things inherently non-comparable, namely the different skills and qualities of labor and the real use-values of its products. Thus, claims Marx, "Capital . . . works towards its own dissolution as the form dominating production."[22]

This requires a little explicating. Labor as a measure of value breaks down for three reasons. First, while mechanization, or we can say, automation, reduces labor costs, increases the productivity of individual labor and so increases surplus value, in the long run this gain is negated. If fewer man-hours are worked, then labor becomes a progressively smaller factor in costs, and progressively less determinative of market prices (of which, for Marx, unlike Ricardo, it is *never* wholly determinative). But as surplus labor and surplus value is one ultimate basis of the possibility of profit, this means that profits too, in the long run, decline. The "abstract labor" of mere machines is inevitably seen as more "natural" and cannot therefore so easily serve as a mythical measure of value in the way that the "excess" added by human freedom with its capacity for auto-renewal is able to do. Also, an automated production requires less human organization and so, given the right finance, is more imitable, while technical innovations in this field quickly become antiquated. These three circum-

20. Marx, *Grundrisse*, 702–6.
21. Ibid.
22. Ibid., 700.

stances together tend to constrain competitive profit and encourage the formation of monopolies.

Because, for Marx, abstract labor and surplus value are the ultimate basis of commensuration, but actual prices are affected by the mediation of the market and the social distribution of Capital, it is rarely possible to give a quantifiable "proof" of Marx's value theory (to demand this is to suppose that it is exactly the same sort of thing as liberal economic theories of value which are "economistic"). Nevertheless Mandel and others have claimed both that firms limit automation to retain profitability, and that sectors that become fully automated often start to show zero profit returns; the logic for their existence is in terms of their role within the total affairs of a company.

The second reason is that surplus value becomes harder to convert into profit because the growing number of poorly-paid marginal workers means a diminishing market for capitalist goods and a growing crisis of overproduction.

The third reason is that when capitalism gradually ceases to be the appropriation of individual labor and becomes instead, as Marx says, the appropriation of "the general productive power" of man, "his understanding of nature and his mastery over it by virtue of his presence as a social body," then the full irrationality of the system is exposed. A scientifically educated populace realizes the absurdity of subordinating the infinite productive power of non-human labor to the short-term interests of a few human beings rather than to the long-term interests of humanity in general.

Of what use today are Marx's prophecies? As I have said, some Marxists, like Mandel, who have resurrected the labor theory of value,[23] believed that, in the late twentieth century we were now entering into the kind of contradiction that Marx describes. Other thinkers on the left accepted the "neo-Ricardian" (the term is only partially accurate) approach of Pierro Sraffa which simply identifies value with prices, and claims that profits are generated entirely by exchange processes. This view tended to suggest that capitalism can survive the transition to full automation, despite the fact that all the empirical evidence suggests that the present system is reluctant to exploit automation to the full.[24]

23. See, for example, Schwarz, *Subtle Anatomy of Capitalism*, and Shaikh, "Poverty of Albegra."

24. See Steadman and Sweezy, *Value Controversy*, especially the article by Cohen.

The Sraffian approach may appear to have a seductive empiricist appeal. Yet it surrenders, not a detail of Marxist economic theory, but rather the main perspective under which Marx grasped the economy as a social process, and under which (as Habermas argued[25]) he was able to see a constantly renewed mode of mystified communication as the point of interconnection between individual action and functioning system. In the Sraffian approach one is tempted to see the economy again in liberal terms as an area of pure technical functioning with its own momentum, and so not to understand how the capitalist economy must constantly reproduce its own possibility as the simultaneous constitution and estrangement of social relations. One loses the sense of capitalism as a lived illusion, in which labor must be reduced to a mythical abstract measure, and yet this ascription of mythical quantities *really* organizes the lived structures of domination.

The latter, Marxist, theory supposes that automation marks a point of crisis where the myth is exposed. When the role of direct labor is drastically reduced there is no ultimate court of appeal for market commensurations. Capitalism becomes inherently unstable. At the same time, in its constant search for new sources of expansion, it cannot avoid the need to automate.

However, even if it is the case that the capitalist base in surplus value is being, or will be, eroded, one may still want to draw back from the third "visible absurdity" argument as used by Marx himself, and by Mandel. The market and the state may very well find devices for hiding this absurdity from view, and we do not after all have a "better educated" population. The possibility of diminution of direct labor in manufacturing may not occasion a transition to socialism but a drastic mutation of capitalism into another, alienating mode of production. This would be one that *continued* to sustain the alienating appropriation of the general productive power of humanity, in a manner that Marx supposed to be impossible. But because this could no longer be sustained by genuine self-regulating competition, and because the essential alienation would be accomplished not in the relations of employment, but in social relations more generally, it seems likely that such an economy could only operate in a totalitarian

25. Habermas, *Theorie des Kommunikativen Handelns*, II:489–548. However, Habermas rightly suggests, in contrast, to say, Mandel (see text, below) that Marx is "economistic" in seeing alienation of individual labor as the finally unique source of oppression, the last barrier to be overcome.

context of strict cultural control. State bureaucratic oligarchy would now start to fuse with the "private" oligarchy and monopoly of capital. Hilaire Belloc's "servile state" would start to emerge. With the current apparent collapse in 2008 of the finance and debt-fuelled domination of neoliberalism in a crisis of the "non realizability" of abstract assets through linkage to more material ones, this specter now looms. State control of banking could easily dictate greater state direction of production and a greater use of technology—yet still in the interests of the market and still involving an extraction of surplus-value from the dispossessed who do not equitably share in the profit of industry, but are bought off with "wages" and "salaries."

If this diagnosis is at all a true one (and the signs are there) then Christians may have to face up to the possibility that things are going to get infinitely worse. We then need to recall that the history of fallen humanity is necessarily a history of increasing catastrophe, despite the "counter-history" of redemption, however we may suppose that to proceed.[26] Marx at his best (without the final optimism, which in its determinism seems scientifically unwarranted) comprehends this, in that while he believes that every phase brings new benefits and awakens human creative powers, he also believes that in each phase alienation and dehumanization become more pervasive, more deep-seated, and above all more subtle. This is why the text of history increasingly requires complex decoding, and why all of Marxism appears as esoteric nonsense to some, while to others it is clear that it is the processes of history which have themselves become esoteric.

In the coming years, there may be very few left who can decode the yet more subtle mystifications. Infinite division of physical and intellectual labor (*and* of reproductive labor), subtle surveillance of persons, and regulation of behavior through mind-control will perhaps render future tyranny non-apparent. Already we have heard the voices of the philosophers like Derek Parfit of Oxford,[27] who believe that a true utilitarian society must abandon the Christian-derived notion of the person (though he

---

26. I am here invoking concepts of Walter Benjamin, which have very much to do with his involvement with Jewish mysticism. See his "Theses on the Philosophy of History" in *Illuminations*. However, I do not myself see "Counter History" as consisting merely in despairing transcendental gestures. For me history is both catastrophe and tradition of human deification, in so far as it is focused on Christ.

27. Parfit, *Reasons and Persons*.

confuses this with the Cartesian subject), in favor of objective states and essentially discontinuous experiences. This ultimate extension of Hume, Bentham and Sidgwick is then given a plausible mystical gloss by association with Buddhist impersonalism.

Work and Culture in British Tradition

In this section I shall deal with the cultural aspects of British industrial decline, including religious dimensions.

One popular account of decline, expressed most fully by M. J. Wiener, has claimed that it is ultimately attributable to a "hostility to the industrial spirit."[28] Much of the "Anglican social tradition" from Coleridge to Tawney to Demant can plausibly be seen as exhibiting such an attitude. Is it really to blame for wrongly despising and denigrating the realm of industry?

I have already said that "hostility to the industrial spirit" is not an all-sufficient explanation. But even Wiener's cultural analyses will not altogether do. There is no single British anti-industrialism; there are several, with overlaps. First there is Luddism, a popular and semi-rational rejection of the inhuman application of technology by Capital. This has little to do with the second strand, which consists in the aping of the gentry and hypocritical disparagement of an industry held at a distance by English *rentier* capitalists. Such an attitude is far from inhibiting international manufacture, and its hostility to industrial Britain is ultimately tactical. Thirdly, there is the much more controversial matter of the "Ruskinian" tradition, which while deploring the mode of operation of "industry," constantly sought (in deed as well as word) to uphold the value and dignity of true craftsmanship. Here I agree with Raymond Williams that the Tory-radical critique of capitalism did have genuine existence.[29] Though its relation to capitalism was ultimately contradictory, it cannot he reduced, on the level of ideological discourse, to apologetic for Capital when it needs to legitimate more organicist attitudes, as Terry Eagleton once seemed to think.[30] The Coleridge-Carlyle-Ruskin tradition gets going before the late nineteenth-century corporatist phase of English

28. Wiener, *English Culture and the Decline of the Industrial Spirit: 1850–1980*.

29. Raymond Williams, *Culture and Society: 1780–1950*, 1–67.

30. Eagleton, *Criticism and Ideology*, 103–11

capitalism, and is distinguishable from Burke's initially agrarian capitalist philosophy. For this reason it developed ideas that were of service to socialists. In any case the contrast with an organicist past is *morally* important even to Marx. In Feudal society, he says, "all social relations appear as relations between persons The diverse kinds of work and their products have in consequence no need to take a fantastic figure distinct from their reality."[31]

When it comes to the attitudes of Tawney, Christendom, et al., it must be admitted that there are some ambiguities. There is an area of over-easy transition between *rentier* attitudes, genuine Tory radicalism, and romantic (not meant disparagingly) socialism. But this fact contains at most warnings; it does not allow us to draw the strong Wienerian moral.

The second cultural myth which has exerted a strong appeal concerns the progressive "demoralization" of the working class. This was especially expounded by Jeremy Seabrook who considered that old proletarian community values have been finally swamped by a tide of consumerism and possessive individualism.[32] There is great truth in this, but the thesis tends to be allied to certain perceptions of British socialism. The Labour Party is seen as having today lost its working class roots, and for many, especially Christians, this means its very *raison d'etre*.

It is a misunderstanding. While working class culture may in the past have put up certain barriers to the ravages of capitalism (e. g., the history of associationism and consumer cooperatives) it was not on the whole a socialist culture, or the culture of the producers of real use-value, but rather the culture of a caste of manual laborers. This was well analyzed by Gareth Stedman Jones in his book *Languages of Class*.[33] Many central aspects of working class culture—cinema, sport, pubs, music hall—have been deeply compromised with capitalism. It was, as Stedman Jones says, a "culture of consolation."

For this reason its decline does not have quite the significance that might be supposed. The future of political radicalism in Britain does not depend on the existence of this kind of class-consciousness. In fact, as Stedman Jones showed, the Labour Party did not simply emerge out of a

31. Cited in Dumont, *From Mandeville to Marx*, 176.
32. Seabrook, *What Went Wrong?*
33. Jones, *Languages of Class*, 243–56.

particular cultural class background, as the older E. P. Thompson account suggested, but rather was the outcome of the construction of a particular political rhetoric capable of binding together sections of the working class with sections of the professional classes. Instead of the threadbare observation that the Labor Party owes more to Methodism than to Marxism, Stedman Jones offered us the view that "Toynbee Hall has as much claim to be counted among the ancestors of the Labour Party as Methodism, Taff Vale or William Morris."[34] Toynbee Hall, we should remember, was in the last analysis a product of liberal Anglicanism which in another, though more orthodox (and sometimes more politically radical) variety provided through Gore, Scott Holland (brothers of those other disciples of T. H. Green who founded Toynbee Hall), and then directly from Tawney the main Labour party ideology of the first part of the twentieth century.

Tawney tried to transcend professional condescension and had a vision of the objective unity of interest between mental and manual labor.[35] But in general the Labour Party has relied on that attitude of professional sympathy for the manual workers which has liberal Anglicanism for one of its sources. Perhaps it is hardest of all for the Church of England to outgrow this attitude of condescension and to espouse a genuinely radical politics of distribution of resources and sharing in economic profits. Certain versions of kenotic Christology in Anglicanism, especially to the degree that they have T. H. Green himself for their source[36] (though this is not intended as any general derogation of Green whose theories of "positive freedom" transcend their statist context), are certainly subject to the criticism that they are an ideological gloss on the charitable road from Balliol to the East End of London. However, the more thoroughgoing kenoticism (deriving ultimately from Pusey's Alexandrianism, and already suggested in Scott Holland's sermons[37]), which stresses that "emptying out" was not a contingent act for God, but rather descriptive

---

34. Jones, *Languages of Class*, 247. He also calls attention to such an essentially Christian socialist creation as the Workers' Educational Association. There is a certain danger, when people claim that Anglican socialism was never "in touch" with the working classes, of falling for laborist illusions about what constitutes the strength and identity of socialism. This is not to deny that a healthy socialism and a healthy Church must include a dynamic relation between intellectuals and popular forces.

35. See especially Tawney, *Acquisitive Society*, 160–76.

36. Green, "Essays on Christian Dogma," 207–20.

37. See for example, Holland, "Meekness of God."

of his very nature, escape these criticisms, and tend to engender a more adequate social theology.

I suggest that it is in keeping with such a theology to recognize that while it is important for the not-poor to identify intellectually or materially with the poor, it is still more important to be "the poor," which means, here and now, to belong to the class of genuine workers, or potential workers, who are all the victims of subtly and deeply embedded evil. This, of course, should not prevent us recognizing that the exploiters of labor are in a deeper sense victims of a system whose true nature they could not dare to comprehend.

Christianity, Labor, Capital, and History

In this last section I shall try to make the theological dimensions more explicit; firstly in relation to the human significance of work, and secondly with regard to the Christian relation to capitalism.

The theological appraisal of work is not merely to be deduced from Christian "principles," but rather is projected forwards by the whole history of Christian thought and practice. In the first place, there is a fundamental difference between the Biblical and the Greek attitude to labor. The latter supposes that the gods have hidden from human beings the sources of abundant provision, and that these must be sought out by cunning, Promethean labor, which has nevertheless an ambiguous status. The great aim is to disguise this labor and enjoy its fruits, which alone give it point. Through Aristotle this attitude enters into Christian tradition, also finding twentieth century expression in such Thomist works as Pieper's *Leisure, the Basis of Culture.*

Of course there is much of value here, and the Aristotelian tradition stresses the absolute priority of ends and use-values over the market processes of exchange. Marx is in this respect very much an Aristotelian.

And even Marx accepts something of the Greek attitude to Labor in general. In Marx's later vision of the socialist society there is an absolute duality of work and leisure. Work has become a totally communal and mechanized process designed to reproduce the necessities of life. On the other hand, the *wealth* of this society is now measured in terms of the free time of individuals, which is time in which they can develop their *individual* intellectual and creative powers. The great aim for Marx the political economist (and therefore individualist) is "Free individuality, founded on the universal development of individuals and the *subordination* of their communal social productivity as being their social resources. . . ."[38] Marx here appears to fail to reflect that this freely developing individual is itself the product of bourgeois culture, and to subscribe to a naïve theory of the creative spirit, which fails to recognize the importance of specific linguistic exchanges, and particular traditions of interpretation for its sustenance. Within the terms of this apparent collective/individual dichotomy, he does not realize that the very division between necessary and pleasurable must break down in a society where purely human, personal values are cultivated. In the last analysis, specifically human work is the gratuitous production of that which is precisely not necessary, namely the difference between nature and culture. All economic necessities ultimately arise *within* the economic system. And in addition there are really almost no jobs which are automatically routine and laborious; these qualities follow almost entirely from the social context of work, the degree to which we allow it to be performed skillfully, and to be endowed with ritual meaning.

The biblical attitude is more profound.[39] Labor is not the consequence of the fall, only the debasement of labor. God himself is fundamentally and primordially a worker, and our work is pleasurable because it is the creative tending of God's universe. Work is an end in itself, although it is not the only end. Hence Benedictine monks, unlike ancient Greek philosophers, sought to combine *theoria* with productive work—both being caught up in liturgy, the *opus dei*. It is clear that the Protestant work ethic is only the remote distortion of this vision.

For the Christian, I want to suggest, there is a reversal of attitudes, a "transvaluation of values" with regard to work. This consists in the fact that we are serious where others are trivial, and comic where others are weighed down with the wrong matters. I mean that for us work is always a form of play (as Creation is for God) whereas so called "spare-time" is the serious time of redemption, of our relation to others and to God. This, of course, was best expressed by Eric Gill when he said "That state is a state of freedom in which a man does what he likes to do in his working time,

38. Marx, *Grundrisse*, 158.
39. See Gordon, *Economic Analysis before Adam Smith*, 65ff. .

and in his spare time what is required of him. This state can only exist when what a man likes to do is to please God."[40]

But even here we must beware of a dualism. The spheres of obligation and gratuity (of *theoria-praxis* on the one hand, and *poesis* on the other) are really necessary to each other. The context of social relationships limits, guides, and makes meaningful our creative work. Production, on the other hand—whether of food, bridges, words, or computers—extends the possible range of human relationships, and also tends to circumscribe their possible quality. Life is "psychogeographical."

Thus when we are trying to project a desirable future, we must think of a "social relations of production" in which relations and production are truly inseparable. The strict divisions of work and leisure would start to break down in such a world, as, needless to say, would the capitalist association of work with paid employment. The strangeness of the female world to men, as Angela Cunningham and others have pointed out,[41] consists partly in the fact that to some degree already it is not governed by these separations. But this vision is entirely at variance with the ideal of "the leisure society." It insists that meaningful work demands social validation, and that such work is integral to the nature of humanity. This is why Christians must never endorse what Gill described as a life of "fretwork and frustration."

Automation has to be seen within this context. Of course we should welcome the mechanization of some "tedious" tasks, and the extension of human possibilities. Automation carried out with human well-being in mind may also create many more possibilities of human labor. It needs also to be said that a fully human society might use all technology selectively, which is to say rationally, according to an assessment of its real suitability for various tasks, and the relative desirability of replacing human labor in any particular instance. Machines do not replace certain skills that a nonmarket society might choose to cultivate more. And, in general, machines do not, strictly speaking, "take away from human labor," because the sphere of possible human labor is as infinite as human personal needs and desire for experience and understanding.

The second theological dimension concerns the relationship of Christianity to capitalism. It is time that this question was reopened at the

---

40. Gill, *Art-Nonsense and Other Essays*, 1.

41. A. Cunningham, "Shall Work Set us Free."

level of seriousness entertained by Macmurray, Tawney, and Demant.[42] And that means at the level of the philosophy of history, the only level at which we can *really* be talking with Marx.

Both Marx and Tawney considered that, in a post-capitalist era, economics and political economy would lose their centrality altogether. But the latter was much clearer than the former that so far the economy had only possessed this dominant role within the capitalist phase. Growing economic determinism is seen as *itself* a product of the Capitalist system.

Tawney (and Demant later, from a more conservative viewpoint) is here following the "sociological" rather than the Marxist tradition. For Weber, the economic rationality of the Capitalist era is self-contained and unchallengeable (Tawney, of course, dissents here), but it had a specific beginning within Western history, a beginning enabled by tendencies within Judaism and Christianity. Tawney rightly narrows this thesis to certain contingent theological developments, and we can now specify: capitalism was partially enabled by a deviational individualist, voluntarist, and nominalist form of Christianity beginning before Protestantism, and then finding its main vehicles not only in Protestantism but also in the (vast) Suarezian inheritance and also in Cartesianism/Jansenism.

The sociologists indicate the possibility of religious determinism, but in the case of Weber (at least) they do so in a very constricted way. Weberian sociology is more narrowly conceived than Marxist social science because it is understood as a "complement" to a newly autonomous (marginalist) "economics." Moreover, because Weber accepts a Kantian fact/value dualism, sociology is either an attempt to explain the empirical functioning of ideas and actions, or an attempt to *understand* ideologies: the conception of "ideal types."[43] Thus religion conceived as an area of subjective value is doubly removed from practice—one step from "society," and two steps from the "economy."

It would be very superficial to say that, by contrast to Weber, Marx underrates the "religious factor." In fact, Marx's conception of the social reality of religion, and the role it plays, is a much more profound one. For he does not simply relate religion and economy as a relation of ideas to practice. Instead, as Lucio Colletti points out, it is always fundamental for Marx that there exists a parallel between the *workings* of the Christian

42. Macmurray, *Clue to History*; Tawney, *Religion and the Rise of Capitalism*; and Demant, *Religion and the Decline of Capitalism*.

43. On this, see Clarke, *Marx, Marginalism, and Modern Sociology*, 198–99.

religion and the *workings* of the capitalist economy.[44] Marx believes that the capitalist economy *actually works like a religion* sustaining itself through the performance of a systematic logic of mystification. Indeed the parallel of economy and religion is the most fundamental of all Marx's thoughts.

This requires explication. It is not, after all, entirely fair to say that Marx projects backwards into preceding ages the dominance of economic rationality. In fact he does interpret the process tending towards the establishment of commodity production as the final triumph of the most purely economic relations, that is exchange relations. In pre-capitalist societies the fetishization of value is achieved in a sphere that is less distinctly economic, but rather also socio-political and religious-hieratic. The real factor of continuity in the emergence of "economic" society from pre-capitalist modes of production is the continuous evolution of a mystifying language, a continuous seduction of human beings through their own signifying productions. Thus Marx speaks of the "language of commodities,"[45] and specifies: "it is value rather, that converts every product into a social hieroglyphic. Later on, we try to decipher the hieroglyphic, to get behind the secret of our own products; for to stamp an object of social utility as value is just as much a social product as language."[46] He also remarks sardonically that "the language of commodities has, besides Hebrew, many other more or less correct dialects."[47]

This last sentence indicates how language is the middle term allowing the parallel religion/economy to operate. Furthermore, it also suggests that anti-Semitism may be for Marx no dispensable element within this comparison. In my view the above observations constitute the basis for a possible "deconstruction" of Marx, such that the priority of economic over religious determinism is no longer absolutely tenable, even within Marx's own terms. This proposed deconstruction would focus on the following points:

(a) Marx *wants* to say that "The religious world is but the reflex of the real world."[48] But the very subtlety of his analysis makes this difficult. For Marx there is not just an ideological concealment of social reality,

44. Colletti, *Marxism and Hegel*, 249–83.

45. Marx, *Capital*, 20.

46. Ibid., 45.

47. Ibid., 20–21.

48. Ibid., 51.

but rather there is an economic-linguistic process that establishes itself as reality by a process of systematic concealment and mystification of this very mode of establishment. Thus, as Lucio Colletti has shown, Marx understands idealist philosophy as really reflecting the idealization and alienations that sustain capitalist reality. When Marx says that "the mutual relations of the producers . . . take the form of a social relation of the products,"[49] the point is not just that the latter disguises class domination but also that this specific form of domination only *exists* through such a disguise, which is effective for all classes.

Given this analysis, Marx cannot really maintain the contrast between a religious alienation that is in the realm of "consciousness" and an economic alienation in the realm of "reality." To do so is to remain half Feuerbachian, not really to understand the religious illusion as rooted in social practice. Here Marx is betrayed by his own (indispensable) metaphors. Economic equivalence is frequently compared to sacramental meaning.[50] But this parallel is all too precise. In a sacramental practice, as in an economic one, there is a fetishization, something is arbitrarily made to "stand for" something else, yet this convention *really organizes* human actions and relationships.

If religion and the economy are both abuses of language (and this is clearly what Marx is really saying), then there appears to be little reason for giving the one causal priority over the other.

(b) Because he pretends to confine religion to the ideological, Marx never sees the need to show why there is economy *and also* religion. In fact it seems that there have been some societies, like ancient Babylon, where the two were virtually identical. But if the basis for the extension of economy into religion, and the ultimate separation of the latter, consists in the need to ground human significance in a transcendent reality, then Marx has not really shown why religion will disappear when contradictory socio-economic forms have been unraveled.

(c) The reader of chapter I of *Capital*, the chapter on "Commodities," is bound to ask why exactly it is that the development of human productive forces must take place through the medium of historical mystification, for Marx certainly does not regard the latter as merely contingent.

49. Ibid., *Capital*, 42.

50. For example: "The fact that it (the linen composing a coat) is value, is made manifest by its equality with the coat, just as the sheep's nature of the Christian is shown in his resemblance to the Lamb of God" (ibid., 20).

This question applies especially for the commencement of the process, for later it is possible to explain changes in terms of the development of the forces of production and consequent or parallel shifts in the social relations of production that deepen and perpetuate established patterns of reification. But why the "mystical veil" at all? Here it seems that the implicit answer of the chapter on commodities is that this is a necessary *linguistic* development. Human beings, for Marx, must pass from a primitive stage where they are narrowly confined to fixed social relations, and to certain constant use-values, to a final stage where their being is seen as co-extensive with the infinite possible range of social relationships and of the transformation of nature into objects of human use and meaning. But the passage from "fixed particularity" to "infinite particularity" can only be *via* the construction of false linguistic universals and equivalences, that is of tropes treated as if they were realities like the piece of linen whose value is taken as equivalent to the coat that is made out of it; the coat "stands for" the linen (this, of course, is a synecdoche). Later, the tropes are reduced to the abstract genera of money and capital.

This for Marx is a universal diachrony. Yet he slightly interferes with the universal diachronic vision, when he mentions that "Trading nations, properly so called, exist in the ancient world only in its interstices, like the gods of Epicurus in the Intermundia, or like Jews in the pores of Polish society."[51] Anti-Semitism can be accommodated only synchronically, but this tends to suggest that there are cultures which constantly possess a different religious-economic specificity.

(d) What is then the real basis for the inevitability of linguistic mystification? Here we see Marx's most complete inversion of Hegel. The latter's model is a kind of "Gnostic Trinitarianism" in which absolute spirit must become constituted in concrete terms, but this process necessarily involves an estrangement only resolvable when spirit "returns to itself," in realization of its absolute self-constitution. It is for this reason that Hegel gives a "heretically Christian" philosophy of history. Yet cannot the same thing be said of Marx? Instead of absolute spirit we have a "human naturalism" which can only "return to itself," though in a "higher form" through the movement of historical estrangement. Marx does not, it is true, like Hegel, see *objectification* as necessarily alienating; instead what is necessarily alienating for Marx is *tropical exchange and abstract universalizing*.

51. Marx, *Capital*, 51.

The claim here then is that Marx does not in fact distinguish an exact decipherment of particular historical fetishization from a general philosophical nominalism (to which, of course, "economics" as a whole subscribes). But this is a very severe failure because it implies that the will beyond fetishization is really a will beyond the sustaining conditions of human culture. Human beings do not live in a world of securely discreet qualities and use-values, because meaning is only constituted through "arbitrary" metaphoric exchanges. In *The German Ideology*, Marx certainly understands individual life as mediated by the social phenomenon of language, but he never reflects on language as a system of signs, subject to the necessary substitution of one thing for another, and the indeterminism of meaning involved in an unavoidably infinite *semiosis*.[52]

This has three implications: first, one requires devices for distinguishing "innocent" from "culpable" *semiosis*. This is a huge problem, but I suggest in general that it is to do with the contrast between metaphoric processes where "polar tension" is preserved, and so there can be semantic deepening and critical appraisal of received meaning, and metaphoric processes which "close off" this tension and conceal the processes of their own becoming.[53] I think that these criteria would reveal capitalism as mystificatory in precisely the Marxist sense, but would not necessarily show the same thing about all forms of sacramental or "fetishistic" practice. Secondly, the way may be opened for a more complex and adequate reading of history, where one distinguishes, synchronically, between relatively innocent, and relatively culpable cultural processes (the "Gnostic" myth of necessary linguistic mystification being thereby overcome). It might he much more possible to make sense of the history of Israel and of Christianity within such a scheme, though one might here have to conclude that specially "innocent" processes also contain especially strong "culpable" potential if they take on distorted forms. Thirdly, this move means that not all "mystery" is automatically "mystification." It is now definitely not the case that meanings that can only be established indeterminately or metaphorically are necessarily manifestations of distorted social processes. Thus religion is not automatically culpable; it requires assessment, and may be itself the site of political struggle, rather than always the target of political critique.

52. On this Piercean concept, see Eco, *Role of the Reader*.

53. See my article "William Warburton: An Eighteenth-Century Bishop Fallen among Post-Structuralists."

(e) There is a further consequence of Marx's attachment to an inverted Hegelian model. This is that (like Feuerbach) his personalism is ambiguous. In the *Economic and Philosophical Manuscripts* Marx is clear that in the communist society our individual being will coincide with our social being; that we shall exist in our concrete relations to nature and to other human beings. However, as we have seen, in later works there sometimes seems to be a suggestion of a liberal romantic individualism. I think that the foundation of this is twofold. In the first place, the point where Marx has the strongest conception of the real, linguistic character of social ties is where he is considering alienated relationships. In consequence, emancipation tends to appear as release of the individual from social distortions. The reason for this, however, is not really that Marx has lapsed into thinking in terms of a pre-social individual, but that he thinks of use-values as existing outside the sphere of linguistic exchange. In the second place, Marx the atheist has to understand human being as entirely "self-mediated" being.[54] But what is the subject of this "self-mediation"? The real answer is "man" taken collectively, but this sounds suspiciously reifying. Hence, I think, a tendency to substitute the individual human subject in this "self-mediating" role.

If this self-mediation were more realistically seen as only partial, then an autonomous humanity, and so atheism, would not be so perfectly constructed. We should be left with the endless series of constituting relationships, and also with a question about how far we can ever totally "reclaim" the objects of our own production. If we are not "in charge" of the meanings we promote, but these are subject to future interpretation, then we have never really done with the Hegelian "cunning of reason." However, we need ways of discriminating this from the mystifying "hidden hand" of the political economists, just as we needed devices to distinguish "innocent" from "culpable" *semiosis*.

(f) The above moves have suggested that Marx's economic determinism can be deconstructed to yield a sort of economic-religious-linguistic determinism. I have then developed this in a positive, rather than skeptical direction, by accepting that while all our knowledge is "aesthetic," "immanent," "indeterminate," and "consensual" in character, it can nevertheless

---

54. Marx, *Early Writings*, 356. Marx has earlier said (p. 350) that one should realize that the individual *is* the "social being" and not set an abstract society and the individual over against each other. Yet it seems that only the one or the other can be the subject of a fully "autonomous" *Durchsichselbstsein*.

be genuine knowledge. This of course suggests a continuity between all knowledge and the mode of Christian faith. It suggests also how any ethically valid practice has to be rooted in a particular tradition that "projects forwards" a horizon of ethical becoming. This implies more than the mere appropriation of historically developed use-values, as envisaged by Marx. For him, the ethically objective and normative is provided by the prospect of "natural-historical" humanity, a humanity fulfilling all real possibilities without alienation or illusion. However, if our being is given in the cultural specificity of linguistic exchange (where there are always certain "arbitrarily" dominant signifiers, allied to particular dominant modes of action), then in addition to the "natural bounds" we are always promoting some order of goals seen as especially desirable. In fact, only within this order are the "natural bounds" mediated to us. Thus a purely naturalist, Marxist ethic is impossible, because traditions continue to stand not only as things which must be initially inhabited and criticized in pursuit of the "natural bounds," but also as things which must continue to be positively accepted and subscribed to (even though they are subject to constant reinterpretation). This could be mere conservative positivism, but the religious, transcendent grounding of the possibility of an imperfectly realized truth will tend to guard against this.

I suggest that this sort of deconstruction of Marx, whereby he is drawn back into the elaboration of a Christian philosophy of history, is the right approach to the problem of relating Christianity and capitalism. It is much more promising than a return to the idealist perspectives of Weber, while at the same time it does permit us to raise again the Weberian question of why capitalism developed in the Christian West. But we may partially overcome the dichotomy of religious versus economic determinism, if we understand religion not as a set of ideas, but as an entire practice which works like an economy (and as a language) distributing and proportioning reality through a series of substitutions and exchanges.

Within this perspective it is possible again to understand the Western separation of the economic sphere from the religious-social-cultural sphere as in part an inner-religious achievement. As Weber described, this emerged through the practice of "worldly asceticism" and a systematic dualism that both insulates the sphere of material gain from religion, and ultimately validates this activity in religious terms. However, this is not just a validation of the secular, this is a religious construction (in theory and in practice) of the secular as the sphere where humanity defines itseif as power, echoing God's self-definition in the Creation. It is sometimes suggested that the fault of technological humanity is an overstress on "human making," but this often implies a denial of the modern understanding of historicity. What is rather needed is a reclaiming of making, not as what gives the bounds of the secular, but as what initially opens up our awareness of the sacred in the presentation of compelling and unfathomable forms. Marx, in undermining liberal dualisms certainly overturned the peculiar post-Reformation constitution of secular and sacred, in the interests of a "single world." He made the arbitrary move of setting human *poesis* and religion over against each other, but a deconstructed Marx can be read as especially over-throwing the basis of secularization.

I hope that I have shown how capitalism is to be regarded as Christian heresy, and Marxism the ally of Christian orthodoxy, in no glib or superficial sense. If these things are the case, then they change our relation to the crisis of late capitalism in Britain, which is in 2008 so intensified and so further conjoined to a global crisis. It is not enough merely to "respond"; we must understand that the crisis is our responsibility; the economic and social arguments are finally theological.

What I am finally suggesting is a Christian-historical perspective on our current situation. The Christian confidence in its ethical tradition is peculiarly strong because we claim that, in the life of Christ, we have already a concrete definition of a perfect social reality, which nevertheless in its to-be-realized fullness we can only imperfectly sketch out. Yet this perfection is a very terrible historical reality. If, after the glimpse of divine glory in the incarnation, we reject or distort Jesus's concretely described way of love and peace which points to the removal of all sacrificial and idolatrous coercion, then instead we are driven to even more desperate measures to disguise, extend, and legitimate our coercive systems. I believe that this is quite literally what has happened in Western history.

If my worst fears are confirmed, and capitalism transforms itself into a subtle totalitarianism, then the world will shape itself into a more definite (though perhaps more disguised) rejection of Christ. Marxism relies partly on a humanist doctrine of the person that it now probably has not the philosophical resources to sustain. It is becoming increasingly difficult on the secular left to perceive how a scientifically critical approach to society can also be an ethical one. In this situation, it may be Christianity alone that is ultimately able to sustain resistance.

This will be because throughout its history, Christianity, besides in its major deviations furthering the processes of catastrophe, has also in its authentic fragments (which also have a tradition) provided us with the scattered elements of the human Republic, and the divine Kingdom. History, as mystification, works towards the further and further concealment of these fragments, which exist also among the people of Israel. But the attempt is useless. The mystifying labor of capitalism or of totalitarianism beyond capitalism can construct only the mystery of the Cross, which, if we bear it, reveals again the secret of the world.

6

ON BASELESS SUSPICION

Christianity and the Crisis of Socialism

In the Western world, at least, socialism has long been in crisis as a political force. But it is has also been in crisis as an intellectual creed, and it is this crisis that concerns the present chapter. Nevertheless, the practical and the theoretical crises are very closely allied; the real political problem for contemporary socialism may be that, increasingly, people no longer know, or have forgotten, why one should be a socialist.

One might want to re-express this as "people no longer see any *reasons* to be a socialist." And the practical response might be to urge us, once again, to convince people that socialism is the truly reasonable path. And yet, I am going to argue that in certain crucial senses there simply are no "reasons" for being socialist in the way that we have tended to imagine in the past. If, I shall suggest, we can overcome the lingering suggestion that socialism is a matter of science, of historical diagnosis, or of universally valid reason, then we shall actually be able to recover the most authentic core of the socialist tradition, and the Christian socialist tradition in particular. In the course of this argument I shall first of all establish a contrast between old-style Christian socialism and new-style Christian Marxism, and then go on to show that Christian socialism is in certain ways more in tune with the radicalism required today. Finally, I shall suggest how Christian socialism nonetheless moves beyond the ambiguity of the postmodern critique of capitalist society.

My thesis, stated in brief, is that socialism is not right because it is "rational" but right because it is just. And the corollary here, to adapt

Péguy, is that the critique of capitalism is a moral critique or else it is no critique at all.

In previous years Christian socialists have been seduced away from the priority of the moral critique in the course of an engagement with Marxism that has too often been naïve and uncritical. It is a mistake to suppose that there is a clear continuity between past and present social-ism, and that the latter has just borrowed from Marxism elements of empirical rigor and of congenial humanism. On the contrary, it would be more accurate to distinguish sharply between an old "Christian socialist" critique of capitalism and a more recent "Christian Marxist" one.[1] The contrast can be set out in roughly the following way.

In the Christian socialist critique there is a distinct confrontation between Christian values and capitalist reality. The critique is seen as pos-sible because of the difference from capitalism represented by Christianity, especially in its past history—the first Christian communities, the mon-asteries, the medieval towns, the guild associations. By contrast with this standard, capitalism appears as a kind of apostasy—according to John Ruskin, "the most remarkable instance in history of a nation's establish-ing a systematic disobedience to the principles of its own religion."[2] For Christian socialism, unlike Marxism, capitalism did not appear as a par-tial, contradictory development of freedom—instead it was denounced as a pseudo-progress, and a mere contingency, whose rise was the shame of Christendom. Capitalism was seen as the practice of a false knowledge which made self-interest moderate self-interest without the intervention of virtue, and secured public order without the architectonic of justice. Ruskin, again, saw the triumph of political economy (i.e., of a "value-free" economics, dealing with wealth creation in abstraction from other considerations) as the promotion of certain quasi-virtues of busyness and frugality in place of true political *phronesis* and Christian charity. And the displacement of the ethical in the public sphere was held to be cotermi-nous with the triumph of secularity. After the retreat of public religion a

---

1. I am indebted here to Stanley Hauerwas, whose trenchant article "Some Theological Reflections on Gutierrez's use of 'Liberation' as a Theological Concept," first suggested to me the importance of this contrast. My thanks are due also to Rowan Williams, Adrian Cunningham, David Nicholls, Kenneth Surin, Timothy Radcliffe, and John Orme Mills, who commented on earlier drafts of this chapter.

2. Ruskin, *Unto this Last*, 162.

vacuum was created in which a merely "economic" regime could "manage" a society, even without a moral or religious consensus.

In certain respects, this critique was a *counter-Enlightenment* critique. It did not locate socialism as the next stage in a narrative of emancipation, or of the genesis of human autonomy. On the contrary, the enlightened goal of the self-regulation of the will according to its own natural, finite desires and capacities was seen as of one piece with the operation of political economy. The rejection of the latter, then, did not rest, like Marxism, on a "dialectic of Enlightenment" or an immanent critique of the present ideals of freedom.

The obvious objection to this would be that of Marx himself: Christian socialism was nothing but "the holy water with which the priest consecrates the heart-burnings of the aristocrat."[3] The implication here is that the only true socialism was that which freed itself from Tory radicalism and medievalist romanticism. Yet nearly all nineteenth-century socialism, outside Marxism, contained counter-Enlightenment elements—as we have already seen in earlier chapters. The case of the French "republican" socialists—like Cabet, Blanc, Barbès, and Proudhon—is the most instructive.[4] In these writers one finds, typically, an attack on the idea that justice can be simply equated with the maximization of freedom, and an identification of religion with harmonious, fraternal agreement, over against the inherent "antagonism" of secular individualism. Their initial appeal to a past ideal was that of the "enlightened" revolution itself—namely to the classical republic. Yet this ideal was qualified in a more associationist, anarchist, pro-familial, and pacific direction by reference to Christian tradition and to medieval exemplars. Where Rousseau's "civil religion" took on a more Christian caste, there, precisely, "socialism" was born. And the appeal back to *both* the antique *polis* and the medieval guilds is made because *only* these contrasts (and this remains true even for Marx) allow one to pinpoint the new and unprecedented factor in capitalist oppression. The appeal had also another and un-Marxian purpose. The republican socialists did not conceive socialism *negatively*, as the unraveling of present contradictions, but *positively*, as a contingent piece of human imagination. In this "positive" and undialectical socialism, the future possibility has to be composed out of the fragments of past justice.

3. Marx and Engels, *Communist Manifesto*, 108.

4. Vincent, *Pierre Joseph Proudhon*, 33–78, 127–65.

"Christian socialism," in short, and even main-line "republican socialism," was not a Whig discourse about emancipation. But this did not necessarily imply a Tory hankering after a merely static hierarchic order (though in many "Christian socialists" like F. D. Maurice, it no doubt did). Even in Ruskin, who stresses the all-importance of parental and pastoral roles, there is a suggestion that these roles will *only* be secured if they are disseminated, and become, as far as possible, reciprocal—a kind of "clerisy of all citizens" in fact.[5] The real point of necessity for hierarchy in Ruskin is the transitive relationship of education, where an unavoidable non-reciprocity nonetheless works towards its own cancellation. Liberalism tends to disguise this necessity, because it makes normative the spatial relationships between adult, autonomous subjects, a habit which achieves its *reductio ad absurdum*, as we saw in chapter 1, in William Godwin's vision of a world of finite immortality, without sexual passion, without birth, and without death.[6] In this sense, then, if Christian socialism has an anti-liberal commitment to collective norms of justice which can only be handed down through time, it has a commitment to hierarchy. However, it also contends that an arbitrary hierarchy, of a non-self-cancelling kind, is partially responsible for the formation of the modern machine of abstract power. This is particularly true of later French ruminators on *trahison des clercs*. For Charles Péguy social hierarchies and especially the Church clergy themselves are most of all to blame for a "reversal" of the divine pedagogic *mystique*, such that right from the Church's very foundation the energies of the many were recruited to maintain the securities of the few.[7] Thus Christian socialism was able both to appeal to the fragmentary justice of the past and to connect present secular injustice with past social and ecclesial error.

By contrast, a wholly different sort of critique of capitalism emerges from "Christian Marxism" as discovered in recent "political" and "liberation" theology.[8] This critique does not really have its origins in social

5. Ruskin, *Unto This Last*, 150.

6. Godwin, *Enquiry Concerning Political Justice*, I, 86; II, 520, 527–29.

7. Péguy, "Clio I," 101–8.

8. I have deliberately presented both Christian socialism and Christian Marxism as "ideal types" for the sake of making my point in a brief space. However, my critique of Christian Marxism applies especially to the writings of J. B. Metz, Gustavo Gutierrez, and J. L. Segundo, and *a fortiori* to those of Alfredo Fierro, See, in particular, Metz, *Theology of the World*; Gutierrez, *Theology of Liberation*; Segundo, *Liberation of Theology*; Fierro, *Militant Gospel*.

theory at all, but rather in the problems of theological epistemology. Following Karl Rahner, German theology sought a starting point in philosophical anthropology, in a theory of human nature and human subjectivity. Once Rahner's own transcendentalist anthropology had been rejected as too individualist and too ahistorical it was hoped that Marxism could supply an alternative foundationalist discourse. Just as Rahner's anthropology focused on a subjective "spirit" whose attention no finite object could finally detain, so J. B. Metz and others declared empirical history to be the growth of human autonomous freedom, albeit with dialectical hiccups on the way. Because political and liberation theology associates Marxism with a Christian coming-to-terms with Enlightenment freedom, it always connects it to a positive evaluation of the secular, and of the modern age. It is a consequence of this that these theologies do not permit a directly *Christian* critique of capitalism. On the contrary, "Christian Marxism" is just another version of the liberal Christian's need to celebrate a marriage between Christianity and some body of supposedly objective empirical knowledge. The great appeal of this enterprise is that the vastly complex problems of being a Christian in the modern world can be nicely simplified if one baptizes a particular social theory and accords to it a "totalizing" application. Thus Marxism will tell one what stance to take, and will allow one to take it alongside other, well-meaning but non-Christian people.

For "Christian Marxism" the critique of capitalism is indirect. Marxism is baptized, because it supposedly decodes human finitude and points to a universal movement of "liberation" on which theology can build. It is Marxism itself, the baptized theory, which then provides the specific critique of capitalism. This leads to three further points of contrast with Christian socialism.

First of all, the emphasis of critique switches from capitalism's denial of justice to its inhibition of human freedom (see Hauerwas, note 1, above). As *both* a science *and* a humanism, Marxism has to ground its critique in theoretical reason. Thus it has a preconceived and unjustified picture of the essence of human nature as unrestricted production and unrestricted fulfillment of supposedly inherent human "needs." As Terry Eagleton in his middle-years-incarnation once all too accurately said, Marxian morality can only open up at the point where the social relations of production are seen as inhibiting the further development of forces of production.[9] Marxism sidesteps the question of justice both on the way to Utopia—where history is reduced to a dialectical means to an end—and for Utopia itself, where the removal of the last barriers to autonomous freedom and unlimited production is supposed to render the perennially renewed question of just distribution finally redundant. This is to subscribe to a myth of apocalyptic negativity, whereas many supposedly "Utopian" socialists have been preoccupied with the detailed questions of justice: what *kinds* of property are allowable, under what conditions; by what *standards* do we exchange one thing for another; how can we outlaw "profits" in excess of just remuneration; how can we prevent money and credit from assuming a self-generating power; and how can we make monetary and market exchanges coterminous with exchanges of moral value. These questions all presuppose that genuine political freedom for the individual involves a sympathetic taking account of the endless demands of others, and that true equality assumes some fundamental agreements about cultural norms. As Aristotle and Aquinas taught, there are no set rules or criteria for sorting out the priority of demands, nor for establishing shared values, the civic "good." But Marxism avoids this crux of practical reason by telling a theoretical story in which history gradually unravels a condition of absolutely spontaneous peace and freedom.

When the stress is on justice, as with Christian socialism, then one will recognize the importance of certain already-existing communities which are able to generate sets of distributive priorities and to project common goals. Such agreements do not necessarily imply equality. Nonetheless a truly social, or socialist, equality does presuppose this kind of non-theoretically prescribable consensus. It is natural, then, that Christian socialism (supremely, with Charles Péguy) has often been a mode of *ecclesiology*—interpreting the mystical body of Christ as itself the incubus of a more just society.

But Christian Marxism finds it hard to place ecclesiology. And herein lies a second point of contrast with Christian socialism. For in its theological conception of *Christianity*, Christian Marxism can be curiously unhistorical. It tends to fall back on the idea that the individual believer is in touch with certain universal values and motivations, but must apply to Marxism to be told how these are to be "objectively" instantiated in the present. There is a problem here, which does not

9. Eagleton, "Marxists and Christians," 465–70.

exist for Christian socialism, about how to relate the "history of salvation" to "the history of emancipation." Whereas, for Christian socialism, the narrative of salvation is one source for the very *conception* of a socialist possibility, for Christian Marxism the historical contingency of this narrative (the departure of Abraham, the Exodus, the life and death of Jesus, Pentecost) must be subordinated to a fated immanence of human development; a story that can he told (as in Segundo) with as many Teilhardist as Marxist overtones.

The subordination of salvation to liberation means that salvation is conceived either purely transcendentally—as a going beyond all finite limits—or else as the secular process of the setting free of the human finite essence. In either case Christian Marxists have fallen prey to what Michel Foucault called "the analytic of finitude."[10] By this he meant a historicism in which it is supposed that one can somehow round upon finitude and "represent" the human subject in terms of its supposed intrinsic limits as what truly "underlies" history and paradoxically permits a continuing development. Thus one can define humanity in terms of the priority of "basic" economic needs, like Marx, or in terms of a universal oedipal economy of desire, like Freud, or in terms of a "being towards death," like Heidegger. These are all variants of "the analytic of finitude," and they were all notably beloved by twentieth-century theology, which was so often confined within an anthropological *episteme* and the illusion of a once and for all "representation" of the finite human subject.

In Christian Marxism, then, unlike Christian socialism, freedom displaces justice, and anthropology displaces ecclesiology. But from these displacements flows another which forms the third point of contrast. This is the displacement of ethics by dialectics.

In the realm of modern natural-law theory, which is also the realm of the secular, an attempt is made to ground the ethical in the pre-ethical, in some theoretically knowable principle like utilitarian benefit or abstract individual right.[11] For Marxism, the theoretical principle is the coming-to-be of human self-possession without heteronomous dependence, through the unraveling of a dialectical logic. But to accept this new natural law is to displace the immediacy of ethical judgment. From a Marxist perspective it is inescapable that capitalist abstraction is fine

10. Foucault, *Order of Things*, 312–18.
11. MacIntyre, *After Virtue*.

and necessary in its own day, and so in a certain sense "moral." It is no good pretending that this Marxist morality has a certain affinity with Aristotelian refusal of the is/ought distinction.[12] For the Marxian question, "How are we to act, given the facts?" betrays at root a positivist attitude to the facts and permits a dualism of means and ends, whereas the "moral facts" of Aristotelian ethics are only read as facts in terms of their inherent value and teleology, a teleology for which means are only ends "in embryo." The means/end dualism in Marxism perpetuates by contrast the Machiavellian indirectness of political economy, the manipulation of vices towards goals of mere coexistence, which are, as it were, false *simulacra* of political community. So dialectics remains caught in the political economy paradigm which always embraces two different versions of means/end dualism; sometimes the manipulator was the Machiavellian sovereign, or the mercantile state, while at other times the manipulator was providence, or the force of nature. And it little matters whether the logic of nature is considered more "ideal" or more "material."

Gilles Deleuze sought to expose the metaphysical illusions of dialectical reason.[13] It is an attempt to subordinate, in the long run, all difference to identity and totality. This is inevitable if one sees difference as emerging through determinate negation—but this is a logicist myth; in reality differences are pure, creative positings, unpredictable "superadditions," in the gift of the plenitude of future time. Likewise, there is no such thing as "immanent critique," where one is led to a deepening apprehension of an already given idea through an unraveling of the contradictions in its present manifestations. "Immanent critique" suggests that, although critique takes time, and can only be realized in specific times and places, it remains the *self-critique* of autonomous reason, which gradually achieves greater clarity and self-consistency. But there is no justification for belief in the gradual disclosure of a standard whose validity will be obvious to an undeceived reason. Instead, critique is always in the gift of the alien, of the other—of differences that are not immanent to the given but always stand "over against it," even if they are completely (but not dialectically) entangled within it. This means that contradictions within any given social system or ideology are never merely objective or inevitable, but only emerge where difference takes the form of a positive challenge. It is true that there are

12. See Eagleton, "Marxists and Christians."

13. Deleuze, *Différence et Répépitition*. And see Foucault, "Theatrum Philosophicum." 164–96.

always differences which can never be totally suppressed, and that there are always tensions between them, but there is simply no limit to the possible functional management of these tensions by any particular system. Tensions have to be politically exploited before they can be accounted as conflicts with the system itself. For example, the struggles of workers for higher pay and better conditions may be just part of capitalist functioning, and need involve no real challenge to the system. It is not even the case, as Marxists would claim, that the interests of the workers are "objectively" antagonistic to capital. For this presupposes that workers have an "essential" identity as human beings which is not fully absorbed by their roles as workers, consumers, and seduced admirers of the spectacle of capitalist wealth and glamour.

To many socialists, and to Christian Marxists, these anti-dialectical and anti-humanist conclusions have appeared to threaten the very "reasons for socialism" themselves. Postmodernists like Deleuze seemed to underwrite capitalism as an infinitely expanding antagonistic game which permits one no real critical purchase. Yet there is another way of looking at this. It is notable that Proudhon, as a representative of "republican" socialism, rejected all theological and secular theodicies which justified short-term ills in terms of long-term benefits.[14] Proudhon's passion against the ingrained evil of history even assumed a Manichaean complexion at times. Likewise he came to half-reject Hegelian dialectics, because he saw that this subordinated the just balancing of the demands of different subjects to the self-becoming of subjective freedom which is at once the will of the isolated individual and the will of the sovereign state (or of the revolutionary proletariat for Marx). Proudhon realized that by insisting on the priority of mutual justice one could actually grasp freedom more radically than Hegel as respect for specific and endlessly different choices. For paradoxically such choices can only flourish in *peace* where they are constantly coordinated with each other through a developing consensus.[15] Thus Proudhon saw the task of justice not as the bringing about of final synthesis, but rather the replacement of tension as antagonism

---

14. Frazer, *Selected Writings*, 188–89.

15. While Christian socialism is committed to positive freedom of participation in the pursuit of commonly-accepted goals rather than negative freedom of choice, it also opposes unnecessary attacks on self-sufficiency which produce a *coerced* dependence. Areas of relative "independence" for individuals and groups are vital precisely for the creative *re-imagining* of the public *telos*; this and not pluralism of values is their real justification.

with tension as equilibrium. For this reason he accords to justice a certain Platonic stature of transcendental unity, which equalizes the unequal, but eludes the formal mechanisms of the dialectic.[16] In contrast to Hegel and Marx, this "Platonism" still permits history its open-ended indetermination. Certainly the republic is *in* history and justice is not discovered prior to particular acts of adjudication; but it is also timeless—the republic *is*, where there is justice.

By breaking with dialectics, one breaks with another version of the modern paradigm which de-ethicizes the public realm. By contrast, any Christian Marxism dangerously qualifies moral responsibility in history. The Canadian theologian, Gregory Baum, declared that while Christians are ethically obliged to side with those who are victims of oppressive social structures, nonetheless these structures themselves are to be thought of in objective, sociological terms, and not to he seen as the avoidable product of human injustice.[17] Paradoxically, this is to subscribe to a very individualist notion of "responsibility." It colludes with political economy's version of the "heterogenesis of ends," where individual decisions are like windowless nomads, having in their self-consciousness no connection with the long-term social upshot. For while no one deliberately "planned" capitalism, it is also true that we *never* pre-discover what precisely we have done, even what we really "intend," until our actions are articulated within public discourse. Our bad intentions seem to "overtake us" by "sur-prize" and have the character of something "always already begun." A bad system is the incremental sedimentation of lots of minor social articulations of selfishness and self-delusion.[18]

So in the light of the postmodernist critique of Marxism one can re-read (for example) Ruskin's strictly moral critique of capitalism, not as a blindness to history, but instead as a penetration to the real level where capitalist assumptions are generated, both in theory and in practice. Christian Marxism does not reach this level, because it ascribes to a metaphysical "priority of practice" and reduces theory to "a second step."[19] This

---

16. Frazer, *Selected Writings*, 223–35. See also de Lubac, *UnMarxian Socialist*, 151–65.

17. Baum, *Religion and Alienation*, 193–227.

18. See Ruskin, *Unto this Last*, 141.

19. If "priority of practice" means simply that theology begins as a reflection on a given discourse (a socio-linguistic complex of thought and action), then one could assent to it. But too often it seems to mean also either one or all of the following: (a)

tends to accord a kind of mystifying rational validity to "action as such" and precludes the realization that no area of human discourse (thought/ activity) is inherently more "fundamental" than any other. The critical task is not to identify a material or activist "base," but to reconstruct what Cornelius Castoriadis called "the social imaginary" or the fluid level at which societies "imagine" the very things that get most taken for granted.[20] Theoretical books can be thought of as intense abridgments of the real theoretical text which is social practice itself.

So when, in *Unto this Last*, Ruskin declares that Political Economy substitutes "balance of expediency" for "balance of justice" he is arguably making a historical diagnosis more profound than that which seeks "fundamental" causes in the shape of an always presupposed, and therefore ahistorical, "material base."[21] Just as historically penetrating is his contention that political economy is the first generally accepted "nescience" in human history, because it aims not to promote, directly, a maximum excellence, but advocates the deliberate exploitation of differences of ability and of knowledge.[22] Relative failure, weak ability, bad craftsmanship and stupidity have a definite function for political economy in the reducing of production costs and the extension of abstract "wealth." One could add here that the promotion of "stupidity" has become infinitely more important within an information-dominated economy where it is essential that knowledge be parceled out and possessed in an independent way by no one in particular. Although Ruskin did not anticipate this development, he realized that right from the outset capitalism was as much to do with a redefinition of knowledge as with a redefinition of political flourishing. As a nescience, political economy broke with the idea that all knowledge should promote wisdom and virtue. It was inextricably accompanied by a new *moral* economy which, as in Hume and Smith, made a sharp division between the private and consumerist sphere of "natural" sympathies based on universal feeling, and the "artificial" sympathies which arise in

---

that a "pure" decision of commitment precedes any theological articulation, (b) that the commitment is in terms of "a material base" and implies a diagnosis of "underlying" and inescapable historical processes which are "prior" to thought, (c) that all theologies are subject to an instrumentally pragmatic test concerning their effect on this basic level.

20. Castoriadis, *L'Institution Imaginaire*.

21. Ruskin, *Unto this Last*, 112.

22. Ibid., 178.

relation to the positive facts of property, possession, and political power.[23] The Scots economists certainly wanted to connect *homo economicus* with public virtue, but they deliberately promoted a new economic *virtù* as an equivalent of the Machiavellian version of political prudence, with its stress on heroic strength, and the functional value of class-struggle for the strong community.[24]

Like the Scots, Ruskin's historical diagnosis assumes the inextricability of economic distribution and moral economy. But his medievalism suggests a different reconciliation of wealth with virtue. Ruskin notes that "manly character" and "production and exchange" are not easily reconciled.[25] Yet (one could add) this commonplace is specific to a classical legacy that subordinates the productive household to political relations in the city between property-owning males. Only the post-Christian tendency to merge the conceptions of *polis* and *oikos* (i.e. to make the household with its "pastoral" oversight of material well-being a basic unit of government) permits Ruskin to demand that production and exchange discover within themselves immanent norms of virtue and *paideia*. The trouble is, he notes, that trade and manufacture have *never* been seen as included within a Socratic "discipline of death"—it has not been recognized that there are here responsibilities for subordinates and for the quality of products which at the limit imply the same self-sacrifice which we see as involved in soldiering, teaching, or medicine.[26] Likewise Ruskin wants questions of the aesthetic quality of objects produced or exchanged to be coordinated with questions of ethical goals for social subjects. Economic value, he says, is properly "the possession of the valuable by the valiant."[27] A just exchange of goods and labor presupposes a match between the ethical capacities of persons and the interpreted excellence of material objects.

Ruskin's moral diagnosis was, therefore, also a historical one. Not only did he see the new nescience as a Machiavellian filling of a moral and spiritual vacuum, but he also located the opening of this vacuum in the failure of Christendom to perfectly realize its own implied integration of *polis* with *oikos*. The search of Hegel for a modern equivalent of the

23. Hume, *Treatise of Human Nature*, Bk III, Pt II, Vol II, 252ff. Smith, *Theory of Moral Sentiments*, 116ff.

24. See Pocock, *Machiavellian Moment*, 462–506; and Hirschman, *Passions and the Interests*.

25. Ruskin, *Unto This Last*, 178.

26. Ibid., 125: "The Merchant—What is *his* 'due occasion of death?'"

27. Ibid., 171.

antique polis only allows him to try to keep civil society (in other words, the economic realm) "in its place." But Ruskin's appeal to the Christian *differentia*—namely, the integration of *polis* and *oikos*—permits a much more radical denial of political economy.

In the light of these reflections on morality, history, and dialectics, one may question the assumption that Christian socialism is really less critical than Christian Marxism. It seems that the former may be in some ways more compatible with the postmodern metacritique of Marxism. This metacritique no longer permits the view that capitalism is to be opposed because it is irrational, or self-contradictory, or self-occluding. I have already indicated some of the many reasons for this, but l should like to add briefly the following three points.

First of all, both the "scientific" *and* the "humanist" versions of the theory of alienation disappear once one denies that man's (sic) labor, or the products of his labor, in any way "belong" to him by nature. On the contrary, ideas of subjective "self-expression" and norms of autonomous production only arise in the context of a set of culturally specific symbolic exchanges with nature and with other persons, which go to make up "liberal capitalism." Hence the notion of self-possession in work is *itself* generated by the capitalist relations of production, so that it is not enough to claim, like Marxism, that this condition is not truly fulfilled by capitalism. For one cannot imagine self-possession as a "natural" state which capitalism falsifies, or unlimited, autonomous production as a "natural" goal which capitalism is holding back. On the contrary, one can only ensure that people's work really "belongs" to them if one not only brings them to fully share in its benefits but also creates a situation where they identify by habit and consent with its goals, in the content of a common culture.

With this a second point is linked—namely, that capitalism is not "mystifying" because it makes an artificial "exchange value" more basic than a natural "use value." As Jean Baudrillard has pointed out, the notion of a "pure" use value, and of sheerly "natural" needs outside the processes of symbolic exchange, is as much an effect of the capitalist economy as the idea of "abstract equivalences" in exchange values.[28] It is like Smith's and Hume's dualism of "natural" and "artificial" passions. Moreover, contemporary capitalism has dispensed with even this duality—increasingly we know that our needs are both socially created and constantly fulfilled,

---

28. Baudrillard, *Mirror of Production.*

but we still consent to this seduction, to the dizzying variegations of a pointless desire.

The third point is that the notion of ideology is no longer always a useful one. This concept presupposes that there is a gap between real social pressures and their ideal representation. Sometimes this is the case—and myths like Margaret Thatcher's "personal choice" serve an important function in capitalist society. However, this society has no need for an *overall* ideology in addition to the assumptions built into economic and bureaucratic relations—on the contrary, it requires only areas of local ignorance, where the spur of illusion can often be functionally useful.[29] And if delusion *is* more than local, then it does not lie only at the superstructural level; on the contrary, it is more importantly located within the workings of the economy itself, as Marx brilliantly recognized in his theory of fetishization and reification (this is why Marx *remains* the supreme analyst of capitalist economy).[30] But Marx still saw fetishization as concealing from view both the process of its own constitution and an innocent, "natural" reality. Yet, in a sense, fetishization conceals nothing at all, either in society or in nature, but through its reduction of everything to equivalence it "prevents" other equally unfounded social possibilities—other, more admirable "fetishizations," since humans *can only* deal with ineffable blends of "idea" and "thing." In particular it occludes the possibility of a "just economy" where things cannot all be measured on the same quantifiable scale, but are seen as symbolically representing each other in a fashion that cannot be translated into a univocal abstract language, whether of signs or of monetary tokens. Marx compared the operations of capitalist economy to those of a religion—but wrongly supposed that one can give a critique of this symbolic system by comparing

29. Thompson, *Studies in the Theory of Ideology*, and Turner, *Religion and Social Theory*. But Turner is wrong to reject the theory of fetishization and the primary location of ideas in power-relations themselves.

30. See chapter 5 in this volume. Although the present chapter stresses the limitations of Marxism and the falsity of a hybrid "Christian Marxism," I still stand behind most of what is said in the preceding chapter about the importance of Marxist *economics*, and the Marxist analysis of the capitalist mode of production, especially in *Capital*, chapter 1. It should be also noted that the outlook I am advocating does not deny the validity of class struggle (however complex a matter that may be in practice). Indeed, social and ideological struggle of all kinds becomes more important once one abandons the notion that capitalist processes themselves will tend, in the long term, towards socialism.

it to a demystified "human nature."[31] Rather, critique is only possible by comparing it to "other religions."

Furthermore, at certain strategic times and places, fetishization may no longer conceal the process of its own constitution. People may come to recognize capitalism for what it is—namely, a nescience and a "lived illusion"—and yet still affirm it and promote it. And this is not irrational, nor ideological, nor unprogressive. While Margaret Thatcher was ideological in associating her market philosophy with "traditional" values, most of her progeny have been out and out modernists who entertain no such illusions. The ideas that neoliberalism/neoconservatism are "backward looking," or that socialism can successfully appropriate the modernist discourse of "individual rights," represent fatal misapprehensions. All the socialisms, including Marxism, which compromise with the Enlightenment, ultimately lose out to capitalism as a more virulent and purer form of liberalism. Socialism is not necessarily on the agenda of history, and its "future" is always bound up in keeping alive a sense of collective purpose linked to objective and transcendent norms. This is *not* to say that these norms are eternally "present" to us in a constant fashion. On the contrary, our normative sense emerges through processes of "tradition," the gradual development of a common real cultural outlook, and collective purpose develops through seeing what is possible at specific historic junctures. But the transcendent reference of developing values is suggested just to the extent that such values are "positively imagined" in the course of unpredictable superadditions to the tradition, rather than being "negatively immanent" to an evolving dialectic.

It is because capitalism may be theoretically rational and indefinitely feasible, and yet not practically rational in the Aristotelian sense (in other words, not ethical), that the Marxist mode of suspicion will no longer do. Both Marxianism and Freudianism claim to investigate the suppression of something supposedly natural and fundamentally human: familially-generated sexual desire, autonomous freedom, or material production.[32] Instead of these modes of "foundational" suspicion, only a Nietzschean "baseless suspicion"—a suspicion not founded on an unquestioned starting point for "truth"—remains possible. Here the contingency of a particular cultural formation is exposed to differential contrast. *Other*

31. See chapter 5 above.
32. See Deleuze and Guattari, *Anti-Oedipus*.

possibilities relativize our own actuality, expose to view its assumptions, which we had taken to be universal norms. So what is "unmasked" here is not the suppression of the universal but the (*sometimes* ideologically disguised) non-allowance of other, equally valid possibilities. Hence there is an exposure of the "arbitrary" through a ceaseless imagining of other, equally "arbitrary" options.

And yet within secular socialism this Nietzschean postmodernism is rightly viewed as ambiguous. As has been seen, postmodernists are no longer able to reject abstract equivalence in exchange because it is "irrational." Instead, Baudrillard and others have favored, over against capitalism, the "symbolic exchange" of primitive societies—where there is a predominance of gift, sacrifice, mutuality, and loss rather than cold accumulation, or totalizing calculation—on ethical and aesthetic grounds alone. Yet what is in evidence here is not attachment to a *particular* cultural set of symbolic practices; instead the appeal to the "primitive" is a surrogate for a nihilistic will to the promotion of difference, the ceaseless breaking of any totalizing claims to "truth," as being the only justifiable goal that remains. Although foundational reason was rejected, the French postmodernists still clung to the formalism of an abstract "difference" itself, as the one remaining source for discriminating judgment. As a value this is poised uneasily between, on the one hand, a continuing celebration of individual choice and autonomy, and, on the other, a reappraisal of heteronomy with the realization that we are always defined with respect to "the other." This hesitation is best exemplified in Jean-François Lyotard, who deliberately foregrounded an oscillation between Kantian respect for personal freedom, and a "pagan" heteronomy where we possess our identity as a role within an inherited narrative.[33] He resolved this tension by proposing a paradoxical inversion of the categorical imperative—one is *always* to will the different, that which *cannot* be universalized.

In political terms, this meant that for Lyotard, as for Baudrillard, there is an imperceptible point of transition at which capitalism is pushed to a logical extreme that makes it pass over into a neo-primitivism or neo-paganism. As more and more things are absorbed into the impermanence of capitalist exchange, the distinction between sign and reality, which an earlier capitalism promoted, is exposed as an illusion, and the prospect of a purely "playful" "de-territorialized" society, celebrating the

33. Lyotard and Thébaud, *Just Gaming*.

limitless variety of possible "truths," is open to view. In this society, the only universal practical truth, according to the transformed categorical imperative, is the upholding of everyone's rights to compete in the potentially infinite number of different "language games." Lyotard's residual Kantianism depended upon an upholding of a distinction between "conflict," or legitimate competition within the rules of the various games, and "terror," which is the prevention of people from playing or the exclusion of certain games altogether. But, as has been pointed out against Lyotard, this distinction relies upon the illusion that there are fixed boundaries between the different language games—as, for example, Lyotard believed, in still curiously Humean fashion, that there is a sharp cleavage between theoretical games about "facts" and the ethical game about "values." Clearly, in a reality dominated by difference, and so by indetermination, "legitimate victory" may be in terms of altering the rules or of shifting the demarcations between different competitive areas.[34]

Lyotard's version of an "agonistic" society cannot, consistently, be subject to any further moral qualifications that would rule out fascism or terror. And, as a result, postmodernism's notion of a capitalism "going beyond its own bounds" just looks like political economy *in extremis*. After all, the stoics, the ancient precursors of the economic paradigm and modern natural law, already compared morality to an agonistic game where the point was not the outcome but "playing well." So it does not seem that postmodernism is a natural ally for socialism. Its version of difference reads difference as "necessary conflict" or as "ontological injustice."

But if my contentions are correct, then the main traditions of socialism were always linked to another critique of Enlightenment—not so much a critique "after" modernity, as rather an "alternative" to it, and in this (though not a reactionary) sense a "counter-modernity." After modernity lies a disappointment with scientific reason and natural law, leaving only a formalistic nihilism as their pale echo. But in the critique that runs, as it were, "alongside" modernity, classical and Christian exemplars help to promote a more hopeful metaphysic. One can trace connections (via Vico, De Bonald, and Ballanche) between the French nineteenth-century radicals' rejection of ontological antagonism (as discussed earlier in the chapter) and Augustine's counter-historical reading of Roman history in the *City of God*, where he exposes and denies pagan myths of the

34. See Weber, "Afterward: Literature–Just Making It," in Lyotard and Thébaud, *Just Gaming*, 101–21.

primacy of conflict which he sees as "enacted" in the lived narrative of the worldly city.[35] Such a "harmonistic" vision provides not just a "baseless suspicion" but also "baseless critique" of the narrative mode of nihilist suspicion itself—namely, the "polytheism" of unavoidable pluralism, deception, and conflict. For this Christian metaphysic—which in the doctrines of creation and Trinity posits an "original difference" without usurpation or rivalry—justice is possible, and the harmonizing of tensions is possible, although there are no rational criteria for these things. Lyotard's continuing attachment to a formalist regulation is superfluous if one is committed—though of a course on no grounds separable from the logic of this commitment itself—to a specific sacred space, the Christian *ecclesia*, whose very specificity consists in the concrete actualizing of a universal eucharistic unity-in-difference. Only through this lived demonstration is such an ontological perspective and such a practical possibility maintained. The demonstration may be thin, yet only this demonstration sustains the possibility of "socialism."

35. See Milbank, "An Essay Against Secular Order."

PART III

Theology and Social Theory:
Responses to Responses

7

ENCLAVES, OR WHERE IS THE CHURCH?

It was not the purpose of *Theology and Social Theory* to imagine the Church as Utopia.[1] Nor to discover in its ramified and fissiparous history some single ideal exemplar. For this would have been to envisage the Church in spatial terms—as another place, which we might arrive at, or *as this* identifiable site, which we can still inhabit. How could either characterize the Church, which exists, finitely, not in time, but *as* time, taken in the mode of gift and promise? Not as a peace we must slowly construct, piecemeal, imbibing our hard-learned lessons, but as a peace already given, superabundantly, in the breaking of bread by the risen Lord, which assembles the harmony of peoples then and at every subsequent Eucharist. But neither as a peace already realized, which might excuse our labor. For the body and blood of Christ only exist in the mode of gift, and they can *be* gift (like any gift) only as traces of the giver and promise of future provision from the same source. This is not an ideal *presence* real or imagined, but something more like an "ideal transmission" through time, and despite its ravages. Fortunately the Church is first and foremost neither a program, nor a "real" society, but instead an enacted, serious fiction. Only in its Eucharistic centering is it enabled to sustain a ritual distance from itself, to preserve itself, as the body of Christ under judgment *by* the body of Christ, which after all, it can only receive. In a sense, this ritual distance of the Church from itself defines the Church, or rather deflects it from any definition of what it is. In its truth it *is* not, but has been and will be.

---

1. The original version of this chapter responded to a special issue of *New Blackfriars*, April 1991, on *Theology and Social Theory*.

And yet it is, or believes itself to be, a true rite of passage from redemption to judgment. The Eucharistic elements are given to the Church, but not only may one eat to damnation, the very eating and drinking of Christ can be nullified by human greed (1 Cor 11:20–22). For even ritual forms are entrusted to our transmission, presentation, and elaboration: to receive Christ, to receive the flow of time as embodied God, is in some minimal way to receive the Church as itself an adequate mode of reception. Since the wine must unavoidably be carried in a chalice if it is not to be spilt, we can only be persuaded that this is indeed the blood of Christ if we are also persuaded by the performance (despite the performance) and persuaded by the preacher (despite the preacher).

Therefore the short answer to where is the Church? (or where is Milbank's Church?) might be, on the site of the Eucharist, which is not a site, since it suspends presence in favor of memory and expectation, "positions" each and every one of us only as fed—gift from God of ourselves and therefore not to ourselves—and bizarrely assimilates us to the food which we eat, so that we, in turn, must exhaust ourselves as nourishment for others. But the long answer could never be completed, since it would be nothing other than the Church's own act (which *also* defines it) of self-judgment and self-discrimination: all the stories of true and failed transmission, of more or less adequate persuasions and receptions; an ecclesiology of the kind that Rowan Williams demands, which involves critical narratives of the (endless) genesis of the Church. Not a judgmental history which measures the Church against the pre-established standard of Christ, but a history which in detailed judging raises us to a better perception of the pre-given standard—which can only be pre-given in the mode of promise. I willingly concede that my steps in this direction have been too hesitant and would only add that such "theological Church history" is not a task for academics only, nor one which finally privileges the first beginnings of the Church, but one which is also dedicated to many obscure, "private," and scarcely traceable happenings. If one neglects the "micro-temporality" of the Church, its proper precariousness, then a new kind of narrative essentialism might intrude, ignoring the fact that the Church is present as much in an obscure but precise act of charity as in the deliberations of epochal councils. Paradoxically, I would wish to argue that the "formalism" of my metanarrative, of my ethics and ontology, operates precisely as a safeguard *against* such an essentialism. For two reasons: first, the metanarrative which declares that all other histories are judged by the story of the arrival of a community of reconciliation is in a sense an "anti-metanarrative" as it tells of an *end* to (the rule of) imagined fateful logics, destined sacred identities and so forth. From henceforward there will, indeed, be only multiple and complexly interweaving stories to tell: what makes these stones nonetheless one is no principle of hypotactic subordination but a peace that (faith experiences and hopes) will shine amidst their parataxis (to adopt the terminology of Catherine Pickstock).

Secondly, the "formal" descriptions (which I do not claim could ever be exhaustive—even within the confines of formalism)—in terms of peace, forgiveness, harmony, etc.—describe structural relations, and *do not* isolate essences (i.e., what substantive ingredients are necessary to an identity), nor prescribe "what is to be done." In a sense, indeed, I am *not* concerned to provide an "ethics" (and doubt even the desirability of doing so) but rather to describe a supra-ethical religious affirmation which recasts the ethical field in terms of a religious hope: we may think of the good as infinitely realizable harmony if we believe that reality can finally receive such an imprint. This faith sustains ethical hope, but it also *overthrows* every "morality": every prescription in terms of such and such an inviolable law, uniquely valuable virtue or exemplary politics. To say "universal peace" is to say that everything has its place and its moment: every person's position can be judged equally by all others and must finally be judged by herself from her own unique and irreplaceable perspective (of course one needs general examples and conventions and norms, but none are *inviolable*). Therefore the ecclesiastical task of judgment (the Church is to judge itself and the world, as St. Paul makes clear) cannot be academically pre-empted. Which is not to deny that the last chapter of *Theology and Social Theory* requires (infinite) supplementation by judicious narratives of ecclesial happenings, which alone would indicate the shape of the Church that we desire.

Nor do I want to deny that between my "formal" or ideal descriptions of the Church (of an "ideal" happening and "ideal" yet real, if vestigial, transmission) and rather minimal attempts at "judicious narrative," there may exist a certain tension—close to the tension between ritualized and improvised (supposedly more, "real" and "historical") action. However, it seems to me that the Church has always lived with this tension and that it already surfaces to view in the New Testament itself. Consider, for example, Paul's letters to the Corinthians. They are characterized by what one might describe as "ritual priority." The Church is only the Church because it imbibes and becomes Christ's body, and re-articulates his earthly performance (1 Cor 10:16–17). What a cumbersome and taxing re-conception of social life! This new community has no "head" but a man once crucified, who only speaks again in the mute form of food. Unlike previous pagan (Indo-European?) rule, he is not, as head, over-against the body as the superiority of reason (which from time immemorial has governed "desire" and "passion" with aid of auxiliary "force"), but also as his (already) own body, at a "distance" from his (not yet) own body, which he rules. His reasons are not commands to his body, but undergoings of his body, by which his body is given to us. This wisdom is not "of this age," and not in this age does it exercise its power (2:6). It is as radically absent as a dead, exhausted body can be, and its power only that of a promise. Such wisdom can therefore only operate as "hidden, foreordained" (2:7). It is the creative wisdom of God, which, as Jean-Luc Marion has pointed out,[2] can for Paul make "to be" the things that are not and "as nothing" the things that are which seem to be solidly before us (1:28). This wisdom ruins the "wisdom of this age," the Greek philosophic wisdom which rests on a secure grasp of what is "present" (and so what "is" simply) to intel-lectual sight (1:18–29).

The crucified Lord only rules by giving himself over to us for our future nourishment. He refused the temptation of *present* power, and his post-ascended availability by no means reverses that refusal. To be gov-erned by this Lord, to internalize his rule, can only mean to come under his sign of the reversal of all worldly norms of knowledge and authority. Self-knowledge (the basis of self-command) is impossible, every image we make of ourselves illusory. But when we love, then we gradually come to know "as we are known," not as we are, but under the transformative gaze of uncontingent love itself. Without self-understanding we should not judge even ourselves, and certainly not others on the basis of our own norms. Judgment has occurred with Christ and is radically suspended till the *parousia* (4:3–5). The Church is, uniquely, not a community consti-tuted by judgment, but by the acknowledgement that judgment is not yet possible. Only out of such acknowledgment, which is its possessing of the mind of Christ, its waiting on love, is it alone fit to judge the world. And its members, for now, should only submit to judgment within the Church

2. Marion, *God Without Being*, 53–108.

(for violations of the suspension of judgment? For lack of love?) To enter into judicial litigation with other Christians is supremely to betray the character of the Church as community (6:1–8).

Without knowledge, without judgment, there can be no economy for the restriction of loss (endemic to our finite temporality). This, presumably, is why Christians are *moroi* not *phronimoi* (*not* prudent, *not* ethical) and only *phronimoi* in Christ according to an economy in which loss turns out to be gain (4:10). Fools, because they give themselves away, and not for a cause, not to a city, not to a place, only as links in a continuous, non-teleological chain of givings-away. Fools, because indifferent to worldly circumstance whose *reality* under the *sign* of the cross is transposed: slavery is freedom, self-giving; freedom is slavery, our bondage to the truly desirable (7:20–23). Likewise, we must be joyful as if sorrowing, for this joy is not ours, does not belong to us. And be sorrowful as if rejoicing (7:30); for every sorrowing misses something, and is our possession after all of love, and can be received as love by whomsoever is thereby loved (2 Cor 7:7). In this way (as Marion indicates) love goes "further" than loss of presence (at least of the other). Faith in creation, in resurrection, is faith in the deeper power of love over the apparent power of destruction.

If the "head" is a self-giving body, then no one is submitted to anyone else, but all are submitted to all. Paul may be an apostle, but the Corinthians can be kings without him and he will be happy to rule with them (4:8). The only rule of the Christian economy must be sharing for the sake of equality (2 Cor 8:2), and in the case of sexual exchange, each spouse must give unstintingly since each "rules" over the other (1 Cor 7:3–4). Most communities are "identified" by legal codes which distinguish the pure from the impure, the ethically allowed from the disallowed (the two categories, ritual and ethical, may not finally be distinct). However, Paul begins to see, tentatively and inconsistently, that this is not properly true of the Church. Those who eat the body of Christ do not eat this food *rather than* other foods, since Christ's food is uniquely not used up and uniquely "claims us" rather than vice-versa (6:13). Other foods are but temporarily useful, even if they have been offered to idols, who have no real power, and therefore are reduced to mere ontological indifference and the innocence of actuality (8:1–13). (In the sexual sphere, Paul's intimations of apurism are problematically less marked: Christ can be the rival of whores, having already paid for our bodies, just as he can be the rival of our spouses [6:15–20; 7:33–34]). To say this (positive being) rather than *that* (positive being) is to say rift, exclusion, and violence: in this fashion only *law* can "empower" sin, which otherwise would remain an inert possibility of destruction (15:56). "Morality" is complicit with death, as it is only the fragility of the world, which requires a coded shoring-up against loss. Death itself, however, or temporal disappearance, or the way we must indeed necessarily feed off each other is not "sin" for it may be the distance of love. Yet as intended or resigned-to death, as absolute loss and diminution, it is to be decoded as venomously invaded by sin, as a self-justificatory will to the annihilation of the other.

All this complex "formal" characterization of the Church is for Paul pre-given in ritual enactment. And *yet* even the latter can only be guaranteed as an authentic repetition if it is genuinely reflected in the improvised "real-life" of those who transmit and perform it. Paul is obsessively concerned with his own credentials as an apostle, in part because only authentic apostleship will guarantee authentic founding, authentic Eucharistic performance. He therefore seeks to supplement the formal categories with rehearsals of his own missions to and dealings with the Corinthians. Sublime imagery of death and resurrection, atoning substitution, and undying corporeality is harnessed without mediation to the diurnal matters of fundraising, moral discipline, and claims to authority. The character of the gospel as gift—the gift that is only of gift—is in part authenticated by Paul's own Socratic boast to have preached it *gratis*, or rather with the support of the Macedonians (9:15–18). Does this impress, as evidence of disinterest? Whether it does or not, the persuasive content of the gospel is here not separable from a persuasive mode of communication. Inversely, severely practical matters depend upon decisions regarding ineffable theological categories. Are the apostles entitled to their bread for working only at apostleship (9:3, 11)? This depends upon their direct knowledge of Christ and their bearing in their lives the Christ-like marks of substitutionary suffering: hence they also—like the body and blood of Christ—stand judgmentally over-against the Church (4:16). Appeal to one's endurances (4:10–13) then constitutes also a claim to power, for all the redefinitions of power as self-denying ordinance, for all the assertions of ultimate equality, and for all the paradoxical vauntings of "the least member," compared specifically to our genitalia, the weakest, most lacking and desiring (and therefore most responsive to Christ?) (12:22–26). Will Paul efface himself (and his "rational" headship) this far? And is such effacement shown in his claim to the right to judge harshly mere drunkards and sexual offenders (5:1–6, 6:9–10)? Does he not fall into the trap of wanting the Church to excel in a purity understood all too conventionally and exclusively? Whatever the answers, it is clear that formal specifications of *ecclesia* do not readily serve to resolve complex issues of everyday routine, discipline, and authority. Nonetheless, the only Christian approach here must be a persuasive attempt to recite particular cases, particular biographies as authentic embodiments of the *logos staurou*, the logic of the cross. Whereas, indicates Paul (in an astonishing reversal) all philosophy is reduced to the level of mere persuasion (*peithois*), this *logos* alone is truly *demonstrative* (*apodeixei*) since it is realized in power in resurrection and the emergence of the Church (2:4). Yet such power is itself first effective through persuasive preaching and this priority constitutes the ineradicable hierarchic claim of the apostle.

However, for his persuasion to become apodeictic, for his gift to be discerned in the Holy Spirit as gift, this authority must collapse in pace with its exercise. Unlike space, which may be democratic and merely consensual, time demands asymmetrical power and aristocratic rule; but unlike space also, which may persist in oligarchy, time demands the handing over of power as the only mark of its achievement. Apostolic power is self-cancelling. And if Christ, by virtue of his proleptic character does, nonetheless (through his apostles), continue to exercise headship over his body, which is his bride, then all the same the distinction of the Spirit, which is *from* Christ, yet also received as that "other" gift in which he may be discerned as gift, concurs with the impossibility of ever including a later, interpretative, temporal moment merely "under" a past authority which it is to interpret. Christ is himself more disclosed through the Spirit at work in the Church. And as mother and bride, the Church asymptotically approaches (without ever reaching) the perfection of the response of the Holy Spirit to the Logos in the Trinity, in which the Logos exists through this response, which not only bears the Logos through desire, but as desire yet in excess of the Logos, becomes its now *equal* bride. St. Paul even seeks to locate gender relations within this suspense. As the Church is for Christ, so woman is for man and should go veiled in church—nevertheless, he can add, in parentheses, *in the Lord* neither are independent, and both are "from" each other (11:11–12). For now, the priorities of time and its subordinations, but eschatologically, mutual generation. How, practically, can one instantiate such a strictly temporal logic? When, precisely, should equality supervene? But no rules, here, for Church governance: rather we are handed over to all the many particular pleas of claimed authority, all the kenotic measures of its truth.

Paul's letters to the Corinthians, therefore, exhibit the way in which extreme attention to formal categories which detail a "heterotopia" of non-exclusion and non-domination, actually demands supplementation by precise and particular appeals to contingent histories, if these categories are not to remain empty. The categories are not, however, purely paradigmatic: in a sense they detail an ideal yet also real diachrony, a "uchrony," or process of peaceful transmission which is *how* time falls out, despite the universal contamination of sin (since this in Christ has been fully suffered, such that even violent abuse and rupture, now traversed by love, can itself be transmitted as gift). In Christ peace has not, indeed, been totally achieved (a building remains to be built), yet it is proleptically given, because only the perfect saving of one man from the absolute destruction of death, this refusal of the loss of any difference, can initially spell out to us perfect peace. The latter validates the individual as being in excess of any achieved totality, so that the community of infinite peace must be first inscribed in this space of the single element, the discarded stone, which yet now frames the whole future construction.

But is this really vacuous? An evasion of the contingencies of time with their unavoidable arbitrariness, violence, and tragic losses? Let me append some remarks on both violence and tragedy. Graham Ward notes that I believe conclusions are arrived at by persuasion not argument, but wonders whether every act of persuasion does not have a violent character. Certainly, to be persuaded is to be forced, is to succumb to what is taken to be superior power. This power is "violent" (arbitrary, domineering) *unless* what is persuasive has the force of "truth" and one is "truly" persuaded. But there is no evident truth, and truth itself (for *Theology and Social Theory*) can be nothing other than a peaceful communication that is not a consensual reception of the same, but a becoming different of what is received, yet without aggressive rupture. "Harmonious" transition is peace, truth. However (and I should have made this clearer in *Theology and Social Theory*) this non-violence is never merely *visible*, any more than violence. An apparently brutal, physical forcing may be play, may be pleasure, whereas the most apparently freely offered consent may be the most subtle, most insidious domination. Of course it must be added that what is in principle a peaceful transition may be resisted, and at this point arises the question of whether it should be imposed: imposition may at times appear the lesser of two evils, yet it always risks a tragic dilution of its own truth. If it cannot be fully received in the spirit in which it is offered, then it cannot be properly received at all. But the possibility of a recipient later "coming to his senses," in retrospect receiving after all, may justify a coercive measure. In no sense does *Theology and Social Theory* recommend "pacifism," and the formal specification of truth as peaceful relation cannot be applied as a criterion authorizing non-resistance. The latter alone may be finally persuasive, finally redemptive, but no use of prescriptive criteria tell us when it is to be resorted to. Which is not to say that a decision for such a resort is just arbitrary. Instead it is a matter of judgment, in these unique circumstances, *now*. Just as discrimination between violent and non-violent (by participant or observer) is also entirely a matter of judgment. And to judge a reception as noncoercive *means* peacefully to receive . . . this action, or this scene before me.

The above remarks indicate that, as shown also in *Theology and Social Theory*, I do admit a certain "tragic dimension." Circumstances can force us to sacrifice some good we feel essential to our integrity, or even some person who must be forever missed. Yet according to Aristotle such circumstances are usually pre-engineered by a tyrant (Betray your compatriots, or forfeit your mother's life!) and one may wonder whether they ever deserve to be baptized with ontological necessity. I agree with Rowan Williams that one cannot *guarantee* the compatibility of goods, yet also feel that to go on having *faith* in this possibility is part of what it means to read the world as created. God sees the whole creation as "good." What does this mean? *Not* the good of the whole over against the parts, not a perfect order that will be eventually achieved, in time, but the entire continuous happening. Sacrifice in time and space, which normally upholds and defines the good, constituting "ethics," is here spectacularly refused. *This* is not worth *that* surrender, and if anything is to be given up it can only be everything for the source, God, which commands even death and non-being. But this renunciation of the whole is paradoxically in favor of every new, particular, and irreplaceable good that God can bring to be over and above the whole (this, I think, is what Kierkegaard tries to spell out in *Fear and Trembling*).[3] The Christian good is precisely not the good that depends on sacrifice and fixed hierarchy, but the equal necessity and compatibility

3. See my "Sublime in Kierkegaard." In this article I also try to spell out an account of "the self," which the possibility of "choice" between nihilism and Christianity in *Theology and Social Theory* seems to demand.

of all goods. Tragedy as a thematic is linked to political space, to the incompatibility of private and familial goals with those of sovereign spatial order, to the monopolization of power reinforced by a myth of scarcity: *limited* space, time, and resources. By contrast, the Church has no sovereign center; it is present "in" individuals and small communities as much as anywhere, and indeed is *not* so long as one coin, one sheep remains missing. Creation *ex nihilo* and the resurrection of the dead are protocols against the myth of scarcity, of limited being. Love opens up every space, fragments every moment; where it is not wanted, steps out, again.

But is it true that only tyrants, only humanly engineered circumstances, deny us the compossibility of all goods? One must discriminate. First, of course, there are some worthwhile roads not taken, perhaps some wonderful planets not created, and who knows whether even God knows that ours is the best of all possible? These are but wistfully mourned. Secondly, there are existing goods destroyed out of tragic necessity in circumstances which, I contend, one can always discover to be themselves contingent. But is not the latter claim patently exorbitant? As Williams says, we *always* live, "at the expense of each other"—not merely at the Eucharist are we habitual cannibals. This point should, however, be connected back to the non-visibility of violence and non-violence: in time there is ceaseless using and using up, yet this may at times be judged love and gift, not warfare. Further: according to the peculiar economy of love, in giving we are replenished; here the moral good is not a self-contained, Aristotelian teleological good of "flourishing," rather the goodness of this good is only *found* in its relation to other goods and to God—relations of supplying and of supplication. The loss of "goods" therefore, is not necessarily or always tragic, since truly moral goods are only good in being lost or sublated. Indeed, this is exactly what the "minimalist" theodicy in Augustine appears to imply (see *City of God* 11.22). Nothing *whatsoever* about tragedy here. Rather the theodicy seems to supplement the rigorously relational theory of good involved in the view of evil as privation. If the latter concerns a kind of "intentional" relation—a certain thing is not all it ought to be in relation to God, the former concerns a kind of "extensional" one: viewed in isolation certain pains, certain tediums, seem somewhat intolerable, but when related to other things they become acceptable. They *do not* then appear as necessary evils, or goods tragically foregone, but purely and simply as aspects of the good itself, as necessarily contrastive elements like light and shade. The life of peace is *not* an anemic life without tedium, and therefore without climaxes: the point being that, on account of climaxes, tedium is not merely tedium, but also suspension and excitement. Of course where theodicy ceased to be "minimalist" (as in the seventeenth century) then the sacrifice of individuals to the whole gets reinstated—but that means precisely a kind of legitimation and rationalization of the (ontologically) tragic. By contrast, individuals and communities are not, for the "minimalist" view, to be overridden, but they themselves can exercise judgment about pains, temporary deprivations and losses which are yet not to be considered *evils*, privations of the fullness that might be. So this fullness also is not visible (like a sort of maximally bloated reality), and not a stranger to restraint and delay.

Moreover, to contrast what is tragically lost with what is selectively established may be again to fall victim to the dominance of a spatial perspective, which affords only an illusory foothold. As we live in time, everything is lost, nothing is established, and this renders politics ultimately futile. It is the *mark* of a radical politics to recognize this, and instead of seizing sovereign power, to work against this power by seeking to save what can be saved for every individual in every moment: for example, to ensure that every transaction is as far as possible just and charitable, and as far as possible robs the capitalist of his profits, the bureaucratic state of its domination. If anything is to be saved, it can only be saved in the passing moment of its loss, and if anything is to remain it can only remain through recollection, which repeats what has vanished and so intimates its eternity. As everything passes and only "is" through the trace of its vanishing, nothing even of what has been violently or tragically surrendered (under force of circumstance) is irrecoverable. If we are not raised, then neither is Christ (1 Cor 15:13).[4]

Were indeed a tragic predicament predominant, then many (most?) decisions would be arbitrary, and the Church's preferences no more justifiable than those of the marketplace—indeed the Church might well have to be regulated *like* a marketplace, and this would be its postmodern form. Useless, here, to speak of the resources of forgiveness and reconciliation, for what could they now mean but a sighing realization that we all are merely obeying a throw of the die? The Church's peace would be

4. In my article, "Problematizing the Secular? The Post-Postmodern Problematic," I try to outline (via a discussion of Spinoza) a somewhat more positive relation of *privatio boni* and Christian eschatology to Nietzschean will-to-power and eternal return. Both outlooks are anti-tragic, but, I claim, the Christian one more consistently so.

somewhat like camaraderie in the bath at Twickenham, once the formalized violence of the game is over.

Against Rowan Williams's "tragic" emphasis therefore, which seems too allied to political projects, the writhings of committees, and the identification of the many roads not taken by a single individual with moral "goals," I would want to stress the "absurdity" of faith, its non-resignation to loss and scarcity, and its augmentation of the Platonic vision of good as precisely the harmonious "fitting in" of all roles and options, where these have come to constitute peoples' very identity. All the same, he is wholly right to say that we only act in a history that is (exhaustively if contingently) "shaped by privation," and if *Theology and Social Theory* appears to play this down, than it is much at fault. Original innocence is indeed wholly lost, and only leaves its trace as suffering. Yet it is still innocence that suffers, and *only* innocence (the children we are to become), because what must be suffered is the senselessness of evil, and those who know evil, having "learned from experience," have learned precisely nothing. Furthermore, to surpass the tragic, to make the Christian gesture of faith beyond (but not without) renunciation, is not to embark on a premature celebration. On the contrary, it is to *refuse* to cease to suffer, to become resigned to a loss. Only at the price of an augmentation of suffering does a complete joy and peace begin to shine through.

And this is why Christ came to visit the lost. He sought out those who dwell in tragic enclaves, those who, through privation, enjoy goods which paradoxically cannot be goods because they are cut off from communication, from universal resonance. I mean something like honor amongst thieves, love in brothels, wisdom in the councils of state, Utopia constructed on the ravaged hunting grounds of Indians. But we *all* dwell in enclaves, within founding dishonesties and deprivations, which no later virtue can truly undo. Christ suffers this enclosure and so loves it and discloses it for us and to us. The enclave is henceforwards our hospital and asylum. Here—nowhere yet—is the Church. Everywhere.

8

ON THEOLOGICAL TRANSGRESSION

The Theological Virtues

Let me commence my own response to certain respondents to my work by interrogating a certain note of outrage and dismay present in some of them.[1] An outrage in excess of mere disagreement. For it is not that they simply reject my Christian reading of social reality, as one might also reject a liberal, Marxist, feminist, or Freudian one; it is also that the very attempt is viewed as reprehensible, perverse, and intolerant in a way that the other named intellectual procedures would not be. And precisely why? The answer seems to be that it is assumed that Christianity can only be appropriately understood as something "particular," as a specific set of cultic or cultural attachments, or else as a mode of rendering a "personal" religious experience, which is valid within the confines of remaining but one perspective amongst many. However, this understanding is, historically, *not* appropriate. As Daniel Boyarin rightly emphasizes, the Enlightenment took over from Christianity itself an unprecedented universalizing thrust, or attempt to indicate that which underlies, supersedes, or else fulfils and mutually harmonizes *all* perspectives. Hence the argument of *Theology and Social Theory* is never *simply* that, in a postmodern world, every perspective is as good as every other, and so a reading from one single Christian perspective remains possible. On the contrary, the postmodern valuation of the unsurpassability of *plural* "difference" or

---

1. The original version of this chapter first appeared in an issue of *Arachne*, vol. 2, no. 1 (1995) partly devoted to *Theology and Social Theory* and the rest of my works.

perspective is upheld: what is contested is rather the mode of this valuation, or the precise construal of the transcendentality of difference itself.

Here one can distinguish between a naïve universalism on the one
hand, and *an inevitably contested universalism* on the other. At first, perhaps, the Enlightenment was a naïve dawn of light: since the sun was one
and men now chose to live by day instead of under nocturnal shadows,
it must be the same sun that all see by. But the impossibility of a direct
gaze should have forewarned of a soon-to-be-contested universal: is it
nature, is it freedom, is it utility, is it power, is it *eros*? Eventually, those
who steadfastly persisted in the desire for a direct gaze—the desire for
enlightenment—decided that the thwarting of this desire, the blinding of
he who would look, the darkness of the sun, is itself the final objective
truth. What is (after all) truly, objectively shown, is the flux of perspectives
against a dark background. Such nihilism is demanded by the very forbidding of metaphysics as ontotheology, a forbidding of the transgression of
the reach of our gaze. Since all we see is from a perspective, and even this,
being temporal, does not *remain*, is not self-identical, then even the claim
to see a single objective thing is transgressive, and all we do see is the passage of sight itself into the forbidden realm, which is sublimely off-limits.
Existence, even knowing existence, is ecstasy, our rehearsal of the return
of all things to that entropic nothing which is the ontological non(Being)
of all ontic appearances, which are so much illusory flotsam, purporting
"to be," to have identities, to delay deferral in the face of the infinite speed
of their always already-accomplished annihilation. Yet it is not, as for
older mysticisms of reason, that temporal appearances may be escaped,
for what eclipses them is merely nothing, a nothing that only exists in its
predation upon that appearance whose being it nonetheless inverts.

Hence the entirely logical triumph of the black Enlightenment, from
Schopenhauer through Nietzsche, Heidegger, and Bataille to their contemporary heirs. For nihilism is enlightenment; its (un)knowing of that which
remains as nothing—which, as Catherine Pickstock points out, most fulfils
a requirement for the perfectly objective and inert—realizes with precision
the desire of reason, which is to say a desire that there should be reason pre-
eminent over desire. By the same token, as Conor Cunningham has pointed
out, it fulfils and perfects, and does not in any measure exceed, the project of
metaphysics as ontotheology (in Heidegger's sense): for its supreme "caus-
ing" being is nothing and this being is (not) in the same fashion as every
being: hence Being as such is univocal, and abstractly graspable for what it

is (not). I do not, therefore, any more than Nietzsche, pronounce the word "nihilism" in necessarily pejorative tones; it is to be respected far more than "humanism," and will always remain the most plausible mode of universal reason, if "plausibility" is that for which one is most concerned.

In our time, therefore (contrary to many superficial diagnoses of "postmodernism" *almost never* ascribed to by its supposed French exponents), enlightenment appears to be at last realizing its dark potential, and to have overcome "the inevitable contestation of the universal" to which I alluded above. The universal is nothing, it is death. It is also the infinite perspectival variety of life, or series of claims to "identity" which always have to invoke a fictional metaphysical background to secure themselves. Since each of these vaunted "realities" lapses immediately into virtuality or mere "simulation" of a projected reality, on account of the continual disintegration of its identity by the hand of time (or else time "manifest" as critical thought) the universal of the flux of life (*difference*, or whatever) is dialectically identical with death. And one must acknowledge here how, despite all its purported pursual of a difference beyond dialectical opposition, postmodern nihilism nonetheless "at its last gasp," when it ponders the transcendental relation of *difference* to what it differentiates, and thereby the transcendental relation of nothing to everything, re-inscribes dialectics, just as it re-inscribes the aim of reason, which is to know with security. *Beyond* the reach of desire, which nihilism must rationalistically reduce to desire for death, sublime desire for self-annihilation, or else inevitably illusory desire predicated upon lack (Bataille or Lacan: the difference is trivial). Beyond *also* the reach of trust, which implies a non-cognitive relation to the unknown; beyond, in addition, love, which continues to hope without reason for a return from the unknown; finally beyond hope itself, which continues to think outside any concern with "plausibility."

The pursuit of reason, therefore, even or rather especially in its nihilistic extreme, is in excess of Platonic *eros*, and in excess likewise of Christian faith, hope, and charity. But can it justify this excess? Certainly, within the terms of "objective" judgment, or in other words, *on its own terms*. But this must presume a privileged relation of reason to the universal. It must assume that the sun is the visible light of reason, invisible only by virtue of its known nullity, and not the *subjective* light of the Good (as it is for Plato), only arising upon or within a certain stance, attitude, or mood. It is, therefore, outside the prerogative of reason to deny the possibility of a universally disclosing mood, stance, or attitude. And at this point it becomes possible to raise once again the question of "a contestation of the universal" as was already in effect done by Luther with his priority of faith, Pascal with his "order of love," Kierkegaard with his disclosing anxiety. It then ceases to be enough merely to use the rhetoric of pluralism, the other and difference, for one starts to glimpse how pluralism and difference as "universal" viewpoints may yet themselves be construed in radically different and competing ways. For example, beyond the *fulfillment* of the modern metaphysical enterprise as nihilism, one could imagine a Platonism yet more drastically focused upon *eros* contesting the nihilistic construal of difference, and in particular its being hollowed out by death. Indeed, certain philosophies articulated within Christian, Jewish, and Islamic contexts have arguably *already been* such Platonisms. Or again one might argue that the transcendentality of difference can be otherwise construed by faith, hope, and charity (the "theological virtues" in the terms of Aquinas) than it is by reason. This was one of the endeavors of the last part of my book, which issued in the claim that difference so construed is "peaceful difference" for precise although complex philosophical reasons which my critics rarely explore or contest, just as they never consider why "the French postmodernists" *cannot* construe difference as "peaceful" and *never* describe it as analogical.

If, therefore, nihilism is not to be the end of the argument, precisely because there are also possible "logics of mood" beyond argument, then this will involve considering the readings of the universal, even of a universal that only "is" in dispersive dissemination, by Christian theology or else a Platonic, Jewish, or Islamic philosophy. The secular contestation of the universal is indeed at its "end" in nihilism, but just for this reason a post-secular contestation of the universal now commences. And to see this claim as opportunist or implausible by virtue of all the borrowings which theology (or another religious discourse) will inevitably be making from "postmodernism" is historically blinkered: for alongside the secular self-deconstruction of Enlightenment into an immanentist nihilism, parallel religious "metacritiques" of reason's claims have proceeded throughout modern times. Moreover, the former has consistently tried to takeover the philosophical moves of the latter: hence the "linguistic turn" itself, or the priority or "expression" over reason was first articulated in *theological* terms by Berkeley, Hamann, and Herder; Nietzsche's transvalued ethics of "gift" manifestly reworks the Lutheran priority of faith over works;

Heidegger takes over anxiety and repetition (in *nuce* the whole discourse on supplementation) from Kierkegaard, *ennui* from Pascal, ontological difference from Aquinas, and the *aporias* of time from Augustine (and in every case the true extent of borrowing is suppressed).

For convenience, one can dub the former, secular self-critique of Enlightenment "immanentism," and the latter, religious metacritique of Enlightenment "the discourse of transcendence." If one asks why it is that immanentism, supremely in the case of Heidegger, has become contaminated with the discourse of transcendence, then the answer must be that the invoking of the immanent whole as a mysterious *nihil* which plays the role of transcendental condition of being and understanding inevitably suggests a re-occupation of the site once occupied by "God," where, by contrast, for a humanist doctrine focused round epistemology (articulating the mere conditions of what we as stable identities might know), this site was strictly off-limits. Moreover, Heidegger's immanentism claims to provide a "philosophy beyond philosophy," philosophy being traditionally construed as metaphysics that represents to itself stable present realities. Yet the site beyond philosophy that is still in some sense philosophical is predetermined within Western discourse as a theological site, such that, for all Heidegger's inaccurate attempts to characterize classical theology as "ontotheological," he is nonetheless impelled to express a "post-philosophical" philosophy on the basis of theological transplants. Indeed, he is quite explicit: from Pascal and Kierkegaard he takes over the idea that not a representing reason but rather "mood" (*stimmung*) is what provides the clue to the illumination of Being, to a possible ontology. Hence in Heidegger himself the project of a contestation of the universal beyond the sway of reason is mooted. But only in a false, contradictory fashion: for he insists (indeed more or less assumes) that the theological treatments of the import of "mood" are uncritical and metaphysical, in the sense of transgressively speculative. Only philosophy can tell the truth of mood. But that is tantamount to saying that only philosophy objectively "sees" what is involved in mood, thereby bringing irreducibly religious attitudes, convictions of desire, of faith, and so forth inappropriately under the sway of knowledge, such that only reason and not mood after all can unravel mood in all its subjectivity to itself. Such cognitive reduction of attitude, which is supposedly not violated in its attitudinal character, can with precision be described as "Gnostic." (And beneath this Gnosticism there lurk elements of anti-Semitism and a diabolical political agenda.)

Hence Heidegger failed to capture from theology the thematic of mood. It remains untamable by nihilistic reason (nihilism which is the true destiny of reason) and now returns to contest its construal of the universal, which, in one valid transcendental denomination, is difference. But why should we listen to this contestation? That itself is ultimately a matter of what happens to be our mood, if I may so indicate the entirely casual and therefore almost missable character of what is truly serious. Nevertheless, our moods today are so often mixed that even theological reason may discover unexpected possibilities for attentiveness to what it has to say. One such possibility may concern the question of social and political hope. For this hope is a mood not *yet* quite stilled, although the hour of midnight (the final night of our Western history) draws steadily nearer. In the mode of another *gnosis*, a previous progressivism (liberal or Marxist) confused hope with optimistic speculation on the basis of facts or plausibilities. Today, by contrast, no doctrine of an inevitable or even possible liberation of a true human essence any longer upholds the hope of a progress beyond bureaucratic and market-dominated society. To the contrary, today's progressivists are hitherto held in spellbound thrall by the spectacle of a still-developing capitalism inexorably commodifying the realms of knowledge, law, policing, and even government itself. Yet, illogically, they cling to a hope for something "beyond," and try to pretend that such hope can still be gnostically grounded in diachronic development. Hence they tell themselves incredible stories about how the way to overcome capitalism is to push it to an excess, to release all the flows, which it renders accumulable and profitable for some by half-releasing and then "re-territorializing." These stories precisely cohere with an attempt to blend nihilism with hope: to view as both oppositional and promising the drive to entropic extinction which is at the same time the release of infinite speed, an unimpeded line of flight. Yet while the invocation and encouragement of such a drive might be arguably subversive of a society built upon accumulation and the marketing of "identities," it cannot be genuinely *promising*. All that it holds out is an exit, not a future, since the strict logic of nihilism, its precise rationalism, posits no actual line of flight other than the ceaseless breaking and re-setting up of arbitrary boundaries. And this line of flight is already the line of our present proceeding, our present unstoppable acceleration. (Here earlier nihilist thinkers were usually more clear-headed: Heidegger taught the inevitable fatality of technocracy; Bataille the necessity for taboos; Lacan the law of frustration within desire.)

Therefore our now at last threatened neoliberal global reality (ludicrously misdescribed by some as "conservative re-trenchment") is essentially at one with our most "radical," our most *avant-garde* thinking. Just as, for the latter, the spuriousness of any assertion requires a supplementation whose process of arrival is liberating ("deferral"), yet whose actual arrival is once more violent, so also, in order to produce surplus value, every physical or informational commodity must for a time proclaim a new and integral identity which holds the key to prestige, health, wealth, or power until its insufficiency is exposed by the arrival of something more "successful," more revealing, more fundamental, ensuring that "the real thing" is forever "yet to come." At the heart of this proclamation resides an emptiness: nothing to be known, no "real" strength that is the basis for power, no real virtues that demand admiration, no truly enjoyable riches rather than merely nominal ascription. Yet to assert this in merely *critical* discourse (the language of reason) is no longer to expose an illusion; on the contrary it is to demonstrate that we now live in accord with the way things are (not). Now, at least, like nature herself, we trundle our fantasies perpetually around the void.

Both capitalism and nihilism, therefore, converge on the same destiny: since no content, or identity of any sort, can be *justified*, a ceaseless variety of content is simply tolerated or permitted according to the formal rules of an agonistic game originally played to the advantage of certain identifiable players, although now we cannot be so certain even of that. Now the game itself rules, with its relays of signs according to precise rules of coding and meta-rules for recoding, and so on *ad infinitum*. The only content desired by the game is the new arrival, yet this newness will be arbitrary, threatening a violence outside the system. In consequence, the future must also be policed in advance as far as possible, the new content received into a prescribed formal position, relatable along a continuum to other positions. It must be positionable, classifiable, re-producible. Hence in defiance of "real" bodies, whether natural or cultural, which are defined *not* (as the "realisms" of nostalgic humanists like Roy Bhaskar suppose) by an—in principle—representable spatial structure or essence, but by ceaseless temporal fading and constitution through non-identical repetition, "virtual" bodies are substituted. These bodies appear (this is the very content and occasion of their appearing) not to fade, they appear to persist—albeit as "traces"—precisely to the measure of our demands and orderings. They permit us the illusion that we live in a pseudo-eternity of space, rather than in the passage of time, which is our "embodiment." Yet if time is not a moving image of eternity, but arises from and proceeds back to nothing, then the reduction of time to spatial convention, a series of written spacings (Derrida) or contents which are paradoxically definable in a fractal manner as the hollowing out of infinite abysses, can be taken as the most genuine manifestation of the essence of time and body. For immanence, the truth of life is death, just as to deny the "after-life" (life in the presence of eternity) means to deny that we have ever lived at all. This is all rational, and I would not *argue* against it. Yet in another mood we can perhaps glimpse how faith in the eternal gives us back what we had supposed to be our real bodies with their endurance through non-identical repetition whose truth is narrative or music, and not an essence, not even essential nothingness—the only precisely-positionable position, that lure and love of every "science."

Nihilism, as the logic of a perfected capitalism and bureaucracy, which are themselves the implementation of reason, is therefore without hope. Yet its proponents still illogically persist in hoping. They still (just about) entertain this mood, and therefore I may still address them. I may still request that they consider whether hope without reason (though not against reason, which in the wake of hope will be redefined) may not of itself provide a clue to the real. And further to this, whether as Kieslowski's *Trois Couleurs: Bleu* seems to enquire, whether the three Enlightenment universals of liberty, equality, and fraternity are not rendered nugatory if linked mainly, as the Enlightenment assumed, to reason, and not to the older trio of faith, hope, and charity? If hope is without foundation in reason, then its positive stance to the future must belong to a wider trust in the unknown, which is faith. However, to advocate faith rather than reason is immediately to invite massive misunderstanding. Many suggest that if reason can be overweening, it nonetheless has the means to check itself, whereas faith has no such means, since its claims to know are from the start without basis. However, this is to misconstrue *pistis* as *gnosis*. Faith does not claim to know anything; rather it trusts the unknown, which certainly renders the unknown eminently personal (personal beyond anything we know as personal), for only the personal meets, or meets with our trust. But it does not "know a person" (not even Jesus), it merely trusts. Therefore it is not a question of "having faith in something," or of making preposterous claims on the basis of faith. And it follows, in turn, that there are not many faiths (the non-existent "world-faiths") of which some might be dangerous. A dangerous faith, purporting to secure the unknown, to provide a demonstrable or else contractual basis for its trust, as in many rites of sacrifice, would not be faith at all. Faith leaves the unknown as unknown and is always inconceivable without the *via negativa* which is not some sort of dissenting "minority report" distinct from dogmatic theology, but was always the path of classical theology itself (at least up to Duns Scotus). Therefore there is only a single faith—to have faith at all is to have faith in the transcendent God, and indeed *pistis* is arguably a specifically Christian rather than even Jewish category. It is a mood of trust that involves a being "persuaded" by the reach of a divine word beyond the scope of dialectics. And far from being dangerous, it has nothing at all to do with danger, since it is that which even in the face of manifest danger persists in hope and in the offering of love, rather than erecting a counter-barrier of dangerous warning against previous threat. Inversely, reason, even in its modesty, always courts danger, since its limited cautious claims are coterminous with its erected barriers of domination, while the counterpart to its mere humility in the face of the unknown is necessarily anxiety and nameless dread, the very thing that drives us into the temporary security of immune self-possession, that accomplice of all violence.

Despite the final uncertainty of reason, faith, unlike reason exalted into an absolutely prevailing mood, does not *hypostatize* uncertainty as an empty nothing or a sublime sundered from the beautiful. Trusting uncertainty, it receives an ecstatic continuity between the unmeasured and the measured, the infinite and the finite. Here the trustworthiness of the measured and familiar, its consoling beauty, is real as promise of an unknown plenitude. And conversely, and far more crucially, the constitutive incompleteness of any beautiful, harmonious identity, any "measure" (as correctly perceived by nihilism) must be read as *itself* the site of beauty, beauty as the allure of a promising depth, beauty as a measure whose rhythm is but the leading back into that depth. A measure whose ruling order therefore concerns not only the given *ratios*, but the unknown *ratio* which is the sense of "how to go on" in surprising yet appropriate ways. The beautiful here appears as the manifestation of a hidden depth which provokes *eros*—against Burke and Kant and the entire modern *de-eroticizing* of the beautiful in order, in Burke's case, to capture *eros* for the sublime and the "homosexual" order of desire for death, which is a desire for the same (your death which is also mine) in opposition to the sexual difference of living bodies. Against this inheritance one must reclaim the beautiful as itself the sublime, and, inversely, the sublime unknown as eminently beautiful for the trusting gaze of faith. (The claim of Lyotard et al. that Burke and Kant "rediscovered" the sublime suppresses the genealogical truth of their *specific construction of a duality of the sublime and the beautiful*, where earlier—for Longinus and Boileau's theological readings—the sublime unknown could also arrive as the surprising event of new participation in beautiful order).

There is therefore more involved in faith than merely trusting the unknown, for trust itself institutes a continuity between unknown and known that allows the trust of the known to be projected onto the unknown, precisely because trust of the known is reconceived, beyond the bounds of pre-Christian superstition or post-Christian reason, as trust in the continuous arrival of the unknown in the known. This latter, crucial inversion, ensures that trust is no longer conceived reactively as a substitute for guarantee-able security, but on the contrary as an active, joyful, erotic risk, a gesture of confidence that we make in the face of apparent security, rendering security also a delight, but thereby more secure than security, since it turns out that there is only security in the mode of hopeful delight in the unknown. Finally, because in the known there is a priority of the unknown, faith involves more than itself as trust, but includes an already actual reception of the event of the arrival of the mysterious in the cognized. Faith assumes also charity, the advent of the love of God which, to receive in due, means not to hold, but with respect to its constitutive depths to pass on as love for the neighbor. From the perspective of charity we see that the unknown never leaves us with mere postponement (that new idol) but has already in part imparted itself, in the little parts of beings, which are nonetheless inexhaustibly redolent of the fullness of the unknown donation. And for this reason we see also that to love, to be virtuous, is not first of all to do, as if there were some necessary duty to perform in the face of some voiding lack, or some violent danger; rather it is first of all to "actively receive," to repeat what has already been begun. As Hegel realized, against Kant, if love or the ethical state is not already there, in being itself, in human social being, if it is not at first, within humanity, a human-preceding gift, the already accomplished perfection of being (since contaminating evil, is, for the perspective of faith, that which takes away, that which voids), then the ethical state can *never* arrive. Instead love will be *reduced* to mere hope for love or faith in love, which itself will be understood as a voiding, or endless negation of barriers which are held to hold back the arrival of the ethical. For the latter perspective, there is no "participation," no love-in-a-measure; it is rather all or nothing, since love is construed as the allowing of absolute autarchy, absolute self-determination (Kant), or securely possessed happiness (Bentham). And these things never arrive, rendering love and the ethical effectively irrelevant. One is left with the god of postponement, as in the drastically extended Kantianism.

Without charity, therefore, a discourse of transcendence involving only faith and hope—trust in the other, hope for the arrival of the other, allowing the other to be other—retains a persisting closeness in practice to immanentist nihilism. Hence the ineffective emptiness of Levinas's "transcendent." Where the Other or the other is rendered immune from visibility—which Levinas arbitrarily construes as *necessarily* the visible as possessed by reason—then the other is actually reduced to and defined by unknowability. He is identified with that void, which as we have seen is the very *condition of possibility* for possession and control. He remains after all the subject of rights, the objective, classifiable subject of modernity, whose freedom is secured by the terror of a never-accomplished work of policing. Here the unknown never arrives in the event of the embodied other, and the other himself never arrives as an event for me, since there is no common measure, no blending of identity and difference which constitutes the beautiful as the continued possibility for justice, or an objectively "right" positioning of people and things, albeit according to a surprising, imprescribable measure. Faith indeed teaches no "rule" of measure, but it nonetheless trusts that there can be shared ruling. At the same time, it already receives and narrates measure according to its own judgment. It already loves: genuine transcendence includes a reception of the event of love as the arrival, in harmony with us, of the other. Hence, as I shall stress below, my insistence on the "presence-already" of the Church and my refusal *simply* to present it as a utopian ideal. For the Church is (*as* Church, not, obviously, when it ceases to be the Church) nothing other than the continuing event of charity, and there can be no non-ecclesiological understanding of the point that "the greatest of these is charity." To say that only charity abides, is also to say that only the community of love abides.

From the above, I hope that I have managed to articulate two decisive reasons that might attract an attention to theology even from those in the mood of reason. First of all, the isomorphism between nihilist thought and late-capitalist practice surely indicates more clearly than ever what John Ruskin already intimated, namely that the rule of formal indifference is precisely *secular* rule. Therefore those who still entertain a hope beyond the sway of capital and "information" (commodified knowledge) ought at least to entertain the thought that there might be something "beyond secular reason." Secondly, should they continue to hope, despite realizing that "postmodern" discourses provide no grounds for hope (*any* hope, never mind utopian hope), and continue to love and trust likewise, they might also entertain the thought that there can be a mood of faith, hope, and charity other than that of reason which construes the universal, or transcendental difference, differently. They might also wonder whether their continued loving, hoping, and trusting after all derives from a Christian legacy, and whether these things are sustainable outside an entire Christian logic. Nihilism, after all, has nothing to do with love or even *eros*, since it only thinks more precisely the bounds of pure reason, hypostatizing as senseless nothing the inevitable transgression of those bounds. Since such a transgression *returns* us to the bounds, or in other words reinstates presence, identity, technocracy, capital, and domination, their non-surpassability turns out to be *precisely* the message of Derrida et al. But supposing there could be a real, not a merely virtual transgression, and a true postmodern? As I have shown, the only possible transgression of current order would be a theological one. So it is not simply that I am not a mere "conservative," it is even that I am one of the few people continuing to uphold the bare *possibility* of a "radicalism."

In the next four sections I shall try to meet my critics by indicating briefly how a reading by virtue of theology, or in terms of the theological virtues of faith, hope, and charity, bears upon secular and Christian theory and practice.

Faith and Secular Reason

"Postmodern" thought represents a heightened form of rational discourse, of "secular reason." Its hyperbolic rationality recognizes that there is no genuinely known present, for a univocally representable object of knowledge is always deferred. Identities continually dissolve in a gesture towards the void. But for many "postmodern theologians," it appears that this void may very easily, or might just as well, be named "God," such that at last we have a kind of universal rational theology, independent of creeds and institutions, but in line with a supposed "separate" tradition of negative theology within Christianity. It is often unclear here whether "faith" is required in order to name the void "God," and if it is, then further unclear why such fideistic re-naming should make any intellectual or practical difference, if not also conjoined with a reception of the charitable event, which implies recognition and insertion within a sequence of loving eventualities, a "tradition of love."

However, this hybrid void/God is by no means subscribed to by the rigorous proponents of differential thinking: not by Heidegger, nor Derrida, nor Nancy. For these thinkers (one way or another) the void is a transcendental object of reason, and faith can only intrude upon this empty scene by "naming" the void in a way that would compromise its transcendental status, and reduce it to something merely ontic. Hence for Derrida, there may indeed be a not-accidental resemblance between his discourse of deferral and the discourse of negative theology, but he also insists that the deferrals of the latter are an asymptotic approach to an infinite *arche*, an ultimate presence, whereas his logic points rather to the ultimacy of deferral itself, so refusing any need to posit a transcendent beyond time. In consequence, not the transcendent God but transcendental Being/Nothing, or the impersonal, unilateral, not-returnable "gift" of time's arrow is the ultimate context for "existing" and "knowing" (the parentheses denote the infinitely deferred evacuation of content by its transcendental preconditions which is crucial for Derrida's position). This outcome, if accepted, then permits theology only three remaining moves if it wishes to preserve its possibility: 1) The void can be named God. But in this case God himself is Being/Nothing, God himself as transcendental nothing is cancelled in the series of ontic appearances, yet preserved in this very cancelling without return. Much in earlier Derrida suggests the possibility of such a "left-Hegelian" death-of-God theology, and some American followers of Altizer dutifully grasped an obvious market opening and put this into Derridean dress (Mark C. Taylor). 2) One can accept *différance* as a transcendental condition for all discourse *without* naming it God, and then seek to elaborate a theological discourse under this rubric. This is the Australian poet and theologian Kevin Hart's much more subtle strategy, but it faces a double problem: is not transcendental *différance* inextricably allied to the reduction of eternity to time, and will not the name "God" articulated within pre-conditions of speaking that are more ultimate than this articulation itself name only something ontic, something regional, and therefore an "idol" *concealing* (like every "presence") its own pre-conditions? 3) With equal subtlety, one may speak, like Jean-Luc Marion, of a transcendent Other, who "gives" both Being/Nothing as transcendental precondition *and* what it preconditions, namely beings. However, the difficulty here concerns the notion of something "otherwise" than Being: how shall we construe this except as a kind of radically purified subjectivity and therefore, after all, as "a being" and moreover *only* a being, something ontic and contained within the ontological difference, which cannot be superseded? Or again, how else but as a pure "possibility" without actuality? But such a possibility can only be effectively imaged within the discourse of being (and we have no other recourse for knowing) either as an impersonal pre-determination of being or else as an empty, characterless "will," neither good nor bad. Even if God is first loved, desired, and trusted rather than known, he must thereby be accorded the "actual" attributes of a specifically loving will, of a giving in the beautiful forms of the desirable, such that he must be deemed to supereminently precontain such forms. This third strategy therefore, by accepting initially a Heideggerean (and so nihilist) reading of Being, finally fails to distinguish God from an empty void. This indicates that the true theological task might be, not to "relinquish" Being to the realm of reason, but rather to ask whether Being (reality, actuality) ought not itself rather to be approached in the moods of faith, hope, desire, and love.

"Postmodernism," therefore, *does not* allow room for theology, and I never sought to speak apologetically in merely postmodern terms. This is rather the trade of the fabricators of a hybrid deferral/*via negativa*. On the contrary, theology has no genuine place on the contemporary secular intellectual scene. The real issue therefore is that of the possibility of an entirely immodest, radical transgression of this scene's assumptions, whose shape I have already sought to sketch out. Instead of *accepting* a critical, transcendentalist approach to Being which rigorously issues in the conclusion Being=nothing (as also life=death and time=flux of deferral), theology questions whether Being is first of all, or supremely, illuminated by the light of reason alone. From the Cappadocians (with much help from Neoplatonism) through to Eckhart, theology did precisely this.

In this context it already uncovered the ontological difference between beings and Being, but construed this (by faith) to mean that Being cannot be taken to be univocally like beings, and that no being, not even temporal flux itself, genuinely of itself "exists." What only of itself "exists" or rather "is" in a primary sense, is Being, in which beings only participate. Therefore, in Eckhart's phrase, *esse est deus* (not the other way round), Being is the utterly unknown, and in this sense indeed it is more than Being. It is in consequence not the object of conceptualizing reason, *even* of an indirect transcendental gaze, but of faith, love, desire. And as such Being is not only Being, but in its "simplicity" is taken to coincide with all those ultimate objects and conditions of all our positive moods, which like Being itself can never be securely and finally present: it is also beatitude (happiness), the good (the way things ought to be), the beautiful (the truly desirable), and so forth.

Contemporary with Eckhart, Duns Scotus was the first theologian to think something different from all this with rigorous consistency. He, in effect, invented a discourse later to be called "ontology" (in the seventeenth century) by arguing that Being could be adequately grasped *prior* to theology as the bare existence of any single existing thing, whether finite or infinite; all thought, he argued, assumes such a grasp of being as a *univocal* term. Thereby, at a stroke, Scotus anticipated transcendental philosophy, idolized God, obscured the ontological difference, and implied (unlike Augustine or Aquinas) that any being can be fully "present." In this fashion the Oxford theologian set us on the intellectual course to modernity. In order to question his long-term legacy, and so to inaugurate something "postmodern," Heidegger had to overtly or covertly retrieve elements in the thinking of Augustine, Aquinas, and Eckhart: specifically the *aporias* of time, the ontological difference, and the evacuation of ontic content by the ontological (this is the Eckhartian strand). These moves *might have implied* (but it is Heidegger's political interest to conceal) the return of thought about Being to theology, and so a return to the "sublimation" of philosophical discourse into talk about God, which was the achievement of the Church fathers and earlier scholastics. However, Heidegger instead sought to think the ontological difference and the *aporias* of time within a purely immanent, temporal horizon defined by a supposedly rigorous "reduction" to the fundamental appearing of the conditions of all appearing. And that is precisely to *maintain* the Scotist project, the modernist project, after all: for, still, according to

Heidegger, there can be a non-theological, non-mystical, discourse about Being, within the bounds of the Scotist *esse objectivum* which disallows an intentional *ecstasis* to a real in excess of appearance. This *metaphysics* (for "metaphysics" or "ontology" has meant, since Suarez, just such a discourse) claims to construe the ontological difference intellectually, as if only one account of this difference were possible. For Heidegger, Being itself appears unequivocally to knowledge, albeit in the mode of non-appearing, which in order to remain known is hypostatized as nothing.

These allusions to Scotus are not imposed from without: Heidegger's formative early work was on a Scotist text, while both Derrida, and more consistently Deleuze, advertise the continuity of a differential philosophy with Scotist univocity. The "postmodernists" explicitly *do not* entertain an "analogical series of differences," because for them Being is not, as for theology, transcendentally in excess of beings, but instead is dialectically identical with them in its negation of them. For the same reason, within their outlook, beings can never increase in Being, can never grow, but always already absolutely are to the maximum degree of illusion. Thus there are no hierarchies of increase (which need not imply a fixed, oppressive hierarchy), no more-or-less-to-be-valued, no exemplary, canonical foci, since everything is at its acme and, in principle, everything arbitrarily dominates everything else. Each difference, therefore, as Deleuze explains, occurs in exactly the same fashion as always uniquely different, always identically privileged along with any other variation. Hence the lack of possibility of increase, of growth in reality, which would be "participation in Being," is one and the same with the lack of mediation, since to change, to grow, to become other, cannot here mean also to remain the same, but simply means to become different, *against* what you were previously. By contrast, horizontal mediation or an ineffable third path between difference and identity is only construable in connection with vertical analogy or the mysterious "likeness" of beings to Being. To see mediation, which is to say, beauty, to hold it for real, is to see it as given by a real whose depth it begins to disclose.

Here, in the thinking of analogical difference, lies a possibility of "contesting the universal" beyond the "conclusion" of nihilism, which is the culmination, and not at all the surpassing of metaphysics. Even reason can acknowledge the possibility of an analogical ontology, although its affirmation can only be made by faith, hope, and love, a particular slant of desire articulating its own logic. Kierkegaard already thought of it as "non-identical repetition" and one should note, briefly, two ways in which it decisively differs from univocal differentiation. First of all, in the latter case difference is only postponed; what is encountered remains always the same, rendering univocal differentiation devoid of political hope. But in the case of analogical differentiation, difference may be bodily met with and not thereby negated. Secondly, univocal differentiation sets presence dualistically over-against flux. Its mysticism is that of "double annihilation," or an infinite shuttle between the present that turns out to be a void, and the void which only "is" in the avoided present. But for analogical differentiation the flux is but the music of harmoniously succeeding presences, which do not stay for an instant and yet are miraculously heard through all their subsequent echoings. Reason can, indeed, make no sense of the *aporias* of time, so must *sacrifice* either presence to flux, or flux to presence, or, with a final logic, either to either. Yet the senselessness of time is easily lived, enjoyed, sung, narrated, surrendered to. Theology chooses to remain with the "truth" of music and not to resolve it, except by suggesting that the *aporias* indicate the lack of being or ground in itself of either flux or presence. Therefore, for those who still hear music, what is heard through time is the echo of the spheres, the tumbling and ceaseless overtaking of the nonsense of flux by the nonsense of presence and vice versa. How *like* nihilism (and theology is half-in-love with its dark twin), yet how unlike, in that both non-senses are played through together in their ceaseless approach to transcendent sense, which is infinite yet not "present" as an *arche* even to itself (*pace* Derrida) since not "boundable." (Thus, to say that God's act does not cancel his power is a negative statement.)

In the contestation of the universal, therefore, there can be two (at least) different versions of our "constitutive incompleteness." Either our nothingness is supported by nothing, or else it is voided and yet simultaneously and ceaselessly restored as gift by an infinite plenitude, which, to be sure, in comparison to our restricted conception of being as "this or that" is indeed "nothing," so long as this nothing is in turn negated and not (as by nihilism) hypostatized. To say that God is "the infinite series of differences," is eminently and simply all "aliquids" as the supreme *aliquid* which is also *non aliud*, is a mode of such negation. This attribution does not define God—provide him with an essence—but the reverse: for if God were outside the series, he would be a single difference, a single thing with an essence. Inversely, were he not "otherwise" at all, he would be nothing and not God, but nonetheless positively defined after the mode of nihilism.

The analogical version of our constitutive incompletion will support political hope and the welcoming of the other. But the univocal version will not: its message is that we can *never* escape the appearance of identity, never give a gift, never make love, never offer thanks, never welcome, never forgive, only piously aspire towards these "impossibilities" as though our refusal of the impostures that substitute for them was itself somehow an achievement.

Faith and Theological Discourse

Faith, hope, and charity construe the universal sway of difference as analogical. To make this construal is to proclaim theology as a metadiscourse, "Queen of the Sciences." This means that such a proclamation is only made *by* faith, such that from the point of view of reason there remain "other claimants" to the metadiscursive role. However disturbing this has appeared to several of my critics, I do not see how this relativity in relation to "pure reason" (which faith regards as privated reason) can be denied.

Since theology is the discourse of the theological virtues (which are "intellectual" as well as "practical" in scholastic terms) it is, of course, not divorced from experience. Indeed, whereas to be in the mood of reason is to claim to be outside a mood, outside the subjectivity of experience, theology makes no such claim, but instead seeks to penetrate further into the logic of the mood of faith. Nevertheless, the experience of faith is not exactly pre-theological, operating as a controlling foundation for theological words, because every experience has always already been judged, always already been given some sort of symbolic articulation (perhaps not in words, but very often in words). In this case, the experience of faith is already understood as having the structure of "trust in the unknown." Experience arrives at the event of an articulation, although our sense of the inadequacy of our articulation, which is more precisely the articulation of our inadequacy in the face of mystery, provides precisely the sense that we are articulating an "experience." In biblical terms "the sense of God" and the hearing of God speak coincide. My conception of theology does not, therefore, as some have alleged, exclude the experiential and ineffable, although it does, indeed, deny that experience is first of all in-articulate and purely "personal." For what is personal in experience is the unique situation of a person, but in that case she experiences, uniquely, what is also other, preceding, and in common. Even the experience of the divine as unique is therefore mediated by our experience of others. We hear differently, but with their words, the words of a tradition or of many complex traditions.

Such an account of theology is not bizarrely postmodern. Traditional theology did not rest on a prior "experience" of God and Jesus. This is a modern, basically nineteenth-century notion, as likewise is the very idea of supposed tradition-independent "mystical experiences." I tried in *Theology and Social Theory* to indicate how sociology often takes over, uncritically, this specifically modern and "deviant" theological construal of religious experience. Such a notion, which confines religious experi-ence to the private sublime margins and so "polices" it, is thoroughly modern and secular, whereas the notion of an already theological faith is pre-modern.

If theology cannot be practiced apart from experience, but articu-lates it, then it is equally true that it is inseperable from narrative per-formance. This is because it is the discourse of love as well as faith, and the love of God can only be received as an event, and therefore as narrat-able. Narrative, along with liturgical praise (expressing faith, hope, and our return of love to God) remains the first-order discourse of theology. Certain critics have overlooked my fundamental *agreement* with writers like Hans Frei and George Lindbeck, who stress that theology is not first and foremost propositional. However, in seeking to *extend* their anti-foundationalism, I insist that no first-order discourse (whether in theol-ogy or otherwise) acts as a foundation for a second-order discourse, but that the latter folds back upon the former, influencing and re-directing it. Otherwise a narrative or liturgy would not be inherently open-ended, and indeed, pre-reflective societies with little second-order discourse (though it is impossible for this to be entirely absent) characteristically limit non-identical repetition at some point, and fetishize a particular narrative order. Second-order reflections on the presuppositions of a narrative, on the "scene" within which it unfolds, actually help to hold a narrative open, albeit they also take certain decisions about the pre-cise "horizon" of its future possible development. Hence a post-reflective narrative will unfold, be added-to or retold, in the fashion of a Baroque masque in which the scenery or "setting" becomes part of the action itself along with the characters. But of course "the setting" (in this case abstract theological reflection) continually adverts to the already given narrative plot, and when Eve Taylor Bannet cites my saying that theology cannot be tested against its canonical texts she omits the words "in any simple manner." The testing cannot be simple, since both narrative and practice remain irreducibly problematic and aporetic: for example, Jesus's divinity could not possibly be unambiguously displayed by the gospels; this, as Kierkegaard pointed out, would beg the question of what it would be to display divinity. The paradox of Divine Manhood can be shown only "indirectly." Nor would a narrative mode, as such, "claim" divinity, since narrative unfolds and displays but makes no claims. Since this divinity is not a visible fact, even within a narrative, only theology can proclaim it.

My insistence on the ineliminable place of theology within the discourse of faith is, therefore, part of an attempt to sustain the openness of discourse. This openness issues in new first-order liturgical developments and new construals of the given setting in which it unfolds—and often both together in "masque-like" fashion. The second-order reflection of theology operates in two ways: first, it holds narrative possibilities open by revealing the setting as a not-fully-determinate *topos* and so as a fontal source. Second, it does further determine the *topos* and so, like further narrative development at a first-order level, it does indeed take decisions that point in one way rather than another. It is this that Bannet and others purport to find intolerant, since there are no preceding rules guiding these judgments: here we have rather the continuous elaboration of rule, which theology conceives to be the operation of the Holy Spirit. But how should there not be any decisions taken? Postmodernism knows that there must be, but insists on their arbitrary cruelty. Here the only escape from decision resides in its postponement, which frees us from its sway not at all. But once more, theology risks transgression: it suggests that one may have faith that there can be right judgments and even points to a reception of a series of right judgments which is charity. It has faith that there may be taken decisions which preclude other paths only in a benign sense. Benign, for two reasons. First, because what is absolutely precluded is any intrusion that would prevent any further growth, any further non-identical repetition of a narrative. Second, because what is relatively precluded is what for the moment is the less desirable trajectory, whose loss it would be neurotic to regret in time, since in eternity nothing is lost whatsoever.

Theology, therefore, is not practiced apart from experience or narrative, although it supplements them in accord with their own, non-alien constitutive lack. Its arguments are faith's explications, not violent in the measure that they are true, violent, indeed, in their effect as critique upon what is false, on the self-governing, other-excluding citadel of reason. But this violence is not received from theology, but from this citadel's own self-dissolution, the painful and curative undoing of its initial violent self-assertion. So there is no inconsistency, as many have claimed, in the occasioning of violence by a discourse of non-violence: the violent result of this true persuasion has the beginning of its end in the moment of the reception of this true persuasion. It need only be added that the mode of persuasion does not stand apart from the content of persuasion, but is itself the occurrence of that which is to be communicated. So inquisitions, tortures, psychological manipulations are ruled out in principle, though wholly to rule them out in practice requires, of course, a constant vigilance.

Can such theology find a place in the University? Yes, if the University, or an academic community of diverse faith-based universities, is reconceived along MacIntyrean lines, but more drastically—not just as a dialectical contestation of different traditions of rational inquiry, but as the site of contestation of the universal among modernists, nihilists, Christians, Jews, Hindus, Buddhists, Taoists, and so forth. Beyond dialectics, how would they converse? They would classify their differences and their overlaps (since there are no truly discrete traditions, and the whole situation is infinitely more complex than the above labels would indicate), and their explications of their own traditions would seek to persuade and influence.

Faith and Ecclesial Practice

That there can be analogical difference, or social harmony ("socialism") beyond the merely formal peace of agreeing to differ (which is sophisticated and continuous warfare), is a matter of faith and hope. Yet this faith and hope is not empty and without effect—the mere aspiration of a "beautiful soul"—precisely because it is accompanied by a charity which already discerns the real to be the continuous event of analogical differ-ence persisting even through the violence that incessantly ruptures it. To already receive charity, and so to have the possibility of repeating it, is to be within the Church. Never once did *Theology and Social Theory* under-take a defense of "a particular Church" since the Church is not particular, not primarily an institution at all, but a dissemination of love which is the repetition of the occurrence of complete love in the world, a bearing of evil and death within humanity to the point of exposure of their predatory unreality by the divine *Logos* itself. This event, which is simply, in appear-ance, a human life (so *not* a particular fetishized institution), continues in, or rather is itself in part constituted by, its "ascended" withdrawal (as Marion has pointed out) which allows us to receive the distance of the divine other, of love itself in the form of Christ's given, infinitely imparted body. In becoming incarnate, the divine *Logos* gives itself in the Church as a dissemination, which, though never foreclosed, is, unlike univocal differentiation, *also* a body. In this Eucharistic community, because it is a supernaturally-constituted community, there is no primary self-govern-ment, no rule of a whole by a part (which stands for the whole) com-manding other parts (whether this whole be individual or collective) and yet there is a continuously evolving "form." Paradoxically (and here I am contesting Nancy in *The Inoperative Community*) the Church is always about to receive again its own body from without, in the Eucharistic event, and therefore it never commands itself or masters itself. And inversely it is not assumed into a commanding body which is Christ, since Christ's own body is itself his self-constituting distance from that which is *also* his own body, his bride, the Church, in a reflection of that eternal distance of Son from Spirit in the Trinity which prevents us thinking of the *Logos* as totalizing, or of judgment as apart from the always exceeding movement of desire. The Church is hierarchically commanded (as Nicholas of Cusa taught in his great conciliarist treatise *De Concordantia Catholica*) not by people but by *signs*, supremely the signs-become-what-they-represent that are the body and blood of Christ. Therefore it is *defined* by its surplus over itself, by its receiving itself into itself before itself as a gift, not just in theory, but in its central constitutive ritual, without which it would not be Church. By contrast, no secular organization has this structure, but is essentially "self-governing" unless it confesses (as even the state should confess, if it can) that to be a part of "community" (analogically different, non-self-governing, receiving itself from before itself) it must defer to, seek even further to include itself within, the Eucharistic community. This means, not "theocracy" in the sense of men claiming to rule with divine legitimacy, but the very opposite, since all claims to legitimate sovereignty are theocratically tainted. It means rather the gradual *end* of human self-government, a kind of ordered anarchy.

For the Eucharist is not one more particular cult: it has a unique and extraordinary structure. Here, we offer all fruits of nature and work to God in sacrifice, and he takes everything—all of creation, all of us—yet instantly gives all back in the mode of himself, to everyone, without distinction. So in this ritual instance, as in no other cult, there is no brokerage, nothing specific is being offered for a specific return, and no divine reality hierarchically above the human realm is established (since transcendent distance is more distant than any hierarchical distance), and thereby no human hierarchies of distribution of unequal portions of the sacrificial remainder are supported. It is a cult against cult, a sacrifice against sacrifice, but still necessary, for resistance to exclusive cults needs itself to be enculturated. Why? Because the merely abstract resistance of reason to cults repeats in its rational self-autonomy, without the excess of desire or of gift, precisely that cultic self-government which cannot turn itself inside out. With the perfected form of reason in nihilism, with Nietzsche and Bataille, reason half-recognizes that it is also a cult, and speaks of the true "essence" of religious sacrifice and of "the sacred" as self-dissolution towards nothing. There is still "self-government" here, since the unknown is bizarrely mastered by suicide or willingness sacrificially to die that regards it with no more than the regard of knowledge *as* unknown (rendering desire a death instinct); and still brokerage, since life is traded for the "reality" of Being/Nothingness and only returns, for a time, at the price of the obscuration of the latter. Reason, in its final form, is still cultic, still pagan, still self-governing. By comparison, the Eucharistic cult escapes the very type of cult. It is *another* mode of universal practice, neither antique nor (post)modern, exposing, from "the middle" of history, the secret kinship of ancient and recent.

But the Church has always been an institution, and an oppressive one, say my critics. How does all this fine talk about the Eucharist relate to reality? The most important point to be made here is that quantity is not at all what is decisive. The Church is all that it has actually been, since it holds no guarantee against the possibility of human corruption, and the corruption of the best is the worst. *Obviously* a hypocritical pretence to act in the name of love will issue in the worst kind of domination. *Of course* the removal of violent cultic limits on human violence risks a yet worse violence (yet who thinks we can return to local cults?). Therefore if Christian tyranny had been the worst of all (although in reality it has not been) it would scarcely be surprising. Yet in one sense, this does not matter: the event of analogical difference needs only to have occurred once (but always) for one to be able to receive love, to enter into charity, and one must remember that "Church" is as present (more really present) with the ordinary men and women who, unrecorded, have gone away from receiving the Eucharist and loved and forgiven their neighbor, as it is in corrupt men who may have been the administrators of that Eucharist.

However, my critics have one important point: since I insist that the Church is *not* simply an ideal, but the already received event of charity, it follows that the Church is constituted by a continuous act of self-discernment which involves a critical reading of its own history. And such a reading would have to go far beyond the confines of *Theology and Social Theory* and is scarcely the task of one person alone. However, I did offer more clues to such a reading than they allow: specifically I suggested that the more the Church despaired of a direct "pastoral" rule, based on a care for the ultimate objective beatitude of both body and soul, the more it substituted (not being able to revert to the norms of *antique* virtue) a merely "formal" regulation, thus nourishing in its heart the nightmare of the modern state, the modern economy, and so forth. With this suggestion I was seeking to overcome what can be described as the "whig gothic" myth, namely that there is a series of "horrors" belonging to a monkish-dominated Middle Ages. For me the term "Middle Ages" does have legitimacy in so far as it denotes an ecclesiastical project of pastoral rule neither "ancient" nor "modern," but only if one accepts that so defined it began to "wane" from at least the twelfth century. As the work of Foucault and others clearly implies, it was the arrival of a greater supposed rationality, of rule by formal classification and predictable control, which led to persecution of "homosexuals" (who were only gradually invented), lepers, and witches, and later on the increasing disciplining of sexuality. The worst evils committed by the Church were already the evils committed also by state and science, and "medieval" and modern horrors form one continuous series. *The Monk* mutates readily into *Frankenstein*.

Then what of the arrival of religious toleration? Here, I think, one can suggest that matters are much more complex than usually presented.

The film *La Reine Margot*, concerning Catherine de Medici, reminds us of the *politique* role in the worst religious atrocities. Religious consensus within a particular space, as William Cavanaugh has famously insisted, was at first especially demanded by the early modern sovereign state, since this state assumed that community was spatial and bounded, such that all within a space must essentially agree.[2] It never abandoned this idea, but gradually discovered the notion of an empty formal consent, just as today there is increasingly one global space, but it is still supposed to be formed by just such a consensus. However, *it is not true* that such a formalism, which "tolerated" religion merely by minimizing it, is the only root of ideas of religious toleration. On the contrary, there is also an authentically Christian root—some Christian humanists, some seventeenth-century Puritans, some eighteenth-century Anglicans of a perfectly orthodox cast argued that Christian belief of its nature requires absolutely free assent, and that the light of the gospel was only able to manifest itself in the relatively free and open period of late antiquity. To view these arguments as secondary to, and consequent upon, enlightened rationalism, is actually anachronistic.

The above two diagnoses—concerning "horrors" and toleration—are not absolutely crucial to my argument, but they do suggest how a theological reading of Church history can precisely show how horror and intolerance follow when the Church ceases to be the Church. It is not, as might be supposed, irrelevant to reality to insist on what the Church is supposed to be—namely a body governed by signs, which are more its body than it itself is—because again and again in history the Church has appealed against itself to this notion and this practice, and thus proved capable of self-reform. It may appear shocking to insist that the true social body is the body of Christ, and yet, *as a matter of fact*, our deepest notions of body to which we still appeal—the "pastoral" concern of welfare for every person and aspect of life, the public place of "gift-relationships," democratic trust in the eventual common sense of the majority (which is evolved from medieval notions of ecclesial infallibility)—trace back to this notion of a sacred body. My endeavor is to show that to lose the sacrality is also to lose the body—for a virtual wasteland.

While writing this, however, I sense Daniel Boyarin's increasing and apparently warranted annoyance: what of those "within" the body

2. See Cavanaugh, "Fire Strond Enough to Consume the House."

excluded from it? But the first point here is that one cannot banish the specter of "the Christian body" by fiat: its imagery will secretly remain, because it is our final common social alphabet—indeed to be a Marrano (witness Spinoza, Rosenzweig) is to half-embrace it, and not simply to abstain from it. However, it has to be conceded to Boyarin that this is not a one-way traffic, because the Jewish body is not simply "alien" to the Christian body. On the contrary, the New Testament declares that it is an earlier body into which the Christian has been *grafted*; hence any theology of simplistic "supersession" completely misunderstands the Church's own historicity, and also *Paul's* understanding of the Church as in part defined by the meeting of Jews and Gentiles in "asymmetrical reciprocity." This implies that to an extent the Church still awaits itself at the *eschaton*, that for its own reasons it cannot simply pre-empt what will be discovered at this conclusion. It follows that the Church will still expect to learn things *about itself* from the Jewish community, and when I was once in Erlangen, a student observed, quite accurately, that my own ecclesiology was clearly marked by certain Jewish construals of salvation as "restoration of everything to its right place."

And further to this there is the question of whether Judaism has not managed, far more successfully than Christianity, to prevent a duality of sacred and secular. Boyarin is right to ask whether my critique of Weber could not be more forcibly made from a Jewish viewpoint. For do not the dualities I oppose of spirit and structure have their origin in a Christian duality of love and law? However, I do not think that Christian love is opposed to structuration; Jewish law is the least "reactive" of all laws since it first of all seeks to propagate and promote the good, and Christian *agape* is but a radicalization of the mercy code. Nevertheless Paul, pursuing the law beyond the law, rid it of a lingering reactive element which still subordinated propagation to principles "securing" propagation against preceding danger.

Finally, I do not think that Judaism and Islam thrive better as fully-fledged modes of life, rather than as privately entertained beliefs, under a liberal regime of reason than under a state including itself as far as possible within the body of Christ. On the contrary, I think the latter has a much better sympathy, from within itself, for the very notion of the integrity of a religious body. Pluralism is better guaranteed by Christianity than by the Enlightenment.

Faith and Secular Practice

I hope that this begins to answer the question concerning what *Theology and Social Theory* contributes to "political causes." If, like an enthusiastic undergraduate, I had trotted out phrases such as "we need a new theology on the side of victims," I would no doubt have been commended for making a "contribution" to the fate of the poor, the environment, etc. But eschewing such rhetorical regurgitation, I was seeking indirectly to tackle our seeming inability to discover any theoretical or practical grounds for opposing the new global sway of neocapitalism, which is the source of the hunger of the poor, the poisoning of nature, obliteration of sexual difference and equality, the lapse of beauty, the loss of historical memory, and so forth. As to theory, I raise the question, which Bataille already raised in a nihilist guise, as to whether the problem is not that capitalism is the practical shape of secularity as such. Of course this means that I pay more attention than usual to "conservative" critiques of capitalism, without by any means taking them over *in toto*. I suggest that this is more creative than the more usual current surrenders of socialism to liberalism, or else the quasi-fascist communitarian hybrid of "free market" plus merely social and not economic consensual ethical practice.

As to the practical relevance of feminism, which I am held to ignore, I suggest that critics reread the section in my book on the Greeks, where I clearly imply that the *polis* or self-governing totality, with its duality of reason and emotion, *polis* and *oikos*, is bound up with a hierarchical suppression of sexual difference, which the Christian critique of the *polis* therefore implicitly opposes. The gradual releasing of an equal sexual difference in Western history is surely much more of a Christian event than often supposed, taking its origins from the high Middle Ages. For example, in Chaucer's *Wife of Bath's Tale*, a strange argument for a *more fundamental* sovereignty of women over men, which precedes a wife's obedience to her husband, is put into a context of kenotic reversal, wherein Christ himself rules by yielding to the condition of "poverty," of self-dispossession by the other, which is paradoxically the one thing of which one cannot be dispossessed. The poem makes a symbolic equation between various modes of the supposedly "emptier" and "lesser"—poverty, woman, ugly old age, loss of self-control—and suggests that an attentive submission to these apparent voids alone brings back a secure plenitude of well-being, beauty, masculine identity, and fulfillment of desire. (I am not arguing the entire adequacy of this sort of kenotic account; simply indicating that it has had a historical effect.)

The whole point of *Theology and Social Theory* is that it argues that the very notion of sheerly "secular" notions of social influences is barely coherent. Yet my critics, seemingly unable to credit that this could really be my thesis, continue to chide me for not sufficiently attending to secular causes *as* secular, to the primacy and independence of purely secular critiques. Concerning the arguments I put forward concerning the real non-secularity of our hopes, and the non-existence of purely secular critique, along with the very idea of a religion-independent "social" or "economic" reality, they are largely silent. For example, Alan Shandro's suggestion that I fail to see that hunger is "basic" to our humanity will not do: hunger is merely an animal precondition of our humanity, which in human animals always issues in collective, ritualized eating practices. It is the essential indetermination of such rituals which gives rise to history—often thereby producing unmet needs to eat which do not exist by nature—rather than the raw urges of hunger, which are therefore not definitive of a *human* essence, nor determinative even in any last analysis.

By contrast to any secular meeting of secular needs, I suggest that political hope can only now be sustained through a practice of the theological virtues. This means the practice of the love of God in worship and of love of neighbor through forgiveness. To worship God is to let time pass as praise and hope to receive it back through further arrivals, finally the arrival of eternity. The *ersatz* modes of feminism and ecology and cosmology, according to Sheila Lappler, "take serious umbrage" at my devaluing of time as merely passing. Of course they can take all the umbrage they like but will not succeed in isolating a single valuable, retainable moment. There can be no finality in time, and "oppressors" are precisely people who seek to isolate a secure "here and now," to "hold" time as a spatial possession, and, rather than sacrificing the economic surplus in a joyful festive ecstasy (as Bataille rightly indicated), instead demand the sacrifice of passing moments to a coming, spatialized future. When time is allowed to pass, it is valued, and its revelation of non self-identity and non-identical repetition is seen to image, more precisely than a secure spatial present, the non-circumscribability of the infinite. Not theology, then, but rather secular reason, devalues time, since it either (modernism) fantasizes a secure space, or else (postmodernism) seeks the abyss into which time sinks as over-against time, such that what passes in time cannot image this abyss and cannot be sacred. Hence for Bataille, work is merely instrumental and secular, though inevitable, and only the orgy of nihilistic sacrifice is sacred. But for a Catholic perspective there is no such duality: work is reconciled to the festival, since the mode of passage may image what it passes into, what returns it to itself, the living.

Thus there is here a flow of worship into social life, which remains liturgical. Something is required today which would be the equivalent of a medieval guild economy, which *already* sought to regulate a "modern," urban market. For secularization does *not* merely affect the Church; on the contrary we now realize that such "gothic" survivals or revivals as universities, schools, the legal profession, medicine, public broadcasting, public transport, even certain modes of "management," *even the state itself*, are all somewhat sacred, somewhat guild-like in their character of *dedication*. That is to say, they are all dedicated to the achievement of certain qualitative states held to be objectively desirable quite apart from the pursuit of power, wealth, or prestige, or the mere question of what individuals may happen to want. Such dedication verges also on a "dedication" of such and such particular task to the common good, as held to exceed the grasp or interests of any present, living member of a society. The common good in time, as something not to be possessed, is nothing other than the making of continuous music, the offering of a spectacle to transcendence. It is to live in the unlimited circulation of gift, which includes a constant giving to others of the educative gifts that will enable them to give in turn. It is also always a forgiving, which is never "premature," awaiting the achievement of justice to which it will be superadded like candy-floss, but always enabling justice itself, since to forgive is *really to restitute the other* if he will accept this, to enable the other to do the justice for which his iniquity has incapacitated him. Only the forgiving of the oppressors by the oppressed could ever alter the status quo, and bring back through the suffering and healing of wounds an original generosity beyond the arbitrary sway of contract.

Is it so implausible that in the face of unprecedented loss of generosity and its supplanting by contract we should ask whether this is not precisely the outcome of a refusal of the religion which most of all enshrines unrestricted generosity? And is not our only recourse now, not a "new god," but a re-dedication of "professional" pursuits, together with a new dedication of *all* pursuits, including "economic" ones, so that each and every one will value herself or himself (since others so value them, and they pursue recognition) not in terms of the accumulation of abstract wealth or abstract influence (the "star syndrome"), but rather in terms of the acquiring through education of gifts, talents received, which continue to be talents only through their further generous imparting? These gifts have untraceable sources and no ultimate temporal destinations, and in consequence they can only be construed as gifts if they are the offering of time itself to eternity, to receive itself back as time. If our society were in future to participate in this offering, it would locate itself once again within the event of divine charity. Only then could there begin to be justice. Only then would "the West" return from its nocturnal delusion of construing its universal responsibility as reason, and remember instead that it is love.

9

THE INVOCATION OF CLIO

History and Vision

"Why is he telling us all this?" asks Gordon Michalson in his response to my work.[1] Why do I provide in my writing such a disparate medley of history, allusion, argument, rhetoric, and textual fragments? The answer is that I do not believe that securely intuited essences or unquestionable methods are available to us. If, nonetheless, I believe that there is final truth; that there exist also essences (albeit elusive), and that there are good and bad ways to proceed even if they are not exhaustively presentable in advance, then one's procedure can only be *ad hoc* and cumulative (though without even a commitment to the emergence of a "probability" from such accumulation). I favor the wild Anglo-Celtic empiricism of Bede, Grosseteste, Wyclif, Cudworth, Shaftesbury, Berkeley, De Quincey, Coleridge, Ruskin, Chesterton, J. C. Powys or Peirce and Royce, not the semi-wild but rationalistically reined-back empiricism of Scotus, Ockham, Locke, Butler, Warburton, J. G. Frazer, George Orwell, or John Dewey. In the latter case, the open recognition of "appearances" is confined by a narrow (usually atomistic) predefinition of what may count as an "appearance." Following rather the methodless tracks of the former approach, my accumulation makes a case that is just this accumulation, or rather of which this accumulation remains a fragment, since the real case is infinite and inaccessible. For this reason, the fragmentary and not

---

1. The original version of this chapter responded to an issue of the *Journal of Religious Ethics*, vol. 32, no. 2 (June 2004) partly devoted to *Theology and Social Theory* and the rest of my works.

systematic character of the literary pile should be explicitly foregrounded: one should exhibit and offer a ruin. The long but fragmentary gesturing to the inaccessible is the key to the natural alliance of the most radical Anglo-Celtic empiricism with Platonism, whereas the weaker version remains confined within immanence, because it non-empirically invokes some sort of imagined *a priori* limits to the scope of its investigation.

Since the accumulation is itself the stuttering argument, inseparable from myriad specificities, it also develops its own criteria for its own success as it advances, and reveals a true method and procedure along with the emergence of the substantive results of its methods, and not otherwise. Its assumption is therefore radically realist: there are no prior criteria for the truth, since in that case truth would be governed by something other than the truth, which would therefore have to be false. Since the truth is the truth, it declares itself, with an apparentness that is only that of the truth, and in consequence self-authenticating. As to method, the only possible clue to how to search for the truth must be if truth itself offers one some advance glimmering of its own character. This cannot be something given in the structure of nature or our minds—since why should such a given be true and not an illusion?—but must rather be a gift from the truth itself: an Ariadne's thread which we contingently receive, and which may take multiple forms, but which reveals itself as an authentic fragment of a hidden tapestry. At the outset of the quest for knowledge lies a wonder and an astonishment inseparable from the lure of something revealed and grace-imbued—something one must love, trust, and have faith in.

The next question validly posed by Michalson is why does so much of what I tell people take the form of historical narrative? In the end I seem to be offering a vision: the idea that Christianity construes the real as ontological peace from which we are contingently and in some sense illusorily sundered, as opposed to resignation to real ontological violence that is inscribed both in the pagan cyclical vision of impersonal fate and the yet bleaker nihilist vision of the endless interchange between nothingness and its masks which both conceal and constitute its nullity. But how does this vision relate to my genealogies? In what sense does the vision require a Christian metanarrative, and to what extent are my historical accounts supposed to encourage an acceptance of my Christian vision?

Well, first of all, it is a question again of Ariadne's thread. It is in fact Clio, who on behalf of truth, acts as our Ariadne. The way to the truth shines out for us one day in some aspect of nature, humanity, or culture.

But this is an occurrence, an event: yesterday the grove was just a grove; today there is a rustling behind the rustling. Moreover, the event is not a replete epiphany: it may be a binding covenantal *symbolon*, but it is also a prophetic *signum* that indicates obscurely a way forward through time. Our further steps toward the truth can only concern how we are again led by the truth through subsequent disclosures. To think cannot, in consequence, be primarily to induce or to deduce in abstraction from events. Rather, our sequence of thoughts keeps exact pace with the sequence of our actions, whereby we try to perform our vision of our place in the cosmos, and so of the nature of the cosmos, and through this speculative performance hope to receive further enlightenment. For we do not really know what we are going to do until we have decided what to do, and therefore have already done the thing. To decide is but to mime the action in advance (and often the decision will coincide with the externally enacted deed itself).

If we do nonetheless abstract from events, this is first of all a speculative "abduction" (after C. S. Peirce) whereby we try to read the permanent situation within which all history unfolds. This abduction itself still takes the form of a narrative, since it concerns such questions as how eternity gives rise to time, how the temporal reverts to the eternal and of where we belong in the cosmos both from the outset and in the course of our current abstractions within these exchanges. Our more refined thinking is by necessity a kind of shamanic voyage and mystical journeying. In this way, interactions only tie knots in the thread of Clio, although these knots themselves help to hold it together. Speculation reaches out before time for a "prehistory," but history is also the history of speculation. More properly, it is primarily the history of speculation, since every culture requires a myth, and to receive the call of truth in advance from the unreachable end of history (which simultaneously invokes the unreachable origin) is at the same time to undergo the suspension of history in a double sense. It is to find history interrupted, but also "let down" and "held up" in its unraveling, from a vertical height.

It follows from this that philosophy must be historicist. Plato opened the history of philosophy beyond speculative physics (or metaphysics not reflecting on the subjective human situation) by pointing out that if we seek to know anything at all, then there is an unthinkable prior relation to knowledge and to thinking which we cannot know and we cannot think. Yet at the same time we must constantly seek to think and to know this relation, if we are to have an inkling as to the character of the call of truth itself, or its gift-in-earnest of our future reward.

Socrates and Plato also constituted philosophy in opposition to the world of myth that tells stories with no authors, stories of the cruel or merciful (with indifference) rule of fate, and therefore authored by fate itself. Instead, they spoke in their own voices concerning the oracles of an always peaceful height of transcendence. Nevertheless, they saw that, since dialectic on its own cannot authenticate its own quest for truth, the new discourse of philosophy must also fabricate new myths of peaceful emergence and return, in opposition to the old myths of fated conflict, intimately linked with sacrificial rituals designed apotropaically to delay power and economically to recruit its benefits.[2] Beyond the pre-Socratics, they reasoned that, if the human *logos* is not an epiphenomenal illusion and if it is yet always a *logos* in quest of the *logos* (the *Meno* problematic), then the circumstances of the disclosure of truth to us must be ontologically fundamental—and they edged somewhat toward the natural conclusion that the final principle of this disclosure must be personal. But speaking about this disclosure—that is to say, the advance offering of truth as Clio's thread through time—they necessarily had to resort once more to myth and to ritual. Since the lure of truth is the *doxa* only of truth, else it would be false, the lure is not *given* and categorial, either ontologically or epistemologically. Instead it is a contingent *gift*, of whose sending we can only speak in mythical terms involving an absolute "prehistory," and which we only re-invoke through acts of devotion designed to sense once again the divine descent and favor. Thus in Plato the "shamanic journey" persisted, and myth supplemented his more abstract imagining of the world of the forms—an imagining which itself exceeded the scope of dialectic, although it also permitted its arguments to reach a conclusion. The abstract imagination was guaranteed not by objectively checkable discourse, but rather by individual vision.

The new myths and the new abstract imaginings then bent back onto the formation of individual and collective biographies. An exotic topography of forms, demons, oracular insects and sublime ascents was communicated, along with stories of erotic encounters and proposals for new civic legislation that would subordinate human activity to liturgical

2. See Hart, "Christ or Nothing."

praise.[3] For since disclosure in time is only ever partial, the myths and the rituals return us to the realm of everyday chances where we meet with new triggers of "recollection"—or as Christianity will later express it, of "illumination."

What the philosopher has to say regarding truth, therefore, is inseparable from her own experience, her own trials of time and in time. Moreover, since she must re-engage with myth and ritual, and these things are inversely a kind of collective and more fundamental *theoria*, her reflections on truth are also inseparable from the narrative of all human history. Even though Plato failed to develop a fully-fledged historicism, nonetheless it is Platonism itself that points toward historicism, just as it is Platonism itself that nourishes a wild empiricism. The deepest British and American tradition has tended to fuse these three elements, even though the traditional intellectual temper of both Celt and Saxon has generally been held down by a kind of academic "Norman Yoke" of cold rationalism allied to base sensuality.

It is this natural alliance of Platonism with historicism and empiricism that provides the clue to the first positive sense in which my "vision" links with my "metanarrative." We possess only a remote, mediated access to the eternal, and our intimations must be ceaselessly revised. Hence our account of eternal truth, unless we are sadly deluded idolaters, must responsibly include an account of how we arrived at some truth, or rather of how some truth arrived at us—and of how at first and then later, and perhaps still today, we misapprehended even this bare modicum. Our weak truths are indeed doubly contingent: something permanent is only disclosed in a passing advent, and this advent itself is only perceived by us through our signifying, symbolic, and verbal response, whereby we seek to express in humanly inaugurated codes what an event portends, what in time it brings together in space ("symbolically"), besides what it signifies, abductively, for always. All these apprehensions are contained therefore by human language, which is itself of long and particular origin, such that even the most abstract human term, such as "substance," still preserves the traces of a metaphor and could not make sense without such a trace: in this case the picture of something "standing under," and in the case of Greek *ousia*, of food. All human terms, including abstract ones, retain some residue of their cultural genesis, which means that even philosophi-

3. See Pickstock, *After Writing*.

cal language deploys the resources of cultural myth-making. For language and thought to commence in the first place, something must already have been said and proposed and combined, else we could not speak at all. Hence even without recourse to deliberate mythic supplementation, the philosophic *logos* is merely the refinement of myth, since it can only re-work the prior speculative efforts of culture as such.

To propose a vision, therefore, must mean to re-propose an inherited vision and simultaneously to refine this vision by re-tracing its epiphany and the ways in which this epiphany has been authentically repeated or else has become distorted. Needless to say, given all that I have just tried to explain, there is no question here of "checking" later redactions against the original first arrival. For us, in the present, the epiphany is always-already repeated by traditional interpretation, and indeed *traditio* is itself the only epiphany, which is not, however, to deny its vertical ecstasy. To compose the metanarrative and re-insinuate the vision, one needs the "sense" of what has authentically arrived and how tradition should authentically go, even though this sense can only be acquired through the effort of composition itself. Clearly one cannot exit this hermeneutically valuative circle without betraying the truth. So the sort of considerations that Karl Barth applied to revelation apply to knowledge as such.

These reflections apply not only to my overall metanarrative but also, *mutatus mutandi*, to my more specific genealogies of Western philosophy, and modern social thought and practice. The supposed "genetic fallacy" would only be a fallacy if we inhabited pure spatial synchrony. Then it would be the case that the "present" meaning of any term, practice, or idea would float free of its murky past and would be exhaustively given by its place in the current structural repertoire of possible semiotic positionings. By the same token, the total mutuality of such positionings would exhaustively supply all shared and assumed presuppositions. Yet, since diachrony is also real, and even, to a degree, prevailing, all meaning and all action involves genealogy. The complex, multiple network of existing synchronic structures is also the interweaving of multiple currents of narrative, constituted through recollection backward and projection forward. It follows that whenever someone asserts a position, her account of the presuppositions behind the position will always appeal in some sense to her own or to collective history. What we "already accept" refers not only to logic, but also to prior experience, if there are no absolute foundations or starting-points (as has earlier been explained). All our concepts are enunciated in words, and words always bear the freight of a specific history, even if, precisely as words (defined by re-applicability) they also exceed this history. We can pretend that our presuppositions are absolute and uninflected by past events, but this obscures not only genesis, but also theory, since it means that we must take for granted what should not be taken for granted.

It follows that, merely by studying a philosophical text in the present, one cannot divine all its presuppositions. To some extent these are only given in previous texts that it comments on, and so one has to read (at least some of) these texts in order to know more precisely what the present text is responding to and so what it is itself saying. Of course, this seems to open up Charles Péguy's prospect of historicist delirium—of a search for an infinite totality of circumstance that would provide truth. However, this may be guarded against in two ways: first, the present response creatively exceeds its presuppositions, and second, divination has the last word precisely because one can never recuperate all contingent presuppositions. Yet it should still be a reasonably informed divination: divination of a historical sequence. We cannot understand Aristotle's *Metaphysics* except as a response to his predecessors, whose positions he rehearses at the commencement of his treatise. And as Alasdair MacIntyre says, the philosophy of the *Metaphysics* includes how he narrates prior philosophy, what it attempted and how it failed. Alternative narratives would not issue in a pure Aristotelianism. Similarly, today, both analytic philosophy and phenomenology assume a certain story of Cartesian and Kantian and then Fregean or Husserlian "breaks" in the history of philosophy (all cumulatively building on each other), which define how we now see what philosophy is and what it can do. One aspect of an attempt to unsettle this reigning orthodoxy is to show that these breaks were more tied to questionable contingencies and in turn to questionable genealogies than is usually supposed. Such an enterprise can often be allied to disinterring an "alternative canon" of philosophic writings. This kind of tracing back is not, I must stress, an attempt to condemn past thinkers (e.g., Duns Scotus) because of "what they have led to." It is rather the reverse matter of discovering how contemporary thought is rooted in certain decisions that it has forgotten were ever made. Most significant here, in my view, are the instances where modern philosophy is grounded in certain forgotten *theological* decisions that doom it to pursue a certain style of anonymous theology in the guise of philosophy.

In the following sections, I will try to respond more specifically to my critics concerning four fragmentary areas of my metanarrative: Augustine and paganism; Kantianism; the history of charity; and the significance of John Ruskin. The next two sections on Augustine and Kant, respectively, concern the question of Christianity and theoretical ontology; the remainder regards the question of Christianity and ethical practice.

Augustine and the Fairy-Tale

So I want first of all to comment on two moments in my genealogy of philosophy. The first regards Augustine, in response to James Wetzel, the second regards Kant, in response to Gordon Michalson.

Our fallen "dispersal" in time was, for Augustine, a matter not of the shadowy intrigue of time itself, but rather the privation of our apprehension of the relation of time to eternity, which nonetheless had, in some fashion, contaminated time as such. To the completion of the neoplatonic realization that evil is privation, Augustine added the distinction between created and fallen time. These two moves are in fact inseparable.

Neoplatonism had begun to see evil as subjective privation. Thereby it diminished ontological dualism and pointed to goodness as ultimate and personal—since it must be both judged and elected. However, only the biblical legacy completed this transformation. The full theory of evil as lack is best explained in Dionysius and Augustine. This apprehension of evil is also part of a picture which renders utterly contingent both the finite world and human reason, and therefore has to re-invoke mythical discourse, in a new mythology without fated violence. Now myth no longer relates itself anonymously, but is the word of God, the kingly instigator and hero of myth. Through his revelation, we echo the real original story of his peacefully speaking the world into being. Since there are no impersonal and fated factors involved here, Christian *mythos* is actually *more purely myth* than pagan *mythos*, whose purity of subjective focus is always paradoxically and tragically undercut by *a shadowy objectivity*, whether of chaos or of obscure fate.

Now, by comparison with myth, some structuralist theorists (beginning with Georges Dumézil) have seen the story or "fairy-tale" as more concerned with objects than with subjects—the girdle, the ring, the vessel—whose circulations move the plot.[4] Myth concerns deeds of monstrous and sublime subjects at the origin—yet subordinate to a fated objectivity. The fairy-tale, especially in so far as it has become romance, concerns rather the exchanges of concrete objects within an umbrageous proto-history (Arthurian Britain, early Ireland, Britanny, Scandinavia, Germany—all notably to do with the shadowy arrival of Christianity), yet subordinate (by an opposite paradoxical reversal) to the operations of missing personages, preternaturally "other" fairy-figures, or else legendary human persons.

Thus we can conclude that myth appears to be about glorious subjects but is really about the tragic undermining of personhood by fate, whereas the fairy-tale is apparently about the tricky behavior of objects (lovers really seduced by love-potions and not each other, etc. as in the Tristam story) but is actually about the final triumph of misty subjects over objects, the ciphers of a pagan fate now somewhat tamed and subordinated.

But if the Christian romances of the early Middle Ages were able to have a new "ultimate" resonance, this was not because older mythical debris was now put to new secular use to produce cults of love and heroic warfare. To the contrary, it was because the logic of Christianity itself suggested the elevation of the fairy-tale concerning objects (but really the triumph of subjects) over and above the myth concerning subjects (but really the triumph of the objective or the necessary). Thus in these romances, erotic love and warfare are allowed some tragic play, but finally subordinated to forgiveness, honoring the other, and peaceful order. Yet this elevation was only possible because the Christian *mythos* itself was really more like a fairy-tale. The latter is *less* proto-philosophic than myth because not commanded by impersonal necessity. In this sense the Yale School had a profoundly correct intuition: Christianity elevates narrative. Here, performers truly are ultimate and not undermined by a process that invites conceptualization; philosophers being in this respect natural heirs of the mythographers. Nevertheless in the Christian story, objects *appear* to make the plot.

How so? Well, initially God confronts no dragon, but shapes a thing, the creation, and then does further things with this thing. Human beings and even angels enjoy no virginal and independent subjective spon-

4. Greimas, *Sémiotique et Sciences Sociales*, 210–13.

taneity, but begin and remain entirely "objects" of the divine shaping. Intellectual beings, normally the "ends" of non-intellectual instruments, are themselves "instruments" with respect to the divine end, according to Aquinas.[5] Later on in the story, the plot is not propelled by the primordial and irredeemable conflict of conflicting personal impulses as in myth: love and war, love and domesticity, Aphrodite and Ares, Aphrodite and Hestia, etc. *Genesis* never suggests that Cain and Abel were doomed to quarrel, but rather than Cain's murderousness had something to do with his possessive approach to the realm of things. The entire later story of Israel concerns their escape from the rule of things (idols); their construction of a more mobile thing (the ark), which realizes but does not entrap their subjective identity; the losses and regainings of this thing; plus their self-identification in terms of a legal handling of things, which was, in a unique way, at once strict and flexible, and throughout concerned with the protection of spirit and life from the arbitrary objectivity of bloodletting. In the New Testament, Christ (as the Russians, following Nikolai Leskov, have often realized) is more of an enchanter than a hero, able to command and subordinate all objects, but under the *ban* (which fully ethicizies and subjectivizes parallel bans in fairy-tales) of not deploying this power for the sake of his own power. As with the original "tale of creation," the entire story of the New Testament concludes to the shaping of a new "thing" of redemptive power, namely the Eucharist, which as *food* is the most exact example (as Hegel realized) of an object necessary for subjective identity, an object that nonetheless ultimately subserves that identity. Consistent with this, it is objects associated with the Passion and the Mass that become the crucial "magical objects" of the grail legends. The original and absolute divine power over things and fate was subverted by human freedom, whose refusal of gift in favor of autonomy re-enslaves freedom to fate and the rule of objects—physical things, like its own body—by which it is lured and ultimately betrayed. In the Eucharist, however, God descends beneath humanity into thinghood, thereby restoring its subordination to subjective freedom, but retaining the truth that this freedom is only fed by the measured use of inanimate reality.

But how does this narrative dimension relate to the issue of evil? Earlier I indicated that the contingency of evil as privation requires a mythical, narrative dimension. In this regard James Wetzel contends that

5. Aquinas, *SCG* III, 112.

while, at the philosophical level, Christianity does indeed refuse "ontological violence," since evil is only the absence of peace, at the *narrative*
level this is untrue, since a story about evil implies a certain inevitability of evil. If there is a plot involving evil, then it must itself be in some
measure "an evil plot." Indeed, one could ask further, what "plot" and so
narrative could there be without the performance of evil? Thus in the case
of *Genesis*, he notes that God commanding Adam and Eve not to eat of
the fruit of the tree of good and evil already suggests that they *will* eat.
Moreover, Wetzel further suggests that *not* to know good and evil would
be not to know evil as lack and so (I infer) not to know good as plenitude.
Hence there is a conflictual element here: God, wishing to protect mankind, refuses something that in the end is more for their good than for
their harm. Yet, at the same time, he could not really wish them harm.
Thus all the actors—God, serpent, Adam, Eve—are here commanded after all by a kind of impersonal fate not entirely unlike that of paganism.
Nevertheless, this is a more benign fate, as the eating of the apple was a
felix culpa leading finally to humanity's redemption.

   Can there then, in the face of this position of Wetzel's, be ontological peace also at the narrative level, remembering as we have seen, that
Christianity (as, already, Platonism) has an irreducibly mythic dimension
and cannot be conveyed into pure ontology? The answer for me is naturally yes. It is nevertheless true that Christianity (though more mythic
than myth, as we have seen) is ambivalent about narrative (and drama).
The final truth is a tableau, a masque, a vision—and a masque only for
dancing, not for dramatic interplay. Initially, though, there is a narrative.
The *most* narrative of all narratives, in so far as it concerns the instigation
of an object—the creation—*entirely* by subjective power. Yet the *thinnest*
of narratives, in that it only describes a process of making, without any
"interesting" oppilations whatsoever. But in this etiolated mode, it is indeed a story of a peaceful unfolding, which peacefully unfolds. A story
without "plot."

   Were the opening of *Genesis* a myth, then there might be an original quarrel between subjectivities over an object. Instead, because it is a
fairy-tale (as Chesterton surmised), there is a proper relating to an object
which is later transgressed, so giving rise to intersubjective hostilities (the
figure of the serpent is subordinate to this, since he is a tempter in relation to the ban). What is the apple? It is the object as such in the mode
of illusion. The illusion is in fact that of univocity, of "mere" existence,

outside degrees of participation. Eve is offered a "pure" object, entirely under her control, which opens upon the infinite (immortal life) not in relation to desire or goodness, but in relation to the "hinge" between good and evil, somehow to be commanded. Of course, then the apple is really *nothing*; since evil is itself nothing, there is nothing to know about it. There is no knowledge of good or evil, though thinking they have such knowledge is the illusion that Adam and Eve fall into, since their previous innocence was not the protected innocence we cherish in children. It was, rather, unprotection in the face of the ferocity of the good, a state lacking nothing whatsoever. Even the divine ban was not really a ban, but an unimaginable ban on banning. What was banned (a ban that would not really have been announced to Adam and Eve; this is simply our weak postfallen narrative conceptualization) was simply all imagining that there could be a consumable object outside divine control which would indifferently mediate to us God or non-God, being or not-being, good or evil. All that was banned was the thought that evil could be a real thing because it is supposed that there can be a "bare existence" that is simply "there" in abstraction from createdness, goodness, and so forth.

Hence Wetzel is wrong to suppose that God really forbade anything (any real thing), or that our first parents in any way gained by knowing good and evil (for Aquinas, summing up patristic tradition, they enjoyed grace and the promise of immortality in Eden). As for the question of narrative expectation, to suppose that the narrative is saying that the Fall was "historically" inevitable, by insinuating that it will arise in the later unfolding of the plot (since why else commence the narrative?) is to confuse the *res gestae* with the *historia rerum gestarum*. Instead, the narrative mode indicates here just the opposite: since evil is contingent privation, only a story, only a *mythos* and *not* an ontology, can account for its arising. But this accounting is of course not literal. Indeed, we only have the narrative and dramatic modes in the sense of myth—of stories about subjects—*because* of the Fall (as Tolkien argued). The story about the origin of evil must perforce be couched in the idiom of stories about evil, which are even somewhat ambiguously "evil stories" (every plot is indeed an intrigue). Thus the mythical arguments between Adam and Eve include the mythical role of Satan—where the true fairy story mode would require the tale of how the latter was previously attracted by the abyss (as later supplied by Milton).

To sum up, *mythos* is a tale of eternal fatality, or *else* of the fall into the illusion of such fatality. A fairy-tale is a tale either of personal creation or of interpersonal redemption. Christian *knowledge* elevates the fairytale into the romance of ultimate human (or transhuman) performance, because it involves, of itself, a cosmic fairy-tale. The structure of romance is utterly consonant with ontological peace, since it refuses the sacrificial and tragic economy of ontological violence. I can therefore readily extend my theory of Christian philosophy into a theory of Christian literature.

Kant and the Angels

Enlightenment however, is in part the banishing of all influence of myth, fairy-tale, romance, and revelation from the realm of reason. Kant remains paradigmatic for this "punctuation" of reason—since by contrast Hume skeptically argued that we are always governed by the irrational, even though that does not relate to the truth. Gordon Michalson has accordingly asked for greater clarification concerning my attitude to Kant and the "critical turn." In my response I want simply to indicate one way in which his supposed critical turn can be unmasked.

Kant first announced his critical project in his polemic against Swedenborg, entitled *Dreams of a Spirit-Seer*. This was no mere "satire," as too many critics have supposed, but inaugurated a strange debate that persisted through Schiller up to Schopenhauer.[6] One needs to locate it against a consideration of the traditional role of angelology. Kant critically banished, not so much God, as rather the angels.

Theologians today may forget this, but there is no Christian theology without angelology. The existence of immaterial spirits who are not God counterfactually ensures that the Creator is more than the spiritual real; the latter, too, can be created. Equally, though, angelology counterfactually underwrites the distinction of metaphysics from physics, as Islamic philosophy particularly well attests. The abstractability of *eidos* from matter in the physical world we inhabit, attests to the conceivability of pure spirit in a purely "metaphysical" realm.

However, it would be a mistake to suppose that angelology was purely a matter of speculative invocation and not also of phenomenologi-

---

6. Kant, "Dreams of a Spirit-Seer," Swedenborg, *Universal Human/Soul-Body Interaction*, Schiller, *Der Geisterseher*, and Schopenhauer, "Essay on Spirit Seeing."

cal experience. Because we are (nearly) *all* post-Kantians, we assume that experience of the "Beyond" is, for monotheists, always experience of God. This assumption, however, ironically encourages the idolatrous sense that God essentially *is* our experience of him—as, in Kant's case, the experience of the holiness of the moral law, or else the sense that our experience is the exact inverse of the divine experience. Thus Schleiermacher's "feeling of absolute dependency" discloses only a God who is the absolute "ground of our being." Likewise Barth's appeal to a "self-revealing" God discloses only a God who exhaustively is this self-revealing.

But for a pre-Kantian sensibility, the apparition of the beyond under multiple aspects could be correlated with the conjecturing of a multiple spirit world (including the relics of pagan deities) and of other "presences," of more subtle body, within our own physical world. Strong individual and collective impulses seemingly possessed of a cosmic force were still experienced as the manifestation of trans-human personalities. The unambiguously virtuous among these were deemed angels. Angels in fact not only secured God as creator and the possibility of metaphysics, but also the idea (refused already by Scotus) of deepening apprehension of perfections as itself the process of ascent toward God. For Dionysius the Areopagite and countless others in his wake, this ascent was also an ascent upward through angelic hierarchies. To dub an experience of the beyond as being only as yet experience of the angelic was to exercise a phenomenological caution that was the twin of the metaphysical caution exercised in "naming God."

The entire loss of a participatory world and of disclosive aesthetic *eidos* tended to remove the phenomenological, experiential side of metaphysics, in relation to God as well as to angels. This inspired in reaction an increasingly marginal and specific mysticism, now driven hysterically to seek out an entirely specific emotional and positively shaped experience, or else counterwise to abandon selfhood to the point of annihilation in the quest for an entirely elusive God dwelling in a darkness that rivals our meager light, and which therefore no longer inwardly shone with a dazzling eminence obscurely glimpsed through the interplay of affirmation and negation. (The latter drift is found in Surin and in Fénélon, yet was earlier avoided by John of the Cross and Pierre Bérulle, who both notably sustained an older, non onto-theological metaphysics.)

But these maneuvers could apply to angelic encounters also. More stringent tests for the validity of experience, reining back wild empiricism by a demand for exactness of description and reproducibility of the occurrence, also affected claims to experience the presence of spirits. It might seem as if Dante's tour of the angelic realms inaugurated a modern fictionalizing of the Christian mythical, while Swedenborg's eighteenth-century tour regressively reverts to mythical illusion. Yet, to the contrary, Dante's vision blends the historical with the genre of mystical-poetic vision of the otherworldly and angelic, as exemplified also in the Middle-English allegorical poem *Pearl*. He resorted to fiction only to conserve *apophasis* regarding the eternal and its relation to the historical. Swedenborg, inversely, adopts the language of literal reporting precisely *because* he is so modern, because he is a Swedish scientist endeavoring to encompass also the spirit-world within the scope of the precisely empirical. His new, more detailed—and social and familial—account of heaven and his search for spiritual evidences continued to be part of modern culture until at least the early twentieth century (the influence on the New England James family being perhaps the most famous instance).

Kant's reaction against Swedenborg was not only that of an outraged skeptic. It was also the reaction of an austere religious sensibility. He was from the outset concerned not only with refuting impossible speculation that violated theory's field of application, but also with safeguarding the purity of the spiritual. Spirits described in grossly material terms could not be true spirits and were unedifying. True spirits could only be encountered spiritually. But for Kant, as a modern philosopher, there was no longer a participatory ascent into perfections that involved an analogical hierarchy. The only way the spiritual realm could be experienced was directly (or at least as directly as possible) through our own subjectivity. This encounter should ideally be contaminated by no material mediation whatsoever; but that was only possible in the reflective relation of free will to itself, since the rest of our cognitive equipment requires a sensory "schematization." God, the supreme spirit, is invoked here in so far as the moral self turns out to be schizophrenic. The self, in its true, purely spiritual nature, is governed by what follows upon the givenness of freedom. At the same time, it is always, in reality, somewhat unfree, mixing in with the aims of freedom the seeking of verifiable empirical results, and never even sure just when this is secretly its corrupted purpose. Escaping this impasse means that to will our own freedom is after all to have faith in the free God who endeavors to give us our freedom. Within our self-division, God emerges as the legislator even of our self-legislation. God's presence is indeed experienced, in so far as the truth of the moral law can only be "felt" as the interruption of our sensual egoity. This is how practical reason interprets the undergoing of the limits of imagination in the "natural sublime."

But there is no room here for the mediation of angels. There is no longer a mystical ascent of virtue, but only the abrupt divine interruption of unfreedom and letting be of freedom. Since practical reason is really the highest theoretical reason, which directly knows freedom on which all ultimately depends, this "banishing of the angels" is not some variety of theological or metaphysical skepticism. Instead, it is a new theological ontology. God relates directly to spirits who are not hierarchically distinguished, but who are rather all equal in their freedom, and among whom we are numbered. In addition, God guarantees the unity and coherence of the phenomenal world, which we partially attest, but in which we must also have faith (as we need faith to believe in our freedom) in order to pursue our scientific investigations in the future. Kant's theology possessed a fully fledged eschatology: to know or to will at all, we have to be guided by the vision of a realized knowledge and of a "perpetual peace" (among mutually recognizing wills). The God who must be there if freedom and its experience are real, is also the God who must be there at least as the unknown guarantor of the order of the universe. So just as the claim to invoke or experience angels would contaminate our encounter with God "posited" as the source of freedom, so also it would contaminate the God required as a "regulative" guarantee for our other spiritual activity of scientific inquiry. For the medieval vision, the angelic interval guaranteed God's divine height as the creator of beings who is himself *esse*, and as the superformality who is the causal source even of the metaphysical (which concerns primarily the realm of being, and not the divine, even for Aquinas, before Scotus). But for Kant this "between" must be disavowed (at least experientially) in order to guarantee the divine as more purely spiritual, autonomous, and self-caused *within* the metaphysical realm, which is the field of being. Kant's discourse remained in this way more uncritically inside metaphysics than Aquinas's. And by discounting the angelic "between," he idolatrously made absolute the relation between divine and human spirit, as if God confronted us merely as an ontic other, indeed as the other constituting our own selfhood. This was to banish also the Platonic erotic *metaxu* that lures knowledge forward to know what it already knows but does not yet know. By contrast, Kant's God only lures the will to know more of its own empty assertion.

Yet to banish the angelic was to usurp it. Kant augmented the "angelism" that Gilson diagnosed in Descartes. For Kant the "I" is essentially a pure *noumenon*, even if (as he rightly saw against Descartes) the true noumenal self is but obliquely "apperceived," since the phenomenologically experienced empirical self can fall under an *epoche* along with the objects that it appears to know. We may not see angels, but out of the corner of our eye we glimpse our own angelic outline. We may not commune with angels, but to act ethically is to act with other human spirits in an angelic kingdom of ends, where we need not take account of goals and consequences—not out of a kind of moral priggishness (the obvious reading) but because here there are no ends or consequences (yet no *eros* either, so these new angels are after all somewhat prudish). Similarly, Kant in his aesthetic writings may have banished the fairies of romance, but instead it seems that the real noumenal essence lurking behind the bush of every phenomenon is itself a romantically withheld sprite, unromantically unknowable.

Kant's *noumena* were the relics of Leibniz's monads. Nominalist rationalism was forced to register its discontent with drained Cartesian space: physical reality still exhibited the shapes of *eidos*, the power of forces that move and bind, ineffable concinnities, and an aporetic fading of the finite into the infinite. Monads are the magical madness of nominalism in the teeth of such evidence. There are only "points," rigorously displaying the reflective rigors of non-contradiction, yet there are endless points within points and each point subdivides infinitely; every point infinitely reflects every other point, thereby nominalistically atomizing the realist implication of artistic perspective. An appearance of a complex web of real relations is saved by recourse to pre-established harmony. Here an improbably counter-intuitive speculation saves the project of an ontology projected by formal logic.

Kant, however, disconnected the points from their surface display. Just as he religiously disliked angelic mediation, so he also religiously disliked the fractal incursion of the infinite into the finite. The "bounds" of the latter should be preserved, primarily in order to conserve punctual purity, as a kind of immanent angelic presence of which nothing could be known save (perhaps) the fact of its instance.

This meant that while, for Kant, deep reality was Leibnizian, sustaining in these depths the law of identity (that sleeping ally of pure moral self-legislation), surface reality was Newtonian. This duality lurks behind his explicit *noumena/phenomena* duality. Phenomenal space was not allowed to be monadic and pre-established in its harmonies, because it was not deemed by Kant to be constituted only by the endless relations (or seeming relations glimpsed in the Leibnizian *vinculum* linking monad to monad) of contiguous bodies, but was taken, following Newton, to be an empty container. It was not exactly a real infinite emptiness though, as it was for Newton. Kant reserves real infinity for the *noumena* and is fearful of contaminating this with anything material or sensory. Since, however, it has, as an empty container, a kind of appearance of quasi-infinitude, such that antinomously, neither its limitedness (what would limit it without being spatial) nor its unlimitedness (by which it would cease as indefinite to be the container of the body which is always limited) makes sense, Newtonian space cannot be "real," but must rather be the sensory super-formality (mentally distinguishable from material body, and so, in still Scotist fashion, in some way really distinguishable) within which we are bound to apprehend appearance. Space therefore belongs, not to real substances (*noumena*) but to a "transcendental esthetic."[7]

Why though, for Kant, should not space be merely relational? If it were, then one could simply imagine the endlessness of the corporeal world as such, including its fractal sublimation into spirit at the *minima* and *maxima* of extension. Kant, as we have seen, dislikes this metaxological mingling, which he fears will dilute the spiritual. But how rationally can he refute it here? How can he oppose the primacy of a relativized cosmos (Leibniz and also Spinoza) over human apprehension, which is just the event of being acted on and reacting? Here his radical finitism requires an anthroprocentrism, a Copernican turn which does not see our decentering as our limited perspective on the real that is commanded by the real, but instead as our confinement to our "own" perspective which circumscribes an "everyday" world without exit of causal sequences and transparent concurrences.

Now, oddly, he shares this new anthropocentrism with Swedenborg, whose heresy was to make Christ's humanity also eternal and original.

---

7. See Kant, "Dreams of a Spirit-Seer," and "What Does It Mean to Orient Oneself in Thinking?"

It is even as if Kant wishes to give an immanent, temporally confined equivalent of this heresy.

This is bizarrely confirmed by the fact that both the excessive and the confined northern seer provide the same ultimate spatial guarantees for their anthropocentrism. For Swedenborg, the mark of the human character of the celestial realms, in contrast to the earthly, is that there, whatever is first on one's right hand (or else on one's left) remains *always* on one's right (or else on one's left). The human is here never relative to direction, but direction is relative to the human. Although Swedenborg had climbed to angelic heights, he also usurped the angelic by falsely subjugating the spiritual to the sensible, and even to spatial, direction.

But is it not just this to which Kant objects, so inaugurating critique? Yes, but things are not so simple; in fact they are very peculiar indeed. If, for Swedenborg, it is "orientation" that enthrones humanity as the measure of all things, then Kant's Protagorean turn is underwritten in a parallel manner. First of all, Kant, like Swedenborg, requires "orientation" by the divine and celestial. For Kant, this term partially alludes to the invocation of God as the "regulative" principle of physical order. Therefore, as with Swedenborg, the celestial is required to confirm our perspective, yet is nonetheless given as this ultimate measure according to our perspective. But what, for Kant, is this perspective, as regards the material world? It is an order in which *a priori* categories of understanding (cause, relation, quality, quantity, etc.) are always fused with the reception of sensory information because they are "schematized" by the transcendentally esthetic *a priori* sensory formalities of space and time. These transcendentally esthetic perspectives on reality are human-centered projections (if also projections that situate the human in its sensory regard) only because space and time are infinite and empty, as we have seen. But what for Kant proves that space is infinite and empty?

Nothing other than a more sophisticated and reflexive version on earth of the spatial experience of Swedenborg in the heavens. Leibniz, according to Kant, was wrong, and space is both absolute and anthropocentric, because right and left are not symmetrically reversible. This is rather an *absolute orientation*. If space were just a sequence of related bodies, then right and left would be symmetrically reversible. But since they are not, space is a matter of pregiven *a priori* absolute directionality.

Therefore, *the entire critical turn reduces to this arcane issue of orientation*. If there is no absolute right–left orientation, then space can be relational and real. If space is relational and real, then the categories it fuses with sense-impressions can be ontologically real as well, and not just epistemologically *a priori*, since there is no longer any reason to think that they apply "only" to the human perspective. In that case, our thinking would open somewhat on an ontological order, which we could take to be grounded in infinite actuality and so this order would be self-confirming. One would not need to "orient" thought by invoking God regulatively in order to guarantee the consistency, up to an immanent eschaton, of purely *our* spatial orientation.

So *are* right and left asymmetrical and irreversible? This is an ancient argument, but most of Kant's reasons for claiming this are bogus. The most problematic circumstance here is also the most to hand, quite literally. As Kant insists, one's right hand cannot be "folded into" one's left hand, in the way that the line to the right of a point can be "folded into" the line to the left of the point, if one imaginatively moves the right line, like a clock hand, through 180 degrees of space that is a third dimension in relation to the original flat line. But since the right hand and the left hand possess the structure that constitutes right- or left-handedness in three as well as two dimensions (the reader needs to consult his hands in order to see this), one would need an unavailable fourth dimension in order to fold the right hand into the left hand. Thus no right hand will ever serve as a proper transplant for a person who has lost their left hand! However, this does not prove that right and left are mystically diverse. What it proves is only that right and left hands differ, like two globes, in three dimensions, and therefore *themselves* embody irreducibly different relations to right and left. Thus the critical turn itself depends on a piece of sublimely mystical and deluded geometry. One opposes the "postcritical" in the name of a hyper-critique carried out by the genuine, historically aware power of reason.

The above argument would be one way in which one could reject the critical turn. However, for Gordon Michalson this would probably suggest that I am a reactionary, refusing philosophic "progress." But that is to miss the point. I am not just rejecting the Kantian "turn," but also the entire metanarrative that helps to insinuate the truth of this turn—the entire idea that there *is* a precritical and a postcritical phase in the history of human thought.

Deliberately, I have just tried to show how this seemingly grandiose perspective can be reduced to the relatively trivial. Instead, I would offer a different metanarrative with, I think, better historical warrants. For this account, Kant is the long-term heir of the Plotinian strand of neoplatonism that stressed the raising of the human soul above the sensory and the material and the inner constitution of the latter within the soul itself. Kant eventually combines such a stress (anticipated already in German Dominicans like Dietrich of Freiburg) with a different mutation of Plotinianism emerging through Avicenna, Roger Bacon, Henry of Ghent, Peter Olivi, and Duns Scotus. This current tended to establish a priority of the consideration of being over the divine cause of being; the idea that being is univocal; a theory of knowledge in God, angels, and humans as "mirroring" the real rather than being in some sort of ontological identity with it; and the view that fundamental causality is efficient not formal or final in character. These conjoined tendencies allowed a "metaphysics" or an "ontology" to emerge for the first time as a fully autonomous and fundamental field of understanding. Basic to this new "ontology" was the idea that being is what is clearly knowable by the mind and that God is the supreme ontic instance of being thus understood. Kant criticized and inverted only *this* metaphysic, which in reality already called of itself for its own inversion. At a deeper level Kant further *secured* "metaphysics," since its inner tendency was already toward the primacy of epistemology and the bracketing of the question of God.

In this fashion, Kant's position merely follows further one already ancient way—and it cannot be held of itself to define "modernity." So in refusing Kant I am not refusing the modern, only Kant's dubious talismanic status for the latter. I would argue that another, albeit more stuttering current of modern thought (exemplified diversely in Eriugena, Aquinas, Eckhart, Cusa, Pico, Bérulle, Pascal, Cudworth, Shaftesbury, Thomas Taylor, Coleridge, Vico, Jacobi, Hamann, Novalis, de Biran, Ravaisson, Kierkegaard) developed further *another* ancient way. As with Kant, the mark of modernity here is an increased stress on the power of the human subject. But here one has an extension rather of the Proclean-Dionysian version of neoplatonism, which thought of the human soul's creative power not as something inwardly exercised on sensation and body in the constitution of theoretical knowledge, but rather as something exercised externally *with* sensation and body in a transformation of the given material cosmos whose structures nevertheless still retained an exemplary primacy.

For this version of subjective power, though the human soul stands in one sense above the cosmos through its intellectual kinship with the angels, in another sense it must make obeisance to the cosmos, which is part of the divine production of being as such, exceeding human capacity. The unfolding of the powers of our mind and body can only, in consequence, be a work of artistic collaboration with a further revealing of the hidden beauties of nature, which are themselves the work of unconscious art, giving rise to settled "habits" (as analyzed by Maine de Biran and Félix Ravaisson). And only in this unfolding does truth as such unfold—a truth which we must have "faith" in, precisely because nothing else guarantees it, and a truth which "metacritically" disallows any clear critical demarcation of our "own" contribution over against that of external reality, that would allow us to affix clear "limits" to our reasoning capacities. The more radical recognition of our confinement by matter, body, image, and sign also requires us to affirm our supernatural destiny and mediation of the divine, if the apparent meanings that we shape in collaboration with nature are to be freed from the shadow of illusion.

By contrast, technological domination of nature, uninflected by any artistic grace, is always as uncreative as it is dogmatic, since it concerns only the "faster," "stronger," "closer," "larger," "smaller," etc. This barren concern with intensified, reduced, or expanded *mimesis* is enabled by the "Plotinian" retreat into the isolation of supposed pregiven *a priori* structures that purportedly "constitute" given sensory realities. In reality, such structures are but the formulas of planned control abstracted from observation of the regular operation of our own artifacts when they exercise a mesmeric and narcissistic fascination upon us.

If the "Plotinian" current gives rise to unjust technocracy, it is rather the "Proclean" current that more fully allows a recognition of the contingency of human history—since it sees the cultural world as that which we have *made*—even if we have always made *more* and other than we know. For this reason, the "Proclean" alternative version of modernity is actually more modern than the ("Plotinian") Kantian version, which in its apriorism is always a conservative attempt to deny radical historicity. (In Hegel both currents are in tension, but the "Plotinian" current wins out, which is why he is less historicist and less modern than the explicitly Proclean Vico.) The truth of the Kantian current is technologism (as the end of the *Critique of Pure Reason* too well shows), yet this is not the deeper truth of modernity.

Therefore I see myself as subscribing to a philosophical current more and not less modern than the "critical" one.

The History of Charity

A similar hyper-critique should be applied to the realm of human practice. Despite many interesting observations and useful modifications of some of my conclusions, Jennifer Herdt somewhat misunderstands the general thrust of my political thinking. In many ways, hers is perhaps a typical misreading by an American liberal of a European radical as if he were straightforwardly a conservative. She misses the ways in which I am clearly in some ways a Marxist, albeit a very heretical one.

Herdt contests my claim that political economy tended to abolish the sphere of charity. Here she appears to think that I would characterize this sphere in terms of (1) the mutual assistance of believers, (2) an *ad hoc* "private" activity, and (3) a direct personal response to immediate distress.

Accordingly, she thinks that my claim that the sphere of charity has tended to be abolished in modern times can be easily dismissed, as clearly these three characteristics continue to be exemplified and advocated. But does she really think that I would be so absurd as to deny this? I do not think of charity in the three ways specified—nor is it true, as Herdt seems to imply, that the early Church confined assistance to believers. However, even its internal mutuality belonged much more to the content of a new sort of polity than to any sort of merely "private" arrangement, as she equally seems to assume.

Much more interestingly though, she sketches a history of charity to rival my own (and I suspect that of Catherine Pickstock) and at points she offers valuable correctives—which nonetheless do not affect the substance of my genealogical case. I will try now briefly to visit the salient moments at issue. My overriding theme is that Herdt treats changes in Christian charitable organization as mere "responses" to changes in historical circumstance and social structure seen as more or less inevitable and innocent. Thus it is clearly she and not I who both "mystifies social processes" and thinks of charity as mere response to arising need.

Crucial here are our respective accounts of the Middle Ages. Herdt describes the system of medieval relief as an *ad hoc* arrangement in a situation where there was little unemployment, though much poverty.

Manorial relief involved practices of adoption and distribution of tithes; this was supplemented by the efforts of guilds, hospitals, and almshouses. Because this system was so informal, it failed later to respond to drastically altered economic circumstances. Therefore I am wrong to "idealize it."

I do not so idealize it, but this thinly materialist account of medieval charity says far too little—and ignores all the interesting historical research. It is worth first of all pointing out how historically *remarkable* are the specifically Christian institutions of hospitals for the sick and dying, almshouses for the aged, orphanages for the parentless, and education for the poor but talented. They did not, as a matter of record, arise simply as the obvious response to a need. Rather they arose because the needs of the sick, of the dying, and of infants, and more particularly their social needs, were for the first time in history recognized, within a particular religious framework. "Idealization," as usual, is utterly beside the point; even if there had only been a few such institutions (and in reality they were very widespread) the fact of their being there at all would be the remarkable thing.

The second point is yet more crucial. Herdt, neglecting entirely the history of mentalities, assumes that the *notion* of charity has remained the same, while the organization of charity has changed. Yet medieval historians mostly insist that in that epoch charity did not yet mean primarily "doing good to those in need," where the neighbor is paradigmatically a stranger. On the contrary, it meant forging or restoring bonds of mutuality between donor and recipient. Here the neighbor (as for Aquinas) is paradigmatically one's kin, since kinship is with the nearest. Beyond literal kinship, there were quasi-kin, those in one's locality and so forth. Although the neighbor was not the stranger, the stranger could become the neighbor by arriving in one's own parish where he was entitled to that gift of hospitality that is well-nigh universal for most traditional cultures. And on pilgrimages one met with many temporary neighbors. Whereas modernity reads the Good Samaritan as one from far away, the Middle Ages read him as the one who has drawn near.

Since charity was thought of as a state of relation rather than as a deed, it was characteristically an exchange. The beggar receiving alms prayed for you, as did the pensioners of the almshouse you had endowed. Indeed, you went on receiving their counter-gift after you were dead. Did this trade in charity contaminate it? Only from our modern perspective, for which charity is a disinterested act of kindness, not for the medieval perspective, for which, over and beyond such acts, "the trade" was itself charity, since it constituted the bonds of community.

Closely linked with the idea of charity as a mutual state rather than as a unilateral punctual performance, was the ritual, festive character of charity. This can be contrasted with the paradoxical character of modern philanthropy: on the one hand, it is supposed to be unilateral and disinterested, and therefore, from the point of view of the charitable actor, the giver, it is something done "for its own sake." Yet where an act is one-way, and there is no concern to forge a bond, the act itself must be instrumentalized. The point of the act, if it is strictly concerned with the other as other and not the other in relation to you, must be to meet the *needs* of the other, those things which strictly belong to him alone. But the more such needs themselves concern the relations in which the other is involved, the more it will be likely that these relations would include also his regard toward you, the donor. Hence "need" here, as what strictly belongs to the donee, is likely to be defined in the most basic materialist terms, or else in terms of the minimum owing to human freedom, such as freedom of movement and the freedom to acquire knowledge. It follows that, paradoxically, the disinterested giver is correlated with a sensual and egotistic recipient. This opens to view an aporetic sociality—who is to be altruistic and when, who is to be egotistic and when? Not by accident, this is akin to the *aporia* that afflicts consequentialism: at what arbitrary point do we cut off the causal chain of actions to define a "consequence" that should be assessed? Who is legitimately a recipient of a consequential benefit and when, rather than an ethical actor looking to benefit others under a consequentialist imperative? The kinship is no accident because, for reasons we have just seen, the "Levinasian" one-way charitable act will tend to be reduced to utilitarian purposes. Such an act performed supposedly "for its own sake" must in reality be cancelled, must fade away, be forgotten about. Since it is really "for the sake of the other," it is in itself, as an act, instrumentalized. But this means that charity is instrumentalized. It cannot be the ultimate, it cannot infinitely "abide," as for St. Paul, if it is only the means to the fulfillment of needs—even the needs of the other. For this reason, every simply "other-regarding" ethic (Levinas etc.) reduces to a mode of utilitarianism, and effaces the ethical for the sake of non-ethical exigencies (such as material needs).

It is for this reason that the festive and ritual character of medieval charity, which appears to be religiously in excess of the ethical, in reality alone secures the ultimacy of the ethical. The offering to the beggar in exchange for his blessing "abides," because the forging of this bond was itself "the point." Of course, there is no genuine forging of bonds without attending to the various needs of the other (including those most merely "his own"), but nevertheless the means adopted to meet these ends themselves participate in a final end (infinite beatified charity) that exceeds these ends. For this reason the gift to the beggar, the endowment of the almshouse, the gifts offered at baptism, the liturgical offering for the dead and so forth, were all occasions for festive celebration. Such celebration was the reflexivity of an act of charity that was indeed "for its own sake." Only the deed, not the actors, can be "disinterested," for, as we have seen, purely disinterested actors are subservient to merely instrumental purposes that paradoxically enthrone purely interested recipients.

So far then, we have seen that Herdt ignores the fact that the medieval notion of charity was ontological, reciprocal, and festive in a way that ours is not. Closely linked to these differentiating features is a fourth one: the poor recipient had a far higher status. From early modernity onwards, the destitute person started to be seen simply as a problem, an excretion, and an untidiness. But in the Middle Ages he had a certain aura of sanctity: fortune had reduced him to the real condition of us all—utter dependence upon grace and favor. And this condition might, indeed, be voluntarily embraced with dignity, as by the three orders of friars. Of course the sacralization of poverty is not without moral ambiguity, but it did, crucially, tend to insist that the materially destitute person is not deprived of the dignity of action. The most *crucial* human actions—gratitude, prayer, and even the counter-giving of concern and well-wishing for donors—were still open to him. A negative assessment of medieval charity might well conclude that this encouraged indifference toward the abolition of poverty, following seemingly evangelical resignation. I do not entirely demur from this assessment. However, the medieval attitude also ensured that those in the present never destined to benefit from future reforms were not dismissed from human rejoicing. Instead of a merely sacrificial relation to future revolution, they enjoyed a proleptic participation in the *eschaton*. Moreover, their seemingly meager part might well be the most essential part. This is not necessarily social conservatism, because the condition of dispossession itself preserves and foreshadows the paradisal condition for true human flourishing.

The second historical moment at issue between us concerns the late medieval and early modern period, "the epoch of reforms"—roughly 1300–1800, which historians now tend to see as more appropriately an epoch than 1450–1800 (and Herdt's own analysis accords well with this division).

Herdt regards the new humanist, Counter-Reformation, and Protestant approaches to charity as simply responding to changed circumstances. She rightly notes that conditions had shifted already in the later Middle Ages, but she thinks that the canonists and clergy lacked the flexibility to adapt. These changes were, primarily: the rise of the money economy linked to the decline of the manorial economy, plus the consequences of the Black Death, leading to a vast increase in the number of wandering vagrants seeking work or higher wages. To these factors were later added, in the postmedieval period, population growth and inflation. In the face of the failure of traditional ecclesiastical and informal patterns of relief, governments were forced to take a new sort of centralized and systematic action. This, for Herdt, is a far more fundamental fact than the traditional view that ascribed the basic shift to the effects of the Reformation. According to this view, Protestantism "desacralized" charity since it no longer held any salvific value. All the festive aspects vanished, and the Reformers supported the centralization of relief systems under the administration of lay magistrates.

In support of her contention that theological and ecclesiastical developments were not decisive, Herdt points to elements of continuity with medieval practice to the extent that this was possible. Charity remained a central Christian imperative for Protestants, and in eighteenth-century Scotland (unlike England) the established (Presbyterian) church took prime responsibility for poor relief, still essentially organized through collection and distribution at the parish level. Only England, among European countries, developed a formal taxation system to deal with poverty, but even here the entire apparatus of personal giving, guild organization of charitable circulation, hospitals, schools, and almshouses endowed by non-profiteering trusts, remained of paramount importance. There continued to be an interplay between more secular, systematic, and state-directed approaches and more intimate, festive, and religious ones. A proof that ideological factors were not the decisive thing at work lies in the fact that the Counter Reformation tended to centralize and deritualize charity just as much as the Reformation.

Now none of the above is "wrong," and one should confirm Herdt's view that the Middle Ages faded only slowly (and indeed, in the current fate of the universities one can see that they are still fading). However, it is also inadequate.

Did new economic circumstances simply "arrive"? One can allow that plague was more or less a pure contingency. But "the rise of the money economy" is something more than a simple change in the weather. Marxists would rightly insist that it concerned an entire new set of social relationships and a new conception of economic value—both of which were at least equally as exploitative as the feudal manorial relationships they tended to replace. Therefore, "the new money economy" was not something morally neutral in the way that Herdt regards it. Moreover, even Marxism is too whiggishly fatalistic: there is no logical reason to say that the rise of a town economy and the increasing instance of free labor had inexorably to encourage an untrammeled capitalist market. To the contrary, the entire medieval guild organization (including guilds of money-changers) was an effort to ensure that the inherent abstractions of money and interest on loans were always reined back by the primacy of substantive and appropriate needs, intrinsically just rewards for labor, and intrinsically just patterns of exchange according to a natural and not "accidentally" resultant scale of values. These efforts were by no means entirely abandoned by the humanists, the reformers, and the counter-reformers, even though one can argue that diminishing the religious importance and rationale of the trade guilds greatly hampered these later endeavors.

One can also argue that a key failure of the Middle Ages was any extension of the guild system to the countryside and to agricultural production. In many ways, it was the modern landlord who encouraged the emergence of the ruthless proprietor and the socially detached capitalist. But again, one cannot see this development as simply inevitable. The problem was that the decline of feudal relations (with the somewhat receding horizon of perpetual local warfare) and the rise of free labor tended to encourage a new sort of aristocratic (or genteel) anarchy and brutality. Not simply plague, but the increasing enclosure of land for sheep-rearing, or other modes of locally monopolizing agriculture in England, drove the late medieval population away from their ancestral lands. Many contemporary commentators, such as Thomas More, were far from seeing this as "inevitable." Perhaps, given human nature, it was all but unstoppable. However, just as the medieval towns and cities bore witness that an urban market economy need not be a nakedly capitalistic one, so also the often non-feudal rural economy of medieval England, especially in East Anglia, bore witness that a rural market economy need not generate a landscape without people. East Anglia remained dominated (as all recent local researches demonstrates) by pre-Norman varieties of an independent yeomanry, some land shared in common, village egalitarianism, and patterns of land distribution focused more upon the village than the manor.[8] Yet this region, vastly boosted by the guild-regulated cloth trade, was one of the wealthiest areas of medieval Europe, as its enormous (now often eerily isolated) parish churches still attest. To see all this as merely a kind of nascent underdeveloped capitalist modernity is to beg a whole host of questions. It is equally plausible to see it as the developed survival of a primitive Germanic tendency to "free association," where the emphasis falls on both these terms.

So it is too simple to see "the new circumstances" as *entirely* inevitable, and certainly too simple to see them as morally neutral. What about the charitable response to these new circumstances? Here, one can question Herdt's downplaying of the importance of ideological shifts, in several different directions. First of all, it is not the case that tendencies to the "rationalization" of charity (looking at the whole picture, diminishing waste, locating the truly deserving, etc.) began only in the early modern period, or were associated only with the secular arm. To the contrary, Eamon Duffy lists ways in which these trends were already under way in the later Middle Ages and concerned religious practice.[9] The "kinship" model hovered between the idea that the nearest kin are the closest neighbors on the one hand, and the idea that the entire human race forms

---

8. See Williamson, *Origins of Norfolk*. Such a more recent vindication of Stubbs and Maitland is not dealt with by Norman Davies, who tends to dismiss their perspectives as English prejudice in his otherwise superb *The Isles: A History*. But Maitland was "pro-Germanic" not simply pro-English, and he developed his ideas in discussion with German legal historians. Moreover, it seems an anachronistic mistake to link the Celtic with the French and European too readily in Davies's fashion. To be sure, the Normans and Breton aristocrats opportunistically revived Welsh cultural thematics. But in Ireland, Wales, and south Scotland, the Norman and not the Saxon was the real invader. See Sheehy, *When the Normans Came to Ireland*. Saxon, Dane, and Celt were very akin, although the former two were perhaps somewhat more constitutionally democratic and lacked any tradition of a non-familial priestly order like that of the Druids. Perhaps the true insular (British-Irish) tradition synthesizes the (Germanic-Celtic) "free association" aspect with the Celtic "religious clerisy" aspects grasped by Coleridge.

9. Duffy, *Stripping of the Altars*, 357–62, 504–5, 510–11.

one kin descended from Adam on the other. For this reason, the arriving stranger could be greeted as remote, lost kin. Hence medieval charity was temporally and geographically stretched between the nearest and dearest on the one hand and the remote and unknown on the other. But Duffy in effect points out how this stretching was disturbed in the later Middle Ages. Charity instead became circumscribed by local space, confined to the parish. The family (one can add to Duffy) started to retreat into a secure space of inheritance prior to charity, while strangers started to be treated as the concern of wherever they truly belonged. Ironically, as people became more and more displaced, a greater and greater attempt was made to locate and confine them. As I pointed out at the end of *Theology and Social Theory*, following Foucault, medieval charitable institutions (even from as early as the twelfth century) started more and more to acquire a sinister disciplinary and classificatory aspect that perverted charitable shelter into coerced confinement.

Even under ecclesiastical patronage, charity began to be "spatialized." Equally, according to Duffy, it began to be confined more to "worthy" recipients. He indeed speculates that this was in part the upshot of a stricter application of sacramental doctrine, since, whereas the Mass works *ex opere operato* and not *ex opere operantes*, the reverse applies to the prayers of others on our behalf: their efficacy depends on their sanctity. Even so, one could argue that an earlier sense of the limited relativity of all human sanctity and the corresponding worth of the prayer and faith even of the sinner has been lost to view.

Whatever the case here, these earlier shifts show that the Church itself helped to reshape charitable practice, and only partially as a reactive measure (for example to the increased prevalence of "strangers" after the Black Death). There was also a certain shift toward a less-festive notion of charity construed now as a one-way gift meeting a need that we must severely judge, while inversely the festive exchange of gifts was, indeed, becoming more debased into a merely calculated contract for which mutual benefit has started to be "the point" and not rather (in addition to mutual benefit) "mutuality as such." (Later, in the eighteenth century the field of benevolence comes to be sundered between one-way giving to the destitute on the one hand and a parodied gift-exchange among "friends" and "neighbors" that shadows market contract by thinking of private relations in terms of a cost–benefit analysis, on the other.) These changes can probably be correlated with the rise of a more voluntarist theology that tended to separate our natural and intellectual quest for happiness on the one hand, from the (supposedly) sheerly chosen acts of our will on the other. Hence Abelard already, and then later Richard of St. Victor, Bonaventure, Peter Olivi and Duns Scotus, tended to advocate a "disinterested" love (indifferent to our own fate and happiness) toward God and toward our neighbors. Scotus had already ceased to think of ethics and politics primarily in teleological and eudemonic terms, and so he exhibits *in nuce* the modern combination of purely "free gift" alongside normatively contractual relations for mutual benefit—the space of "gift-exchange" being thereby obliterated. Since, for Scotus, "justice" is now in excess of "seeking happiness," it tends to concern a formal respect for freedom and contract, and a substantive respect only for the meeting of the more obvious, material, and sheerly "owned" needs. (As is increasingly observed, this is proto-Kantian.)

One can therefore plausibly suggest, *contra* Herdt, that if there is a strong resemblance between Reformation and the Counter Reformation charitable practices, then this is not simply because they are both adapting to the same exigencies. There is in addition a shared theological legacy that reflects an earlier shift that was ideological as well as practical.

Hence there are several features of early modern charity that Herdt ignores, features that are not merely responsive, but rather belong to deep structural shifts at once in practice and outlook. Festive charity showed a sharp decline: in Calvin's Geneva the practical counterpart of a theological insistence on God's grace as one-way free gift and our love of God as equally unidirectional (such that even the non-elected should still love him) was a disapproval of the exchange of gifts at baptism. Inseparable from this decline was a loss of the celebration of mutuality as such.[10] Charitable gifts were now more to strangers whom one never met—and strangers, moreover, in one's own locale. One should *not* regard this change (initially under humanist *aegis*) purely negatively—the concerns for a more integrated and rational approach does indeed exhibit more concern with specific need and with eradicating poverty. Here again, I am

---

10. See Pickstock, *After Writing*, 135–67; Davis, *Gift in Sixteenth-Century France*. See also Johns, *Women's Utopias of the Eighteenth Century*, 105. Johns discusses the Utopian writer Sarah Scott considering whether to be friends with a sickly person who may die is or is not "a bad oeconomy in happiness"! This seems like the *acme* of fake mutuality. For the earlier Abelardian, Victorine, and Franciscan undermining of the "mutualist" model of charity, see Rousselot, *Problem of Love in the Middle Ages*.

no simple dreamer of a medieval golden age. Nevertheless, one can argue that these new dimensions did not *have* to lose sight of the festive dimension. Moreover, this loss was directly connected to the cold, incarcerating character of the new approach (as described by Foucault) and to the new stress on the (always futile and morally dubious) attempt to discriminate between the worthy and the unworthy poor (as disastrously revisited in our own day by both Clinton and Blair).

So Herdt says nothing about either new confinement or new moralizing. Nor does she say anything about new spatialization or insistence that the poor be dealt with only in their own parish. Instead of kin in near and remote time and the remote stranger approaching, one has now the strict mapping of a present human geography that binds men and women to their own parish pump. According to a 1598 Statute of Elizabeth, a vagabond in a parish or "Tything" was to be openly whipped and returned to the parish he was born in. Not all contemporaries, unlike Herdt today, thought that this sort of measure was a mere adaptation to the "new monetary economy." Thus in King Lear, that radical reactionary William Shakespeare speaks of "[Poor Tom] . . . who is whipped from tithing to tithing and stocked, punished and imprisoned."[11] For Shakespeare, everyman, including kings and nobles, are implicated in his fate, as the plot of the tragedy shows. "Who gives anything to poor Tom?" means therefore—where now, in modernity, is *agape*? Precisely my question.

"Poor Tom is a cold"—this is what Herdt seems incapable of grasping, in its many dimensions. It is not simply a matter of the harsh early modern restriction of mobility from parish to parish. It is also a matter of a license to local exploitation of supposedly "free" laborers (who had in reality nowhere else to go). As William Cobbett much later noted in *Rural Rides*, they were often reduced to little more than beasts of burden by "improving" landlords, whereas only *old-fashioned* farmers treated them well. By Cobbett's day the tithe system, in the context of a married clergy and a church which had mostly abandoned asceticism and sacred poverty, had long ago ceased to nurture equality rather than disequality. The link between social justice and a sacral control of the economic surplus (which otherwise may be abstractly capitalized, as Bataille pointed out) had been broken. Instead, the poor, to Cobbett's rage, were now bearing a disproportionate burden of support of the clergy, while the latter tended

11. Shakespeare, *King Lear*, 3.4.50, 3.4.129–31, 281 n. 130.

to uphold high rents to landlords, for fear that the landlords would otherwise withdraw support for the tithe contribution. (There were widespread rural anti-tithe riots in England as late as the 1930s, on the eve of the Second World War.)

Herdt also ignores these Cobbettian issues of the new naked exploitation of rural labor in a money economy—a mode of capitalist slavery in fact—and the increased recruitment of the ecclesiastical economy also to the interests of new capitalist hierarchy. Of course, the Church continued to promote and administer "charitable enterprises"—but these were now less festive, less mutual, and less protective, while they were conversely more distant, judgmental, and incarceral. At the same time, the regular mode of the ecclesiastical economy was more divorced from charitable circulation.

The latter point is an aspect of a larger issue between Herdt and myself. When I say "the sphere of charity was abolished," I do not, of course, mean that charity as a "mopping-up operation" came to an end. Rather I mean that the idea that charity was the *primary purpose* of economic and social circulation was explicitly abandoned, in contradiction of the gospel. Moreover, charity confined to the reactive margins tends to be denatured as unilateral, non-festive, and instrumental. The whole of Charles Dickens's *opus* diagnoses this circumstance, as Chesterton surmised: his main exaltation is of the festive *domus* and the festive peregrination, while his sharpest satire is reserved for the purveyors of cold charity, at a distance. This *opus* was born out of horror at the workhouse. But Herdt, finally, says nothing about the nineteenth century evolution from "outdoor" to "indoor" relief, which consummated the disciplinary perversion of charity. With the advent of the workhouse, the supposed assistance of the neighbor was exposed as being a means to control the population in general.

The History of Sympathy

I would further contest Herdt's claim that eighteenth-century benevolence and sympathy were in general valid extensions of the Christian notion of charity.

Because the paradigm of subjective right lies in absolute possession, modern political theory already accorded an apolitical primacy to the economic—as most clearly appears with Locke. However, the stress on subjective right was not enough to give rise to political economy, and Locke remained rather an economistic political theorist. For the economy concerns exchange as well as ownership and production. To stress only the latter can somewhat invoke a life of sturdy pastoral independence, untrammeled by the market, as one sees already with the Stoics (an earlier source of subjective rights theory), somewhat also with Locke, and more later with Rousseau. The mercantilists in the late seventeenth century were, for this reason, *not* Hobbesians delighted by notions of natural rights and contract, since they favored rather artificial contracts in which they thought human beings were always already untrammeled by natural and a-rational inclination.

The Scots political economists sustained this aversion to political individualism and natural contractualism. As Herdt indicates, they followed those critics of Hobbes who invoked the theme of "sympathy" against him. These critics were, in the first place, the Cambridge Platonists and certain latitudinarian divines. Benjamin Whichcote already argued that sympathy is not, as it was for Hobbes, an imaginative putting oneself in the place of the other—no more than a mode of self-projection. For Whichcote, sympathy is more primary than the reflexive imagination, since we often exhibit spontaneous feeling for others in circumstances we would never imagine ourselves inhabiting. (This is especially true of children as, according to Herdt, Henry Grove later pointed out in the 1714 *Spectator*.)

This, however, as Herdt has well said, gives rise to a kind of *aporia*. Can sympathy ever be moral, much less the root of morality? On the one hand, if it is the reflexive exercise of the imagination, does it not reduce to fantasized self-interest? On the other hand, if it is a spontaneous instinct of an animal kind, how can it exhibit true moral consideration?

According to Herdt, this *aporia* was evaded because a synthesis was arrived at.[12] Both Hume and Butler argued that, to have moral relevance, a conscious imaginative reflection must be built upon the basis of instinctual sympathy. In this way, supposedly, the "moral sense" tradition that flowed from Whichcote through Shaftesbury and Hutcheson was both continued and transcended.

"Sympathy" relates both to the market and to charity. The latitudinarian divines thought of sympathetic instincts as providential placements, which the divine reason coordinated beyond our immediate rational

---

12. Herdt, *Religion and Faction in Hume's Moral Philosophy*.

sight. In this sense, morality itself was subject to the operation of a hidden hand. Similarly, for the Scots economists, "demand" was not simply natural, but influenced by our spontaneous sympathy for the tastes of others and our sensible fascination with the glamour of wealth. On the other hand, for the same thinkers, sympathy ensured that the victims of the market were not neglected, but given charitable assistance.

For Herdt, however, imagination comes to replace the hidden hand in Butler and Hume and later Hazlitt, to engender a fully secularized account of sympathy, which forms the basis for a secularized practice of charity. This practice can potentially achieve, through imaginative sympathy just that "harmony in difference" which I see as a theological prerogative.

My question to Herdt at this point is twofold: first of all, can she be so sure that her resolution of the *aporia* is secure; second, does she tell too simple a historical story?

She herself rightly differentiates Whichcote from some later moral sense theorists. He had borrowed the theme of "sympathy" from the Stoic tradition, but nonetheless given it a Platonic gloss. Thus, as Herdt accurately says, for Whichcote human compassion was a participation in the divine compassionate nature. As such, it was not simply a sensible instinct, but was somewhat conscious. In fact, for the Cambridge Platonists, "moral sense" belonged to the field of "common sense" that mediates between the sensory and the rational in Aristotle. This, however, suggests that *the initial* critique of Hobbes was not in terms of "sympathetic instinct" prior to the exercise of imagination, but in terms of a sympathy that is already imaginative, but also spontaneously instinctual in such a way as to render fantasy more than mere self-projection. And indeed, later Cambridge Platonists like Cudworth were among the first to develop a doctrine of an actively shaping imagination.

These stresses, however, were largely perpetuated by Shaftesbury. For him also, in his *Characteristics*, moral sense is no raw feeling, but more an exercise of *sensus communis*. As such, it balances out the instinctual claims of both self-interest and benevolence in a fashion that is really not so unlike the workings of Butler's "conscience" (even if Butler failed to see this).

Although Shaftesbury's duality of self-interest and benevolence is all too modern (since it rescinds from the question of true teleological self-interest, which is not an "alternative" to the well-being of others), his notion of moral sense still genuinely avoids the reduction of the ethical to either pre-ethical freedom or pre-ethical happiness (deontologism and utilitarianism). Instead, moral sense involves a feeling for appropriate social harmony, and the objectively right state of human existence, still seen as a participation in divine harmony (and also seen as sometimes incorporating the inescapably "ruined," and the "strange beauty" of the tragic). Shaftesbury's neopaganism actually contained more echoes of the genuine notion of *agape* as ontological state than most modern Christian ethical theories.

Including Joseph Butler, that overrated divine! Imagination actually plays less of a role in his account of sympathy (*contra* Herdt) than it did in the Whichcote-to-Shaftesbury tradition. This appears to light in the Bishop's comments on Hobbes. He objects to the latter's notion of a prerational imaginative putting ourselves in the place of the suffering other, that if this be really prerational then it *would* be but a sympathetic instinct. As such, it would no more belong to self-love than to benevolence, since both these notions involve rational reflexivity. Therefore Butler did not think of the imaginative as rising above the instinctual.

This role he rather reserves for the more coolly rational conscience. He failed to see that for Shaftesbury the imagination and the moral sense belong to the *sensus communis*. Hence his basic critique of moral sense theory—namely, that strength of feeling is no proof of its altitude—is actually somewhat vacuous. The strength of feeling can indeed provide its own warranty, just because it derives from its intimation of a binding together of the sensible and intellectual throughout the cosmos (remembering that Shaftesbury preserves some echo of Cudworth's view that it constitutes an "intellectual" [i.e., meaningful] system).

In Butler's own view, conscience substitutes for, or rather overrules, moral sense. The latter is now reduced to the merely instinctual, whether one is speaking of raw self-interest or the passion of benevolence. Both these instincts are "ours" in a non-reflective sense, and neither enjoys a natural primacy. But true moral self-interest and benevolence must take a cooler and longer view. Hence the balance and the mediation between the two instincts concern fundamentally a utilitarian calculus. This, however, is more possible concerning our own future than that of society as a whole, where our knowledge is too limited. It is here that—somewhat as with the latitudinarians—Butler holds that God has providentially placed in us not merely certain benign passions but also certain *absolute* feelings of conscience, independent of any consequential estimation. These concern such things as honesty and respect for life and property. Often noted here is a kinship with Kant's deontology; far more significant is another resemblance—namely, the failure of both thinkers (more honest in Kant's case) truly to distinguish rational duty from moral sense after all. For how is one to comprehend self-authenticating conscience, save as a kind of cooler disclosive passion?

If we are too finite to operate a utilitarian calculus regarding society as a whole, this cannot apply to God. In the *Dissertation on Virtue* accordingly, it appears that God is a utilitarian. In the *Analogy of Religion*, however, God also is subject to the absolute of "conscience." Why should this be the case for Butler? One should invoke here the fundamental liberal *aporia* of alienation. Pure social utilitarianism (as later with Bentham) can alienate every right of self-interest. But Butler, historically prior to a utilitarian doctrine harnessed to the nation-state, seeks to keep both the absolutes of self and of the social whole in play. Indeed, this is his reading of the Pauline doctrine of the body of Christ! Hence the private and the public are privately balanced by our concern at once with general utility and with respect for person, property, and contract—since Butler's "conscience" is curiously alert only to modern subjective rights. But they are *publicly* balanced by the divine respect for the same rights (God being the supreme Anglican landlord) combined with his (as it were) occasionalist co-ordination of our respective passions. Market society is therefore the shallow secret of Butler's supposed subtle balancing of diverse moral philosophies.

Deconstructed in this way, it turns out that Butler's account of sympathy as strictly finite does not at all temper sympathetic instinct with the imagination and continues to require supplementation by a divine hidden hand. Therefore we do not discover here, as Herdt claims, any development toward a theory where imagination might displace God as the guarantee of genuine charity. To the contrary, one discovers instead the typically early modern combination of apparent human self-sufficiency that has to be rescued by an idolized onto-theological God acting within the same ontic space that we occupy.

By contrast, sympathy was more tempered by imagination in the "Cambridge Platonic" tradition, where human virtue was not finitized, but seen as a participation in the divine infinite virtue. Here God was not invoked to supplement our deficiencies within a single univocal ontic plane, because imaginative sympathy was seen as a genuine, partial "anticipation" of the mind of God. It was not therefore invoked as a pre-moral ground of virtue, as it was by Butler, along with freedom and utility, those other two modern candidates for such a role. Herdt wishes to find some authentic secular basis for charity, but my point in *Theology and Social Theory* and here is that that means, precisely, to seek a pre- (and therefore un-) charitable basis for charity! For true religion declares nothing more than this—that charity is its own ground, since it is the supreme reality.

Without the framework of participation, sympathetic charity *cannot* resolve the *aporia* of sympathy and imagination. If there is only myself and the other, and no God, then sympathetic imagination reduces either to animal instinct that regards purely the other, or else to a rationally reflexive projection of my own self-interest. Imagination can only be a discerning recognition of the other for his own sake, and for the sake of his entire set of sensible and intellectual relations, including his relation to myself, if it is an active anticipation (to use a favorite Cambridge Platonic word) of the divine *telos* for humanity and the cosmos.

Neither Hume nor Hazlitt is an exception to this conclusion. In the case of the former, there is no real learning from Shaftesbury with regard to the imagination. Instead, there is a combination of merely instinctual sympathy with an imagination projected from self-interest and in no way actively expanding the range of individual insight. Indeed, Herdt expresses this well herself: Hume distinguishes a sympathetic feeling for the glimpsed stranger from an imaginative entering into his "interest." But all that this means is that Hume offers a basically utilitarian ethic, linked to an account of the imagination just as egotistically projective as that of Hobbes, but on a more Stoic and less individualistic foundation, namely, prereflexive sympathy. The latter by no means substitutes for a "hidden hand" coordinating our diverse passions, since immanent nature still plays this divine role. Nor is Hume's sympathy an *architectonic virtue* like Christian charity. It provides a foundation but not the capstone, since beyond the sympathetic base it is a matter of a utilitarian calculus. And the virtue of benevolence which sympathy grounds is not architectonic either. For Christianity, charity must suffuse all political ruling, all economic distribution, as well as all private activity. For Hume as for Adam Smith, however, our sympathy for the distressed is a weaker emotion than our sympathy for those unjustly treated; our sympathetic fear confronted by those punished by the law; and our sympathetic admiration for the lives of the wealthy. Hence society is built mainly upon justice and accumulation—not upon benevolence. This is confined to the margins. Benevolence—as marginal, as unilateral, or as non-festive—is a *fake substitute* for charity. This is why I argue that the space of charity was abolished.

In the case of Hazlitt, certainly sympathy is wholly taken up into the imagination. But the latter is now purely projective, though in an idealist ("Fichtean") and not utilitarian mode. The imagination does not reach to the new, since we do not just reconstruct the sensorily given, but imagine our own future, re-imagine our own past, and so forth. However, imagination has now so overtaken sympathy altogether that the imagination of the lives of others is itself simply an enlarging of our own inner identity. Here, then, we have another immanent and secular alternative. But like the utilitarian one, the price of secularity is obliteration of the other: she can only be taken account of in so far as her needs correspond to those which my own subjectivity can comprehend. This contrasts with a theological approach that can allow for appropriate communion with an other whose concerns remain somewhat mysterious to me, since both her and my own subjectivity, and the interaction between them, are seen as but a remote approximation to the life of the Trinity. One can find such an approach in the mature Coleridge, who thereby genuinely fuses sympathy and imagination and sees their operation at once as empirical and yet as "idealistically" exploratory of the mind of God.[13] Coleridge, not Butler, Hume or Hazlitt, resumes the British-Irish Platonic tradition (which is significantly other to the German idealistic one).

It is true that, in Hazlitt's case (as in that of the early empiricist Coleridge), sympathy could help to fuel social radicalism. But it is then only a starting point. To say that the causes of poverty must be eradicated requires a sense of distributive justice and of appropriate teleology which sympathy alone cannot provide. More usually, when the treatment of poverty was foundationally sympathetic, it was also merely reactive, immediate, and remedial. This is the conservatism of benevolence compared with the radicalism of charity.

---

13. On Hazlitt and sympathy, see Natarajan, *Hazlitt and the Reach of Sense*. On Coleridge and sympathy, see chapter 1 in this volume.

Contemplation, Production, and Exchange

Jennifer Herdt also upbraids me for confining *poesis* to the esthetic realm. Again this is quite contrary to my intention. What I wish to promote is rather all *techne* as *poesis*. Just as, in every act of charity, there should be a surplus of festive gratuity that alone renders the act charitable, so, similarly, in every historical making there should be a surplus of the decorative that exceeds the technical and establishes the poetic. Otherwise, the very "madeness" of the artifact is suppressed in favor of its usefulness for reinforcing a merely given natural end—such as speed, or reach of eyesight.

David Craig echoes this critique somewhat in his comments on my reading of Ruskin. In general, he comprehends this well, and even usefully extends my analysis. But something in him holds him back from both Ruskin's vision and my version of this vision.

Craig, like Herdt, is troubled that my vision is too esthetic, though he allows fully that it is also a social vision. According to him, even Ruskin did not go this far: he allowed that there was an inherent agonism to the money economy. This is not, however, true: for Ruskin the prevalence of just prices and wages can ensure that the formal mechanism of money subserves justice. And even if we cannot, for Ruskin, ever repay "the debt" of labor, this does not—given his vision of the possibility of universal dignified work—imply that work is an undergone violence. Although the debt persists, it appropriately meets with the counter-gift of provision for the worker.

In addition, Craig claims that I ignore the dominance of *theoria* over *poesis* in Ruskin. Yet I do in fact mention that Ruskin's revision of social virtue is twofold and doubly revolutionary. In the first place, Ruskin insists that all labor be treated as a site of virtue—with its own internally generated and collectively recognized standards of operation. All work is now for him noble, precisely because he fully grasps that all cultural knowledge and political practice is mediated by *fabrication*: of churches, roads, bridges, houses, etc. His somewhat "Masonic" (and of course *theurgic* sounding vision) extends also to religion: liturgy is only possible through the human shaping of stones, sounds, and gestures. As Michael Wheeler has well demonstrated, it was this insight that accounted for his "deconversion" from evangelical Christianity in midcareer.[14] A deconversion not to agnosticism, but to a mode of Catholicism for which Ruskin

14. See Wheeler, *Ruskin's God*.

(like Charles Péguy and Simone Weil later) saw no clearly adequate institutional embodiment in his own era.

But in the second place, Ruskin wished to see *theoria* as *more* than a theoretical (intellectual) virtue. His grasp of the practical imperative of *theoria* renders him the most important ecological thinker of all time. Again his insight concerns something simple yet overlooked: unless esthetic estimation enters into all our regards upon nature, upon human products, and upon each other, all ethical practice will vanish, because only utility, subject to base calculation by the self-interested will (individual or collective), can then remain. One might say that this extends the legacy of Shaftesbury's estheticized ethics—but Ruskin's insight only became obvious in the midst of the mid-Victorian degradation of taste in all fields: landscapes, interiors, clothes.

So Ruskin does indeed speak of given natural value. But we have to *discern* this—and without detailed rules, even though one can, he thinks, distinguish a steady "typical" beauty which reflects the eternal divine attributes, from a "vital" beauty which more exhibits God's specific creativity in a given instance. In the case of nature, we must discern the value—at once esthetic and moral, at once decorative and fitting to proper human purposes—of the divine work of art. But equally, in the case of human works of art, we must exercise the same discernment and purchase and use only the intrinsically valuable. Even though we are dealing here with new arrivals in time, shaped by human hands, nevertheless an intrinsic nature—good or bad—is apparent to our view. Equally, the original shaping of these things must be guided by such discernment—and here it seems a reasonable gloss on Ruskin to say that *poesis* discerns within the very process of making, since it does not discern something simply pregiven. It is guided by the very end that is imagined (inadequately) only through the poetic act itself. Indeed, when Ruskin says that value is the "use of the valuable by the valiant," something like the coming-together of the theoretical with poetic discernment seems to be intended. We must respect the natures intrinsic in things (natural or artificial) but to do so we must also actively and rightly deploy our own capacities (as artisans, consumers, politicians, economists, fighters).

Craig also thinks that I overlook and would disapprove of Ruskin's belief in some measure of state activism—for example, with respect to pensions, care of children, job training, education, and public museums and trusts. To the contrary, I have often indicated my support of such things.

Like Ruskin, certainly, I do not see state activism as the prime means to bring about a socialist condition, but rather local-scale agreements among producers and between them and consumers. Yet like Ruskin again, I fully recognize that this is only possible within a wider institutional framework (including public banks, price and wage regulating bodies, intertrade councils, etc.) culminating in the state, which should appropriately have oversight in some areas (national transport, e.g.) and a role in others (like education and providing of an ultimate welfare safety net). Ruskin was also one of many nineteenth-century figures who encouraged the growth of national-level trusts and corporations not under government control, yet not subject either to the whims of the market: in Britain the National Trust and the BBC have emerged from this tradition. To me this belongs to the Christianization of the state and subsumption within the *ecclesia*: its rule begins to be pastoral. I am an Anglican, not an Anabaptist!

In other respects, Craig feels that I do not separate myself enough from Ruskin. He does, I think, take my point that without the collective recognition of intrinsic goods, we are left at the mercy of the manipulations of power. Yet, mysteriously, he wishes to build society at the most fundamental level on the possibility that different groups recognize diverse and mutually incompatible goods. The riposte here is obvious: in such a society, at the macro-level, the mere rule of arbitrary power will still apply. Society must not be resigned to this prospect, although such non-resignation does not forbid free discussion, nor the temporary resignation to a certain division of peoples who are unable for the moment to reconcile their diverse values. In reality, no formal code of "rights" ever orders these matters according to an *a priori* blueprint; it is rather a matter for pragmatic negotiation.

Again I am upbraided for not breaking with Ruskin's account of hierarchy. Yet Ruskin advocated no fixed hierarchical social order. Certainly he believed in a hierarchy of values, since he was not a nihilist. Certainly, also, he thought that the distribution of power, property, and money should be somewhat linked to the human possession of values; otherwise people are given scope for harm, not scope for the good. This is a less *utilitarian* version of "to each according to his needs, from each according to his means," which recognizes that "needs" and "means" are not simply material "givens." It is incredible that when one advocates such a thing—the possession of the valuable by the valiant—one is accused of "elitism," etc., whereas the application of such a principle would shatter (and is the only thing which could shatter) the gross because entirely arbitrary hierarchies and inequalities of our current society. People seem not to realize that global society today is the *most* hierarchical and unequal there has ever been.

Then Craig complains that I endorse through silence Ruskin's hierarchy of gender. Here, I am afraid, he is woefully ignorant of the excellent recent feminist work on Ruskin which long ago questioned Kate Millett's favoring of J. S. Mill over Ruskin.[15] *Sesame and Lilies* was well-received by the women's movement in Ruskin's own day and this is not surprising, as it closely reflected the feminist work of Anne Jameson whom Ruskin had met in Venice. Ruskin effectively adopted Jameson's refusal of a utilitarian education for women, which he, like her, felt would inhibit the spontaneous sympathetic and imaginative strengths of the female mind as especially exemplified in Shakespeare's heroines (they both noted that Shakespeare has no real heroes). Ruskin's fear in "Of Queen's Gardens" that formal education in specifically *evangelical theology* will corrupt women's natural spiritual instincts is cousin to this sentiment. And if Ruskin notoriously thought men should exercise military, productive, and architectonic virtues, while women should exercise more economic and political ("ruling") virtues, Jameson had already (more conservatively) said that men should "govern, sustain and defend," while women should "cherish, regulate and purify."

In either case, the stress on women as naturally best at exercising social, economic, and distributive virtues was not conservative but radical, especially in the nineteenth-century context. For the idea was that the domestic, distributive, and "exchangist" needed to play a far greater *public* role than hitherto, as compared with the productive and directing.

In modern terms, both thinkers are recognizing (what many parents know) that male humans operate more in person–thing terms and female humans in person–person terms. Moreover, *Ruskin* clearly saw himself as exercising a *womanly* role—as weaving a kind of patchwork of disparate ideas and tasks together, indeed as one made a eunuch for the sake of the kingdom of heaven. As the poet Geoffrey Hill so memorably puts it: "Ruskin's wedded incapacity, for which he has been scourged many times with derision, does not render his vision blind or his suffering impotent. Fellow-laboring master-servant of *Fors Clavigera*, to us he appears some

15. Peterson, "The Feminist Origin of Of Queens' Gardens"; Birch, "Ruskin's Womanly Mind."

half-fabulous field-ditcher who prized up, from a stone-wedged hedge-root, the lost amazing crown."[16]

For Ruskin, the symbol of Athena (and behind her the Egyptian goddess of wisdom) was a weaver's shuttle. Proportionate exchange between people was for him perhaps the most *supreme* wisdom; hence we must add a third discovery to ethical *theoria* and generalized *poesis*: long before Bataille, Ruskin envisaged a generalized *exchange* or economy. And this he associated with a new handing over of more social power to women.

In this context, the question of legal rights and professional education for women (as supported by Mill) seemed to Ruskin distracting and irrelevant. No doubt he was wrong about this. However, contemporary feminists rightly tend now to see that Ruskin's vision of women in relation to society and education was at once more eccentric and more drastically critical of patriarchy than that of Mill. Moreover, his practice with regard to female education was more radical than that indicated in "Of Queens Gardens." Perhaps modern college professors need to hesitate before priggishly finding fault with the "attitude to gender" of a Victorian man who helped to bring about the foundation of Whitelands College for women in south London, in addition to girls' schools in Cork and Cheshire.

Finally, the idea that Ruskin associated sacrifice and charity with women, especially, is untrue. The former association he roundly repudiates in *The Ethics of the Dust*. "Old Lecturer" to young Violet: "The self-sacrifice of a human being is not a lovely thing Violet. It is often a necessary and a noble thing, but no form nor degree of suicide can be lovely." Nietzsche could not have bettered this, but would scarcely have thundered out the sequel: "I hope you will never marry anybody, Violet, who expects you to make him happy in that way. Men help each other by their joy not their sorrow. They are not intended to stay themselves for each other, but to strengthen themselves for each other."

As for charity, *Fors Clavigera*, is unambiguous and ungendered: "we dark-red communists . . . exist only in giving."[17] I suppose that is the real rub for certain heirs of a landowners' revolution.

16. Hill, *Triumph of Love*, 80. This canto, like *Theology and Social Theory*, links Ruskin with Augustine's *Civitas Dei*.

17. Ruskin, "Fors Clavigera," 283–86.

The Logic of Persuasion

I have provided in this response some examples of my interlinked meta-narrative and ontology. Yet Michalson legitimately asks, why do I see them as merely persuasive and not apodeictic?

The answer is that they are not "merely" persuasive. I do not, however, need "criteria" for persuasion, else it would not be truth that persuades. Since truth is also the good and good is also peace and harmony, it is the latter which persuades. Whom would they not persuade? If people are not so persuaded, then speech (the *logos*) falls silent.

But, my critics will protest, here it is a matter of being persuaded *of their ultimate reality*. And do I not seem always to say that one may equally opt for the ultimacy of the agonistic—either in a resigned or a perversely celebratory tone?

Here I feel I can now go a little bit further. To opt for truth and peace is also to opt *for reason*—for the ultimate reality of reason. If peace is the ultimate reality, then reason sinks roots into being; it goes all the way down. Reason then allows that the world we inhabit is to a degree real (the most degree possible for the finite) since it shares in the real-of-itself. It reveals that all the actuality of this world and all its potentialities (passive and active) are given "to be" by an infinite actuality of "to be." And this provides a genuine ontological difference between what "is" of itself and what merely exists as granted a contingent being from this ultimate source.

Since reason goes all the way down in this way, our reasoning is not epiphenomenal—any more and by the same token that our moral and esthetic sense is epiphenomenal.[18]

However, if the world is not created and all is really war—for a human understanding—then the appearance of reason is not sacred. Here reason itself has opted for the ultimate reality of unreason or non-meaning, as any rigorous nihilist will openly tell you. If all has no source, all springs from nothing. This means that the actual and the possible spring from a prior possible which "is not." But an "is not" is not "there" and can activate nothing—as far as any reason (that we know of) can conceive. Moreover, if the appearances we know arise from nothing, then they are themselves "really" nothing. They are nothing as appearances since they conceal the nothing that is their real substance. Yet the nothing only shows itself, only

18. My remark here should be taken as qualifying but not denying my treatment of reason in chapter 8.

"is" in the appearances. So reality is a shuttle (not that of Athena's loom) between one hidden illusion and one surface illusion.[19] One cannot stay for a moment in either sphere, since each is equally *irrational*. On this atheist (nihilistic always) account, reason is just as much an epiphenomenal illusion as the moral or the esthetic sense. Moreover, the ontological difference is here only acknowledged in a crippled sense that must invoke a meaningless "pre-ontological." The arrival of being in the flux of time is still surely ontic: being is only ontological as the source of both temporal flow and temporal presence. Yet on the nihilistic view, being as source "is not," is nullity. Hence the manifest reality that there is "being as such" (not just this thing or that) is here evaded and actually deemed an illusion.

Can reason rationally opt for a position that recognizes its own ultimately illusory character? Perhaps. . . . Theologically this means that one denies the ontological "spirit" (Origen's *pneuma*) of reason. Between the ultimate ontological truth of reason and unreason, only persuasion can choose. But only the persuasion to the ultimate truth of reason is rational . . . all the way down.

So the historical lure of love is also the permanent witness of the understanding.

---

19. C. Cunningham, *Genealogy of Nihilism*. See Hart, "Offering of Names."

PART IV

Political Theology Today

10

SOVEREIGNTY, EMPIRE, CAPITAL, AND TERROR

Concerning the immediate aftermath of the events of September 11, 2001, the initial question one should ask is exactly why there was outrage on such a gigantic scale? After all, however shocking this event may have been, it was only a terrorist attack carried out by a few individuals, unusual only in the extent of the physical damage inflicted, and the number of innocent lives that were lost. So why this unprecedented outrage? There may be two answers here.

The first answer is the threat to sovereign power that was involved. It is, after all, sovereign power that is supposed to have the right over life and death, whether in Islam or in the West. The sovereign state can execute people. It can pass laws that increase the lives of some and decrease the lives of others. It can fight wars. It can impose sanctions that kill. Individuals who take upon themselves this right of life and death are considered to be criminals. But to kill on this scale throws everything into confusion. Was this a crime? No, it seems, because killing on this scale is something only the state is supposed to be capable of. Was it then an act of war? Well, if so, then we are talking about a different kind of war, because only sovereign states can wage war. It actually seemed to be worse than normal war waged by a state, because it was a threat to the very idea of the state itself, and so to sovereignty itself.

One must here ignore the pieties about the dreadfulness of terrorism. The West and Israel engage in or covertly support many acts of terror all over the globe, and indeed terrorism has only arisen as a tactic of minority resistance in imitation of the new late-nineteenth and twentieth-century deployment of unabashed physical and psychological terror against civilians as a primary instrument of war, in contradiction to all traditional Christian teaching and even practice, up to a certain point. (These horrific new tactics were arguably first taken up during the American Civil War.) The terrorism that was seen in the attack upon the twin towers as being uniquely evil was the terrorism that assumes a power that is supposed to belong to states alone. I am not at all saying that the people who blew up the World Trade Center buildings were anarchists. No, they were perhaps indeed Islamic totalitarians who wished to establish something like an Islamic International (this applies to Al Qaeda; whereas the Egyptian Hamas organization aspires to Islamic nation-state-hood). But their *mode of action threatened* the very idea of the state.

So that is my first answer. But answer two is that there was a hidden glee in the official outrage on the part of at least of some, though certainly not of others. The attack seemed to give an opportunity to do things that some factions in the West had wanted for a long time. An assault on so-called rogue states; a continuous "war" against "terrorists" everywhere; a policing of world markets to ensure that free-market exchange processes are not exploited by the enemies of capitalism. But, above all, the attack provided an opportunity to re-inscribe state sovereignty.

The modern secular state rests on no substantive values. It lacks full legitimacy even of the sort that Saint Paul ascribed to the "powers that be," because it exists mainly to uphold the market system, which is an ordering of a substantively anarchic (and therefore not divinely appointed in Saint Paul's sense) competition between wills to power—the idol of "liberty," which we are supposed to worship. This liberty is dubious, since it is impossible to choose at all unless one is swayed one way or another by an influence: hence a supposedly "pure" free choice will only be a cover for the operation of hidden and uniform influences. People who fondly imagine themselves the subjects of their "own" choices entirely will, in reality, be the most manipulated subjects, and the most incapable of being influenced by goodness and beauty. This is why, in the affluent Anglo-Saxon West today, there is so much pervasively monotonous ugliness and tawdriness that belies its wealth, as well as why there are so many people adopting (literally) the sing-song accent of self-righteous complacency and vacuous uniformity, with its rising lilt of a feigned questioning at the end of every phrase. This intonation implies that any overassertion is an impolite infringement on the freedom of the other, and yet at the same time its merely rhetorical interrogation suggests that the personal preference it conveys is unchallengeable, since it belongs within the total set of formally correct exchange transactions. Pure liberty is pure power—whose other name is evil.

The nation-state itself creams off and piles up this pure power in the name of a people. Every modern state therefore is inherently semi-racist because it proclaims the supreme interest of a discrete populace, defined by legacy as well as territory. This semi-racist holding together of a people requires an exterior—a potential enemy. As Carl Schmitt argued, the occasional emergency of war is crucial for the (one must add, modern) state's legitimacy. But globalization puts the modern state into crisis. There is now the prospect of no more exterior, no more real foes. Sovereign power is consequently threatened. If it remains merely domestic, it will wither away in the face of multiple loyalties. If it exports itself and drives toward a globalized set of interlinked "market states," then it still needs an enemy who is other. Without an external enemy, the enemy must now be internal, lurking everywhere. Without the possibility of the occasional emergency of war, there must be perpetual war against an internal danger. As Jean Baudrillard has said, globalization inevitably evokes its own shadow: the irruptive challenge of suppressed singularity, which when all other resources are lost to it, can still make the symbolic gesture of sacrificial death: suicidal self-sacrifice or the sacrificial murder of others—the two being often combined, as on September 11.[1] A monotonous totality both requires this opposition and tends to provoke its unexpected instance.

Because of its history of expanding frontiers—its internal wars against native Americans, African Americans, British loyalists, Spaniards in the South and West, the dissenting Confederate states, Southern and Central America, dealers in alcohol and drugs, and Communists in the 1950s, the United States had in a sense been long preparing for this new sort of global conflict. As Michael Hardt and Antonio Negri argued in their *Empire*, American neo-Roman imperialism works by a constant subsumption and inclusion of "others," such that difference is apparently welcomed, yet actually subordinated to an unremitting uniformity. This subsumption coincides with an obliteration of the older distinction between colonies as the extra-capitalist sources of "primary accumulation"

1. Baudrillard, "L'Esprit du Terrorisme," 13–18.

and the fully capitalized home markets. Now all comes to be within the unrestricted one world market.

This contrasts with older European imperialism, which held the other at a subordinated distance, permitting its otherness, even while subordinating it for the sake of an exploitation of natural and human resources. And one should I think add to Hardt and Negri that, in the case of Britain and France, there were also certain utopian imperialist schemes that went beyond even this subordination and tended to deploy the peripheries and "savage" to mock the center and "civilized" (see, for example, Rider Haggard's *King Solomon's Mines*). Such nuances are often overlooked in pseudo-left-wing American "postcolonial" discourses, which actually assist the ideology of the American Right by implying the original "innocence" of the United States as a once-colonized nation, and it's natural solidarity with all the colonized. It is also overlooked that British and French imperialism was in part initially instigated by the need to control the activities of freebooters and provide relative protection to the people they were already exploiting.

These collusions and oversights tend to conceal the fact that American neo-colonialism is yet more insidious than the older variety. It does not attend to cultural difference (like, for example, the British law code for India, assisted by the historicist and comparativist work of Henry Maine); it pursues no substantive goals of the political and social good (however deluded the ones of old empire may often have been) and seeks instead both pure economic exploitation and the absolute imposition of American signifiers. Under French and British colonial law, child labor was banned; now within the "American Empire," but of course with total European connivance, it is everywhere rife. One can also note here that in the cases British imperialism was purely economic, it tended also to be more corrupt and oppressive, as in the case of China and the opium trade (see Kazuo Ishiguro's novel *When We Were Orphans*), or the ruthless policy of divide and rule pursued in the Near East, which the United States and the UK now jointly perpetuate.

While Hardt and Negri concede that neoempire in certain ways outdoes old empire in vileness, they still subscribe to a dialectical myth that renders this more nakedly capitalist phase of empire somehow a necessary staging post on the way to socialist utopia. Surely we need instead more sober reflections on the temporary need for some sort of more benignly parentalist assistance for the South from the North? So much of the South is devastated in its internal resources and in any case so bound up with the North that only global solutions enabled by a West newly committed to global equality will be viable. But of course these solutions require a long-term restoration of local initiative and resources, freed from exploitation by globalized capital, industry, and agriculture.

But what we have seen is the very opposite: an attempted fearful extension of American Republican Imperialism, in terms of a logic that is impeccably Machiavellian. The unity of the republic, snatched by fate out of time for the sake of its own negative freedom (and the negative freedom of its citizens insofar as this is maintained through their absolute submission to the republic) can only be secured through constant reunification in the face of a threat to this freedom. Given that the republic is isolationist and has no interest other than its own freedom, it is not able to mediate with the other, even in an old-European hierarchical fashion. Instead, it can only withstand by subsuming and by expanding at least its frontiers of cultural reach. Commentators who have tended to think that Bush was jolted out of isolationism by the catastrophe miss the point that isolation and hysterical expansion are two halves of the American Republican dialectic.

Moreover, the American sense that what is isolated and expanded is unquestionably the *acme* of human political achievement, frozen forever in an ideal constitution, disallows the self-denying ordinances, the sense of temporariness, of passing expediency, and of fearful desire to avoid *hubris* that is expressed, for example, in Kipling's poem "Recessional." American imperialism never supposes that the Captains and the Kings must one day depart.

This is why, in an emergency that tends to release the unspoken truth, there was at first so much apparently insane language concerning "infinite" processes: an infinite war, infinite justice, infinite retribution—sustained in George Bush's terrifying post-September 11 address to Congress. There he declared, for the first time perhaps since Hitler's announcement of the Third Reich, a kind of state of perpetual emergency. He announced a new sort of war without aims or a foreseeable end, often to be fought in secret. Those not with the United States and Britain in the war were declared to be against them and allied with terrorists. This was potentially a license for totalitarianism, and quickly, for the sake of fighting a vague conflict explicitly projected to last almost forever, it became for a time almost unquestionable that basic legal procedures and respect for people's privacy should be suspended.

The existence of a state of emergency was witnessed in the statement by Donald Rumsfeld that non-Afghan Taliban should be "either killed or taken prisoner." This was more or less a license to the Northern Alliance to kill these people like dogs, on the very dubious assumption that they were somehow implicated in the attack on the Twin Towers. Of course even if they had been, the proper response would be to arrest and try them; yet implicit in Rumsfeld's statement was an exceptional suspension of all normal legality: *both* the norms of criminal legality *and* the norms of military legality. Because one is dealing with a threat to sovereignty as such, regular legality no longer applies, since the merely formal, decisionistic basis of law in a state that exists mainly to undergird the market cannot appeal to a natural equity beyond itself. Without the state, there is, for the modern outlook, no political good and evil, and therefore against the enemies of the state, neither morality nor law applies. They are neither warriors for another power (or an internal counterpolitics), whom one must respect as individuals, nor transgressors of the law whom one must respect as malefactors deserving punishment and the instigation of repentance.

No, they have sunk beneath humanity, as Dick Cheney later confirmed. Captured "terrorists" he declared "don't deserve to be treated as criminals. They don't deserve the same guarantees and safeguards that would be used for an American citizen going through the normal judicial process." This exclusionary logic was then impeccably realized in the confinement of Al Qaeda suspects in animal cages exposed to the elements in Guantanamo Bay off Cuba. Such a stark denial of the *imago dei* for "terrorist suspects" tends to expose the concealed racist basis of the usual talk of "human rights." This "universal" notion was originally invoked by the West in order to intervene in the internal affairs of nonwhite countries, from Turkey in the case of the Armenian massacre, onward. But as soon as the white West is threatened, it becomes clear that rights are things that archetypally belong to "American citizens" under "normal," which means local and not at all universal circumstances. This is all a very far cry from Harry Truman in 1945, who insisted, against Churchill's unreflecting proposal to shoot the Nazis in a corner, that "this would not sit easily on the American conscience."

The suspension of all norms of legality was further confirmed by the stipulation that future secret executions of those covertly convicted of terrorism could be watched by the relatives of victims of September 11. Here one was confronted with the purest barbarism: in the past, or in the Islamic present, public executions possess at least the primitive rationale of visible justice and warning, while unwitnessed modern execution exposes a certain proper shame and hesitancy on the part of the state; but *selectively* witnessed executions obliterate the line between punishment and vengeance, since all that matters here is the death of the other power threatening "domestic" power and lives. How is one to interpret this as anything other than a kind of sop to a mass psychopathology?

Such emergency measures were not really being proposed because of the unique character of terrorism, but rather because of the perception of a new threat to sovereignty and capital. Hence the new European anti-terrorist laws, which defined as terroristic any actions intended "to destroy [European] political, economic or social structures" and include "the illicit capture of state or government installations, the means of public transport, infrastructures, public places," appeared designed more to inhibit militants than to catch terrorists. As Alima Boumediene-Thiery put it at the time in *Le Monde*, "Bin Laden and his friends aren't in the habit of walking about without papers with bombs in their pockets; nor of occupying *usines* and banks: they direct them."[2]

So one was confronted with an unspeakably bizarre turn of events, whereby, in a matter of months, one single terroristic assault led to the permanent suspension of ancient Anglo-Saxon liberties, including *habeas corpus*, in both Britain and the United States. How does this shockingly abrupt transformation relate to the idea of a war of civilizations, which had been hovering for some time in the overheated air of American Politics departments?

Within the perspective of Samuel Huntington, who first spoke of this type of war, Islam has been seen as the other, outside the Western legacy and somewhat immune to Western post-Enlightenment values. However, Islam should be thought of as both other and yet not other.

Revived Islamic civilization is in some ways a challenge to the Western secular state, but it is also much more like a rival twin than we care to imagine. Recent scholarship is showing just how Islamic the West itself has been. When the University of Oxford was founded in the late twelfth century, some scholars there took over an essentially Islamic proj-

---

2. Boumediene-Thiery et al., "Europe: vers l'état d'exception?"

ect for the experimental control of nature that was at first to do with op-tics and alchemy. The Cartesian turn to the subject, the idea of knowledge as detached representation of spatialized objects, the exposition of being as univocal, all have their long-term origin in, ironically, the Oriental thought of Avicenna (ibn Sina). To say, as many do, that Islam was only accidentally, and for a time, the bearer of a Mediterranean civilization to which it was essentially alien is quite untrue. Even though philosophy was less easily assimilated within Islam than in Christendom, Avicenna and other philosophers were still concerned with "prophetology," or the nature of inspiration, and this profoundly inflected their rendering of Aristotelian and neoplatonic understandings of the soul. In this crucible, protomodern ideas concerning subjectivity were forged and then handed over to the West.

In the year 1277, the Christian West reached its crisis: certain drastic edicts issued by the archbishops of Paris and Canterbury meant that it decided more or less to outlaw the common Hellenistic legacy of Aristotle fused with neoplatonism, and blended with allegorical readings of the Hebrew Bible, which it shared with Islam, Judaism, and Byzantium. A common culture of mystical philosophy and theology, focused around analogy and ontological participation—which has also tended to favor social participation—was rendered impossible. The West and Islam part-ed along fideistic lines, since Islam, too, inclined in this period to outlaw this perspective. Islam became a doctrinally orthodox, scriptural, and legalistic civilization to the exclusion of dialectics and mystical theology (apart from newly enhanced mystical Shi'ite and Sufistic tendencies).

The conventional view is that, from that point forward, the West became secular and Islam became theocratic. But that seems to me to be a half-truth. In fact, by abandoning the shared mystical outlook, Western Christian theology started to look more and more itself like Islamic or-thodoxy; it started to read the Bible more like the Quran, allowing only the literal meaning and construing that meaning more narrowly than it had. The new stress, in the fourteenth century, that only God's will makes things true and right, echoed earlier Islamic *Kalam* theology and some of the ideas of Al-Ghazali. The West's attitude toward evil, with ironi-cally the Cathars safely defeated, started to become more Manichean, again taking over the unfortunate Iranian contamination of Islam by the primordial Zoroastrian tradition. But, above all, in the political domain (as Pope Benedict has indicated), the Sunni linking of the absolute will of the Caliph with the will of Allah, and with the right to fight holy wars, was taken over by Christian thought. As earlier in Islam, so now also in the West, a merely *de facto* grounding of state sovereignty in absolute right to do what it likes is linked to its mediation of the will of God. Thus the early Western nation-state started to fight holy wars within Christendom itself. Modern Islam and Christianity are not after all so dissimilar in certain ways.

What I am wanting to suggest here is that theocratic notions of sovereignty are not simply something archaic within Islam that stands over against our Western modernity. In many ways theocratic notions are specifically modern in their positivity and formality (as Carl Schmitt explained). Bush in a crisis has appealed to the supposed divine destiny of America, and it is modern Judaism that has lapsed into a statist, Zionist form.

In recent years a terrible symbiosis has arisen between Zionism and the American Protestant and un-Christian literalistic reading of the Old Testament in the Puritan tradition, which equates Anglo-Saxondom with Israel. Both ascribe to an idolatrously non-typological and non-eschatological reading of God's "free election of Israel," as if really and truly God's "oneness" meant that he arbitrarily prefers one lot of people to another (as opposed to working providentially for a time through one people's advanced insight—as Maimonides rightly understood Jewish election); and as if he really and truly appoints to them, not just for a period, but for all time, one piece of land to the exclusion of others. (Regina Schwartz's *The Curse of Cain*, which tries to distinguish true from idolatrous monotheism in the Hebrew Bible, is relevant here.) There is also an unfortunate tendency within contemporary theology to play down the Christian "going beyond the law," a tendency which incoherently and anachronistically seeks a kind of alignment with post-biblical Rabbinic law, as if this somehow had obviously more status for Christianity than Islamic law (even if we may well often find the former to be nearer to Christian charity).

Meanwhile, the Islamic Wahhabi, based in Saudi Arabia, to whom bin Laden and the Al Qaeda belong, are themselves in some ways very modern. They are opposed to all iconic images, all auratic manifestations of religion; they are urban, middle-class, fanatically puritanical. They are prepared in practice to compromise the Islamic tradition insofar as it stands firmly against usury. And they are thoroughly in love with technology. Bin Laden in the desert with his gun is surely an American antihero: perhaps a sectarian first cousin to Joseph Smith. For it is not an accident that the Mormons—that archetypical American sect, according to Harold Bloom—express such explicit kinship with Islam. And the covert kinship and alliance of Bush and Blair with the Saudis—the worst succorers of Islamic terrorism—is the darkest theme of all in this entire story.

But of course the West and Islam have construed the legacy of theocratic sovereignty in very different ways. The West has invented a secular sphere that is neutral and unmystical: the sphere of a pure balance of power whose control is still nevertheless, in the last analysis, divinely sanctioned. Strict Sunni Islam knows only an expression of sacrally-backed absolute sovereignty supplementing non-negotiable *sharia* law. One may not much care for either variant. But on what basis can one decide that an Islamic sacral state, especially if it took a more sophisticated form than that envisaged by the Taliban, is not permissible? In reality our apparent concern for women and others persecuted by these unpleasant people has been fantastically hypocritical: as recently as 1998 the Californian oil giant UNOCAL, with the backing of the United States, was trying to enlist Taliban support in building an oil pipeline through Afghanistan from the former Soviet territories to the north.

The only possible basis for refusing the legitimacy of an Islamic state would be if Islamic men, and especially Islamic women, themselves decided that they no longer wanted such a thing. This decision would amount though to a new construal of Islam, and a redefinition of Islamic community apart from the sanction of coercive law. Islam would then have to proceed in a more Sufistic or else mystical Shi'ite direction. It is certainly not in principle up to the West to decide, although the West must also properly guard its own religious-political legacy against the various modes of Islamic territorial incursion.

As has already been suggested, a perpetual war against terrorism can be seen as an effort to resolve the crisis of state sovereignty in the face of globalization. Since, in a real sense, both the Western and the different Islamic state forms face the same crisis, one can go further and say that both terrorism and counterterrorism, which have become commingled, are attempts to resolve this crisis. To see globalization on one side and anti-globalization on the other (as Baudrillard perhaps tends to do) is too simple.

But there is also another aspect to the crisis of globalization—the economic rather than political. The West had expanded its economic hegemony since the end of the Cold War. Once there was no longer any need to pander to third world regimes in order to counter Soviet influence, the United States, mostly supported by Europe, proceeded to set up economic structures that operated entirely in its own interests, with the result that global inequality has vastly increased as well as environmental damage, which is sometimes the direct result of U.S. intervention. These structures have included the liberalization of markets and the removal of all inhibitions on stock exchange speculation, as well as the scandalous patenting of genetically altered (and thereby probably contaminated) crops, allied to the outlawing of the natural varieties produced, particularly in South America.

But by 2001 hegemonic economic structures showed signs of impending implosion: supply had been outrunning demand; computer technology had been overinvested; Western interests in older manufacturing had been rashly sold off; and domestic shares and economically crucial information had gotten into the hands of people who are potential enemies. The United States and Europe were consequently faced with a need to implement more internal regulation—but also with the specter of having already let things slip beyond their control. We appeared to have reached the moment in history prophesied by Franz Steiner in his essay "On the Civilising Process," when so many forces of danger have been unleashed in a "civilised" society without taboos, that these dangers must be relentlessly policed. Steiner conjectured that this would simply drive the dangers "inwards," so that as humans become more and more subject to terroristic counterterror, the more they will all tend to become pathological, potentially terroristic subjectivities—one thinks here of the dystopian novels of J. G. Ballard.

The assumption prior to this new turn had been that the market and freedom simply line up with Western dominance. Now, however, we saw how a small number of hostile, politically motivated investors can reap devastating effects. September 11 was a kind of chiasmus—a crossing over and reversal. During the 1990s, Western power had became more and more abstracted and virtual in character: dominating the pathetically real and material lives of people in the South. Now, suddenly, the West was reduced to the Paleolithic. We realized that the abstract was still partly stored in two fragile standing totems with less resilience even than neolithic standing stones. This still-fixed capital was simply knocked over. But meanwhile, in the face of the failure of Western information to stop this catastrophe, the terrorists were manipulating information in order to seize the maximum abstract advantage.

Given the sheer convenience of war and military emergency to forces wishing to resolve the twin crises of Western sovereignty and Western capitalism, one has of course to ask to what extent these forces were, subconsciously or consciously, urging war before September 11? This was now a war against terrorism we were told, which had suddenly become a global and immediate threat, though we had not been generally told this before the catastrophe. And in fact there is much evidence that global terrorism had been recently in decline rather than to the contrary. Therefore there is every reason to suspect that the war was not simply a war against terrorism, but also a war against multiple targets, designed to ensure the continued legitimacy of the American state and the global perpetuation of the neocapitalist revolution of the 1980s.

Ever since January 2001 at the very least, crisis had surely been in the air. Bush withdrew from international agreements on ecology, weaponry, debt, and the pursuit of justice—most ironically of all he refused to acknowledge that any American could ever be a war criminal, thereby undercutting the legitimacy of international juridical procedures against someone like bin Laden. Meanwhile, anti-Western politics in Russia in the East had been reemerging, anticapitalism was reasserting itself in Western Europe and under the banner of antiglobalization it was starting to coalesce with resistance movements in the South. Right along the Atlantic seaboard from Britain to Portugal a growing irritation with America in the face of economically disastrous flooding probably linked with global warming was evident, but was scarcely reported in the United States at all. Anti-Americanism in France and Italy was increasing at an alarming rate. In Great Britain the conservative party faced possible extinction and public opinion, moving to the left of Tony Blair, now favored action drastically to reduce corporate greed. More seriously still, the socialist president of Venezuela (and friend of Fidel Castro), Hugo Chavez, had been flexing considerable political muscle in the face of the general failure of neoliberal regimes in his sub-continent. In the face of American and European opposition, he had encouraged the OPEC countries to sustain a middling level of oil prices where market demand would have forced a drop. This, obviously, had implications for Middle Eastern politics and for the U.S. hegemony in that region. For some time now, reliance even on Saudi oil had become dubious.

Suddenly then, American and capitalist hegemony looked surprisingly fragile—although of course this should not be exaggerated. But it must have appeared fragile enough to powerful right-wing think tanks, who are in any case prone to apocalyptic scenarios: a frightening possible convergence of a protesting South America, Islamic nations rich in oil, revivified Russia, and a Europe more wobbly and more prone to anti-U.S. sentiment than at any time since World War II.

Finally, the United States was and is itself a potentially unstable polity. Cultural and political shifts in South America would have ripple effects among Latino populations in the United States; low election turnout reveals a vastly indifferent and often alienated population; an eighteenth-century constitution produces constant stasis and deadlock that cannot deliver normal modern state infrastructures and welfare provisions that form a buffer against dangerous discontents of the underprivileged; the culture wars reveal incompatible accounts of American identity; edgy rival oligarchies do not trust democracy to deliver security, but believe they have to manipulate the outcome of elections (as occurred in November 2000). In the face of this potential hydra, it was clear that the U.S. establishment and the Bush administration were deeply divided and inconsistent. Pure isolationism had been one response, yet it was clear to many that this is a very risky course. Those advocating a more aggressive and interventionist strategy on the assumption that American supreme power must never be challenged (a doctrine initiated by Madeleine Albright) were delivered, by good fortune or otherwise, a supreme present on September 11.

Not only could national security henceforward override democracy without question, but the immediate threat of terror for the moment pulled Europe, Russia, South America, moderate Arab States, and China in line behind the United States. They were enlisted with varying degrees of enthusiasm and begrudgingness behind a military action that would assault all those who resist the sway of the global market, as well as behind police deployments to ensure that the market and flow of information were not themselves used against the market and against this flow. In addition, a new unity of Americans, rich and poor, behind a resurrected patriotism, had been put into place. The fractures lurking ever since November 2000 were for the moment sealed, although any manifest failure of "the war" might cause them to appear again with a vengeance.

At the very center of this strange and multiple conflict stood oil. Detailed and objective analyses by *Le Monde* and many other reliable sources showed that what was initially played out in Afghanistan was not a war against terrorism nor a response to the attack on the Twin Towers, but *le nouveau grand jeu de Kipling*. Multiple interests were trying to seize control of one of the largest pools of natural resources in the world in the former Soviet and largely Islamic territories to the north. There was also an attempt by the Gulf states to reestablish the ancient silk route to China, which would link these states all the way to Islamic Chinese communities; an attempt that the West was clearly anxious to resist. Hence the economico-political stakes were enormous and also deeply confused. I have already mentioned that the United States initially sought to cooperate with the Taliban in building oil pipelines. But they proved to be far too unreliable, especially after the 1998 bombings in Kenya and Tanzania.

It became instead imperative for the United States to lay oil and gas pipelines through a more manipulable Afghanistan. In the face of a rebellious OPEC, the United States badly needed a new pool of tame oil suppliers besides the increasingly edgy Saudis. At the same time, this new North-South resource route would cut through the middle of the potential Islamic East-West trade and political axis as well as inhibiting the American-feared eventual emergence of a Eurasian power-block. The new Afghan wedge indeed initially involved also a new cooperation between the United States and Russia: the naïve British were surprised to discover after the retaking of Kabul that they were not much welcome; and Russian forces were creeping back in. The trade-off for the Russians was, of course, license to pursue their own brutal policies in Chechnya; just as the trade-off for India was a stepping-up of its quarrel with Pakistan.

Oil, therefore, is the clear focus of a crisis that has wider political and economic dimensions of the kind that I have described. As long ago as December 2000, experts in the United States were suggesting that an American-Russian action against bin Laden and the Taliban in Afghanistan was being planned. This war and the "war on terror" in general were not simply in response to September 11. There are also unanswered questions about the somewhat implausible tardiness of the U.S. reaction to the terror strike at every level. However, one does not need to suppose any sort of conspiracy theory for my main theses to stand.

Reactions to September 11 in the U.S. government were admittedly various and variously motivated. Even George Bush kept on changing his tune as to whether a police or a military response was the more appropriate. Yet one must ask why so universally and immediately the attack was compared to Pearl Harbor, when, after all, it was only a terrorist attack, albeit of an unprecedentedly appalling kind. One man destroying New York with a nuclear bomb would still be a criminal and not a warrior, and one treats all warriors with more respect than criminals. Usually one avoids seeing terrorists as engaged in war, because that is just how they want to be seen, and starting a war is generally their aim. In the annals of terrorism, Al Qaeda has now been uniquely successful: the West has played their game at every turn, including providing the conditions for it to return to its bases in Afghanistan. For as Baudrillard declared, they aim to pose against the regime of formal exchange and technological war without losses the symbolic capital of death for a singular and substantive cause, gambling on the likelihood that, pushed to the limit of questioning, the West must still trade in the capital of death if it is to legitimate itself, which has indeed proved to be the case. Yet, as Baudrillard further contended, the West tends to lose in this exchange: the extermination of innocents with zero loss of combatants on a somewhat arbitrarily chosen stage (Afghanistan and Iraq) cannot really outweigh the suicidal targeting of a supremely significant site. For this reason it must inevitably foster many more potentially self-sacrificial terrorists in the future, and in this way the West is itself sucked down a suicidal path, and led away from formal equilibrium. Thus, while indeed in one respect "the war" is not simply to do with September 11 and is commanded by the West's pursuit of its own economic interests, in another respect its specific mode has been dictated by the need to react symbolically and cathartically in the face of public outrage, and in this respect the terrorists have truly dictated the pace and character of the events of recent years. A balanced analysis must do justice to both the economic and the symbolic aspects, and try to comprehend just how they interact.

In neither aspect, however, is one really talking about the tracking down of evildoers, as we have been led to believe. Supposedly "the war" in Afghanistan was pursued against bin Laden, and yet it does not seem likely that if he were ever caught he would be treated in accord with the Geneva Convention. If terrorism were really the issue, then much the safer thing would be to stick to the discourse of crime and the practice of regular policing and due juridical process. Anything else, as the bitter experience of the French and British shows, only tends to increase the support of terrorist groups and legitimate their operations. The ethical evil of terrorism is that, more than certain modes of conventional warfare, it directly instrumentalizes human life. But as Kenneth Surin and Rowan Williams have pointed out, this means that any response that tends to do the same thing is uniquely ineffective: in losing the ethical high ground, it also tends to lose the strategic high ground.[3] This quickly happened to America in Afghanistan, once it had bombed and killed innocent villagers supposed to be "harboring" terrorists; together with Britain bombed a prisoner of war camp; caused all the major aid agencies to flee Afghanistan for the duration of the conflict; and finally delayed the arrival of humanitarian aid even after the fall of Kabul. Even were those who say that only "massive force" stops terrorism correct (and they are unlikely to be proved right in the long term because of the delayed "blowback" phenomenon), the implication would be that only a permanently terroristic state can stop terrorism—once again wiping out all moral distinctions between the respective parties. Baudrillard rightly pointed out that this levelling effect between crime and punishment is vastly reinforced by the power of filmed images (when they are available), which tend to convey violence and its results rather than the reasons for violence. In this way they assist the human propensity to sustain a spiral of revenge.

The use of cluster bombs, of heavy bombers where there were no hard targets, and the attack on unquestionably non-Taliban places like the village of Gardez quickly showed that one is not even speaking about "collateral damage" here. The real purpose was not to capture bin Laden, nor even to overthrow the Taliban, but rather to exhibit a show of terror intended to cow the entire region for the foreseeable future and bend it and parallel terrains to the Western will. From the war against Spain to capture the Philippines, through Hiroshima and Vietnam and the Gulf conflict, the United States has deployed the terrorizing and murder of civilians (five million dead in the Vietnam conflict in the whole of Southeast Asia), the massacre of disempowered individual combatants, and the use of poisonous or torturing weapons (condemned ever since antiquity by civilized nations) as a primary instrument of military and political policy. Cumulatively, this reveals the relatively genocidal tendency

3. Surin, "September 11th and the Ethics of Violence." Rowan Williams, *Writing in the Dust*, 37.

of specifically Republican imperialism (commencing domestically with the treatment of native Americans—who, in Virginia at least, had been significantly chary about the original break with Britain), and it amounts to an atrocity almost on a level with the Holocaust and the Gulags, raising the suspicion that U.S. and indeed European domestic democracy is a kind of harmless theatrical indulgence for the globally privileged. And this circumstance reveals to us that the trouble is not "totalitarianism" pure and simple, but the emptiness of the secular as such, and its consequent disguised sacralization of violence. There is a desperate need for the United States to reach behind its current Machiavellian, Hobbesian, and Lockean norms for its deeper and more truly radical legacy of Christian (and at times Jewish) associative agrarian and civic republicanism, which has truly to do with just distribution and the inculcation of social virtue. Among much of the American populace, the spirit of this legacy is still extraordinarily and creatively alive, as anyone who has lived in the United States can testify. Yet it is today rarely able to achieve any conscious political articulation.

But was there no true *jus ad bellum* in the case of the Afghan war, if not the Iraq one? But the oft-used analogy here with medieval wars against pirates is not really right. Pirates in the Middle Ages were in many cases treated like criminals, in a period in which war itself was seen as a kind of police action—at least justified war. And because pirates were mostly afloat, they were a kind of isolatable antistate in any case. Terrorists, by contrast, live like criminals in the pores of society, and cannot readily be reached by military means. There cannot be a just war against terrorists, because they are neither a sovereign state, nor do they necessarily represent a true rebel cause that will justify talking about civil war in some sense. Thus it is not surprising that, as the conservative politician Wayland Kennet pointed out in Britain, there was only a "rhetorical declaration of war" in Afghanistan, rendering it an illegal conflict from the point of view of international law.

Were this continuing "war" a war mostly against terrorists it would not be a just one, primarily because it would be a lunatically "disproportionate" action. In any case, not the prime perpetrators (still mostly at large after thousands of deaths and the sowing of the seeds of untold future misery and future terroristic movements) but two sovereign states have been attacked. As I have already said, the idea that Britain or the United States cared about the iniquities of the Taliban is ludicrous: they helped to create them; they have been happy to tolerate the convenient Islamic atrocities of the Saudis; and having totally failed to carry out their own ground war in Afghanistan, they were ready to let the Taliban be displaced by the equally obnoxious Northern Alliance.

One must assume that the powers that be are cynically aware of all this. So one must also assume that the war against terrorism is a cover for other operations and purposes of the kind that I have described, as well as being an unpremeditated symbolic response to an overwhelmingly symbolic event. Indeed, as Rowan Williams pointed out, since terrorism is a now permanently possible form of behavior, the idea of a "war" against it is as absurd as the idea of a "war on drugs."[4]

Unfortunately, the chance for the Western state and the Western market to ensure its continued hegemony in the face of dire symbolic and real threats is also the chance of specifically modern Islamic fanaticism. Bin Laden's following among those who in other circumstances would deplore him has been vastly increased by the recent actions of the West and Israel.

A war against a civilization cannot be won. And Islam could still prove to be more united, less decadent, and more resilient than we imagine. Its potential for concerted action might well be enhanced by the current financial crisis, which may possibly prove catastrophic. So the time has come to abandon our global idolatrous worship of sacralized absolute sovereignty and the formally neutral market, with their empty pursuit of power, in West and East alike.

Both empty secular power and arbitrary theocratic power, in their secret complicity, show us no way forward. Neither enlightenment nor "fundamentalism" can assist us in our new plight. Instead we need to consider again the biblical and Platonic-Aristotelian metaphysical legacy common to Christianity, Judaism, and Islam. We should ponder ways in which this legacy may provide us with a certain area of common vision and practice, including economic practice, while at the same time respecting social and cultural spaces for exercised difference.

Such a common vision would eschew all idolizations of formal power, whether in the case of individual "rights" or of absolute state sovereignty. Instead it would trust that human wisdom can intimate, imperfectly but truly, something of an eternal order of justice: the divine *rapports* of

4. Rowan Williams, *Writing in the Dust*, 37.

Malebranche and Cudworth. A shared overarching global polity would embody this intimation in continuously revisable structures dedicated to promoting the common good insofar as this can be agreed upon. It would also embody this imperfection through the maximum possible dispersal and deflection of human power.

Perhaps then the noble and at times heroic perpetuation of the local and embedded also could be a proffered gift to the whole globe, which would reciprocate with a measured influence and support, instead of an obliterating equivalence. Perhaps then we would cease to sacrifice the substantively particular to the generally vacuous, ensuring that there was no need for the particular to incite in response the suicidal sacrifice of everything, forever.

11

LIBERALITY VERSUS LIBERALISM

The recent history of political theory is strange. The welfare of this world has been wrecked by the ideology of neoliberalism and yet its historic challengers—conservatism and socialism—have been mostly in total disarray. Socialism, in particular, appears to be wrong-footed by the discovery that liberalism and not socialism is the bearer of "modernity" and "progress." If the suspicion then arises that perhaps modernity and progress are themselves by no means on the side of justice, then socialists today characteristically begin to half-realize that their own traditions in their Marxist, Social Democratic, and Fabian forms have been themselves too grounded in modes of thought that celebrate only utility and the sup-posedly "natural" desires, goods, and needs of isolated individuals.

For these reasons, there is no merit whatsoever in the contention of the ageing Left (Habermas, Hobsbaum, etc.) that we have been faced with an abandonment of progress and the enlightenment by a postmodern era. To the contrary, it is clear that what we have experienced is rampant enlighten-ment, after the failure of secular ideologies derived from the nineteenth century—socialism, positivism, romantic nationalism, communism—that sought to some degree to *qualify* enlightenment individualism and formal-ism with organicism, distributive justice, and socio-historical substance.

Instead, in the face of the mismatch I have indicated, we need to take the risk of thinking in an altogether new way that will take up the traditions of socialism less wedded to progress, historical inevitability, materialism, and the state, and put them into debate with conservative anti-capitalist thematics and the traditions of classical and biblical political thought which may allow us to see the inherent restrictions of the parameters of modern social, political, and economic reflection. Our perspective may remain basically a "Left" one, but we need to consider the possibility that only a re-alignment of the Left with more primordial, "classical" modes of thinking will now allow it to criticize currently emerging tyranny.

This should include at its center an openness to religion and to the question of whether a just politics must refer beyond itself to transcendent norms. For this reason, in what follows I have undertaken the experiment of thinking through a Catholic Christian (Roman Catholic, Orthodox, High Anglican) approach to the social sphere in the light of current reality, in the hope that this will have something to offer not just to Christians, but to a degree also to Jews, Muslims, and people of no religious persuasion whatsoever. I do not choose to insult the latter by concealing in any way the religious grounds of what I wish to say, nor my view that a predominantly secular culture will only sustain the neoliberal catastrophe or cause it to mutate (after the credit crunch) into a new form of state-market oligarchy.

The documents of Vatican II, especially *Gaudium et Spes*, appear in retrospect to have been in some ways over-accepting of modern liberal democracy and market economics.[1] This is historically understandable— since the Church needed to move beyond a previous endorsement of reactionary and sometimes absolutist monarchy, and static and hierarchical economic systems linked to unequal landholding.

Today though, we need to recognize that we are in a very different situation. First of all, recent events demonstrate that liberal democracy can itself devolve into a mode of tyranny. One can suggest that this is for a concatenation of reasons. An intrinsic indifference to truth, as opposed to majority opinion, means in practice that the manipulation of opinion will usually carry the day. Then governments tend to discover that the manipulation of fear is more effective than the manipulation of promise, and this is in keeping with the central premises of liberalism which, as Pierre Manent says, are based in Manichean fashion upon the ontological primacy of evil and violence: at the beginning is a threatened individual, piece of property, or racial terrain.[2] This is *not* the same as an Augustinian acknowledgment of original sin, perversity, and frailty—a hopeful doctrine, since it affirms that all-pervasive evil for which we cannot really account (by saying, for example, with Rousseau that it is the fault of private property or social association as such) is yet all the same

---

1. See Rowland, *Culture and the Thomist Tradition*.
2. Manent, *An Intellectual History of Liberalism*.

a contingent intrusion upon reality, which can one day be fully overcome through the lure of the truly desirable which is transcendent goodness (and that itself, in the mode of grace, now aids us). Liberalism instead begins with a disguised naturalization of original sin as original egotism: our own egotism which we seek to nurture, and still more the egotism of the other against which we need protection.

Thus increasingly, a specifically liberal politics (and not, as so many journalists fondly think, its perversion) revolves round a supposed guarding against alien elements: the terrorist, the refugee, the person of another race, the foreigner, the criminal. Populism seems more and more to be an inevitable drift of unqualified liberal democracy. A purported defence of the latter is itself deployed in order to justify the suspending of democratic decision-making and civil liberties. For the reasons just seen, this is not just an extrinsic and reactionary threat to liberal values: to the contrary, it is liberalism itself that tends to cancel those values of liberality (fair trial, right to a defense, assumed innocence, *habeas corpus*, a measure of free speech and free enquiry, good treatment of the convicted) which it has *taken over*, but which as a matter of historical record it did not invent, since they derive rather from Roman and Germanic law transformed by the infusion of the Christian notion of charity—which, in certain dimensions means a generous giving of the benefit of the doubt, as well as succor, even to the accused or wicked. For if the ultimate thing to be respected is simply individual security and freedom of choice (which is not to say that these should not be accorded penultimate respect) then almost any suspensions of normal legality can tend to be legitimated in the name of these values. In the end, liberalism takes this sinister turn when all that it endorses is the free market along with the nation-state as a competitive unit. Government will then tend to become entirely a policing and military function as J. G. Fichte (favorably!) anticipated. For with the decay of all tacit constraints embedded in family, locality, and mediating institutions between the individual and the state, it is inevitable that the operation of economic and civil rules which no individual has any longer any interest in enforcing (since she is socially defined only as a lone chooser and self-seeker) will be ruthlessly and ever-more exhaustively imposed by a state that will become totalitarian in a new mode. Moreover, the obsessive pursuit of security against terror and crime will only ensure that terror and crime become more sophisticated and subtly effective. We have entered a vicious global spiral.

In the face of this neoliberal slide into despotism, Catholic Christianity needs once more to proclaim with the classical tradition it carries—and which tended to predict just such a slide of a "democratic" ethos into sophistic tyranny—that government is properly mixed. Democracy, which is "the rule of the Many," can only function without manipulation of opinion if it is balanced by an "aristocratic" element of the pursuit of truth and virtue for their own sake on the part of some people whose role is legitimate even if they remain only "the Few," although they should ideally be themselves the Many. Democracy equally requires the "monarchic" sense of an architectonic imposition of intrinsic justice by a transcendent "One," however constituted, that is unmoved by either the prejudices of the Few or those of the Many. (One can think here of the legitimate European outlawing of capital punishment, against the wishes of the people or certain activities of the unelected European commissioners in protecting the minority interests of European Atlantic fishermen.) In addition, the Church needs boldly to teach that the only justification for democracy is theological: since the people is potentially the *ecclesia*, and since nature always anticipates grace, truth lies finally dispersed amongst the people (although they need the initial guidance of the virtuous) because the Holy Spirit speaks through the voice of all. *Vox populi, vox Dei* alone legitimates democracy, not the view that the collective will, simply because it represents a lowest common denominator of arbitration, should always prevail.

But to say this is to ask that we subordinate contract to gift. A government may be contractually legitimate as elected and its laws may be legitimate as proceeding from sovereign power, but such arrangements can be formally correct and yet lead to tyranny—as the Nazi example and now the Bush example so clearly show. So beyond this it needs to be supposed that the truth lies with the people somewhat in the way that truth lies in the Church for St Paul: namely that the body of Christ receives from the Holy Spirit—who is life and gift—a life of circulation which is the exchange of gifts. Different people and groups have different talents and insights—these they share for the good of the whole body. The people give their goods to the head of the Church who is Christ; in like manner the people should give their gifts of insight and talent to the sovereign representative who acts in their name.

Inversely the sovereign power must think of itself as distributing gifts—gifts of good governance and ordering, not simply as imposing a fiat in order to expand the utility and productiveness of a nation-state. This is an outrageous notion—for example New Labour's racist view that Britain should only accept "skilled" immigrants and refugees who can increase the gross national product. A government that gives must rather pursue the intrinsic fulfillment of its citizens. To rule in this way means that the subjects of rule can participate in this ruling, can appropriate its task to themselves. To be ruled renders them indeed "subjects" even in the ontological sense, since thereby something is proposed to them that can form their own integrated good if they respond to it. And no one is self-originated.

This means that to be a subject of a "crown" (in an extended sense) is actually a more radical idea than to be a citizen of a republic possessing "natural rights" in the contractualist sense of Rousseau (not necessarily in the ancient Roman sense). For the citizen is a natural individual be-fore the state comes into being and only a citizen as co-composing the state. This means that he is always implicitly threatened by what Giorgio Agamben calls "the state of the exception": if he lapses back into being a natural individual like the denizens of Guantanamo Bay, he now lacks all human dignity.[3] This will only be granted to him as long as the contrac-tual co-composition of the state holds good. Moreover, since in practice individual freedom of choice must always be limited, an appeal to "hu-man rights" as an unassailable norm will always mean in reality a covert allowance of specific freedoms for some and certain converse inhibitions of specific freedom for others for interested reasons of power-politics.

By contrast, if one has what one may metaphorically describe as "constitutional monarchy" (I am not necessarily advocating it in the lit-eral sense) then according to natural law and not just natural right, the sovereign authority is only "subjecting" men because it is obliged to offer them the gift of good coordination of diverse talents and needs. St. Paul desacralized and redefined human rule as only concerned with justice and not with the protection of religious power or a domain—hence no human animal can fall outside a beneficent subjecting (in principle) which is in excess of contract.

For this reason, the Christian principles of polity stand totally op-posed to any idea of the "nation-state" as the ultimate unit and rather favor at once the natural pre-given "region" on the one hand, and the universal human cosmopolis on the other. Likewise they oppose the ma-

3. Agamben, *State of Exception*.

nipulative politics of human rights and propose instead the distribution of specific liberties, offices and duties to certain individuals and groups in certain circumstances according to the discernment of what is specifically desirable and has a tendency to cement human solidarity. Such a principle refuses the dangerous double-tendency of the nation-state now becoming a global superstate-cum-global market. This double tendency is on the one hand to exalt the "rights" of many diverse cultural groupings, an exaltation that ultimately encourages the rise of terrorism rooted in particularism, and on the other hand to limit public norms to empty, abstract ones. Since these alone have to do the business of mediating the unmediably diverse interests of multiple cultural sub-groupings, they enjoy unlimited respect which must encourage the growth of a universal tyranny, since such abstract principles have no grounding save in the maintenance of power and some sort of peaceful order (which is in reality but suspended hostility) for their own sakes. Because they cannot really mediate the diverse interest groups, these will continue to be aggrieved against each other and against the central power, which will never be perceived as conceding to them "enough." Thus postmodern terrorism of the particular and the different feeds off modernist terror of the formally universal and vice-versa. In neither secular otherness nor secular universality now resides any hope.

To the contrary, the only ground for hope lies in the rediscovery of a more positive mode of mediation between regional interests and between the regions and the cosmopolis. Such a mediation involves the sense that differences are not valid as such, but are rather valid in their partial but necessary monadic intuitings of an elusive universal. Conversely, universality cannot be valid as a claimed finished grasp of ultimate principles, but only as a very remote intuition of the shape of a global and cosmic community in which all differences are reconciled and mutually flourish. But such a genuine account of unity and difference only makes sense if it appeals to a ground of their blending that is the true universality beyond the human, toward which we may genuinely journey. Transcendence must here be invoked, and indeed it is clear that only the notion of a Trinitarian God who is eternally relation and eternally the expression of unity in difference provides the adequate thought of a grounding for human association that would point us beyond the current mutual complicity of state terror with anarchic terror.

Such an anticipation of Trinitarian transcendence can only be mediated by a mixed government which includes a monarchic concern with unifying charitable synthesis for the sake of its intrinsic justice and not simply because a majority desire it. This positive feature of "monarchy" does not of course mean that the "monarchic" power should not be elected. To the contrary, it should be regarded as able to give rule because it has first been constituted by the mass donation of varied talents and points of view.

This perspective, however, should encourage us to revisit notions of "corporate" authority that are characteristic of Catholic thought and linked with the principle of subsidiarity. Not all bonding and grouping happens at the central level, and there is not first of all an aggregate of isolated individuals. To the contrary, people forever form micro-social bodies, and governments should treat people not according to formal abstraction but as they are—in regions, metiers, local cultures, religious bodies, etc.

To re-insist on monarchic, aristocratic, and corporate dimensions is in one sense conservative. Yet I remain a socialist of sorts. My case is rather that democracy will collapse into sophistic manipulation, as Plato taught, if it is not balanced by the element of "education in time" which requires a certain constantly self-cancelling hierarchy. The hierarchies of liberalism are in fact absolute spatial hierarchies of fixed power: one can climb up the ladder of power but only to displace someone else. The purpose of control here is simply utility and not the sharing of excellence. By contrast, the genuine spiritual hierarchy (after Dionysius the Areopagite) is a hierarchy that for human spiritual beings is endemic to time: in which pupil may overtake master and yet there should be no jealousy by the hierarch of the potential of the temporarily subordinate, because excellence is intrinsically shareable. Today, especially in Britain, all education is being subordinated to politics and economics. But a Catholic view should teach just the reverse: all politics and economics should be only for the sake of *paideia*.

This means: make time equal to space or even primary. Unqualified democracy has a kind of spatial bias—it supposes that we are all contracting individuals within a sort of eternalized *agora*. But this is to deny *life*—indeed it is part of the culture of death of which Pope John Paul II spoke—for life flows as a perpetual *glissando* through time. Life is not simply democratic, because it is both spontaneously creative and giving:

with the arrived child, something new emerges. We must give to this child nurture, but from the outset the child reverses this hierarchy by revealing his unique creative power of response. No democratic contract can be involved here. Pure democracy tends to deny the sanctity of life, the importance of the child, the procedure beyond mere political participation to old age and death—its "normal" person is rather the freely choosing and contracting autonomous thirty-one-year-old. But *no* human person is forever like this; it is rather only a moment in a coming to be and passing away.

A politics subordinate to education—and so to the various traditions of wisdom, including religious traditions which can alone undertake a real *paideia*—can be truer to life as such, and also will be bound to ask questions about the final end of life. For only if life is deemed to have such a final end can every moment of life in fact be granted value. At this point it is not, after all, that one is straightforwardly advocating the primacy of the temporal dimension over the spatial one. Nor an aristocracy of *paideia* over a democracy of the *agora*. Indeed there can also be a bad modern, liberal mode for the dominance of time over space. For it is actually the case that pure spatialization will *also* tend to subordinate every given spatial form to the process of time leading towards the future. But not the time of gift: rather the empty time of pointless accumulation of a new spatial hoard of "wealth"—a hoarding of capital whose investment in the real is infinitely postponed.[4] By contrast, time can only be the time of gift where time is providing gradually the way to eternity beyond time. From this perspective every formed spatial stage of the way has an aesthetic value in itself and is not subordinate to future production.

Hence pure contractual democracy is spatial and yet in fact it nihilistically evacuates material space in favor of an abstract time always to come and so always perpetually postponed. On the other hand, a mixed government grounded in eternal law sanctifies local spaces in their actual temporality and does not subordinate them to the pure *glissando* of mere process.

So in the face of the crisis of liberal democracy, Catholic Christian thought needs to return to certain older themes of its critique of liberalism, but for radical and not conservative reasons. The "modernity" of liberalism has only delivered mass poverty, inequality, erosion of freely

4. See Guardiola-Rivera, *Being Against the World*.

associating bodies beneath the level of the state and ecological dereliction of the earth—and now, without the compensating threat of communism, it has abolished the rights and dignity of the worker, ensured that women are workplace as well as domestic and erotic slaves, undermined working-class family structure, and finally started to remove the ancient rights of the individual which long precede the creed of liberalism itself (such as *habeas corpus* in Anglo-Saxon law) and are grounded in the dignity of the person rather than the "self-ownership" of autonomous liberal man (sic).

The only creed which tried to challenge this multiple impoverishment—communism—did so only in the name of the subordination of all to the future productivity of the nation (in practice also to the oligarchic power of a few technocrats), and ignored people's need's for an aesthetic and religious relationship to each other and to nature. What must rather challenge liberalism is a truer "liberality" in the literal sense of a creed of generosity which would suppose, indeed, that societies are more fundamentally bound together by mutual generosity than by contract—this being a thesis anciently investigated by Seneca in his *De Beneficiis* and in modernity again reinstated by Marcel Mauss.

This is not, of course, to deny that merely "liberal" measures of contract are not ceaselessly necessary to safeguard against the worst tyrannies, nor that we do not often have to resort to them in *lieu* of more substantive linkages. For these reasons I am *not* seeking to push a liberal approach altogether off the political agenda. Instead, the argument is that contract can never be the thing that fundamentally brings people together in the first place, nor can it represent the highest ideal of a true distributative justice. So before contract, since it is more socially real, lies the gift, and ahead of contract, since it is more socially ideal, lies, once again, the gift.

But considerations about gift are relevant also to a second context for contemporary social reflection. This concerns the economic realm. Recently, at least up till late 2008, we have lived under the tyranny of an unrestricted capitalist market. We have abandoned the Marxist view that this market must inevitably collapse and evolve into socialism. So we have thereby bid *adieu* to immanent, secular, historicist hope. But we have also largely abandoned the social democratic idea that the capitalist market can be mitigated. Here a Marxist analysis still largely holds good: social democracy was in the capitalistic interest for a phase which required a Keynesian promotion of demand; but it was abandoned when the excessive demands of labor, together with economic competition between nation-states ensured that the generation of profits became problematic. It is nonetheless true that neoliberalism has scarcely solved the problems of relatively slow Western productive growth since the 1950s, and now it faces its own crisis of excessive capital build-up, unable to realize itself in investment and real assets and so transferred to the funding of debts that have now become unpayable. What we now face is the likelihood of a new round of doubtless different Keynesianism, which may this time threaten a new market-state totalitarianism.

Here again, Catholic social thought needs to remain true to its own genius which has always insisted that solutions do not lie either in the purely capitalist market nor with the centralized state. There is in fact no "pure" capitalism, only degrees of this mode of production and exchange, even though one should still aspire eventually to go beyond the capitalist system. Small-scale local capitalist economies are only in truth semi-capitalist, because they often exhibit a competition for excellence, but not a mutually-abolishing drive of companies towards monopoly (as was rightly argued by Fernand Braudel). This is because, in such cases, for example in parts of North Italy and of Germany, a certain local culture of design-excellence ensures that there is *no* pursuit of production *only* to make money, nor any exchange of commodities *only* determined by supply and demand and not also by a shared recognition of quality—such that supply and demand plus the accumulation of capital for the future and offering of loans at interest for reasonable social benefit are themselves involved in an exchange in what is taken to be inherent value and not just formal, market-determined value. (This is not at all to deny that there will be always be a never foreclosed *debate* as to what constitutes intrinsic value.)

Given such a consideration, one can see that an element of "gift-exchange" can remain even within the modern market economy. Producers of well-designed things do not just contract with consumers. The latter give them effectively counter-gifts of sustenance in return for the gifts of intrinsically good things, even though this is mediated by money.

From this example one can suggest that more of the economy could be like this. This requires indeed that one favors local production of locally suitable things linked to local skills. We should import and export only what we have to, or else what truly can only come from elsewhere—for I am not advocating asceticism! Rather the true hedonism of the genuine and its interchange. But if we receive only the exotic from elsewhere, then here, too, there can be a form of gift-exchange in operation. In actual fact, global communications and transport favor this: within a global village those in Europe wishing to receive the good gift of organically-farmed food can in exchange pay a fair price for this which is a counter-gift ensuring that producers should not be exploited. (Nevertheless, one should be on guard against situations where consumers are made to pay excessively in order to compensate for inadequate investment or excessive profit-making on the part of exploiting owners of production.)

It is also likely that Islam and Judaism will be sympathetic to this way of looking at things and in fact the best hope for Europe is the re-emergence, beyond the dominance of a worn-out *Aufklärung*, of a certain religiously informed but shared philosophic culture built around a wisdom tradition that re-awakens the old Western fusion of biblical with neoplatonic (Platonic plus Aristotelian and Stoic elements) tradition. This alone will be able to provide ontological grounds for the possibility of a future achievement of social participation that is a real consensus—rather than the liberal semi-suspended warfare of plural co-existence. These adequate grounds concern the affirmation of an ontological participation of the temporal in eternal peace and justice; the "memory" of a pre-fallen and uninterrupted mediation of this eternal peace to time; and finally the hope for an eschatological re-disclosure of this peace here on earth.

Things like the economy of fair-traded food-items may not sound dramatic or decisive and indeed they remain pathetically marginal and often compromised, but nevertheless the extension of such gift-exchange bit by bit is the sure way forward rather than revolution, government action alone, or else capitalistic solutions. Groups linking across the globe can ensure that something is given back to the earth and that genuine goods go into planetary circulation. We need once again to form systematic links between producer and consumer co-operatives and we need to see an emergence of cooperative banking, social credit unions, trade guilds, and voluntary economic courts (perhaps supervised by Church, Islamic, and Jewish bodies) to regulate and adjudicate the interactions between many different modes of cooperative endeavour. Only this will correct the mistake of all our current politics: namely to suppose that the "free market" is a given which should be either extended or inhibited and balanced. For if the upshots of the free market are intrinsically unjust, then "correcting" this through another welfare economy is only a mode of resignation; moreover its task is Sisyphean and periodically doomed to go under with every economic downturn.

Instead, we need a different sort of market: a re-subordination of money transaction to a new mode of universal gift-exchange. This requires that in every economic exchange of labor or commodity there is always a negotiation of ethical value at issue. Indeed, economic value should only be ethical value, while inversely ethical value should be seen as emerging from the supply and demand of intrinsic gifts.

For ethical value is not for Christianity just "virtue": rather it is supremely informed by charity and therefore it is the forging of bonds through giving and receiving. Virtue is here ecstasized and therefore its context ceases to be simply, as for Aristotle, political, but rather becomes, as for St. Paul, also economic—the virtue of a new "social" in the middle realm between *polis* and *oikos* that is equally concerned with political just distribution and with domestic care and nurture (the equality of women, which stems from Paul, even though he could not see how far this must go, has profoundly to do with this). St. Paul does not mention *arête*, though he does talk of the person who is *phronimos*. The latter is now more a giver and receiver of gifts than he is the attainer of a certain inner balance between reason and passion (as for Aristotle), as Philippians especially shows. For St. Paul, in speaking of *ecclesia*, proposes a new sort of *polis*, which can counteract and even eventually subsume the Roman empire—as the heirs of Abraham, Moses, and Plato must today subsume the American one. This new *polis*, as Bruno Blumenfeld shows, as with Philo, is at once monarchic, headed by Christ, and drastically democratic in a participatory sense—the people are the body of the King; the King can only act through the people.[5] Since virtue is now newly to do with the wisdom of love, virtue with Christianity gets democratized, and is indeed dispersed amongst the diverse gifts of the body of Christ which, as talents, also need to be constantly exchanged in order to realize the solidarity of the whole. As much later in Christian history (the seventeenth century) Pierre Bérulle suggested (though too much in the sense of Royal absolutism), human kingly rule is entirely Christological, since it echoes the kenotic and deificatory exchange of worshipping and worshipped (the King manifesting in a faint degree the glory of divine rule as such) that is fused in one corpus by the Incarnation.[6]

5. Blumenfeld, *The Political Paul*.

6. See Morgain, *La Théologie Politique de Pierre de Bérulle*.

The latter event creates a new paracosmic reality—a new order somehow embracing both God and the Creation and a new order which abolishes the previous absolute dominance and semi-universality of the law, of *torah, lex*, and *nomos*, and so of all political process as such. The participation of the creation in God through the newly realized cosmic body of Christ ruled by the new order of love is utterly self-abandoning toward the good of the cosmic community of *esse* (as for Aquinas, there is only one divine *esse* in Christ for Bérulle). And it meets all the time with an equivalent divine kenosis: such that God now is—or is also and so is even in himself—simply a sharing of himself with the Creation, and yet this by free gift of love and not by inexorable fate of immanent pantheistic process which would tend always to appropriate the beings of the Creation. No. As created, things exceed both temporal process and fixed form; out of these they constantly weave the exchange of *relation*, and relation persists all the way down, because the created thing is at bottom outside itself as relation to another, namely God who gives it to be. But the God who creates affirms this within himself as generation of the *Logos*, and affirms also the worshipping response of the Creation within himself as the procession of the Holy Spirit.

Yet to this infinite good within the Trinity is added the ecstatic mysterious "extra" of finite dependence and finite worship. God, as both Philo and Bérulle in different eras said, lacks worship of himself, since he does not, as ontological rather than ontic, depend even on himself anymore than he causes himself. Yet in the Incarnation, suggests Bérulle, God ceases to lack even this and in coming to share God's life we are returned by God in Christ always back to specifically finite excellence. The invisible points back to the visible as well as the other way round, as Maximus the Confessor says in his *Mystagogy.*

So with the Incarnation, for all that God, it seems, can receive nothing, it happens that God comes to receive our worship of himself by joining to the personhood of the *Logos* our human worship. Thus in some mysterious way, it is not just that the finite receives unilaterally the infinite, nor that the finite returns to the infinite a unilateral praise. It is now rather true that there is an infinite-finite exchange of gifts—as St. John of the Cross affirmed was the case in his experience of deification. And in this way Christ is now King upon the earth, so that it follows that there should be always also a secular fusion of democratic dispersal with monarchic liberality and objectivity. Indeed this should run almost in the direction of monarchic anarchy, as clearly recommended by Tolkien in the *Lord of the Rings* (no law in the Shire; but the orderly echo of remote kingship). Or perhaps in the spirit of Robin Hood: like other legendary outlaws of the time of King John he had been declared "civilly dead" (*civile mortuus*) outside the law and therefore outside humanity, with the price on his head equivalent to that of the head of a forest-wolf. He had been declared so by a feudal king who tended to reduce his rule to the self-interested formation of contracts, and so was eventually restrained by the counter-contract of the Baronial *Magna Carta* to which he was forced to submit. But Robin Hood in legend appeals to the King in exile (in later re-tellings this becomes John's brother Richard, away on crusade), the King of natural law from whose legal domain no living human being can possibly be excluded. It is this natural law of fair distribution and generous assistance that Robin in the forest seeks to uphold, under the knowledge that its earthly sovereign representative remains in existence and may mysteriously show up at any time.[7]

In order for it to be possible that sovereign authority can exercise such a light touch, there must, however, be a collective interest in a sustainable and stable economy in which each person enjoys what is legitimately his own because it meets some of his basic needs and allows sufficient scope for the exercise and marketing of his talents. Property, as Hilaire Belloc taught, needs therefore to be as widely and equally dispersed as possible, in order to ensure that people have real creative liberty, little interest in greed and a tendency spontaneously to form self-regulating mechanisms of exchange of benefits. Today very few people, even middle class "well-off" people, possess any real property as opposed to a mass of temporary commodities that they have been more or less constrained into buying. For all the neoliberal talk of freedom, it is not an accident that so few are allowed the kind of property that permits one to leave a creative mark in the world. This is above all true of land—but we are made to pay most dearly of all and on almost life-time lease for the very space in which it is possible to sleep, make love, be born, die, prepare food, engage in play and in the arts. We should instead seek a way to provide people as widely as possible with real property, commencing with landed property itself.

As I have just indicated, property that is to do with self-fulfilment rather than accumulation is the foundation for a free giving and receiving

7. See Pollard, *Imagining Robin Hood.*

that begins to compose a wider social household. But here gift-exchange is not just a mode of economy, but also a mode of politics; its spontaneous formation of an ethos and of tacit conventions restricts, without entirely removing, the need for the operation of codified and enforceable law—though this is still somewhat required, especially in order to prevent any breaking of the norms of wide dispersal. Monarchy in some sense, as Belloc like Tolkien taught, enters into the picture here, because mass popular movements along with the centralizing ambitions of the few can—as in fact occurred in the early modern period—tend to subvert the more genuine operation of local participatory democracy that is linked to the dispersal of property, whether in town or countryside. (In the Medieval case, especially in the towns.) Here the function of a somewhat "transcendent" single power should be to secure, uphold, and intervene occasionally in favor of, the subsidiary dispersal of power to its levels of appropriate exercise.

In this way, the function of the rule of "the One" that I am invoking runs against, rather than in support of, the modern doctrinal and practical upholding of an absolute sovereign center, which tends to ensure that even a supposed rule of the Many—"the sovereignty of the people"—is in reality an *over-emphatic* rule of the One.

We have seen that *ecclesia* names a new sort of universal polity, primarily democratic, yet also monarchic, which was invented by Christianity. But just how is this *ecclesia* constituted and how is it supposed to work? For St. Paul it seems to be a kind of universal tribalism of gift-exchange over-against both local polis and universal empire. But how can this be? Gift-exchange is normally of sacred things amongst friends. With relative strangers one needs formal rules of contract to ensure mutual benefit. Things exchanged here get secularized. How can one return to tribalism and exchange gifts with relative strangers? Well, I have already indicated that there may be a virtuous dialectic at work here: the more we become strangers also the more—potentially at least—we become universal neighbors. For when strangeness becomes absolute—as, for example, when Captain Cook encountered the Maoris—then there is no conceptual context for contract and the spontaneous familiarity of gift must once more be resorted to. We cannot today achieve this spontaneous familiarity as isolated individuals, but we can achieve it if across the globe localities and kinship groups still retain identity—as they tend to do, to assert themselves against anonymity—and yet ceaselessly exchange this with other groups: the way for example different folk musics remain themselves and yet constantly borrow from other folk musics.

But there is another and specifically theological point. Christianity renders all objects sacred: everything is a sign of God and of his love. Moreover in Christ this is *shown again,* and he provides the *idiom* for rendering all sacred. Hence there need be no more neutral commodities just as there are no more strangers—not because we are citizens, even of *cosmopolis,* but because we are sons, daughters, and brothers in Adam and now in the new Adam who is Christ. We are literally one kin, as the Middle Ages saw it—one kin both physical and spiritual; one kind under Christ. Thus we live by an exchange of blood, and charity is just this exchanging.

But is it? Is not charity the free one-way gift? But this makes love always sacrifice. But what is sacrifice, the ultimate free one-way gesture of love for? Surely to re-establish exchange. In this way sacrifice by no means escapes an economy, nor should it. And yet in gift-exchange, though there is equivalent return, the same thing does not come back. Something passes never to return at all. And for this reason no counter-gift ever cancels a debt but always inaugurates a new one. In the New Testament one finds both repeated unease (in both the gospels and the epistles) about gift-exchange as something pursued for the power of the benefactor, unlike the grace of God, and yet at the same time a continued insistence that God's grace must be actively received and responded to, and that the mediators of this grace, like St. Paul himself, deserve acknowledgment and support—the tension between these two stresses underlies many tortured passages in his writings.

For this reason the gift is not a straight line, but nor is it a closed circle. Rather it is a spiral or a strange loop. Beyond the law of non-contradiction it is both unilateral and reciprocal. It spirals on and on, and there is no first free gift, because to give to another one must have received at least her presence. Likewise one cannot be grateful without a gesture, which is already a counter-gift.

And when one gives, for that unilateral instance one is a monarch. One stands, as it were, hierarchically above the one who cannot choose what you are going to give to him, say to him, etc. No contractual liberalism can ever bind the oscillating aristocracy of mere conversation. Likewise when one receives, for that instance one is a monarch receiving tribute, even if the roles will be reversed in the next instance. Thus to give, or to receive, is hierarchically and unilaterally to help continue a process that is nonetheless fundamentally democratic and reciprocal. Indeed charity as welfare and justice as equity have always been the prerogative of kings and empires rather than city-states, all the way from Babylon to Elizabethan England. But charity is not just welfare, it is also, as the Middle Ages taught, the festive "between" that binds people, like the state of grace between the beggar who blesses you and you who give your coin to the beggar.

We, today, have totally divided reciprocal market contract from private free giving. And yet the latter remains secretly a contract and the former is also like the crossing of two unilateral gifts whose objects in no way mingle. Our situation therefore has crazy undercurrents that go unrecognized. Giving is, by contrast, only really free and liberal where it respects and helps further to create reciprocal norms. Contract is only really fair where there is a judged equivalence of objects and also a free mutual promotion by donation of the welfare of the exchanging parties.

Judged equivalence of objects. If all objects are sacred then, as for primitives, they possess a kind of animated force. Objects or their equivalents must return to their first owners or primal origins because they have in some sense personality. And this is the ecological dimension of gift-exchange. Humans identify themselves through the production and exchange of things: Marx was right. So inversely things are imbued with the story of human comings and goings. Objects naturally carry memories and tell stories; only commodified ones do not—or they tell shameful tales which they also conceal. In a modest way, even the packet of fair-trade coffee can start again to be a mythical object with personality.

For Catholic Christians, this is as it should be. Every thing is sacramental; everything tells of the glory of Christ, and therefore every economy is part of the economy of salvation and every process of production and exchange prepares the elements of the cosmic Eucharist. This was true for St. Paul: his thought about grace is indissociable from his thought about the human exchange of talents and of material benefits. But the latter can only be a just exchange where there are constantly re-negotiated and agreed upon standards concerning the human common good: of what should be produced and with what standards; of whom should be rewarded and to what degree for the sake of further beneficial action by individuals. "To each according to his needs and from each according to his means" should still be our aim; but outside a completely crass materialism the question is about legitimate and desirable needs and means and the ordering of diverse needs and means. Here the crucial paradox so often ignored by socialists (but not by John Ruskin) is that only where there is an agreed hierarchy of values, sustained by the constantly self-cancelling hierarchy of education, can there actually be an equal sharing (according to a continuous social judgement as to who will most benefit from such and such a gift, etc.) of what is agreed to be valuable. Without such an agreement, sustained through the operation of professional guilds and associations as well as cooperative credit unions and banks, there can only be market mediation of an anarchy of desires—of course ensuring the triumph of a hierarchy of sheer power and the secret commanding of people's desires by manipulation.

For where there is no public recognition of the primacy of absolute good as grounded in something super-human, then democracy becomes impossible, for it is no longer supposed that one should even *search* for the intrinsically desirable. It then follows that people can only find out what they "should" desire, or even about the possible objects of desire, from the very "mass" processes that are supposed to represent only the general desires of the people. Liberal democracy is then doomed to specularity: the represented themselves only represent to themselves the spectacle of representation.

Moreover, a *purely* participatory democracy, without representation, is surely an illusion under any conditions, ancient or modern. For prior to the complex decisions made for itself by the multitude lie always per-suasions by the Few and the many "ones," while the execution of these sovereignly autonomous decisions involves once again heteronomous interventions by the One and the Few, since all cannot attend to the busi-ness of all, for all of the time. If there are no criteria for the legitimate operation of these processes of "aristocratic" and "monarchic" education and mediation, then the covert operation of these processes will corrupt any ventures in democratic participation, which most certainly should be promoted.

Indeed the allowing of the instance of the aristocratic and monarchic moments actually ensures a tempering of any attempted purely represen-tative democracy, because it will tend to balance the element of the pass-ing of the gift of trust to representatives with a return-gift of self-ruling to the people themselves in their diverse regions and smaller groups—a self-ruling exercised directly in terms of an organization of the resources for economic and cultural life, and not primarily through the ballot-box.

For there is simply no truth in the Marxist assumption that, once freed from the shackles of oppression, people will "by reason" choose equality and justice. To the contrary, in the light of a mere reason that is not also vision, *eros*, and faith, people may well choose to prefer the petty triumphs and superiorities of a brutally hierarchic *agon* of power or the sheer excitement of a social spectacle in which they may potentially be exhibited in triumph. This is exactly why the vast numbers of the American poor are not waiting to rise up in revolt.

For the same reason, "pure" democracy would be a *mise en abyme*: one would have to have endless "primaries" before "primaries" in any electoral process. Instead, in reality, at the end of the line always, someone puts herself forward as a "candidate" (in some sense), someone stands up and says something that no one has voted on or contractually agreed that she should say. Gift always precedes both choice and contract, because no formal pre-arrangements can entirely control the content of what we impose upon others in our words and symbolic actions which inevitably sway them in a certain fashion.

In the United States, part of the problem is that there is a yearning for the madness of pure democracy: thus there is no "monarchic" body that organizes boundaries of voting districts, because this would be considered "undemocratic." In consequence this task is left to the reigning political party and the resultant gerrymandering is seen as just a fact of life. Thereby the lure of the democratic abyss abolishes democracy, whereas some admission of aristocratic and monarchic principles (as in Canada, for example) actually secures the space of the possibility of democracy. Similar considerations apply to the dangerous United States practice of systematically replacing all government officials with party-placemen after every change of the party in power. This encourages a subversion of the democratic process by career interest and the narrow perspectives of the professional technocrat and manipulator over the more genuinely mandarin, wide-ranging interest in objective justice and human benefit of the unelected civil servant. It should finally be insisted, as Michael Lind has pointed out in *Prospect*, that the United States' "division of powers," while it was in part inspired by a genuine Harringtonian desire for mixed government, was from the outset contaminated by Montesquieu's modern simulacrum of this principle: namely a division of powers that would permanently pit richer and poorer, federal and more local, urban and landed social forces against each other in a balanced and eternally sterile *agon* that precisely mirrors the stable conflict of the marketplace.

The same abyss exerts its fascination when the New Labour government—as obliquely indicated by Archbishop Rowan Williams in his Dimbleby lecture—obscures the irreducible moment of non-democratic decision which it should be obliged to take responsibility for, in the name of appeal to "opinion-soundings" and the like which purport to gauge not just what the people want, but more crucially what they will permit a government to get away with. Such apparent sensitivity to public opinion in reality subverts democracy, because it fails to acknowledge that democracy operates through a gift-exchange of *trust* that also exceeds an impossible "absolute" democracy. A government has been trusted to take its *own* decisions on the basis of justice and integrity, precisely because the electorate has previously endorsed its general principles, record, and ethical character. No plebiscitory process of whatever kind can displace this "monarchic" need for self-grounded decision taken "under God," for the reason that the people can never collectively be placed in the exact position that an executive power should occupy: of being (ideally) of the right human type, having enjoyed the right experience, receiving the right information, being able as an individual or small-group mind to arrive at a complex conclusion on the basis of complex reasoning.

In consequence, for a government to pretend not to decide, or not to have to decide, will always be in reality to decide in a disguised way through manipulation of opinion, plus the following of the most debased mass-opinion or of the course that it can most easily get away with. And where a government has no sense that it has a duty to decide for justice and the long-term global and national good that is in excess of democratic norms, then its horizon for decision will be only that of increasing its own power and influence to the degree that this is seen to be compatible with remaining in power, retaining the good-will of its temporarily most powerful allies and procuring a sufficient continued popular assent or being able to ride-out temporary public discontent. One can argue that the over-weaning recent power of the British governmental executive, as manifest especially in the lead-up to the invasion of Iraq, is linked not *just* to its contempt for accountability to the elected sovereign body of Parliament, but also to its evasion of a properly executive responsibility which would be to take decisions and guide Parliament on the basis of intrinsic justice and the most long-term legitimate interests of the people on whose behalf it takes decisions. In the case of Iraq, this included the long-term inevitable British relationship to continental Europe, as opposed to its short-term beneficial links to the United States.

One could of course protest here that the problem was rather Blair's "monarchic" commitment to his own judgment of the overwhelming need to overthrow tyranny, even in the face of mass unpopularity. Yet if there was indeed an element of this then it was essentially delusional, since it had earlier ignored the need to remove other tyrannies when this was less clearly in the perceived U.S. interest and the British interest if it wished to remain in American good graces. Such delusional decisionism appears surely as a kind of bastard version of true "monarchic" leadership and itself as an outgrowth of delusions of grandeur fostered precisely by the notion of leadership as the courtship of mass adulation. At a deeper level the latter, evasively non-monarchical logic was surely still in force: Blair aligned himself by instinct with the further advancement of Western neoliberalism and Western global dominance now undertaken by military means in the face of economic and political adversity. Thus he aligned himself in addition with a political culture that necessarily has to seek legitimacy in terms of popularity—in the old times of the secure nation-state in the mode of material and spectacular increase, in new globalized times of uncertain boundaries in the mode of the warding-off of continual threats to human security. Even if the war in Iraq can appear contradictorily to have increased those threats and so to court *un*popularity, by the very fact that it increases global insecurity in the future it helps to sustain the new currency of political legitimation which is fear. And I have already explained why this currency is the extreme outworking of the principles of liberal democracy, not the classical ones of mixed government.

We need then, in the Europe and the World of the future, a new conception of the economy as a non-zero-sum game that is engaged in for mutual benefit: that is to say, as an exchange of gifts in the sense of both talents and valued objects that blend material benefit with sacramental significance. We need also to encourage a new post-liberal participatory democracy that is enabled by the "aristocratic" process of an education that seeks after the common good and absolute transcendent truth. Finally, we need to see that it is equally enabled by a monarchic principle, which permits a unified power at the limit to intervene in the name of non-codifiable equity—the liberal alternative to this being the brutal exclusion of those, like the inmates of Guantanamo Bay, who escape the nets of codes and are therefore deemed to be sub-human.

Does all this sound fantastic? No, the fantastic is what we have: an economy that destroys life, babies, childhood, adventure, locality, beauty, the exotic, the erotic, people, and the planet itself.

Moreover, if we refuse a profound and subtle theological social carapace, we will not in the future necessarily recover secularity: instead we may witness the effective triumph (in power if not in numbers) of religious fundamentalism and especially Protestant fundamentalism, in cynical alliance with a liberal nihilism. For the formal emptiness of the liberal market and bureaucracy is now apparent to all: its heart will be filled with something, and especially with a neo-Calvinistic creed that justifies this emptiness, because cumulative success in the reckoning to oneself of its void sums is seen as a sign of favor with another eternal world that alone really matters—although that, too, is conceived in terms of preferential absolute success in contrast with absolute failure.

Most, including myself, have hitherto supposed that the religious conflicts in Ireland are an anachronistic echo, in a remote corner of Europe, of ancient European conflicts. But then why have they flared up again so recently (the latter half of the twentieth century) and persisted so long? Is not Ireland somewhat like the United States, where a "belated" avoidance of secular ideologies has turned imperceptibly into a foreshadowing of a time when those ideologies are exhausted? Here again, there is no progressive plot to history. What one has seen in the province of Ulster has often been a conflict between a bigoted, puritanical, and hyper-evangelical neo-Calvinism on the one hand, and a largely reasonable, socially and political-aspiring Catholicism on the other—the murderous fanatics on the "Catholic" side have tended to be so for socio-political rather than religious reasons. Moreover, Government responses to this conflict now seem, in retrospect, like dummy-runs for a global suspension of civil liberties in the name of anti-terrorism.

Certainly not in any straightforward fashion, but nonetheless in a real one, it could be that the Irish conflict is in fact a harbinger of a wider, future, and much more complex and many-faceted new struggle for the soul of Christianity itself—which may yet dictate the future of Europe and even of the world.

12

STALE EXPRESSIONS

The Management-Shaped Church

The man next to you on the London-to-Edinburgh train going north, wired up to his laptop and his mobile simultaneously: issuing instructions about hiring, firing, sidelining, expanding here and reducing here, letting so and so in on the latest developments, leaving so and so out of them, making cautious inquiries concerning new development opportunities, closing down an unprofitable field before it sinks too many resources. Yes, he may well be a systems manager for an information technology firm. Or, he may equally well be a Baptist minister. . . .

What is going on here? Quite simply a new mutation of Protestantism in its mutually constitutive relationship with capitalism. The latter has hitherto depended upon a sharp division between the formally free human subject who can produce and exchange, and the inert commodity-object which is simply to be managed or manipulated. However, the system also depends upon placing many or most human subjects in an uneasy border zone between subjectivity and objectivity. The worker is to be treated as an expendable function; the consumer is treated as a means for the realization of profits and the recycling of resources. The contest of the market is the struggle of individuals to augment their subjectivity and decrease their objectivity. On either side of the struggle profit is generated: the objectivization of some human beings means profit for others; the subjectivization of human beings means an increased capacity for initiative and so for investment. But within the point of transition from one status to the other in either direction resides a purely inter-human *agon* that is not of itself generative of economic value. That person x control person y is functional for the system: whether x controls y or y controls x is a matter of indifference to the system. The system requires an interpersonal struggle to occur, but the oscillations of *dramatis personae* are sterile so far as it is concerned.

There is only one business that can capitalize even this unavoidable point of transitional indifference. It is the trade in souls as perfected by evangelical Christianity.

Here we must first of all grasp the point that the Reformation was from the outset not only reciprocally linked—especially in England—with nascent capitalism, but also with the emergence of absolute state sovereignty. A merely abstract currency, removed entirely from moral and ontological evaluation, requires that there be a single mint, along with a single law, which both comprise a single absolute guarantee of monetary evaluation. In a similar fashion, the Lutheran or the Calvinist God, who no longer acts out of any recognizable love, but rather by force of inscrutable decree (in fulfilment of the general Western Christian tendency to endorse double predestination and to limit the scope of the harrowing of Hell) is the unmediated guarantor of spiritual redemption. He promises to redeem on the last day the pledge of faith in the cross of Christ. This ensures already that the Church is diverted into the channels of business. For if the crucial thing is no longer the gradual inculcation of the *habitus* of charity, as for a genuine Catholic understanding, but rather the nominal imputed status of "being saved," then logically the task of the Church becomes simply one of mission, narrowly understood as the recruitment of ever more souls. Just as God is no longer primarily seen as a giver, but rather as an elector, so also the prime business of human beings becomes not the performance of works of charity, but rather the communication of faith as the offering of a redeemable pledge. Previously, the love of God for us was also our love for him and composed a sort of ontological bond. Likewise, love between human beings was a reciprocal binding together in a harmonious society. Now, however, the love of God is an elective indulgence against the background of his sovereign inscrutable reserve. God, evangelicals still tell us, whether with respect to the creation, redemption, or atonement, is not in any way bound in justice to love or to show mercy—which means of course, quite simply that he is not self-bound to goodness, as the Catholic faith has always understood goodness. Similarly, human love becomes after Luther a gratuitous and unilateral performance, surplus to our ontological or redemptive status and therefore supposedly all the more loving in its very non-necessity. Love is not to be exercised only to the loveable in its various degrees, as according to Augustine's *ordo amoris*. Rather, love is sheer subjective gesture towards anything whatsoever. But this distorts *caritas*: it sunders it from judgment and renders it irresponsible. In the real, primary, responsible social world of binding exchanges, contract now rules: voluntary election and mutual pledge for the sake of mutual interest without the real affectionate binding together of human persons.[1]

None of this was realized all at once. Most of the history of Protestantism is the history of a Pietist reaction that restored some of the spirit of genuine, Catholic Christianity. The same restoration is continued by the Charismatic movement insofar as it allows post-apostolic miracles, so removing one of the doctrinal pillars of the magisterial Reformation.[2] However, modern Protestantism has tended to bifurcate between a Pietist-become-Wesleyan holiness emphasis on moral sanctification on the one hand, and an emotivist Pentecostalist stress that gives a more affective stress to the experience of salvation as such. Of course there are complex mixtures, but the tension holds in general. More recently the latter stress would seem to have become predominant.

With the decline of the Pietist-Methodist impulse, the original logic of Protestant practice is reinforced. The point of Christianity becomes mainly the production of more Christians. God, through an arbitrary mechanism, has redeemed us from his wrath. The news of this redemption must be spread to as many as possible. I have already hinted at the way in which this model of practice echoes and itself reinforces the model of the capitalist market and of absolute state sovereignty. But today, as with the Baptist minister on the train, we see the perfecting of this continuum. Christianity is reduced to a readily graspable product: the promise of a mysterious relationship with Jesus, the absolute authority of a printed book, the reduction of complex doctrine to formulas about atonement, a single punctual act of faith which is like an absolute banknote, redeemable in eternity. The point is that as many people as possible should buy this product—the interrelations, the social practices of these people are more or less beside the point. Likewise the habitats of these people, or

1. See Hénaff, *Le Prix de la Vérité*, 351–80.
2. See Mullin, *Miracles and the Modern Religious Imagination*.

their cultural styles. The same product, since it has a merely formal content—namely imputed justification—can be translated into a thousand different styles and guises. The only *ethos* that it absolutely requires is the *ethos* of hypocrisy, in an ontological sense—like Mr. Slope's smile or the surface of Victor Hugo's morally ambivalent sea in *Les Travailleurs du Mer,* which conceals for a while everything, including the irruption of the monstrous.

If, however, evangelical Christianity tends for logical reasons to operate like a business, this does not yet reach the heart of the contemporary fusion between religion and business practice. This heart lies in the way in which Church as business actually *further perfects* capitalist practice. For it removes the interval of indifference that lies in the transition of person as object to person as subject. The product of the evangelical business is the redeemed soul—its commodity is itself a subject, and here the only business analogy, though it may be a remote one, would be with the slave-trade. However, the redeemed person, unlike the enslaved one, has not in any way surrendered his subjective freedom. No: to the extent that he has become an object he has here remarkably increased this freedom. What we are dealing with then is a horrendous parody of Paul's words about how in Christ we become free although we are slaves. For in the parodic case, the gained soul is free just in the measure that she is seen as the potential source of gaining yet further souls. So there is here realized a kind of gain in efficiency as compared to the ordinary firm: workers who submit are now at once and without pause or struggle also entrepreneurs who can immediately innovate. Moreover, the raw materials of accumulation, being simply people, are much more readily available. Competition between evangelists and churches of course remains, but the transition of this or that specific person from the objective to the subjective pole, since it has now become immediate and seamless, is itself rendered productive of value—both spiritual and economic. In this way a church business can perhaps spread faster than any other.

Perhaps this analysis goes some way towards explaining why the further unleashed free-market capitalism of our time is everywhere accompanied by the revival of evangelical religion. On the one hand, the very inner logic of capitalism is genealogically in part a Protestant one, for reasons which I have tried to indicate and which recent research has tended to confirm in new ways, beyond Weber.[3] The more a purer capitalism tends to emerge, the more that its incipient nihilism of empty formal

---

3. See Hénaff, *Le Prix de la Vérité.*

evaluation can only be disguised through appeal back, once more, to a voluntarist theology. Even liberal Christians are starting now also to make this appeal.[4] On the other hand, as I have just endeavored to show, capitalism can further perfect its own logic through the practice of a trade in souls which in effect fuses the emptiness of the commodity with the emptiness of the supposedly free, non-teleologically-determined subject. The "saved" individual has an infinite abstract redeemable value. Without this religious overlay, the capitalist machine is palpably unjust, nihilistic, and ecologically destructive. One might espouse it out of a kind of perverse *jouissance,* but that is perhaps only an option for a liberal elite. The masses require something more consoling: a world-view in which even market losers are in some sense genuinely market winners, because their salvation literally constitutes a certain social capital. The saved need not despair, not only because they still have Jesus even in the direst straits; but also because this belief can always be cashed-out socially and economically.

Today then, Protestant Christianity may be functional for capitalism. But equally, capitalism is functional for the logic of Protestant Christianity carried to a new extreme. So also is the sovereign state, now already somewhat internationalized. Ever-faster flows of transport and information, ever increased convertibilities of different localities and cultures, ever increased control by an international military-police force, ever-increased deracination, all provide perfect circumstances for evangelizing. The more that the lost are lost, then the more that they can be offered a virtual security, underpinned by the infinite.

What I have been describing in contemporary Protestantism is not, however, all that is going on. So far I have given merely half the story. The other half concerns what one can call "the generalization of the Oxford Movement." It is completely wrong to see the latter as a kind of English aberration or archaism. To the contrary, Newman's initial recognition of post-apostolic ecclesiastical miracles, was, as I have already intimated in this book, part of a crucial development in the history of modern Christianity. Once Hume, Darwin, and biblical criticism had cast further doubt upon the possibility of the miraculous as such, the temptation was to endorse their continued contemporary possibility. This applied as much to Protestantism *en masse* as to nineteenth-century Catholicism.[5] But

4. This becomes explicit for example in the work of Marilyn McCord Adams.
5. See Mullin, *Miracles and the Modern Religious Imagination.*

where the Oxford Movement's further divide with received Protestantism came was with respect to the impact of biblical criticism, which was in reality Pusey's starting point after his youthful sojourn in Germany. Either one endorsed its speculations, or one became suspicious of the entire Protestant quest for an early "pure" Church prior to Catholic corruption. Might not this be the pursuit of a phantom? Why should one assume that the only early Church for which one has any evidence, and which already appears substantively Catholic in practice and outlook (as any Grand Tour east of Dover will readily confirm) was not in itself in continuity with apostolic times and the teachings of Christ himself? In a somewhat similar fashion, an assimilation rather than rejection of evolutionary science required a return to a more Catholic, more metaphysical understanding of the doctrine of creation as the origination of being as such, not specifically temporal existence, and a more metaphysical doctrine of the Fall as a lapse so drastic that it ensured a totally untraceable continuity with ontologically original perfection. And in general, if Darwin and higher criticism had proved the shipwreck of literalism, then the only alternative to a totally fideistic mode of such literalism was to explore once more, again in a more Catholic mode already revived by Romanticism, the symbolic, allegorical, and imagistic mediations of religious truth.

Ever since then, I would submit, specifically *educated* Protestantism has undergone a process of re-Catholicization which has come to a higher valuation of the sacramental, and of the Church as a spiritual society whose purpose is to *be* the body of Christ and not simply to "bring people to the resurrected Jesus," as if this reality could be encountered outside sacramental and ecclesial mediation. One can see this re-Catholicization in diverse ways in Barth, in Bonhoeffer, in Tillich, in H. Richard Niebuhr, besides more obviously in most twentieth-century Anglican theologians. One sees it today in Scandinavian Lutheranism and one sees it overwhelmingly, and in a manner that goes well beyond Barth, in learned American Protestantism—amongst Lutherans, Baptists, Methodists, Nazarenes, Presbyterians, besides Episcopalians. It has become normal in Protestant graduate schools to study Maximus the Confessor, (all of) Augustine, Bonaventure, Aquinas, Cusanus, and John of the Cross in a way that fifty years ago would have seemed extraordinary.

Am I saying, then, that mass and elite Protestantism are going in two different directions? In a way that conclusion is unavoidable. Yet when, for example, Pentecostal Christians in the Third World start to study, one often sees the emergence of the same Catholicizing direction. At the same time, within European Catholicism itself, especially in Italy and France, we are already witnessing a strong lay revival, especially amongst the young. Again, this is notably a highly educated, minority group revival. Yet it shows signs of spreading, at least amongst the middle classes: at mass meetings of lay organisations like *Communione e Liberazione* one is amazed to see huge audiences of ordinary laity and the presence of national media who treat the occasion like a party conference. There has arguably been nothing like this since the widespread impact of Marxism, and there is now some reason to believe that Catholicism will once more take a leading role in shaping the European future—though the big question is, in what way?

All the same, there does seem to be a kind of drastic division between a popular, mainly Protestant mode of Christianity and a more educated, mainly Catholic one. The sentimental temptation is of course to side with the popular. But what we have here is not a genuine folk-expression of faith, but rather something that appeals to passive, deracinated persons, all too liable to become the victims of religious manipulation. In a sense, we have today lost (perhaps quite recently) the possibility for an authentic popular religious voice, rooted in the soil and so in a spontaneous registering of abiding ontological realities.[6] We can no longer make Chesterton's appeal to authentic common-sense, but instead have to struggle back reflectively to some mode of sanity. It has therefore become inevitable, for the time being, that authentic Christianity will more reside amongst what the current Pope has called "creative minorities."

But where, in all this, is the Church of England? I think in a very peculiar and a very dangerous place. At the precise moment when the intellectual heirs of the Oxford movement within Radical Orthodoxy find themselves helping to shape the international theological mood, they also experience a certain marginalization within England. This is because Anglicanism is now dominated by a tense partition or sometimes an uneasy alliance between old liberalism and the new "mass" Protestantism, in

6. For an extended (and wrongly neglected) argument that decisive educated secularization in this country was not whiggishly "inevitable," but has happened quite recently and for contingent reasons that have to do with power struggles and propaganda wars, see Cowling, *Religion and Public Doctrine in Modern England*. For the argument that mass secularization is equally recent and contingent and has decisively to do with the changing roles and attitudes of women, besides the mistaken defeatism of the clergy, see Brown, *Death of Christian Britain*.

a way that perhaps reflects both English anti-intellectualism and the ethos of economic neoliberalism.

So conservative evangelical currents which, in the United States belong mainly to new denominations or to non-episcopal churches, are in England strongly present within the established church itself. They have little interest in this establishment, nor in its inherited parish system, nor in prescribed liturgical worship, all of which they even tend to regard as inimical to the way in which they understand the process of mission.

But their attitudes have often become strenuously blended with those of post-1960s theological liberals who were already given over to a "management" paradigm, because they had become in effect resigned to the mere "managing" of what they perceived to be an inevitable decline—having uncritically accepted the view that secularization is necessarily on the agenda of history. Such liberals had also imbibed the egocentric bias of the 1960s and tended to regard all the physical and social manifestations of the church as unnecessary encumbrances to the true work of self-knowledge and self-realization.

The projects known as "fresh expressions" and "mission-shaped church" are, therefore, the outcome of this evangelical-liberal collusion.[7] For all the protestations, they are a clear conspiracy against the parish. Perfectly viable parishes, especially in the countryside or the semi-countryside, are increasingly deprived of clergy who are seconded to dubious administrative tasks or else to various modes of "alternative ministry" such as "ministry to sportspeople" or "ministry to youth." In all this there lies no new expression of Church, but rather its blasphemous denial. The Church *cannot* be found amongst the merely like-minded, who associate in order to share a particular taste, hobby, or perversion. It can *only* be found where many different peoples possessing many different gifts collaborate in order to produce a divine-human community in one specific location. St. Paul wrote to Galatia and Corinth, not to regiments or to weaving-clubs for widows. He insisted on a unity that emerges from the harmonious blending of differences. Hence the idea that the Church should "plant" itself in various sordid and airless interstices of our contemporary world, instead of calling people to "come to church," is wrong-headed, because the refusal to come out of oneself and *go to* church is simply the refusal of Church *per se*. One can't set up a church in a café

7. Cray, *Mission-Shaped Church*.

amongst a gang of youths who like skateboarding, because all this does is promote skateboarding and dysfunctional escapist maleness, along with that type of private but extra-ecclesial security that is offered by the notion of "being saved." (In reality one gathers, the only participants in these "new" expressions of Church are in any case existing church members.)

The real, universal Church is found always paradoxically in one place, within one circumscribed boundary and in one sacred, consecrated building, for very good theological reasons. We do not, as Chesterton pointed out, choose the whole of reality, even though it is very specific and has its own strange set of rules, and therefore we cannot compare it to anything else that might be better or worse. We simply accept it and therefore love it and try to improve it.[8] But this means that the cosmopolitan attitude of comparison and ceaseless discontent is further from the ontological truth than belonging to one specific place. One's feelings about one's native village are closer to one's feelings about reality as such than one's feelings about European civilization, for example. Hence the accidental givenness of place is exactly what the Church must be primarily associated with. Only in one specific place can one erect a building which, as Maximus the Confessor taught, images at once the cosmos, the human person, and the transition of human history from old to new covenant through to the eschaton.[9] *Only* in such a building can Christian worship be fully realized. And only in such a building can human beings come together simply as human beings, rather than as political, economic, or religious beings. To some degree this importance of sacred place was slightly lost sight of in the West even as far back as the rise of the mendicant orders, especially in the case of Franciscan practice which the Dominicans then imitated. For all the justified importance of their itinerant preaching, it sometimes tended already to encourage a sense of liturgical mobility which played down the role of the entire physical setting for worship and also the diverse contributions made by different clerical and lay participants in favor of a clerical "leading in prayer."[10]

Human beings *cannot* come together as such in the same way even in a mosque or a synagogue. This is because in a church we come together simply in order to join ourselves to perfected humanity which is transformed through the Incarnation as more than humanity and not in the

8. Chesterton, *Orthodoxy*, 103–30.

9. Maximus the Confessor, "Church's Mystagogy," 181–225.

10. See van Dirk and Walker, *Origins of the Modern Roman Liturgy*.

name of any law, custom, or specific tradition. Nor do other religions conceive of a spiritual society like that of the Church which is in principle self-sufficient and all-embracing.

In this manner the logic of parish organization is simply the logic of ecclesiology itself: the way for the Church to include all is to operate the cure of souls in such and such a specific area. It is pure geography that encompasses all without exception. Equally, it is the located place in the sacred place of the buried bones of the martyrs, or even the place of obscure pagan anticipations of the coming of Christ, that extends this embrace back into the mists of historical time and forward into a trusted future.

So the point of the Church is the assembly of humanity as such in order that it might govern itself by love. Once one has this "church" idea, no other basis for human society can be regarded as fully legitimate. Caesar is in a way irrelevant, only to be appeased, until, after Constantine, he has himself derived the more aspiring aspect of his authority from the authority of the gospel. Hence in the European West, terrain first of all was mapped out by the Church. And so we should never imagine that terrain is somehow more secular than it is sacred. To the contrary, terrain, as part of Creation, exceeds the scope of the state but does not exceed the scope of the Church, since this is destined to be coterminous with the redeemed cosmos, as H. J. Massingham rightly argued back in the middle of the previous century.[11] Christianity *is* Christendom, as the older history of the coinciding usage of these words suggests, else it is disincarnate and so not really the religion of the Incarnation at all. And place, ever since the dawn of humanity, as the early twentieth-century Catholic historian Christopher Dawson contended, is first of all sacred place.[12] Hence the most ancient socio-political units of the realm of England are the ecclesiastical parishes. As recently as the eighteenth century it was the parish council that often organized the division and the order of the tasks of ploughing and harvest. Even if parishes have now legally lost their civil administrative status, since the legitimacy of the civil realm is still officially dependent upon the anointing of the monarch, England remains, as a political body, a body within the ecclesiastical body, and the latter body is grounded upon its physical division into parish units. England as a realm is still in theory gathered together only because of the gathering

11. Massingham, *Tree of Life*.
12. Dawson, *Age of the Gods*.

of humanity as such in love, which is the Church. And this universal gathering can, for reasons I have already outlined, only be variously realized in specific places.

People's orientation to the places where they live is supposed to be in decline, according to the exponents of "Fresh Expressions," but there are two responses that can be made to this claim. First of all, it is much exaggerated, because the desire of people to identify with where they live is so innate and so strong. The more people live in far-flung villages, the more they aspire to a kind of postmodern re-creation of village life and rural community which is not artificial, but merely new. Thus the contemporary proliferation of book-clubs, yoga-groups, local history societies, and local rambling associations. Very often, church members are to the fore in these groupings. One can also conclude that, in the postmodern village, people simply associate because they happen to be there and that this lies close to the universal church-idea of which I have spoken. My own observation is that up and down England postmodern villages tend to lead to a revival of parish life, but that a church in hock to rich evangelical suburbs fails to encourage this and ignores its rural heartlands, just as it is increasingly inclined also to ignore the equally rooted (but often precarious and "unprofitable") communities in inner-city areas. The former neglect could be compared to that of a Tory party that had decided to ignore entirely its core countryside vote. It is surely a death-wish, if one wishes to retain the Church in its true Catholic semblance. And I also think that in large measure church attendance in Britain has declined because of sheer clerical half-belief and incompetence. There is a remarkable failure to do the obvious: in cathedral towns, unlike on the continent, colorful festivals are not advertised with big posters in local shops. Fascinating continued practices like beating the bounds are not integrated into local life, nor into tourist schedules. However, there are many signs that this is beginning to change, especially with respect to cathedrals which are correspondingly showing an upsurge in attendance. It is also precisely the relative anonymity and formality of cathedrals, as opposed to the closed in-group of many suburban churches, which encourages outsiders to attend.

The second response is that the dislocation of people is not something that the Church should simply endorse and encourage, even if resistance seems well-nigh impossible. There is no cultural neutrality, and not just any-old organization of human relationships and communications is compatible with the gospel. We are told that young people today inhabit

there own peculiar culture which the Church must endeavour to understand and not try to integrate with adult life. Exactly how the children of
baby-boomers can have found a novel cultural space of yet further alienation and generational rebellion is left curiously unasked. For the reality
is that their more dissipated and listless mode of being alienated is but a
result of earlier generational rebellion gone seriously awry, which has left
Britain with an age-divided society that has no parallel elsewhere—not
even in North America. This state of affairs is quite manifestly *evil*, and
for the Church to propose to underwrite it is little short of incredible.

Clearly networking, associations based merely on shared interest,
contacts in virtual reality, and so forth are not *per se* bad, and may even
lead to good, but they are nonetheless fraught with danger and cannot
be effective substitutes for real, embodied human contact. After all, what
they mainly offer are frustrating substitutes for the latter. They tend to
promote the illusion of endless possibility, rather than the satisfaction
and the true potential of a limited actuality. Hence part of genuine mission would be the struggle *against* networking, not a working with it as if
it were a neutral means.

The alternative encouragement of the local parish favors a good spiritual ecology—a balance and mingling of diverse personal forces, which in
turn encourages a good physical ecology.[13] The more local community
is developed, then the more we can promote beautiful physical environ-
ments, and the sustainable production of all that can be well-produced at
a local level. This sort of ecology and economy then preserves, to come
full circle, the possibility of a genuine personal and local human independence and freedom which is the soil within which the act of free religious
assent is best nurtured.

One irony in all this is that the Church of England is uniquely well
placed to defend the role of the parish today, which ordinary people
most desperately need, and the health of the English polity and the
English countryside, towns, and cities also requires. This is because we
have both married clergy and women priests. Without the latter, parish life in some areas on the continent is threatened for reasons other
than those which apply in this country. Laity sustain parishes in France
in the face of a dire shortage of priests, and even if this tends remarkably
to encourage a more educated and active laity, too often the latter is becoming divided into rival lay movements. I have already spoken of these,

13. See Massingham, *Tree of Life*.

and I think that the Anglican Church indeed needs something akin to movements like *Communio e Liberazione,* which has a genuine charisma and ethos, rather than the new church expressions which I have been denouncing. On the other hand, such movements require a balancing by strong parish life if they are not to degenerate into politicized factions. And I repeat: the irony is that England is much better placed than the continent to sustain parish life focussed round the traditional role of the parish priest.

So the issue here is not one of "ethical management" of ecclesiastical life. It is rather one of sustaining a true Catholic *ethos* against the barbarism of instrumentalizing reason. "Management" cannot be ethicized, since the term denotes merely the meaningless but efficient manipulations which are all that is left to do with things once they have been de-sacramentalized. And it denotes also all that there is left to do with persons, once they have effectively ceased to be regarded as manifesting the image of God and so as bound finally to return to unity with him, along with the rest of living things, and the cosmos itself—since God is not willful decree, but the eternal bond of love.

PART V

Theology and Pluralism

13

THE END OF DIALOGUE

It is a little surprising that all the contributors to the now classic *The Myth of Christian Uniqueness* agreed to write under this rubric. For at various moments in the book, an alternative, more legitimate agenda, which might be entitled "the myth of Western universalism," was struggling to get out. Several of the essays denied that there is any Archimedean point of theoretical reason from which one can objectively survey all religious traditions, or that religions are "about" an ultimate reality specifiable independently of their traditional modes of discourse.[1] This placed their authors at a certain distance from the "pluralist" position of John Hick, Wilfred Cantwell Smith, et al., which was also represented in this volume, and does indeed seek to downgrade the "unique" aspects of particular religions to the status of historically conditioned mythic garbs for timeless experiences of "reality-centeredness" (Hick) or else ultimate "mystery" (Samartha).

However, despite apparent disavowals, *none* of the contributors to this volume had in truth fully distanced themselves from "pluralism" and its undergirding confidence in a timeless *logos* enjoying time-transcending encounters with an unchanging reality. It is only this residual pluralism, I shall argue, which led so many of them to believe that practical (ethical or political) reason can provide a common starting-point for interreligious dialogue that theoretical reason cannot supply.[2] This "solution" (henceforward "the praxis solution") fails to comprehend that "the Enlightenment

1. Hick and Knitter, *Myth of Christian Uniqueness*. See the essays by Kaufman, Gilkey, Panikkar, and Knitter.
2. See the essays by Gilkey, Ruether, Suchocki, Knitter, and Driver.

project," which since Descartes has sought to overcome the supposed prejudices and limitations of "local" reasonings, and to place reason upon a secure and universal foundation, is at least as strongly manifest in political practice, and social and ethical theory, as in epistemological reasoning. This project has tended to disguise two important facts: first, that the characteristic "liberal" values of the modern West are in specific yet complex ways related to its Hellenic-Roman-Christian-Jewish inheritance; second, that they are also related to certain pragmatic necessities and reconfigurations of power, which ensued upon the disintegration of Christendom. Tom Driver in his epilogue[3] confessed that the proposed basis for dialogue in practical reason involves an ascription to modern liberal Western values, but he did not acknowledge the traditional and continuing political substructures which perpetuate these values, a recognition that tends to undermine their claim to universal relevance.

The same recognition exposes to view a stark paradox. The terms of discourse which provide both the favored categories for encounter with other religions—*dialogue, pluralism*, and the like—together with the criteria for the acceptable limits of the pluralist embrace—social justice, liberation, and so forth—were themselves embedded in a wider Western discourse become globally dominant. And the implication of this paradox is evident: the moment of contemporary recognition of other cultures and religions optimistically celebrated by the *The Myth of Christian Uniqueness* is itself—as the rhetoric of its celebration makes apparent—none other than the moment of total obliteration of other cultures by Western norms and categories, with their freight of Christian influence.

Mostly evading this paradox and its implications, none of the contributors to *Myth* went so far as to be suspicious of the very categories of encounter—dialogue, pluralism, and so on—themselves. However, Raimundo Panikkar did appear to reject the circumscribing of dialogue by Western norms of practical reason.[4] Panikkar offered an alternative to the praxis solution in rejecting all modes of universal mediation and instead espousing a plural account of ultimate reality itself. However, I shall argue below that Panikkar's unwise desire to fuse neo-Vedantic pluralism with Christian Trinitarianism exhibits a residual wish to affirm

---

3. Driver's essay in Hick and Knitter, *Myth of Christian Uniqueness*, 207.

4. Panikkar, "The Jordan, the Tiber, and the Ganges," in Hick and Knitter, *Myth of Christian Uniqueness*, 89–116.

such a pluralist ontology independently of any tradition or any time-bound vantage point.

In the subsections which follow I wish first of all to expose to view certain assumptions which reinforce the pluralist ethos, and which were not called into question by *Myth*. I then want to show, in the second place, how it is only these false assumptions that make the praxis solution appear viable. In the third place, I shall argue that yoking the causes of socialism, feminism, anti-racism, and ecologism to the concerns of pluralism, actually tends to curb and confine them, because the discourse of pluralism exerts a rhetorical drag in a so-called liberal direction, which assumes the propriety of the West-inspired nation-state and the West-inspired capitalist economy. This is not, however, to suggest that these causes can come into their own when released from their Western moorings; on the contrary, I shall contend that another bad effect of pluralism is to disguise the truth that even the most radical Western notions of justice and freedom can only be made sense of, and articulated beyond the confines of a liberal, post-Enlightenment perspective, if they are relocated within the context of Western religious traditions. This is particularly true, I shall claim, of the notion of the recognition of the "other" itself, which is so important an imperative to dialogue. Hence, in the fourth place, I shall argue against Panikkar that a postmodern position that respects otherness and locality, and yet at the same time still seeks the goals of justice, peace, and reconciliation, can only, in fact, be a Christian (or possibly a Jewish) position.

Religion Is Not a Genus

Paul Knitter protested that if religions are as diverse as apples and oranges (he meant apples and vacuum cleaners) then it is impossible to understand why they should seek dialogue with each other.[5] This is surely naïve; in the course of history, the major religious traditions have occasionally entered into polemical debate, sometimes even involving a "trial" of their respective claims, but this has usually been occasioned by immediate exigencies of cohabitation, and has assumed only a local common ground between adjacent traditions, as, for example, a common monotheism between Christianity and Judaism. No assumptions about a religious genus,

5. Knitter, "Toward a Liberation Theology of Religions," in Hick and Knitter, *Myth of Christian Uniqueness*, 185.

of which the various traditions are species, was necessarily involved here. Such an assumption, by contrast, certainly undergirds the more recent mode of encounter as dialogue, but it would be a mistake to imagine that it arose simultaneously among all the participants as the recognition of an evident truth. On the contrary, it is clear that the other religions were taken by Christian thinkers to be species of the genus "religion," because these thinkers systematically subsumed alien cultural phenomena under categories that comprise Western notions of what constitutes religious thought and practice. These false categorizations have often been accepted by Western-educated representatives of the other religions themselves, who are unable to resist the politically imbued rhetorical force of Western discourse. To take a few examples: John Hick could speak of "many roads to salvation," yet it is clear that Eastern religions do not on the whole seek deliverance by divine grace from a sinful or merely natural condition;[6] the Hindu practice of *bhakti* is frequently represented as an instance of worship, when in fact it is mainly concerned with a systematic appeasement of, and seeking of favors from, the various deities;[7] Hindu-Buddhist *ahimsa* is often translated as "nonviolence," when it really means something like "selective coercive pressure through refusal";[8] the Eastern religions are often seen as highly mystical and spiritual in character, yet the practices misallocated to these exclusively Christian categories are not concerned with a quest for beatitude or unity with the godhead, but with attainment of power and liberation of/from the self with its accompanying limitations and liabilities.[9]

The usual construals of religion as a genus, therefore, embody covert Christianizations, and in fact no attempt to define such a genus will succeed, because no proposed common features can be found, whether in terms of belief or practice (gods, the supernatural, worship, a sacred community, sacred/secular division, etc.) that are without exceptions. The most viable, because most general, definitions ("what binds a society together," and so forth) turn out to be so all-encompassing as to coincide with the definition of culture as such. Any conception of religion as des-

6. Hick, "The Non-Absoluteness of Christianity," in Hick and Knitter, *Myth of Christian Uniqueness*, 22–23; Surin, Kenneth. "Revelation, Salvation, the Uniqueness of Christ and Other Religions," 136–59.

7. Chaudhuri, *Hinduism*, 90–95.

8. Ibid., 326–28.

9. Ibid., 311–29; Potter, *Presuppositions of India's Philosophies*, 3–15.

ignating a realm within culture, for example, that of spiritual experience, charismatic power, or ideological legitimation, will tend to reflect merely the construction of religion within Western modernity. By contrast, what we are often talking about when we speak of the religious are the basic organizing categories for an entire culture: the images, word-forms, and practices which specify "what there is" for a particular society. The commonness that pertains between the different religions, is, therefore, not the commonness of a genus, or of a particular specified *mode* of human existence; instead it is the commonness of Being, or the fact of cultural— as opposed to natural—existence itself. And there is nothing *necessarily* analogical within this community of cultural Being; instead, Being—both cultural and natural—or "what there is," can get construed in sheerly different and incommensurable ways by the many religions.

It follows that comparative religion should give way to the contrasting of cultures (although the implied ahistoricity and ignoring of shared roots, infractions, and overlaps in this program must be in turn superseded). From such a perspective the entire agenda concerning the "problem," or "the challenge of other religions," simply evaporates. For if we think that we have discovered that there may be other roads to our definitively religious goals, then we are under a profoundly ethnocentric illusion. The whole notion of dialogue is itself bound up with such an illusion, and lies adjacent to the program of comparative religion. For the event of dialogue, since its Socratic beginnings, assumes a commonly recognized subject matter and certain truths that can be agreed about this subject matter by both (or all) participants. Because of this initial common focus, it is expected that one partner will be able to progress to a sympathetic comprehension of the perspective of the other's point of view. However, in Plato, the initial common focus is extra-dialectical-mythical or cultural. In modern dialogue this is lost and so dialogue is hypostasized; it is dialogue itself which, according to Rosemary Radford Ruether, enables us to develop the facility to "enter deeply into two or three" alternative perspectives.[10] The very idea that dialogue is a passage for the delivery of truth, that it has a privileged relationship to Being, now assumes, contrary to Socrates and Plato, that many voices are coalescing around a single known object which is independent of our biographi-

10. Ruether, "Feminism and Jewish-Christian Dialogue: Particularism and Universalism in the Search for Religious Truth," in Hick and Knitter, *Myth of Christian Uniqueness*, 142.

cal or transbiographical processes of coming-to-know. It then follows that the many different biographies (experiences) and traditions can be appropriated by all as angles upon the truth, which are themselves radiations from the truth.

Yet as it is impossible neutrally to specify such a reality independent of biography—the "writing of life"—dialogue obscures the truth-of-difference. One can only regard dialogue partners as equal, independently of one's valuation of what they say, if one is already treating them, and the culture they represent, as valuable mainly in terms of their abstract possession of an autonomous freedom of spiritual outlook and an open commitment to the truth. In other words, if one takes them as liberal, Western subjects, images of oneself.[11]

Here sympathy turns out to be a mode of betrayal. One should beware of sympathy, because too often we sympathize with what we can make to be like ourselves. In this connection it is salutary to read Nirad Chaudhuri's remarks about how sometimes missionaries were more accurate observers of Hinduism than philosophers, questers after "Eastern wisdom," or later Christians no longer seeking to convert, precisely on account of their hostility. They noted correctly that Hinduism is often dominated by this-worldly concerns, that it is thoroughly magical in character, that it finally subordinates ethical practice to the pursuit of independent power, and that it does not necessarily see asceticism as incompatible with worldly pleasure and success. Of course, the missionaries put all these things in pejorative terms (and translated into Western language they are *bound* to sound deplorable), and failed to comprehend, like Schopenhauer and Nietzsche, how Indian religion might actually challenge the "naturalness" of the Western orientation to goodness and unchanging truth and the arguable dubiety of claiming the supremacy of love—a "bestowing" virtue which assumes you have something to bestow—without according an even greater supremacy to the pursuit of power and freedom.[12] Nonetheless, missionary hostility registered a difference often invisible to the glossating gaze of the well-wisher. (And of course, at depth I really agree with the missionaries!)

If today we wish to register again this difference, then we have to understand that it is not something which will be "confessed" to us by

11. See Surin, "A Politics of Speech," 192–212.

12. Chaudhuri, *Hinduism*, 104–18; Nietzsche, *Thus Spoke Zarathustra*, Part 1, "Of the Bestowing Virtue," 99–104.

the living voice of an interlocutor, whose very willingness to speak will probably betray an alienation from the seamless narrative succession of a tradition which never felt the need for dialogical self-justification, but whose words and acts are held valid in their very repetition of previous roles and sequences.[13] Rather, it is we ourselves who have to conjure up this difference, not by listening to the most articulate of the living, but by an attentive reading of "dead" texts pre-dating Western intrusion and practices relatively uncontaminated by Western influence.[14]

As I have argued, the practice of dialogue incorporates the assumption that religion is an area of universal human concern that we can consider, contemplate, and talk about. Because this area is often specified in terms of suprarational belief and personal experience, one tends to assume that the varieties of religion remain pristinely available, whatever the vagaries of political and social processes. However, religions are subject to subtle extinction, since, as the fundamental logic of a culture, their modes of reasoning are as much inscribed in a people's mode of habitual action and social organization, as in their reflective thoughts. If religions concern "what there is," then it is evident that a person's relation to such an imagined ontology will be for the most part practical and nonreflective. It follows that any adequate description of a religion must attend to practice at least as much as to theory. Yet when one focuses on practice, the sheer range of religious divergence tends to stand out more starkly. The religious community may sometimes coincide with the political community (Islam); it may be relatively independent of political associations and of particular social regulations and class divisions (Christianity, Buddhism); it may not even be an essentially unified community in terms of either belief or practice (Hinduism). These contrasts entail incommensurable social projects, whose differences are only mitigated once these projects—and hence the whole original reality of the religions themselves—are heavily subordinated to the universal sway of the liberal state and the capitalist market.

Very little attention was given in *Myth* to the idea that religions can be considered as social projects as well as worldviews. This is particularly apparent in the assumption, which pervades most of these essays (and made the book a successor to *The Myth of God Incarnate*) that Christian

13. Lyotard, *Differend*, 152–56.
14. Halbfass, *Indien und Europa*, 433–38.

uniqueness resides essentially in its Christocentric claims. There are two things wrong with this. First of all, it is apparent that at least as important a site of uniqueness is the ecclesial project itself; no other religious community comprehends itself (in theory) as an international society, independent of political regimes and legal codes, including as equal members (in some sense) men, women, and children, without regard to social class and committed to the realization, within this society, of perfect mutual acceptance and cooperative interaction. Even if this has only applied in theory, the sheer theoretical force of this project has had, historically, an immense "deterritorializing" effect in terms of disturbing existing political, social, and legal barriers, and it is clear that however much the contributors to *Myth* wished to water down their Christology, they still betray some degree of commitment to the singularity of the Christian project in terms of their will to carry forward such a deterritorializing process.[15]

The second thing wrong with the Christocentric fixation is that it implies that christological claims are only to do with the fetishization of the particular, rather than with the very constitution of the Christian mode of universality and the Christian social project. Yet the gospels are not actually all that much concerned with Jesus as an individual, but rather present him as exemplifying perfect humanity, perfect sonship, and through this exemplification making a later repetition of this sonship possible in the Church. This new and universal pattern of humanity is, however, presented to us not only in terms of concepts, but also in terms of (highly spare) narratives and (really rather abstract) metaphors. It is, in effect, because the narratives and metaphors are fundamental for defining the new and universal pattern of life that Jesus was regarded by the early Church as identical with the divine *Logos*, not because he had become the random object of a cultic attachment. Were this not the case, it would be difficult to understand how the proclamation of Jesus's divinity in John and Paul goes along with the furthest extreme of removal from the cultic and legal aspects of Jewish religion. The particularity of Jesus is insisted upon *only* to define a new framework of more than local relevance.[16]

By contrast, most of the contributors to *Myth* implied that their own devotion to Jesus is essentially a matter of cultic attachment or perhaps just force of sentimental habit. When they become their superior jet-hopping,

15. On "deterritorialization," see Deleuze and Guattari, *Thousand Plateaus*, esp. 351–474.

16. See Milbank, "Name of Jesus."

dialoguing selves, this level of devotion is transcended and recognized as the mere outward garb of a more essential and purely human commitment. Similar misconstruals of the place of the Buddha in Buddhism, the Koran in Islam, and even of the *Dharma* in Hinduism were implied. In all these cases, crucial aspects of the major religions were misrepresented as local pieties, when in fact they are basic elements of a grammar which intends to rise above, fulfill, or regulate such pieties in the course of defining the rules for a universally relevant cultural articulation.

For every major religion is *already* the result of a confronting of the fact of religious differences and an attempt to subsume such differences. (Although the ways and degrees of constructing "universality" themselves vary enormously; for example, in the form of a codification of mythology and of ritual practice—Hinduism, or in the concentration upon one supreme creator God rather than on an entire pantheon—Judaism). By comparison, genuinely local religions (and of course relative isolation does not betoken primitiveness) may scarcely have had to confront the question of whether their beliefs and practices are relevant beyond the confines of their own society; this is presumably why they are so liable to conversion by, or accommodation within, the terms of a major religion, which is in part the result of such a confrontation. The major religions are notoriously not so susceptible to conversion or accommodation, precisely because they already embody a more abstract, universal, and deterritorialized cultural framework, although they do not usually succumb to the temptation of trying to found this universality in a reason independent of all particularized memory. Just because of these universalizing aspirations, their conceptual frameworks cannot readily be dissolved through dialogue, whose only possible outcome must be either disguised conversion by the rhetorically strong discourse (Christianity), or else a new hybridization, yielding a new, and of course just as *particular*, elite religion for the votaries of dialogue themselves.

The contributors to *Myth* showed no signs of attending to this difference in character between local and major religions and its negative implications for the dialogical venture. Instead, they consistently confused elements of grammars of universality with mere cultic particularity. This error was then compounded by their association of religio-political imperialism simply with the global imposition of a local point of view, notably that of the Christian West. But from a world-historical perspective (the level to which they encourage us to aspire) all the major religions are associated one way or another with the "imperial," nomadic ventures of the Indo-European peoples, and this expansion has never meant merely the exportation of local views, but always the attempt to reinvent or expand these views in universal terms. So to celebrate universalism, rationalism, and humanism on the one hand, and to disapprove of imperialism on the other (like the contributors to *Myth*), is contradictory. For both phenomena are deterritorializations, such that universal humanism is constituted by the power of (modern, Western) empire, while inversely, empire is the work of an impulse to rational "comprehension." To my mind (and I think I am being much more Marxist than *Myth* here), most empires are ambiguous rather than sheerly deplorable. They reduce the instances of internecine conflict, interrupt the seamless narratives of unquestionable local tyrannies, and establish new central courts of appeal, both of constituted legality and abstract reason. Yet at the same time they tend to exercise a more stable and effective sort of tyranny by purporting to enshrine power less in force than in natural order, or in principles. In the capacity of principles to migrate can lurk the sheer *force* of migration.

In this section I have identified four assumptions which undergird pluralism, and which no one in *Myth* sufficiently repudiates or substantiates. These are:

1. Religion is a genuine category.

2. Dialogue gives a privileged mode of access to truth.

3. The uniqueness of the major religions consists in their cultic attachments rather than in their social formations.

4. Imperialism is simply the arrogance of locality, especially Western locality.

In the following section I wish to show how, by calling into question the first three of these assumptions, one also undermines the praxis solution.

Practice Is Not a Foundation

In the first place, it is clear that the idea of religion as a categorial area of human life encourages the view that its scope is always distinct from that of ethics, aesthetics, and politics. This pluralization of discourses/

practices, and denial of their intra-convertibility as affirmed by Christian tradition (so that aesthetics may now validate the unethical, religion the unaesthetic, politics the nonreligious, and so forth) is, of course, a key feature of Western modernity, notably described by Max Weber.[17] Weber also realized that if there is a universal discourse in modernity, then it is that of formalized law and constitutional politics, which attempts to police and keep within their proper bounds all the other discourses. The idea expounded by Knitter, Gilkey, Ruether, Suchocki, and Driver in *Myth*, that it is a politico-legal discourse about justice and liberation that the religious traditions can now all share in common, is a somewhat ideological presentation of this circumstance of modernity, which seeks (not unlike Weber himself) to give to a contingent construction of reality the status of an emergent, universally valid *logos*.

The uncritical embrace of modern norms of politics and legality led the contributors to gloss over, and even to try to deny, the obvious fact that religions have differed over political and social practice quite as much as anything else. Their newfound consensus in this area, where it exists, does not proceed from a multiply immanent convergence, as *Myth* implied, but from their general acceptance of political and social secularization with its accompanying so-called liberal values. Even Raimundo Panikkar, who was by far the nearest in the book to emancipating himself from pluralist presuppositions, spoke of a new turn of the religions to the public, political realm, as if this realm was always in essence present, prior to, and independent of, the religions themselves.[18] Concomitantly, Panikkar thought that a "politicization" of religion is today accompanied by an equal "personalization" of religion, which means that the true springs of religiousness are discovered to lie within religious experience, inspired by a somewhat free-wheeling, not community-guided, engagement with a particular religious tradition. Here Panikkar betrayed something which he shared with the other contributors, and which is surprisingly characteristic of liberation theology in general: religions themselves are *not* conceived in political terms as social projects; again and again, religion is confined to the sphere of private inspiration for the individual activist.[19]

---

17. Weber, "Politics as a Vocation," 77–128; idem, "Science as a Vocation," 143–45.

18. Panikkar, "The Jordan, the Tiber, and the Ganges," in Hick and Knitter, *The Myth of Christian Uniqueness*, 101–5.

19. Milbank, *Theology and Social Theory*, chapter 8.

Although an embracing of modern secular politics and legality is the real key to what is going on in the praxis solution, its advocates do not fully face up to this and contrive some extraordinary legerdemain. Paul Knitter, for example, suggested that religions have never been as far apart in their soteriologies as in their theologies (this of course ignores the fact that these categories are actually alien to most religions). Such a claim can only imply that a common secular realm of human aspiration, relatively free from mythical and metaphysical elaborations, has always been latent within the religious traditions, and that the modern distinguishing of the political category has always been somehow present, albeit often obscured. Yet if this is the case, the political and social agreement only arises insofar as the political gets *separated* from religion, or at least its more particular aspects. Even were one to grant this, a perplexity would remain. How can a consensus about social justice, which is relatively independent of religion, possibly help to mediate the differences between religions? The religions may agree upon common action, but this will neither help nor hinder a process of specifically religious dialogue.

In the second place, the idea of dialogue as privileged mode of access to the truth has its practical, political equivalent in the essentially liberal (and certainly not socialist, or radical-feminist) view that the sole principle of justice is the according to everyone the rights of free action and expression, whatever their natural-social status. The *character* of this status, and its mode of social constitution, is here essentially irrelevant. Thus while it may appear that Marjorie Suchocki made social justice to be a normative reference point for dialogue, in fact she *defined* justice in terms of dialogue: "Liberation theology has pointed to the invidious effects that follow when one mode of humanity is made normative for others."[20] The implication of this statement (which is a misdescription of liberation theology) would seem to be that the viewpoint of the oppressors in Latin America has been imposed upon the viewpoint of the oppressed, an impression confirmed by Suchocki's later claim that "when justice is defined from the perspective of the oppressed, certain consequences follow."[21] But the viewpoint of the oppressed (as oppressed) is only *constituted* through their oppression; the aim of justice and liberation should therefore be to obliterate this viewpoint. Of course, the oppressed may so far transcend

20. Suchocki, "In Search of Justice," in Hick and Knitter, *The Myth of Christian Uniqueness*, 149.

21. Ibid., 154.

their oppression as to imagine such a liberation, but there again, they may simply collude with their oppression. The criterion for justice cannot therefore be the occupation of a vantage-point from which oppression will be exposed in all its obviousness; there is no such vantage-point, no such obviousness.

Dialogue, therefore, is not relevant to the poor and dispossessed, because justice toward them is not primarily a matter of listening to them, but constructing for them and with them the circumstances in which they can join in many conversations, no longer as the poor. Curiously, both Suchocki and Ruether, by ignoring the "different kinds of difference," and equating the poor, women, blacks, and religions as "voices" which have the right to be heard, appeared almost to will that the poor be always with us, as a category as natural as that of (biological) race and (biological) gender. Of course this is not what they meant to say, but the adoption of inadequate, liberal language for the project of justice and liberation in the Third World casts doubt upon whether they desire any truly postliberal outcome. And a similar apparent naturalism, tending to undermine their radical rhetoric, appears in connection with their making religious difference to be equivalent to gender and race difference. "The idea that Christianity, or even the Biblical faiths, have a monopoly on religious truth is an outrageous and absurd religious chauvinism,"[22] thunders Ruether from a post-patriarchal Sinai, which is still far from the postmodern Jordan. The economic metaphor gives her away: "religious truth" is not to be monopolized, because it is a "commodity" that should be in free circulation, producible and consumable at any point upon the globe. Christianity is only permitted to supply innocuous cultural variants in this process, just as women and men, blacks and whites are supposed to experience a single human reality in diverse ways. It seems that religion really is no more than what one is born with, like one's gender or the color of one's skin. If religions are natural and diverse manifestations of an essential humanity like the two genders and the many races, then culturally invented characteristics are being ascribed to the permanent character of various different human populations. And that of course suggests racism. Thus the equation of claims to religious superiority with racial or sexual chauvinism is itself deconstructible as a racist assertion.

22. Ruether, "Feminism and Jewish Christian Dialogue," 141.

Because a religion is not a natural manifestation of species diversity, but embodies in its practices and beliefs a continuous reading of the world, there is nothing in principle objectionable, as Ruether implies, in claiming that a particular culture is crucially in error at some point, nor that another culture is intrinsically superior, even though these claims can only be made from the perspective of another, non-neutrally justifiable cultural reading. Indeed, if it were accepted that all cultures (religions) have equal access to the (religious) truth, then all critique, including critique of sexist and racist constructs, would become impossible. And since religions are such readings, deeply embedded in habitual practices and attitudes, it is clear that the idea of a universal religion free from cultural attachments, or even of an essential Christianity that could be expressed in non-Western cultural terms, is just nonsensical.

In the third place, if the uniqueness of the major religions resides as much in their social formations and projects as in their cultural attachments, it is clear that questions of justice will not provide the gateway to consensus. Only by significantly altering its traditional attitude to sacred law, and thereby its entire received character as a social product, can Islam, for example, bring its treatment of women into line with modern Western, never mind feminist, assumptions. Or again, the abandonment of earlier pro-aristocratic sentiments and the traditional Indian sacralization of untrammeled royal power by modern Hindus has always been accompanied by a significant "ethicization" of their received philosophy under Islamic and Christian influence.[23]

Agreement in the socio-political sphere nearly always betokens the triumph of Western attitudes and a general dilution of the force of traditional religious belief. Where, by contrast, as in the case of Islamic conservatism (insofar as this is genuinely a revival of traditional Islam and not a reactive invention of an Islam made apparently safer than the tradition could ever have been against foreign and critical incursions), the full "difference" of a religious outlook is insisted upon, then there not only arise theoretical conflicts with Western understandings of economic, social, and gender relations, but the claim to a space for the full exercise of Islamic practice tests the bounds of—and perhaps reveals the spuriousness of—the crucial Western commitment to religious toleration. For the Western toleration of a diversity of religious beliefs and practices (so long

23. Chaudhuri, *Hinduism*, 95–98; Potter, *Presuppositions of India's Philosophies*, 3

as this means merely practice of *rites*) assumes a concomitant secularization of law, politics, knowledge, and for the most part education, which often renders impossible a complete modern manifestation of religions in their guise as social projects. Practice, therefore, turns out to be no neutral meeting ground, but rather the place where the other religions, and even Christianity itself to some degree, have been most engulfed by the dominance of secular norms. (Christianity however, *of itself*, demands and originally first produced a certain relative but crucial desacralization of law and politics.)

Yet while it is true that the modern consensus tends to disguise the differences among traditional social projects, it is also the case that some coincidences in outlook between these projects, which together contrast with the modern outlook, can get relatively ignored. A good example would be the widespread opposition to usury within the various traditions. In certain circumstances, and in the context of a search for modes of cultural existence not under the aegis of liberal capitalism, and more respectful of religions as social projects than the sovereign liberal state can dare to be, these coincidences could indeed provide the religions with something useful to talk about. However, this sort of thing is not what appears to be envisaged by the praxis solution.

Cooperation in the causes of socialism, human rights, feminism, antiracism, and ecologism, will not therefore further the aims of religious dialogue. On the other hand, as we have seen with regard to Ruether and Suchocki, the model of dialogue may actually obscure the character and purpose of these causes. In the next section I want to reinforce this contention by arguing that they have an ineradicable relation to specifically Western culture. Here my refusal of the fourth assumption of pluralism—namely that imperialism is simply the arrogance of locality—will be invoked.

Pluralism Does Not Serve Justice

If the "contrasting of cultures," not to mention "the comparison of religions," is to be surpassed, then this might be in the mode of tracing genealogical deviations from a common root. In the case of a contrast between the Hindu-Buddhist traditions and the Greek-Roman-Christian traditions (complicated by the Semitic influence) one can observe, with the aid of the work of Georges Dumézil, how they diverge in offering completely different religio-political solutions to an originally more-or-less single, Indo-European problematic. The incommensurability of these solutions helps to reconfirm the futility of "dialogue."

What East and West really *do* share in common, at root, is a three-fold class structure (fourfold if one includes outcastes), comprising rulers (sub-divided into kingly and priestly), fighters, and tillers of the soil or laborers.[24] This three or sometimes fourfold classification is repeated in the generic grouping of the gods and in the description of the divisions of the human soul. The problematic which this classification gives rise to is roughly the following: how can sovereign, commanding "wisdom," which is at the top of the hierarchy both in the social and the psychological realms, constrain the military or energetic powers without any force of its own? Should sovereign rule concern itself with such an effort at all? Another aspect of the same problematic concerns how sovereign rule can deal with the family feudings of the military powers or psychological drives, and cope with the rebellious tendencies of the peasants and of our unruly desires.

The solution of the East runs roughly as follows. Each class is tightly bound by ritual and ethical regulations comprising the fourfold *Dharma*, but the *Dharma* is both secured, and is subject to alteration by, the sacred king, who is like a kind of floating signifier, of no prescribed caste, and standing above every caste, including the priestly-judicial brahmins. Religious law, like the land itself, is "owned" by the king, and his authority works because his untrammeled and total power is seen as evidently god-like and as channeling a sacred force. Similarly, as the *Bhagavad-Gita* makes clear, the supreme aim of individual action is to arrive at a king-like (Indian gurus have always been treated like kings[25]) mode of action totally exempt from the normal consequences of action, bound by the conventions governing the "four stages of life" (which correspond to the divisions of the soul, the caste divisions, etc.).[26] The family feuding in the *Gita* is not transcended by retreat from the battle, or by legal settlement, but instead by a perfect plunging into this agonistic action that yet leaves one unaffected by its outcome.

24. Dumézil, *Mitra-Varuna*; Chaudhuri, *Hinduism*, 82–83.

25. Chaudhuri, *Hinduism*, 303–6.

26. *The Bhagavad-Gita*; Sharma, *Ethical Philosophies of India*, 79ff.

By contrast, this is the solution of the West. In place of the king and the "Asiatic mode of production," the aristocratic sovereign class band together and exercise between themselves a republican authority in the name of an abiding justice, which is supposed to reflect a stable cosmic order in a way that the *Dharma* is never conceived as doing. Family feuding (see the end of Aeschylus's Oresteian trilogy[27]) is to terminate under the aegis of the law of the *polis*, and the military classes are to be curbed by educative training in ethical and legal norms, which, according to Plato's *Republic* are finally secured by the vision attained to by the wise (and partially by others) of the abiding form of the Good.[28] The sovereign "good person" is not simply to neglect the unruly classes, nor simply to ignore his unruly inner desires, but neither is he to become reconciled to their endless untempered reproduction, like Arjuna under the counsel of Krishna. Instead, the "lower" classes, powers, and desires must be made to participate as far as possible in the supra-reality of "the Good."

Thus the contrast between East and West extends to what we in the West take to be most basic and most valuable. (And one may note here also how absurd it renders the suggestion that Christianity might view, for example, the *Vedas* as a propaedeutic to Christianity to the *same extent* as it has viewed Platonism.) Simply, in the East there were absolute kings and no cities, and this meant *also* no "Good," no ultimate justice, but rather transcendental power or freedom and no ultimately significant "ethical" action, but instead the way of action free from consequences. (It should be noticed here that because the East does not counterpose the sacral and the power-motivated in the same way as the West, the entire mode of Western *suspicion* of religion is redundant in Oriental terms).

The above account gives a brief schematic contrast between the respective imperialisms of East and West. Neither is self-evidently true, and each can be made to cast suspicion on the other. However, it is evident that the East has no resources within itself with which to contest as a matter of justice Western imperial incursions upon its terrain. On the contrary, justice and the Good are themselves the vehicles of Western imperialism, and while this means that they may sometimes be construed as the masks of dominant power, their *supposed* surplus to power also means that they can always be invoked against that which is exposed as having no legitimating grounds other than its own arbitrariness. Thus if the West is the

27. Aeschylus *Eumenides* 752–1047.

28. Plato *Republic* books 6 and 7.

great modern poison, it is also the only available cure; nearly all the revolts against the West have been in the name of the West—even Islamic revolution finds this hard to avoid, and Islam is, in any case, strictly speaking, Western. And if this consideration applies to the East, then it applies still more strongly to local societies, which have still fewer inner resources for arriving at norms for relations among cultures.

It is also notable that while Eastern, "magical" approaches to power tend to place many sacral limitations upon power, whereas the Christian desacralization of power has led unintentionally to its purely secular manipulation, engendering an unrestrained scientism and technologism, it is nonetheless the case that the Eastern concentration upon power leaves it relatively unable to resist (look at Japan) the more successful magic of the West. The compatibility of Eastern thought with a post-Darwinian philosophy is all too often noted by the averagely agog, and essentially unreflective, Anglo-Saxon theologian.

For these reasons it must be sheerly illusory to associate evidently Western concerns with social justice, social equality, and the freedom of the other (the latter two being reinforced beyond the Greeks by the Jewish and Christian traditions) with a tradition-transcending pluralism. But it is more than illusory, it is dangerous, for two reasons. First of all, this association implies that one can found justice and freedom in universal detached human reason. The now general realization that this is impossible, will tend to bring disillusion and despair in its train, unless one returns justice and freedom to their mythical contexts of religious imagining in the Platonic vision of the Good, the Jewish vision of God, and the Christian vision of the Trinity.

Secondly, the pluralist attempt to found justice and freedom will tend to ossify them in their liberal imperialist versions, which stem from the Enlightenment. By contrast, the Christian social project (as Hegel distortedly saw) envisages not just liberty and equality, but also perfect reconciliation in and through freedom. This means that an agreement beyond mere mutual toleration is aimed at, but an agreement constituted through the blending together of differences, which thereby cease to be oppositional. As Emmanuel Levinas argued, the biblical tradition conjoins to the recognition of a transcendent Good the idea that what must be respected as the always-beyond is the face of the Other—although he too little comprehended that this encounter can only be peaceful via the negotiation of a *common space* of intersecting and overlapping practices.[29] It is true that Western imperialism has sought to deny and obliterate "the other," yet this does not mean that the other cultures themselves are thereby the innocent sources of a discourse validating otherness, or any the less "totalizing" in their ambitions, than the more successful totalizing aspirations of Western foundationalism. On the contrary, here also the West has to supply its own antidote, because the Platonic-Jewish-Christian mode of social-intellectual imperialism itself contains protocols for respecting the otherness of the other. And this does not mean merely, as for the liberal mode of dialogue, respect for the freedom of the other as abstractly identical with one's own freedom, but respect for the content of this otherness and its unique contribution to Being. This of course involves notions of *methexis* denied by Levinas—notions which more distinguish the human other from God, yet also validate the specific concrete *appearing* of the other in its partiality as a mode of participation.

Trinitarian Difference Is Not Neo-Vedantic Difference

This reflection leads me to a final consideration of the alternative to the praxis solution as articulated in *Myth* by Raimundo Panikkar. For Panikkar there was no neutral point of convergence among the religions, whether theoretical or practical. Yet he still laid claim to a supra-traditional vantage-point by proposing that reality itself is "plural," and that this circumstance is *itself* "the primordial myth," preserved in one fashion in the christological and Trinitarian doctrines of Christianity, and in other fashions elsewhere.[30]

The ontological pluralism proposed by Panikkar is in fact at once neo-Vedantic and Trinitarian. However, my schematic contrast of East and West suggests that this is an impossible union: neo-Vedantic pluralism, insofar as it has not become evidently permeated by Christianity, will propose a "univocal" or "indifferent" presence of transcendental power in the many diverse and often competing formations of temporal reality.[31] Trinitarian pluralism, by contrast, remains in the "ethical" line of the West, and can perhaps be construed (especially in its Augustinian

29. Levinas, *Otherwise Than Being, Or Beyond Essence*, 11.

30. Panikkar, "The Jordan, the Tiber, and the Ganges," 102.

31. See Deleuze, *Logique du Sens*, 208–12.

version, bearing in mind here both the theory of "substantive relation," and the psychological analogy) as effectively a reworking of the Indo-European triadic structure that de-hierarchizes and temporalizes it. For this reworking, sovereignty is only present in and through its assistance by "the second term" (the military-energetic power, now fully pacified as *Verbum*), which is therefore no longer a potential "threat," and this second term of auxiliary reason is itself only realized through the promptings of "the third term" of desire, which now so far from requiring a military or psychic "discipline," is itself the principle of right direction to the proper, but now infinite goal.[32]

As Panikkar rightly indicated, the non-subordination of desire, or the Spirit, suggests a "difference" within Being that is never contained by a once-for-all totalizing operation of the *Logos*. Yet at the same time, the Augustinian theories of substantive relation, and of the difference of the Spirit as itself the infinite communicability (as community) of the love that binds Father to Son, indicates that the Trinitarian series, in which Christian life participates, is an ethical, peaceful series, which constantly repeats and reinvents a nonviolent consensus. This is incompatible with the "agonistic" pluralism of neo-Hinduism (which is perhaps congruent with a nihilistic postmodernism). Yet such an agonism seems reflected in Panikkar's claim that "pluralism allows for a plural and tensile co-existence between *ultimate* human attitudes, cosmologies and religions. It neither eliminates nor absolutizes evil or error."[33]

What, in practice, does tensile coexistence mean? What else but infinite resignation to war (as opposed to a temporary embracing of necessary conflict and debate), or in other words to the regulated conflict of market and bureaucratic procedures? The problem with Panikkar's position is similar to that arising from many postmodernist proposals that resistance to liberal modernity should take the form of multiple uncoordinated local struggles. The double difficulty here is that localities themselves can never, on the mere basis of their locality, contest an imperial sway, and that the incommensurable differences between localities—which will necessarily intersect and overlap—can only be mediated by the instrumentalist neutrality of the market and the bureaucracy. The neo-Vedantic pluralist claim that all local differences represent some aspect of an ultimate plural

---

32. see Milbank, "Sacred Triads: Augustine and the Indo-European Soul."

33. Panikkar, "The Jordan, the Tiber, and the Ganges," 110.

reality will tend ideologically to reinforce the pluralism of liberal society, because a claimed theoretical equality will disguise the gross global inequalities resulting from a market whose "tensile balancing" only records the relative dispositions of economic and political coercion.

These theoretical and practical problems with the ontologically pluralist position reveal that, while religions may be incommensurable, this does not mean that they can be envisaged as lying peacefully side by side, without mutual interference. For although they do not provide varying accounts of any "thing," or aspect of Being, they *are* different accounts of Being itself, or of "what there is." As such an account, each religion has to reclassify other, incommensurable accounts when it encounters them, according to its own perspective. Even a philosophy respecting difference cannot avoid such an account together with such imperializing reclassifications, precisely at the point where it has to decide whether difference must involve conflict or can mean reconciliation. The neo-Vedantic option acknowledges differences as realities to be constantly encountered, overcome, and held at bay; it does *not* arrive at a valuation of the other, and this is not a traditional facet of Eastern culture. (As Wilhelm Halbfass insists, Hindu pluralism has little to do with toleration.[34]) With an apparently extreme degree of paradox, one must claim that it is only through insisting on the finality of the Christian reading of "what there is" that one can both fulfill respect for the other and complete and secure this otherness as pure neighborly difference. Then, at last, a conversation is established, which is itself the goal of true desire, and not a detached debate about truth, in the manner of "dialogue." But of course the Christian encounter with the other cannot commence as conversation. First of all, Christian theology must continue to subvert other discourses at the very point of their denial of otherness, by searching for internal tensions and *lacunae* which permit it to interpellate "typological" anticipations of the Christian *Logos*, and to set free a spiritually "different" response, which yet must be a specifically Christocentric one. (For example, in the case of Buddhism, one could attempt to show how the Buddhist commitment to compassion and nonviolence inconsistently exceeds the Eastern goals of power and freedom.)

Let me conclude this chapter with a double proposal. As regards the general furtherance of the critical understanding of discourses (the

34. Halbfass, *Indien und Europa*, 430.

minimum that religions can truly share in common) it will be better, and more in the interests of peace and understanding, to replace "dialogue" with "mutual suspicion." As regards Christian theology and practice, we should simply pursue further the ecclesial project of securing harmony through difference and a continuous historical conversation not bound by the modern constraints of dialogue around a neutral common topic. In the course of such a conversation, we should indeed expect to constantly receive Christ again, from the unique spiritual responses of other cultures. But I do not pretend that this proposal means anything other than continuing the work of conversion.

14

THE CONFLICT OF THE FACULTIES

Theology and The Economy of the Sciences

The first thing which members of a modern theology or religious studies department must face up to is that a large percentage of their atheist or agnostic colleagues in the academic world probably consider theology or any other mode of religious reflection as none other than a fantasizing about the void. As to the study of religion, they may very well consider it valid to ask just why it is that humanity has systematically pursued so many will o' the wisps, but they are far less likely to be convinced that one requires an entire separate department devoted to this task. If religion is a human phenomenon, they may be inclined to argue, then the human sciences—psychological, social, and even biological—must take it within their purview for the sake of completeness. A separate department of religious studies, however purged of theology, still wafts behind it a trace of the odor of sanctity: for if the human sciences cannot deal comprehensively with religion, this still implies that there is something "religious," something transcendentally in excess of the biological, historical, social, and psychological.

In the face of such doubts there is, in the end, no convincing apologetic ground upon which theology and religious studies can stand. In secular terms, they should not exist. One might protest at this point that the question of God, or of other religious beliefs, remains something that can be given objective, rational consideration. And that may be fair enough, but such an issue is adequately dealt with in terms of the philosophy syllabus. Another, more valid, objection would be that there are other examples of subject areas organized by *field* of studies, rather than field plus angle of approach: urban studies for example, or environmental studies, which are unified only by an object of inquiry, to which several different disciplinary approaches may be taken. This is, of course, the case, but such subject areas are inherently vulnerable to collapse from within and take-over bids from without. They tend to exist at all only for temporary or expedient reasons. Moreover, in the case of religion, a third cause of strain is the question as to whether "religion" defines with sufficient precision any discrete area of inquiry whatsoever.

Thus one is returned to the truth that self-justification of theology or religious studies before a secular court is well-nigh impossible, and that religious studies is in no better case here than theology. Nonetheless one should not despair, for one reason that is entirely cynical, and for another, which is entirely theological. The cynical reason can be dealt with in a short paragraph, the theological one will occupy the rest of this essay. The cynical reason is that utter incoherence and lack of ability to withstand the critical trial of reason does not matter so long as one can come up with cash and customers. In our postmodern era, the "free, rational inquiry" of the Enlightenment which could reveal only formal truths as objectively real, thus handing over the whole realm of the substantive to the play of agonistic forces, has itself been inevitably invaded by such forces, since form feeds only on the substantive and never perfectly inhabits its own purity. Enlightenment, therefore, has necessarily evolved into the postmodern mixture of the purest, most unbounded, and therefore most *rigorous* logic, plus the most untrammeled sway of vanity and fashion. In many ways a "religious studies department" is well adapted to our era; but we should be warned: the point of fashion is to change, and religious constituencies may well yet further wither away, or more probably mutate and take their custom elsewhere, far away from universities (or what in the future will remain of them).

The cynical reason for not despairing, as outlined above, may be entertained by religious studies, and even by theology, so long as it remains aware that it is, indeed, cynicism. However, the second and alone substantive or genuinely *hopeful* reason for not despairing is not available to religious studies. It is a theological reason alone. This is the possibility that the secular atheist or agnostic consensus might be challenged. And the grounds for this challenge would be simply that they have got everything the wrong way round. They claim that theology, alone amongst purported academic disciplines, is really "about nothing" But theological reason, if it is true to itself, replies to this with a counter-claim: all other disciplines, which claim to be about objects regardless of whether or not these objects are related to God, are just for this reason about nothing whatsoever. This claim holds true for theology however much these disciplines may assist us, in both good and evil fashion, in practical negotiations with the objective appearances of things, for if we take an appearance as a mere "object," that is to say if we take it in *abstraction* from the question whether or not it discloses in some degree God as being his creature, we treat it *effectively* in an atheistic manner, whether or not we remain agnostic as to the answer to the question.

And atheism is but a polite English name for what on the Continent has more often been called what it is: nihilism. It is not, in any sense, as its own apologetic insinuates, the negative doubting of God. On the contrary, it is the positive affirmation of the absoluteness of the void, and the capacity of that void to generate the appearance of a solid something—for all that this appearance, if it arises from nothing, must be without ontological remainder, and must at every instant vanish. For any object, concerning whose participation in infinite actuality—God—we maintain a gnoseological suspense, is an object construed as indeed a will o' the wisp. If it is taken apart from God, as something in itself, then this must mean a something arising from nothing. Therefore the object—the very objectivity of the object as that which appears to the evidence of sight without reference to its origins, or its inevitably hidden aspects—is constituted by its *disguise of the real*, a real which is really nullity. By contrast, the only "something" for this secular outlook is the appearance of the object which is *mere* appearance or illusion, since there can be no *disclosive* relation between something and nothing: of nothing there is nothing to disclose. It seems that atheism turns out to be much more difficult and indeed mystical than theology, as serious atheists, unlike smug thoughtless ones, have always known.

Thus for theology, purely secular disciplines, even if they can show us how, amorally, to more and more seek *to possess* a realm of illusion (though such possession will finally defeat us) and although they can refine more and more the increasingly bizarre and nihilistic paradoxes of logic and mathematics, as well as physics divorced from metaphysics and biology divorced from teleology, are, precisely *as* secular disciplines (although they will nearly always possess also an implicit and redeeming supernatural orientation) through and through nihilistic. By contrast, theology understands itself as alone studying things as ineliminably *real*, in that they are taken as having their source in an original, indefeasible actuality. A consequence of this view is that theology also understands itself as alone able *to remain* with the question of truth, without running into inevitable *aporias*. For theology, indeed, truth is an adequation or correspondence of knowledge with the real, since the one entirely real reality, God, is itself both infinitely actual and infinitely knowing. As real, he is also manifest and self-aware, or truthful. For us to express a truth means that to a degree we correspond in our being to God via an awareness of aspects of the creation to whose lesser reality we also correspond, since the creation is rooted in God, and its being is entirely from God. From this theological perspective alone it makes sense to say that knowing corresponds to being even though we have no access to being other than via knowing, and thus a claim that our knowledge "corresponds" can never be checked up. We cannot compare what is known with the knowledge of it, since what is known is not available other than through knowledge. Hence a claim to know truly, a claim to know at all, does indeed, as Plato argued, only make sense within the framework of *methexis* (participation), for it amounts to a faith that what one shows or expresses in knowledge radiates mysteriously, and a in a limited measure, yet not deceptively, from a plenitudinous origin that is both the source of all things and the genuine depth of all things.

Outside this theological framework, the redundancy theorists of truth are right; "truth" is an eliminable term since it only means that what is "is," and "is" in this context must mean that which appears to us (in terms of both nature and culture) to be, the world as we either pragmatically or conventionally reckon with it.[1] However, there is no secure phenomenalist resting point here, no safe version of transcendental "limits of human reason" within which there may persist a certain sort of certainty concerning the real. For behind the complacency of so-called redundancy or disquotational theory lurks the more fearful specter of "diagonalization." Within the diagonalizing perspective, to say that true statements pertain to the world as we pragmatically or conventionally handle it raises the reflexive problem of how that statement itself is legitimated, since it

1. See Fine, *Shaky Game*, 112–71; Putnam, *Pragmatism*; Davidson, "Structure and Content of Truth"; Rorty, "Pragmatism, Davidson and Truth"; Marshall, "'We shall bear the image of the Man of Heaven.'"

cannot itself be pragmatically or conventionally grounded or disquota-tionally reduced.[2] It seems that in one instance we cannot substitute for the word true—that is the instance when we say, "it is true that all uses of the word true can be translated into other terms." For even if we say instead, "all uses of the word true can be translated into other terms," the fact that we need to make this assertion shows that to affirm the redun-dancy theory is to assert that the redundancy of use of the word "truth" corresponds to the way things are, such that after all we encounter here an unavoidable speculative gap between knowledge and being where use of the word true or equivalent phrasing still has an irreducible function. In a corresponding fashion, if we elect to think that it is true that "true" indicates only what appears to us to be the case, then—as Plato pointed out in the *Theaetetus*[3]—we still have to say, "It *appears to me* that truth reduces to whatever appears to anyone to be." And here again truth is not disquotable nor reducible to appearance, since an "appearance" which establishes that truth resides only in appearings-to-be cannot itself be within the normal plane of appearances, but is rather a meta-appearing which establishes the absoluteness of this plane. Yet at the same time a meta-appearing must after all be regarded as also just another contingent and subjective appearing and so as contradictorily belonging on the same first-order plane after all. In this way it is, in principle, open to challenge by another appearance which could disclose the non-ultimateness of mere appearing-to-be itself. So here once again, there arises an unavoidable—if undecidable—*issue* about correspondence and thus about truth.

It has now been seen, both from the way in which "truth" is not re-dundant in asserting its redundancy, and the way in which the theory of truth as appearance both is not and yet is itself an appearance, that these theories are beset by deconstructive paradox. Thus to uphold the limits of pragmatic or conventional reason, and a disquotational theory of truth with its accompanying phenomenalism, one must also transgress those limits or "diagonalize" out of them, to use the jargon, and risk the notion that one's decision to regard the world only pragmatically or else con-ventionally *does* after all correspond—beyond mere pragmatism or con-ventionalism—to the way things are. This "way things are," this implicit ontology, would be that the world is through and through phenomenal

2. On "diagonalization," see Priest, *Beyond the Limits of Thought*.
3. Plato *Theaeteus* 161C–162A.

without disclosure of anything deeper, that is to say that, for working purposes, it is a meaningless and partially manipulable flux floating above a void (an implied "center" of lack of reasons and non-origination). So after all, phenomena without truth, that is to say, phenomena containing no inner impetus to self-disclosure (as in a theological theory which accepts an ontological dimension to truth) do nonetheless disclose the truth of the void. But as we have seen, this is a self-cancelling form of self-disclosure, which announces the equal untruth as much as truth of what is disclosed, since the void discloses nothing, and in consequence the truth entertained here is a truth crossed out, a contradictory untruth, just as the result, as Hegel realized, of any merely transcendental limitation of possible knowledge is a constitutive contradiction. For if, as we have seen, in the theory under consideration, all truth relates only to appearances, then according to the logic of set-theory this statement itself both must and yet cannot be merely phenomenal; it is simultaneously groundless, floating in a void, and yet grounded within the phenomenal horizon. Hence, just as for secular knowledge all appearances equally are and are not, so also reality is disclosed truly and yet as entirely untrue. Plato, followed by Augustine, Dionysius, and the whole Christian tradition up to Aquinas and Eckhart (and in his wake Nicholas of Cusa) was right: in the mere finite flux taken in itself there resides no truth, and the principle of non-contradiction, of logic itself, cannot be upheld or grounded logically, but only through assent to the realm of eternal unchanging forms, or of the ideas in the mind of God, where what is actual abides, and as infinite or "outside itself" escapes all set-theoretical contradictions—while at the same time (as Eckhart and Cusa saw), appearing in finite terms to be "contradictory."

The above reasonings suggest that theology, in the face of secular attack, is only on secure ground if it adopts the most extreme mode of counterattack: namely that unless other disciplines are explicitly ordered to theology (assuming that this means participation in God's self-knowledge, as in the Augustinian tradition) they are objectively and demonstrably null and void, altogether lacking in truth, which to have any meaning must involve some sort of *adequatio* (for mere "coherence" can only concern the coherence of conventions or appearances).

But one might well protest, how does this picture relate to the real situation in today's universities where it is simply not the case that with 100% consistency secular academics say to students of theology or religion "you speak of nothing" and even less true that those students solemnly intone in reply, "no, it is rather you who speak of nothing." However, to understand why what I believe is the real situation rarely emerges to the surface, one needs to consider briefly the historical emergence of modern theology and religious studies, and in particular the often hidden *role of the state* in this emergence.

There are four significant dimensions here that I want now to enumerate.

First, around 1300 or so, theology itself perversely invented the possibility of an entirely non-theological mode of knowledge. Duns Scotus and his successors through Suarez and Descartes to Kant elaborated the notion that it was possible adequately to think of Being as such apart from its instantiation as the infinite actuality of God. In consequence, it became legitimate to think of the being of a creature *apart from* its creaturehood. But this alters altogether the meaning of contingency. No longer is the apparent being of a thing taken as God's willed partial disclosure of himself, instead it is taken as raw possibility. For if God has been bracketed out, the being of a creature is exhaustively that which appears to our knowledge, and that which appears to our knowledge, that which we can clearly and distinctly grasp, is simply that which is thinkably coherent and so possible. Thus a being taken in abstraction from God is immediately reduced to its enablement by *possible* being, rather than prior actuality. But if possibility is prior, then a "might not be" or "nothing" is on the same level with being, and meontology as fundamental as ontology. As J.-F. Courtine puts it, the contention of Eckhart (but also of Augustine and Aquinas)—which was the inner kernel of orthodoxy tragically rejected as heterodox by the Catholic church itself before and around 1300—that in its most actual self the creature in some sense is God, and of itself is nothing, is negatively demonstrated to be correct by all subsequent deviant scholasticism. In this later and decadent development the inner essence of a finite being becomes nothing as much as something, so that in Suarez and then in Wolff and even in Kant's first critique, the real subject of ontology is not *ens*, but *aliquid* (something) or *objectum*, the "transcendental" reality that might equally be or not be. I have already indicated how this, the substructure of all modern pragmatism, most phenomenology, and most analytic philosophy is implicitly nihilist, rendering the question of "postmodernism" a trivial irrelevance.[4]

4. See Courtine, *Suarez et le Problème de la Métsaphysique*; Alliez, *Capital Times*, 141–241.

The second dimension is closely related to the first. Once the fundamental Augustinian-Dionysian-Thomist structure of analogy of being and participation in being had been destroyed by the Scotist view that finite and infinite being "are" in the same univocal sense, theology gradually changed its character. For Aquinas, to talk adequately of anything, one had to speak of it *as a creature*, to refer its being to God as alone truly being in himself. In consequence metaphysics, understood by Aquinas primarily as ontology, diagonalized out of itself in dealing with *one* topic—namely the first cause, God—that fell within its purview. Paradoxically this one topic, God, is for the Thomist view of metaphysics (as not for Aristotle who remained with a strange aporetic tension) bigger, of greater scope than its supposed all-comprehensive subject matter of *ens commune*—"being in common."[5] There is however no *real* paradox here, only because this subject matter of metaphysics, *ens commune*, is itself provided by a higher cause, which is the subject of a higher science. But here, uniquely, the cause and the science are at one. They are the first cause and its own self-knowledge: God himself and his *scientia Dei* which is theology, utterly ineffable and beyond our grasp. The basic conclusions of metaphysics, including that there is a cause of being which is itself a plenitudinous being, are for Aquinas flickering and uncertain, just because we only ever weakly participate in being and truth, and are, besides, fallen creatures. They are only truly confirmed, established from their ground, by God's imparting to us, to the degree that we can receive it, his own self-knowledge, through his entry gradually into human time (the typology of the Old Testament) and finally with Christ at the Incarnation. This entry not only confirms God as first cause and *esse ipsum* to our wavering reason, but also discloses the inner reality of God as Trinitarian, namely *as* an infinite will to give being, to be known and loved through self-manifestation which pre-grounds the creative act.

But after Aquinas and Eckhart, this sense of theology as participation in the science of God and the blessed gradually evaporated and indeed was subject already to a kind of secularization, such that theology as such was really already abandoned. How? Because instead of the most fundamental determination of being as theological, one now has a theologically neutral determination of being, and theology is forced to

5. See Courtine, *Suarez et le Problème de la Métsaphysique*; de Libera, *Le Problème de l'Être chez Maître Eckhart*; Booth, *Aristotelian Aporetic Ontology in Islamic and Christian Thinkers*.

work *within this framework* as if, idolatrously, there were something more
ontologically fundamental than God. For the figure of participation is
substituted the figure of *distance*: as if God were a very remote, infinitely
large *object*. And where the term "infinite" was traditionally a negative
description of God, it now, in the late Middle Ages, became a positive
definition of his *essence*. And of course a God whose defining nature is to
be unbounded, and a God of which nothing finite necessarily discloses
anything, since its finite essence is simply a logical or grammatical "might
not be," is a God who quickly becomes hypostasized will or force. The
late medieval imagining of a reality divided between infinite arbitrariness
on the one hand, and finite contingent possibilities on the other, already
projected in advance a nihilistic imagining of a blind flux undergirding
meaningless and delusory appearances. Increasingly the Scotist "proofs of
God" in terms of the necessary priority of infinite Being, did not seem like
proofs of God, as opposed to proofs of some sort of immanent absolute
or even immanent absolute void: a conclusion eventually arrived at by
Spinoza. As a result, theology was thrown more and more back on a new
sort of foundation in positive revelation. But in this case also, it was just
as true that theology took for granted a *philosophical* preestablishment of
what an object or a fact was: something clear and evident, without depth,
unambiguous and provable according to "evidence." Revelation had first
to be shown as "possible" in these terms. Then, as regards the actuality
of revelation, God was now seen as disclosing himself in facts which,
increasingly, to distinguish themselves as divine facts, had to be miraculous facts, or else their recognition depended upon an entirely separate,
internal—and only accidentally related to the revealed object—movement of our understanding by the Holy Spirit.[6] The traditional integrity
of theology was thereby lost, for previously theology was not a secondary
reflection upon *data*, whether of scripture or tradition. On the contrary,
theology *was* the event of divine disclosure, a happening in which inner
inspiration and outward expression in signs were seamlessly and intrinsically united. Instead of this sophisticated and believable notion that theology concerns the gradually renewed disclosure of God himself through
creatures which makes use of the ceaseless becoming of creation in time,
an entirely *superstitious* and *contemptible* notion of an arbitrary and blind
faith in certain supposedly revealed facts was substituted. Yet this strange
fideistic superstition is itself captive to the emerging secular idolitry of

6. See Dulles, *Assurance of Things Hoped For*; Latourelle, *Theology of Revelation*.

a God reduced to the status of an object and so able to disclose himself according to his arbitrary will, through lesser objective possibilities. Thus, although this circumstance was for a long time hidden, the mainstream of learned theology effectively ceased *to be* theology long ago. Above all, it ceased to be about God, because it ceased to be itself the existential event of divine illumination, and became instead a second-order reflection on facts or practices of some sort.[7]

The third dimension concerns the state. Scotist distance from an absolute, voluntarist God from the outset meshed nicely with, and was used to support, a new conception of earthly authority as legitimate according to the exercise of power by a single sovereign center if constituted by, and exercised in, the right formal terms, quite apart from the question of the inherent justice of its acts. This meant that public life, as falling entirely under such sovereign sway, was subject to a paradoxically *theological* secularization in that its ordering, though divinely legitimate, no longer in any way reflected divine order or cosmic hierarchy. Partly as a result, "religion" ceased to betoken specific patterns of individual participation in public practice, ceased, in short, to be a "virtue," and became instead a private attitude, not even any longer a disposition to virtue, but rather an act of assent to certain emotionally neutral "beliefs" in certain revealed facts and propositions. Moreover, in the early modern period, while the state was unable altogether to escape the assumption that the practice of religion alone held society together, it quickly came to suppose that the state simply required general assent to some set of beliefs for the sake of disciplined and uniform public worship, plus the supernatural sanctioning of morality and its own positive laws. In that moment the notion of "a religion" and of a plurality of "religions" was born, and later inappropriately used to classify the practices and inherited wisdoms of other cultures.[8] Even today, the state retains some vestigial interest in the usefulness of a private sphere of piety, and therefore tends to encourage the notion that there is a "religious" dimension of life, which assists the

---

7. Even Barth does not entirely escape this sort of positivity and while he recovers the idea of revelation as "self-revelation," this is too much in terms of an idealist projection of the primacy of the finite knowing subject onto God with the result that how God reveals himlself tends to be identified with how God is in himself. I am indebted to discussions with Johannes Hoff here.

8. See Harrison, *'Religion' and the Religious in the English Enlightenment*; Asad, *Genealogies of Religion*; Cavanaugh, "'A Fire Strong Enough to Consume the House,'" 397–420. I am also indebted to discussions with Nicholas Lash on all this.

state's own ends without trespassing on its sovereignty. Concomitantly, it still prefers the public dimension of religion—mystical attachment to corporate bodies and organizations of social practice—to be alienated to its own domain: hence the continued phenomenon of "civil religion."

The fourth dimension, after those of modern ontology without God, modern debased theology, and the modern theopolitical co-determination of the state and religion, concerns the emergence of a notion of "ritual" activity. In the Middle Ages and in most traditional societies all proper action is ritual in the sense that it reflects a cosmic order: as Talal Asad has stressed, the monk's writing in the scriptorium or laboring in the field was as much liturgical as his saying of the offices in chapel.[9] And all these ritual acts were no mysterious symbolic language for some sort of psychological secret attitude; on the contrary they were simply plain, ordinary, transparent acts, whose structure nonetheless pointed to an inexhaustive depth of divine mystery. But later, with the reduction of religion to mean primarily a set of beliefs, actions related to those beliefs started to be thought of as strange, as hovering between real, normal actions, and certain hidden psychological dispositions. In this way a realm of "ritual" or "symbolic actions" was born, which helped to strengthen the illusion that there *are* religious phenomena, available for study and inquiry. Yet in fact, this is a modern Western projection: traditional Hinduism, for example, was not a religion, not an aspect of the Indian way of life, it simply was that life or rather plural lives in their specific totality, their specific structuring and specific visions.

Taken altogether, these four dimensions have helped to shape the modern disciplines of theology and religious studies. Theology has been regarded, unlike philosophy, as a "positive science" concerned with a certain delimited field, rather than as the very consummation and transfiguration of philosophy or the science of being as such. It has also been frequently regarded by the state as primarily functional and practical in character. In Kant's last strange published work, *The Conflict of the Faculties*, he argued that the *higher* university faculties, theology, law, and medicine, can be allowed only limited freedom, since they serve the practical and legal purposes of the state, whereas philosophy, a lower faculty, as being without public responsibilities or direct public consequences, is

9. Asad, *Genealogies of Religion*, 125, 171.

free to pursue pure truth without hindrance.[10] But this, we can now see, is the perfect political equivalence of nihilism: philosophy which can only after all for Kant attain the truth of *appearances* can think what it likes (is a kind of adventure playground, without upshot, for adults), and yet beyond philosophy, and beyond appearances, in the noumenal void, a strict formalism for the safeguarding and sacralizing of an empty freedom, of the void as the essence of subjectivity, pertains. And it is finally theology justified by practical truth that upholds this politically amoral realm of strict and empty formalism. It is no longer by Kant allowed, beyond the formal exigencies of state legal practice, to think the *ratio* between the unknown and manifest appearances (thanks to Kant's strict duality of the sublime and the beautiful) despite the fact that this is the only true site for Christian theology.[11] Within the bounds laid down by the state, theology is instead confined to upholding a supposedly universal morality and to better scholarly establishment of the facts which are taken to ground belief. Thus theology in the course of the nineteenth century acquired wholly questionable sub-disciplines which were no longer expected to participate in God's self-knowledge, but were instead expected simply to establish the foundational facts with pure historical neutrality (on which the Church as department of state depends): biblical criticism, Church history (as no longer a reflection on divine providence), historical theology, and so forth. Even after the decline of public belief, theology has hoped that this self-desiccation of its unity into *non*-theological components will win it general respectability. But it is a short-term strategy and in the end theology is here only preparing its own *auctioning off* to other faculties: to history, oriental studies, classics, etc. The task then *now* for theology is not, of course, to abandon historical scholarship, but to reinvent biblical studies, Church history, and so forth as also attempts, beyond scholarship, to participate in the mind of God.

Alongside theology, religious studies has emerged as the study of a questionably (for reasons we have seen) discrete area of human existence. To that extent, it is not a readily defensible discipline, even if history of religions at its best has attempted an interesting sort of historical ethnography and *histoire totale* of human culture. But what alone *really* drives the study of religion as a distinct discipline is either a vacuous and impossible

---

10. Kant, "Conflict of the Faculties," 233–329.
11. Milbank, "Sublimity: The Modern Transcendent," 258–84.

pluralist theology—whose impossibility I have already explained[12]—or else the atheist or agnostic attempt to explain whatever in human culture falls outside the norms of Western, post-Scotist reason. It is perfectly all right to admit such attempts within a theology and religious studies department, as long as one insists that the department is *still*—as a whole and primarily—committed to theology. For otherwise, if one adopts a neutral stance, one is really giving *free rein* to one inevitable ambition of such inquiries, namely to get rid of theology as an academic venture. By all means, we should include in our endeavors, for example, the psychology of religion, but *never* should we be under any illusion that this is partially in order to encourage a dialogue between theology and psychology. Why not? Because while theology is perfectly open and always has been to discourses about *physical* influences on the soul (the traditional theory of melancholy and so forth) it regards *itself*, in one central aspect, as the discourse about the soul's psychic reality. Hence psychology, outside of physical science, is a rival of theology: indeed it is easy to show genealogically that it is itself but the faint trace of religious belief in the soul, an absurd attempt to talk about the soul without God, despite the fact that the soul as "spiritual" has only been historically constituted in terms of our point of contact with transcendence.[13] Such an attempt is strictly analogous to all post-Scotist attempts to talk about actuality apart from God, and with the same result: finite actuality, here spiritual actuality, must fade away. And, furthermore, the attempt *also* inherits a theological privatization of religion whereby, instead of the "humanly psychic" simply being taken as coterminous with all specifically human outward activity as the spring of "life" and principle of order in such activity (as the psychic is also the principle of life and measure of all other, non-human, realities), it is seen as denoting some elusive, mysterious, supposedly "internal" aspect of our existence. Accordingly, the "psychic" is supposed to be more manifest to laboratory investigation of an isolated individual under artificial experimental conditions than in ordinary interpersonal everyday life.

Thus in relation to secular inquiries into religion, theology should never surrender its hegemony. But ironically, nor should the practitioners of such inquiries want it to, at least if they wish to remain focused upon religion or *a forteriori* to remain located within a religious studies depart-

---

12. See chapter 13 in this volume.

13. The point is well made from a stance hostile to religion by Richard Webster in his *Why Freud Was Wrong*, esp. 457–77.

ment. For without theology's unique assertion of a *raison d'être*, namely maintenance of at least the possibility of an alternative to secular nihilism, the long-term threat of an "auctioning off" of such secular studies of religion remains.

And rather similar considerations apply to the study of other religions (though that is the wrong term). One should say here, first of all, that theology itself should of course include a reflection on the theological meaning of the history of religions. Alongside this, departments will validly include "neutral" studies of such history, besides where possible encouragement of interior intellectual developments of other traditions by practitioners of such traditions themselves—although I think we need to be aware of the degree to which the tradition of such reflection in the case of Hinduism, Buddhism, and Islam has been historically ruptured, and we must not be taken in by inauthentic modern simulacra of such reflection. The facts of history and simple pressure of numbers dictates that such reflection will continue to be more carried out by Christians and by Jews. But there are also two further points. The first is that the very *rationale* for allowing a pluralist encouragement of different traditions of reasoned inquiry *also* demands continuing Christian theological hegemony. Why? Because this *rationale* denies that reason can ever be divorced first from a more than rational commitment and second from the specificity of time and place. Thus this *rationale* itself requires that, as Christian theologians, we sustain our tradition of reflection as a matter of more than rational commitment, which means in turn that we have to insist that a faculty of religion is, whatever else it is, *at least* a faculty of theology, meaning of course Christian theology, as well as that more simply "metaphysical" theology inherited from the Greeks and common to the three monotheistic faiths. But in addition, the realities of time and place to which a theory of "traditioned" reason is committed, still in Europe and America for the moment requires the culturally prior role of Christian reflection. And since the notion of traditioned reason alone can withstand the sway of a supposedly neutral reason, and since this notion demands for the above reasons that we sustain the distinction of Christian commitment and assert its priority for theology and religious studies, then it is paradoxically this priority alone which *shelters* other modes of traditional or religious reflection. By contrast, a strictly secular, neutral regard would simply sweep them away in the wake of Christian theology itself.

It is inconceivable and simply idolatrous to suppose that theology could ever be a component of some supposedly more inclusive and hybrid discipline of religion and theology in general (even though, of course, it is possible to imagine that a Christian theology "track" within a department of religion and theology could readily share in common courses on, say, the Old Testament, Greek Philosophy, and Medieval Philosophy with Islamic, Jewish, and History of Religions tracks).

And yet, I can hear a Muslim or a Jew protest: "Is there not something very strange about what you say? How can Christian theology shelter other religious visions if it is within *this* tradition *alone* that secular nihilism was pre-invented?" There is no answer I can give here which they will find acceptable, and yet I think there is an answer, which is highly relevant for Christians. This is that *despite* the fact that Christian-learned theology abandoned the framework of analogy and participation for a kind of proto-nihilism, it was nonetheless Christian thinkers alone in the Middle Ages who fully succeeded in elaborating such a framework. Without the encouragement of the Trinitarian sense that God is in himself the God who expresses himself creatively, and the christological sense that God only speaks from within history and can only restore a broken history by kenotically entering personally within it, the Arabic and Jewish scholastics (as well as the Jewish kabbalists and even the Islamic mystics) tended not to be able to reconcile God's simplicity and supremacy of will with his eminent possession of the excellencies of goodness, truth, and beauty manifest in the creation (despite their intense will to do so). With the abandonment of participation by Christian theologians, such an inability invaded Christendom also, with the inverse consequence that the Trinitarian and christological doctrines started to lose their centrality and inherent logic, becoming the subjects of mere authorized belief.[14] For this reason it can validly be asserted that the call to recover analogy and participation, which is equivalent to a call to reinstate the hegemony of theology as an alternative to nihilism, will tend to be also a call to recover specifically Christian theology.

---

14. See Milbank, "History of the One God," 371–400; and Burrell, *Knowing the Unknowable God*, and idem, *Freedom and Creation in Three Traditions*.

15

FAITH, REASON, AND IMAGINATION

*The Study of Theology and Philosophy
in the Twenty-First Century*

Monotheisms and Study-Methods

The social and cultural context for the study of theology is changing drastically. Traditionally, theology has been studied as a vocational discipline, subsequent to the undertaking of other studies, in different fields. Characteristically, this has encouraged the view that one undertakes first of all secular studies, guided by the light of reason, before turning one's mind to the higher matter of reflection upon revelation. A corollary of this is that one first of all deals with what is ultimately the classical (Greek and Roman) legacy before turning one's mind to the biblical (substantially Judaic) inheritance.

This pattern then accords with a fundamentally dualistic and hierarchic division of Christian culture between the horizons of Athens and Jerusalem. This division has good aspects (as I shall presently suggest) as well as more questionable ones. At any rate, it contrasts with the educational legacy of both Judaism and Islam, wherein the entire course of learning is more fundamentally guided by hermeneutic engagement with sacred and legal texts. The much increased presence of Islamic culture in Europe therefore presents a challenge to the traditional Christian pedagogic arrangements. On the one hand, it may well be important to sustain our commitment to humanistic learning; on the other hand, the Islamic presence throws a stark light upon the general absence of the biblical legacy within the general run of Western culture. This is by no means simply the result of secularization. On the contrary, it is the result of the specifically Western (not Eastern, at least in origin) conception of the nature of *laicité*. Because the laity have generally been somewhat excluded from the affairs of the Church, the spheres of secular politics and reasoning, founded often upon the classical legacy, have been seen as their "proper" domain.

However, a new socially-induced pattern of theological study provides us with the opportunity to re-think this model. Increasingly, theology is studied not as a postscript to the humanities, but rather as itself a humanistic discipline. Here the issue of theology versus the objective study of religion is proving to be, within Anglo-Saxon countries at least, something of a side-issue. In practice, departments combining both have emerged and the course of a student's study tends naturally to oscillate between a relatively detached view of religious history, belief, and practice on the one hand, and attempts intellectually to develop faith perspectives (whether Christian or otherwise, though Christian perspectives normally predominate) on the other.

More important than this division is surely the newly "humanistic" approach to the combined study of theology and religions. By this I mean, first of all, that theology is now often undertaken as a first undergraduate Arts degree. Secondly, I mean that "systematic" approaches to its study based upon presumed philosophical "foundations" have largely been replaced, within the Anglo-Saxon world, by more eclectic textual and historical study, which includes also attention to literary and artistic religious works. This study certainly builds up to a speculative engagement, but the elaboration of systems according to a method from clear foundational starting points has largely been abandoned. If such an approach was always alien to the Anglo-Saxon mentality, it can also be argued that it was in any case specifically modern and that the newer approach tends to re-work in a "postmodern" way something of the premodern, more piecemeal and commentary-orientated approach to doing theology.

So theology is now predominantly studied as a first humanities degree by students of both sexes who are generally not destined for the priesthood, nor even for academic careers.

Far from this suggesting straightforwardly a secularization of the discipline, it rather suggests its "laicisation," and even a certain popular will amongst younger people to achieve a more religiously informed culture at large, besides a Christian culture wherein reason and politics are guided by the biblical as well as the classical legacy. This overcoming of an inherited Athens/Jerusalem duality can be achieved without abandoning that valuation of Greek and Roman literary classics which is peculiar to Christianity and which, I think, relates to the validation of the "human as such" by the doctrine of the Incarnation. It is in fact the case that the more Judaism and Islam are exposed to a secular literary culture, the more they have implicitly (and usually without knowing it) embarked upon an engagement with the Christian legacy also.

Yet if Judaism and Islam can learn from Christianity the value of relatively independent humanities (since the human as such is latently imbued with the sacred), then inversely Christianity can perhaps learn from the other two monotheisms the importance of a more integrated culture. All the same, in Christian terms this implies a biblical culture that gives far more place than is traditional for either the Jewish or the Islamic mainstream to both the philosophical and the secular literary legacies. What is required now in the West is a more developed Christian human-ism, which, as Pope Benedict has suggested, would allow for a still greater mingling of faith with reason.

This mingling has always been part of the Christian genius, for while Islam later re-discovered philosophical reason, it was never able to inte-grate this within the dominant tradition which remained largely fideistic, so ensuring that philosophy in reaction saw itself as the esoteric preserve of those with superior insight. For the Christian notion of *doctrina* by contrast, an integration of philosophical reflection with biblical interpre-tation was crucial from the outset. And in addition, the typological ap-proach to the partial truth of the Old Testament provided a model which was readily extended to other literatures and cultural practices. This is partly why the universalist thrust of Christianity is more extreme than that of Judaism and Islam, besides being more complex. For on the one hand, the final revelation of God as Man suggests that the traces of truth are found everywhere within the *humanum*. On the other hand, it sug-gests that humanity can only be re-united through the common recogni-tion of this one man, Christ, as the concrete event, beyond all laws and prescriptions, of the arrival of fully restored human truth.

For all the above reasons it seems to me that what is now required, in an age when religion has re-asserted itself within the public realm, is a new sort of Christianized *Literae Humaniores*, to be undertaken either at undergraduate or at Master's postgraduate level, such as is being developed within the Centre of Theology and Philosophy at the University of Nottingham (at Master's Level).

The three major components of this would be theology, philosophy, and literature, assuming that theology would comprise also biblical criticism and Church history and therefore be inevitably engaged in addition with the entire question of history as such. Literature should form the third component, because both theology and philosophy also exist in poetic and narrative modes of representation, while since the Romantic reaction to the Enlightenment these have often proved to be the most important idioms for the defense and development of orthodox doctrine. Since textual study properly predominates in the academy, and because literature tends to mediate between concept and image, the literary mode of artistic representation should assume pre-eminence within this re-conceived syllabus, although this by no means implies the exclusion of a theological and philosophical consideration of music and the visual arts.

Theology *and* Philosophy

But the core of this new syllabus, or "the Nottingham model," is theology *and* philosophy. This deliberately loose conjunction "and" is crucial. For one is no longer talking about "philosophy of religion," nor even about "philosophical theology." The former is a legacy of German idealist thought and tends to suggest that philosophy, beyond doctrinal theology, can tell us the final truth about religion or offer a critical commentary upon it, from an alleged superior vantage-point. But this begs the question about the degree to which the invocation of a Creator God must transform one's understanding of the entire natural order, and also the degree to which the acknowledgment of a historical revelation must revise even that understanding.

It is nonetheless clearly the case that a great deal is to be learnt from idealist philosophy of religion, especially insofar as it insisted on the speculative value of the doctrines of the Trinity and the Incarnation after these had been reduced to mere positive data by professional theology. There is also much to be learned from more recent phenomenological theses in Continental philosophy about the foundational character of "donation," as well as from phenomenological readings of the Bible. However, the question arises in all these instances as to how far an interpretative bias rooted in a particular theological tradition is smuggled into a supposedly philosophically objective account. Has the boundary with theology not already been covertly transgressed, and if so should not this trespass be confessed and then theoretically re-legitimized?[1]

As to "philosophical theology," it is a wholly redundant term: all Christian *doctrina* is involved in discursive reflection, which appeals to traditions of philosophical reflection. Conversely, the more "philosophical" aspects of theology, such as reasoning to God's existence, the so-called problem of evil, the divine attributes, and the nature of talk about God, are every bit as much a matter of "doctrine" that interprets revelatory events as are such topics as sin, grace, redemption, incarnation, and the Trinity.

Where this is forgotten, as in recent manifestations of the "analytic philosophy of religion" in the writings of Richard Swinburne, Thomas V. Morris, et al., then theological approaches to these matters tend to be mis-described in ontotheological terms which treat God as simply a "supreme being" and the consequent discussions of supposedly Christian theses are, as a result, as worthless as would be the discussions of the belief-systems of an imaginary tribe.[2]

Within analytic approaches the exception to this tendency has been the Wittgensteinian approach to religion, which, to the contrary, tends to emphasize that a religion has its own unique form of linguistic coherence and standards as to what can count as true. By comparison with the dire general run of analytic approaches to religion this is highly salutary and valuable. The problem, however, with this approach, is a result of the general problem of Wittgenstein's linguistified Kantianism and finitism, which tends to regard the grammatical rules of religious, as of other discourses (however obscure these may be), as marking out transcendental bounds for correct reasoning which cannot be speculatively transgressed. This scheme suppresses the fact that, since no such boundaries can be clearly identified without a contradictory crossing over to their other side, all human discourses have to cope with *aporias* that arise from the irreducibly indeterminable nature of things with which human beings are confronted and which a *really* rigorous linguistic analysis—as has been

---

1. See, for example, Janicaud et al., *Phenomenology and the "Theological Turn."*
2. See, for example, Swinburne, *Coherence of Theism*; Morris, *Logic of God Incarnate.*

shown all the way from Plato to Derrida—tends to augment rather than to reduce.[3]

Wittgenstein's still Lockean view (rooted ultimately in his mathematically dubious mathematical finitism), that metaphysical conundra will evaporate once we clarify verbal usage, however plural and mysterious he later allowed this to be, seems by comparison somewhat shallow, and only to apply to relatively banal instances. In the case of religion, it is, by contrast, clear that ritual practices not only confront the sublime margins of the meaningful, but also already attempt to reckon with and resolve the irresolvable—and yet linguistically and culturally unavoidable—problems of the relation of the invisible to the visible and the absolute to the relative—as many ethnographical analyses, for example those of Lévi-Strauss, have shown. Accordingly, theological speculation sustains at a more reflective level what is implicit in pre-reflective religious practice and is not a redundant misunderstanding of religious language games, as Wittgenstein and some of his followers like D. Z. Phillips have tended to imply. A more useful application of Wittgenstein is that of Fergus Kerr, who has pointed out how Wittgenstein saw human religiosity as irreducible because rooted in our specifically human mode of animality.[4]

But by contrast with both "philosophy of religion" and "philosophical theology," the point of "theology *and* philosophy" is that the Nottingham model is concerned with the entirety of philosophy, not just its "application" to religion or theology. This is because theology claims to speak about everything in relation to God, which is to say being as such and all of the fundamental modes of being, besides those decisive historical events of divine revelation which are held to re-construe our very interpretation of the ontological. Yet "philosophy" is first of all the name of the discourse which reflects upon being and the ways in which things can be (according to Aristotle). The secondary aspects of philosophy—namely the ways is which being is apparent (phenomenology) and can be known and spoken about (logic and grammar) as well as acted upon (ethics) follow from this understanding of first philosophy as ontology or metaphysics. In this way, theology remains always concerned with philosophy, even if it transfigures it.

3. See Conor Cunningham's decisive essay, "Language: Wittgenstein after Theology," in Milbank et al., *Radical Orthodoxy*, 64–90.

4. Kerr, *Theology after Wittgenstein*.

This concern with philosophy in its entirety does not mean, however, that philosophy straightforwardly provides a foundation upon which theology builds. One could even say that the latter model at once accords too much autonomy to philosophy and too much superiority to theology.

The notion of philosophy as foundational and autonomous is too ahistorical. In practice this usually means that Christian theology becomes subservient to the dominant philosophy of the day, as still usually prevails. The problem here is that these philosophies frequently turn out to be not at all theologically neutral, for example in their conception of the relation of God to being, or of the nature of language and human understanding.

And the fundamental reason for this is that an entity called "philosophy" has never, as a matter of fact, really existed in pure independence from religion or theology. One can even go further to claim that the idea of a sheerly autonomous philosophy is twice over the historical invention of certain modes of theology itself. In the first place, as Pierre Hadot and others have shown, Greek philosophy was always a mode of spiritual practice and never an "interest free" enquiry involving a "view from nowhere." Paradoxically, it might seem, it was only when Jews, Muslims, and then Christians re-discovered aspects of Greek philosophy, especially Aristotle and certain fragments of neoplatonism, that they projected back onto antiquity a purely "rational" enquiry that was somewhat of their own invention. This was because antique philosophy could be viewed as at least problematically legitimate if it was taken as the work of human reason, but not if it was taken as linked to pagan religious reflection. In this way a category of "pure reason" started to come into being only as the shadow of the notion of "faith."

In many ways this re-discovery of antique thought disturbed an older Christian model for the integration of philosophy within Christian doctrine. In the case of the Greek Fathers and of Augustine, little distinction was made between *philosophia Christiana*, "doctrine" and "theology." Truth was seen as one and revelation as the restoration of a fullness of truth, insofar as this is accessible for finitude, to fallen human beings. In Aquinas certainly, in the wake of Maimonides, Ibn-Sina, and Ibn-Rushd, there is apparently a much greater distinction made between philosophy, including its rational mode of doing theology, and *sacra doctrina* which reflects upon revelation. But to regard this apparently clear distinction as simply a gain, with time, of a greater clear-sightedness about the distinction, is surely naïve. For the new distinction rather reflects the challenge posed by Aristotelianism as a philosophy seemingly true according to reason, and yet less easily assimilable with the conclusions of faith than an earlier Platonic mode of thinking. Often, of course, this circumstance gave rise to various modes of a "double truth" doctrine; later it helped to encourage a new mode of theologico-philosophical reflection which not only dared to criticize Aristotle, but also the entire Greek philosophical legacy, by vastly extending the scope of logical possibility. I am thinking, of course, of Scotus and then of the nominalists. However, in the case of Aquinas, the new circumstance rather encouraged him to show how basically Aristotelian reasons, when properly considered, themselves supported the conclusions of faith.

However, Aquinas was only here successful because he was able to show that the implications of Christian doctrine were more "materialist" than had hitherto been supposed. The material creation was not only good, its material character was also for us vital in assisting the processes of mental deliberation, reasoning to God, and the bringing about of our salvation. Even if most certainly Aristotle assisted him in making these conclusions bolder, they are nonetheless supported both by a more accurate reading of Augustine than that provided by spiritualistic and dualistic interpretations (including those of Bonaventure), and by Aquinas's deployment of the Proclean strand of neoplatonism (mediated in part by Dionysius) which already permitted an integration of a more "materialist" view within a framework that remained fundamentally emanationist and participatory. The picture Aquinas is always arguing for concerns fundamentally the logic of creation *ex nihilo*, along with the gracious raising of spiritual creatures to a supernatural end that is, nonetheless, paradoxically an integral implication of their spiritual existence as such.

Thus while Aquinas appears to deploy "purely rational" arguments, the conclusions which he is supporting are always those consistent with faith, like, for example, the diversity and autonomy in different created spirits of the operation of the active intellect, which, against the Arabs, he took to be required in order to sustain both the freedom of spiritual creatures and the ultimate significance of the material distinctness and individuality of human spiritual creatures. Furthermore, Aquinas was not a modern rationalist: he understood good reason to be an attentive reception, via the mediation of the senses and discursive operations, of the divine light of the *Logos*, in fundamental keeping (despite many scholarly denials) with the view of St. Augustine. Finally, for Aquinas, good reason can only be such if implicitly it desires, and therefore mysteriously intimates in advance, that which can only be received as a gift: namely the supernatural light of faith.[5]

In these ways Aquinas effectively restored the Patristic integration of philosophy with theology, albeit he now more distinguished to unite. This is reflected in his pedagogic practice, which rarely shows a strong division between the two modes of discourse, but rather tends constantly to shuttle between both. Reason, for him, always has an obscure onlook towards faith, while faith, which is relatively more intuitive, can never, in this life, fully leave behind the discursiveness proper to philosophy.

It follows that, for Aquinas, philosophy is not straightforwardly foundational and neither is theology straightforwardly superior.

Instead theology, whenever it intimates the heights, must humbly return to the depths and forever in time start all over again with the relatively prosaic problems posed by philosophy. Its transcendence of the philosophical perspective is always, for now, merely provisional. Inversely, philosophy offers no secure self-contained foundation, because it always necessarily gestures beyond itself, in accordance with the Augustinian version of the "Meno problematic" which Aquinas several times invokes: we can only seek God who is beyond all reach if in some strange sense we have already arrived at this destination because he has already reached down to us. The scope of this problematic for him embraces both reason and revelation and transcends their division, just as does likewise the entire framework of the participation of beings in Being and of spiritual beings in the divine light, which is in itself one and simple.

It can be argued, then, that Aquinas warded off the threat of duality posed by those Islamic philosophers with which he was familiar—even if one should point out that various Shi'ite and Sufi thinkers offered more integrating perspectives. Aquinas even, at times, when assessing the rational opinions of Plato and Aristotle, suggests that one must take account of the pagan character of their thought, though no doubt, with historicist hindsight, he did not do this to anything like a sufficient degree.

---

5. See for this and the entire account of Aquinas here given, Milbank and Pickstock, *Truth in Aquinas*. Lydia Schumacher, of Edinburgh University, is writing a genealogy of illumination doctrine that shows that Aquinas was closer to Augustine here than was Bonaventure.

For these reasons it is not entirely clear that Aquinas fully accepted the retrospective invention of the rational autonomy of philosophy. However, this autonomy was much more decisively confirmed in a second historical moment. In a gradual process stretching from Scotus to Bañez, theology started to conclude that human beings have two separate final ends, a natural and a supernatural one, and that the first remains substantially independent of the former. If previously the notion of a purely rational philosophy was shadowed by a sense of something pagan and unredeemed, now this is seen as an entirely legitimate exercise, within the bounds of "pure nature." A fully autonomous rational philosophy had at last arrived.[6]

Yet the paradox is that the secularizing gesture which permitted its arrival was entirely a theological gesture, and even one which sought to conserve the transcendence of God and the priority of the supernatural, by insisting on the sheer "naturalness" and self-sufficiency of human beings without grace, as a backdrop for augmenting grace's sheer gratuity.

This circumstance then poses a crucial question for theology today. Far from it being the case that theology is necessarily at the mercy of philosophical fashions, theology is now in a position to ask whether the fundamental assumed shape of modern philosophy as such is not the result of now buried past theological decisions. Decisions which, in theological terms, were highly questionable, if, indeed, not outrightly erroneous. Here the question of the invention of a double human end may itself be embedded in earlier and equally doubtful theological options, which all tended to suggest the comprehensibility of finite being, essences, knowledge, and causality entirely in their own terms, without reference to their created and supernatural origin. These were, primarily, the substitution of univocity for analogy in ontology; of mirroring representation for knowledge by identity in epistemology; of the primacy of possibility for the primacy of actuality in modal theory; and, finally, in the case of the theory of causality, of the "concurrence" of created with divine causality on the same ontological plane for an earlier notion of equally "self-sufficient" finite and infinite causation operating synergically on different ontological levels, with the latter conceived as transcendentally all-determining of finite causes in their very independence.[7]

6. See Milbank, *Suspended Middle*.

7. See for this and much of the following, Boulnois, *Être et representation*; Nef, *Qu'est-ce que la métaphysique*, 314–415; Schmutz, "La doctrine médiévale des causes et la

In all four cases one has a new set of philosophical theses, which dictate the entire consequent course of modern philosophy. But in all four cases also, it is arguable that the most fundamental reasons for the adoption of these theses were theological. As regards univocity, Avicenna and later Scotus were concerned not just with logic but with the security of the proof for God's existence which, in order to be fully apodeictic, can be held to require a stable middle term. Scotus was in addition concerned to defend the coherence of predicating terms like "goodness" of God by insisting upon their core stability of meaning. Finally, he also regarded the idea that being in the abstract rather than materialized being is the natural first object of human understanding as both guaranteeing our spiritual nature and indicating the difference between a pre-fallen and fallen, sensually debased exercise of intelligence.

As regards representation, the new model was much encouraged by Scotus's view that one can formally distinguish the divine intellect, as representing truth, from the divine being, which enjoys a certain metaphysical primacy. It was equally encouraged, from Scotus through to Ockham, by the view that God, through exercise of his *potentia absoluta,* can sever the normal link between our mind's understanding of things and the way they are in themselves.

In the case of the modal priority of the possible over the actual, it is, once again, a matter of stressing the divine *potentia absoluta* as his primary attribute, along with an elevation of the divine will over the divine intellect, as well as, still more significantly, the formal distinction of the two. The latter notion ensures that reasoning, sundered from the erotic, will be more and more thought of in terms of the consideration of an *a priori* repertoire of logical possibilities, while equally willing, sundered from an intrinsic determination by the rationally best, starts to become reduced to an arbitrary choice that precedes any necessities endemic to an order of actuality.

In the case of concurrence, the more divine freedom is construed in univocal and so ontotheological terms as guaranteed by its power to out-compete and trump created freedom, then the more, paradoxically, created freedom is also granted an autonomous space outside divine causation.

---

théologie de la nature pure." Pickstock, "Duns Scotus." Milbank, "Thomistic Telescope." Burrell, "Aquinas and Scotus" in *Faith and Freedom,* 91–113.

Thus it is plausible to argue that the modern philosophical preference for univocity, for representation, for possibility, the sundering of will
from intellect, and the picture of divine and created causality as being in
competition with each other, possesses not fully-acknowledged theological roots. From a Christian point of view, the buried theological stratum
of modern thought represents not obviously a progressive advance in
Christian reasoning, but is rather thoroughly questionable.

In brief: univocity breaks with the entire legacy of negative theology
and eminent attribution, which also undergirded doctrines of deification.
It obliterates the sense that creation is through and through a divine gift
through its claim that being as such, as opposed to finite being, is not
created, since the term "being" has now become a logically transcendental place-holder that precedes any existentially actual reality. Hence both
infinite and finite being are now held to presume the formal possibility
"to be."[8] For Aquinas, by contrast, the divine infinite being is an absolutely
unprecedented and mysterious simple actuality that is identical with infinite intelligence, while abstract being in general, *ens commune*, is first of
all a created actuality and only thereby a subject of possible becoming or
even of fictional speculation.

The theory of knowledge by representation is likewise theologically
questionable—first because, in God, since he is simple, intellect cannot
"follow," even metaphysically, upon being. Secondly, because the harmonious continuity between the way things exist in matter and the way they
exist in our mind embodies a certain pan-sacramental order that is part
of the divine government of the world, reflecting the divine reason as
such, and therefore not liable to be interrupted by even a divine whim.
Thirdly, because the theory of knowledge by identity respects the partially spiritual, because integrally formed character of all created things
as proceeding from God. Knowledge, from a theological point of view, as
Aquinas taught, has the spiritual purpose of raising and enhancing reality; it is not primarily, in its *raison d'être*, a neutral Sherlock Holmes-like
capacity for observation and accurate inference.

Meanwhile, the priority of possibility denies the traditional sense
that there can be a kind of necessity in actuality as such which is a beautiful, harmonious, grace-imbued good order, recognizable by wise, rightly-
ordered judgment. It also tends, in purely philosophical terms, as David

8. See Honnefelder, *La Métaphysique comme science transcendentale.*

Burrell has pointed out, unrealistically to think of choices in terms of pure logical availability, whereas in practice certain initial choices drastically preclude later ones, whether for pragmatic reasons or for reasons of the formation of a habit.[9] The same theory finally leaves mysterious the question of what sways any choice: in reality there is no "pure will," but only the persuading of desire by some reason or lure that appears to a subject as more convincing or persuasive.

Finally, the theory of causal concurrence idolatrously reduces divine power to being merely a supremely big instance of the power that we know about, and denies the eminent capacity of divine power fully to determine even created freedom, while leaving the latter as free in its own terms and on its own level.

The above set of reflections suggests an initial agenda for the field of "theology and philosophy": a need, in the wake of the writings of recent historians of philosophy which all tend to converge on the same conclusions (some of which I have tried here to summarize), to reflect upon the buried theological origins of modern philosophy and the implications of this both for theology and for our current global culture.

But not just for our culture, also for our entire society. Pope Benedict in his great Regensburg address, and the materialist philosopher Quentin Meillassoux in his little book *Après la finitude,* are significantly at one in diagnosing the ideological problem of the twenty-first century.[10] The philosophy of the twentieth century was predicated on the autonomy of pure reason and the impossibility of metaphysical speculation. Latterly, however, we have seen the deconstruction of the attempts even to define the limits of what can properly be known about, whether in the case of Derrida's critique of Husserl, or Rorty's consummation of the critique of the analytic enterprise. Conjoined to this is the collapse of the ideologies of finitude: positivism, Marxism, Freudianism, even Darwinism. But this has left an appalling vacuum. Without metaphysical mediation, various modes of fideistic religion were covertly emerging throughout the last century, and now, in the new one, they rush in to fill the cognitive void because societies cannot exist without some sort of account of what is real and desirable. The only alternatives now to fideism and the growth of arbitrary theocracy of whatever mode are an entirely nihilistic mode of

9. See Burrell, "Al Ghazali on created freedom," and "Creation, will and knowledge in Aquinas and Duns Scotus," in *Faith and Freedom,* 156–89.

10. Meillassoux, *Après la Finitude.*

market society on the one hand (which will require increasingly authoritarian policing), or else a return to prominence, as the Pope advocates, of metaphysical discourses capable of mediating between faith and reason. To recover and renew such discourses we need to commence with an understanding of how, in the Islamic and Christian West, reason and faith first became separated from each other.

Imagination, History, and Literature

Recovery however, is not enough, because, as Pope Benedict also indicated, modernity is not simply to be rejected. The modern emphases upon strict logical identity, the independence of thought from being, the scope of possibility and freedom, have indeed increased our sense, albeit in a distorted because Promethean or else relativistic fashion, of the primacy of cultural mediation—the way human beings through sign, image, and artefact create their own world and are in turn shaped by this world. There is no avoiding this new awareness by longing for the impossible return of a totally fixed, hierarchical, cosmic, and social order wherein all knew their place.

On the other hand, as Bruno Latour has pointed out, modernity rests upon one supreme contradiction. *Nature* is supposed to be given and fixed and to run according to immutable laws, while *culture* is supposed to be entirely mutable and to pursue no pre-assigned ends whatsoever.[11] Yet today we realize that there may be nothing fixed about nature and that her supposed "laws" may merely apply to certain regional natural republics of habit within a more fundamental sea of chaos. Moreover, we have discovered that there may be no intrinsic limit to our capacity to transform also the physical world for good or ill. Nature, too, it seems, turns out to be cultural. But on the other hand, if that is the case, then our cultural reality is conversely entirely natural—it exhibits, as it were, on the surface of the earth, a strange fusion of nature's capacity both for unpredictable fluidity and for the imposition of order.

Once again, in postmodern terms one can read this scenario either nihilistically or theologically. In the latter perspective the question "how should we be?" turns out to make no sense if it does not also mean "how should the whole of nature be?" since nature is no more given than cul-

11. Latour, *Politics of Nature*. See also Serres, *L'Incandescent*.

ture. On the other hand, the discovery that there is after all no "nature" in the sense of a given order, can lead us back to the view that all finite reality is not "nature" but rather "creation." As created, all things participate in the divine creative power which is at once order-making and yet unpredictable, like the flow of music. Human beings simple command this power more intensely and consciously and this is the valid sense in which they are cultural beings.

A renewed metaphysics should not seek to suppress the primacy of becoming and the event either in nature or culture. It should not recognize divine order in the world despite the flux but through and because of it, albeit in its series of complex and always relatively stable and consistent punctuations. The participation of finite being and intelligence in the godhead needs now to be re-thought in terms of the vital flow of historical becoming which will take account of the way in which, while ontological structures provide the setting for events, the latter can also exceed the import of pre-given structures. This is in fact allowed for by Aquinas's view that *essentia* is actualised by *esse*, but the implication needs much further drawing out.[12] One can say here that the neoplatonic sense of metaphysical genealogy, namely that the "how" of the way things are must be traced back to the "why" of their ultimate ontological derivation (whereas for Scotus and his legacy the "how" of things is complete as a description without advertence to origin)[13] needs to be infused also with a sense of historicist genealogy, namely that the "how" of things must also be traced back to their temporal derivation.

The issue then is to understand just how the process of temporal becoming participates in the eternal procession of the creation from the divine Trinity, which is itself a kind of eternal and perfected process of emanation and yet equally a process of internal "becoming." The Son emanates perfectly from the Father, but the latter "becomes" Father retrospectively (as it were) only through this perfect imaging. The Spirit then expresses, one could say, the perfect unity of metaphysical origination from the perfect with "historical" evolution from an origin to further explication (even though, in God, this *explicatio* is perfect eternal *complicatio* which renders the origin replete from the outset).

As a participation in this doubly-inflected genesis, one could speculate, creation is atemporally and emanatively given to us always through

12. See Rosemann, *Omne ens est aliquid*, for an important attempt to do so.

13. On this point, see Perrier, "Duns Scotus Facing Reality," 619–43.

the eschatological achievement of the new Jerusalem, the perfected heaven and earth, and all our lesser, spoiled historical realities depend for their very existence upon this mediating source. On the other hand, a slow coming to be from Adam, contingently interrupted by the fact of sin and the process of redemption always at work (for even our ontological sustaining), unfolds through time the "becoming" aspect of the Trinitarian life. One can dub the first aspect "Oriental apocalyptic," and the second, the "Occidental historical." This division then roughly corresponds to the role of the imagination in respectively "literature" and history. I will take the second first.

A more historicized metaphysics must give more attention to the role of the imagination. As Aquinas already knew, the latter is for us the threshold between matter and spirit: it is the mysterious alchemical point at which mind, in order to think at all, must produce its own shadowy sensations that must always be "returned to" in order to complete a thought (*conversio ad phantasmata*). Normally we see "right through" these phantasms in order to re-establish contact, via our senses, with the physical world outside us. And yet they are always secretly at work and this is exhibited in the way we not only sense the world and all it includes, but necessarily and "fantastically" sense it "as something." It is just this capacity which renders us consciously historical creatures and one can say that "history happens in the primary imagination," in Coleridgean terms.[14] What makes a historical event an event is precisely the fusion of sensation and thought which imagination, and not reason alone, brings about. And to this is added the work of the secondary imagination when the mind, in the absence of present physical realities, is capable of projecting its shadowy sensations back out into the sensorily perceived world in order to modify it. This gives rise, in the first place, to those fictions that we believe in, those fictions that we inhabit, and which also, along with imaginatively perceived natural realities, help to compose our human history.

And then there are those fictions that we do not inhabit, or not fully, or which we know that we could never inhabit. Pictures of what has never been; symbols of the intrinsically absent and ineffably secret; stories that are simply "made up" and may never be fully enacted. This is the realm of literature, where the secondary imagination absolutely rules. But together with the historical, now intrinsic for both philosophy and theology, the literary is also, in postmodernity, inescapable.

14. For Samuel Taylor Coleridge on the imagination, see his *Biographia Literaria*.

Why should this be? It has to do with the double import of the imagination. The latter, as I have said, is the mediating twilight threshold between spirit and matter, or between reason and the senses. Its strangest characteristic as a "between" phenomenon is that it resides "in the middle voice," at once passive and active.[15] Whereas we can control even where we direct our gaze, images flood into our mind when our eyes are shut, often unprovoked. All the same, we can to some degree learn to conjure these images at will and to shape the precise from which they take. However, at the point of seemingly most control, when we are being "creative," it is more as if we must find the trick of "summonsing" in to the chamber of our mind elusive hidden realities that are seemingly in some sense "already there." (This is why, in mystical Islamic thought, the imagination is seen as opening onto a realm of intermediate beings, or *genie*, rather as rarefied reason opens upon the angelic realm;[16] similar considerations are found fragmentarily within Christendom in terms of the intrinsic link between imagination and "faerie.")

But this double aspect both renders thought more real, and reality more spectral. And this is exactly why modernity, which ever since the Renaissance has more and more opened up the power of the imagination (including the technical imagination), is at once more historical and more fantastic than were the Middle Ages. For a greater sense of our reliance upon the primary imagination grounds thought back in sensation and image, and makes us realize that our thinking is inseparable from our corporeal living and from all that has really happened to us. On the other hand, the further release of the secondary imagination (escaping from ecclesiastical, political, and sexual censorship), reveals to us the fluidity of physical nature as such and the way that form and image is far more intrinsically spectral than even rational speculation.

This release can, of course, be part of a scenario whereby "art" usurps the place of religion in the long-term wake of the *religious* refusal of the icon, which helped to secularize the image.[17] On the other hand, it can also serve to point up the very core of the religious impulse in a clearer way than for the often more abstract reason-dominated Middle Ages, which towards the end became very iconoclastic in its dominant specula-

15. For "the between" (*metaxu*), see Desmond, *Being and the Between*. For "the middle voice," see Pickstock, *After Writing, passim*.

16. See Corbin, *Alone with the Alone*.

17. See Boulnois, *Au-delá de c'image*.

tive theology. (And it is probably the case that only an appeal to the logic of the imagination allows the "great tradition" of theology from Origen to Aquinas adequately to counter the more consistent rationalism of the nominalist revolution.) For the secondary imagination is also the very point at which reason and faith become conjoined. This is because the theological necessarily links rational reflection with the contemplative regard of historical events and visualized pictures or symbols. Its elusive blend of idea and image belongs precisely to the realm of the imaginative "between." Moreover, it is by exercise of the secondary imagination that we have to try to connect historical becoming (including the Incarnation and the emergence of the Church) with the descending emanation of all of nature and culture from the perfect Godhead. Rationally informed faith, therefore, is the exact place at which thinking about history (inhabited fictions and real-ideal occurrences) and thinking about literature (uninhabited fictions) comes together. Since religion concerns "believed-in fictions" or fictions *that might be inhabited or in some sense already dimly are*, it transcends the contrast between literature and history, just as, in the life of Christ, *mythos*, as narrative saturated with meaning, and *historia*, as real event deficient in meaning, *really* (and not just in our supposing) come together.[18]

In the light of faith, therefore, history and fiction both appear as different kinds of ontologically real realms, since they are both situated in the more all-embracing world disclosed by the light of faith: the world in which imagination discerns the link between emanative derivation (which we can only "fantasize") on the one hand, and historical becoming on the other. Merely fideistic faith, by contrast, tends to ape a rationalistic reason without faith and a positivistically-conceived history, ignoring its constitutively ideal dimension (the way in which "what happens" is always in part "what people think has happened"). Fideisms or fundamentalisms always notably downgrade imagination, or go for the kitsch, because they reduce *revelata* to factual assumptions and theology to a few simple and rigid rational deductions from those assumptions.

The reflections in this third section are intended to try to explain why, in the modern era from Hamann through to Tolkien via Claudel and Péguy, it has been literary works that have often most successfully defended and rethought the orthodox Christian legacy. Having understood

---

18. For this thesis, see Milbank, *Being Reconciled*, 94–95.

this, we can in the future take more systematic account of the literary-imaginative dimension.

By the agenda of "theology, philosophy, and literature," therefore, I propose in the first place a reflection on the theological origins of modern philosophy. In the second place a theological critique of modern philosophy. In the third place an attempt further to incorporate temporality into metaphysics. And in the fourth a realization that a rationally informed faith requires the imaginary perspectives of literature as well as the imaginative perspectives of human history.

PART VI

Theopolitical Agendas

16

POSTMODERN CRITICAL
AUGUSTINIANISM

A Short Summa *in Forty-Two Responses*
to Unasked Questions

1. The end of modernity, which is not accomplished, yet continues to arrive, means the end of a single system of truth based on universal reason, which tells us what reality is like.

2. With this ending, there ends also the modern predicament of theology. It no longer has to measure up to accepted secular standards of scientific truth or normative rationality. Nor, concomitantly, to a fixed notion of the knowing subject, which was usually the modern, as opposed to the pre-modern, way of securing universal reason. This caused problems for theology, because an approach grounded in subjective aspiration can only precariously affirm objective values and divine transcendence.

3. In postmodernity there are infinitely many possible versions of truth, inseparable from particular narratives. Objects and subjects are, as they are narrated in a story. Outside a plot, which has its own unique, unfounded reasons, one cannot conceive how objects and subjects would be, nor even that they would be at all. If subjects and objects only are, through the complex relations of a narrative, then neither objects are privileged, as in pre-modernity, nor subjects, as in modernity. Instead, what matters are structural relations, which constantly shift; the word "subject" now indicates a point of potent "intensity" which can re-arrange given structural patterns.

4. The priority given to structural relations allows theology to make a kind of half-turn back to pre-modernity. One can no longer commence with modern inwardness: this is only marked negatively as "intensity" or potential, and the things that can truly be spoken about are once again external. However, this externality is no longer, as for pre-modernity, so clearly an organized spatial realm of substances, genera, and species, but rather a world of temporary relational and habitual networks, always being re-distributed, with greater and greater "freedom," as one passes from mineral to vegetable to animal to cultural animal. So the point is not to "represent" this externality, but just to join in its occurrence; not to know, but to intervene, originate.

5. Externality is therefore a kind of process. One cannot look at this process as a whole, but one can try to imagine what it means, its significance. All cultures, all "religions," in effect see their temporal processes as microcosms of the whole process. Of course, postmodernism denies the point of doing this, except as a game. Yet to understand one's own proffered words or actions as just arbitrary, itself implies a speculation on the arbitrariness of the process in general: its universal production of the merely contingent. Christian theology, by contrast to nihilistic postmodernism, yet with equal validity, imagines temporal process as, in its very temporality, reflecting eternity; as the possibility of a historical progress into God, and as something recuperable within memory whose ultimate point is the allowing of forgiveness and reconciliation. This speculation is utterly unfounded, is inseparable from a narrative practice of remembering, and yet, in postmodern terms, it is just as valid or invalid as claims about supposedly universal human needs, desires, or modes of interaction. Modernity dictated that a sensible theology would start from "below"; postmodernity implies that conceptions of the "below"—of human subjectivity and relationship—are only constituted within the narrative that simultaneously postulates the "above." Once the epistemological approach from the subject is shown to be *more* foundationalist than premodern metaphysics, the latter makes a strange kind of return: but as a necessary "fiction" concerning the unseen relation of time to eternity, not as a modern record of "observation" of this relationship.

6. Postmodern theology does not, therefore, begin with an account of the subject, for this is not neutrally available. By the same token, it is not seriously challenged by modernist discourses claiming to narrate a

universally fundamental genesis of the subject in individual lives or in human history: Freudianism, Marxism, sociology. On the other hand, it has faced a new and perhaps more severe challenge from the implications of a more thoroughgoing perspectival historicism which is what intellectual postmodernism is really all about. If Christianity is just one of many possible perspectives, then why believe any of them? Is not each perspective a strategy of power, every discourse but the means to assert that discourse? Postmodernism seems to imply nihilism, albeit of a "positive" kind, embracing contingency and arbitrariness as the real natural good.

7. Whatever its response may be to nihilism, postmodern theology can only proceed by explicating Christian liturgical practice. The Christian God can no longer be thought of as a God first seen, but rather as a God first prayed to, first imagined, first inspiring certain actions, first put into words, and always already thought about, objectified, even if this objectification is recognized as inevitably inadequate. This practice which includes images of, talk about, addresses to, actions towards "God," can in no way be justified, nor be shown to be more rational, nor yet outside its own discourse, as more desirable, than nihilism, even if it alone "saves" the reality of both desire and reason.

8. But is this really all that can be said? That Christianity is just "on a level" with other practices, other discourses? Not quite. First, it may be argued that Christianity can become "internally" postmodern in a way that may not be possible for every religion or ideology. I mean by this that it is possible to construe Christianity as suspicious of notions of definably fixed "essences" in its approach to human beings, to nature, to community, and to God, even if it has never fully escaped the grasp of a "totalizing" metaphysics. Through its belief in creation from nothing it admits temporality, the priority of becoming, and unexpected emergence. A reality suspended between nothing and infinity is a reality of flux, a reality in the end without substance, composed only of relational differences and ceaseless alterations (Augustine, *De Musica*). Like nihilism, Christianity can, should, embrace the differential flux.

9. Yet here arises the second point regarding whether Christianity is just "on a level." For nihilism, the flux is a medium of perpetual conflict, a pagan *agon* where the most powerful rhetoric will temporarily triumph, only to succumb to an apparently or effectively more powerful discourse in the future. Because there are no fixed categorical areas for different

discourses/practices, they ceaselessly overlap and contest for influence. Lyotard and others rightly did not envisage a peaceful co-existence of a plurality of discourses alongside each other, without mutual interference. The best that can be hoped for is some mitigation of the severity of conflict, a set of formal rules of engagement such as is provided by the market or bureaucracy—forms which can survive many changes in the actual content of "truth." For this reason, postmodern nihilism remains in continuity with liberalism and the Enlightenment. Christianity, however, unlike many other discourses, pursued from the outset a universalism which tried to subsume rather than merely abolish difference: Christians could remain in their many different cities, languages, and cultures, yet still belong to one eternal city ruled by Christ, in whom all "humanity" was fulfilled. In this way it appears as a "precursor" of enlightenment, and any claim of outright Christian opposition to enlightenment is bound to be an over-simplification. But the liberty, equality, and fraternity latent as values in Christianity do not imply mere mutual tolerance, far less any resignation to a regulated conflict. On the contrary, Christianity is peculiar, because while it is open to difference—to a series of infinitely new additions, insights, progressions towards God—it also strives to make of all these differential additions a harmony, "in the body of Christ," and claims that if the reality of God is properly attended to, there can be such a harmony. And the idea of a consistently beautiful, continuously differential and open series, is of course the idea of "music." In music there must be continuous endings and displacements, yet this is no necessary violence, because only in the recall of what has been displaced does the created product consist. Violence would rather mean an unnecessarily jarring note, a note wrong because "out of place," or else the premature ending of a development. Perhaps this is partly why, in *De Musica* and later texts, Augustine—who realized that creation *ex nihilo* implied the non-recognition of ontological violence, or of positive evil—put forwards a "musical" ontology. Christianity, therefore, is not just in the same position as all other discourses vis-à-vis postmodernity; it can, I want to claim, think difference, yet it perhaps uniquely tries to deny that this necessarily (rather than contingently, in a fallen world) entails conflict.

10. Explication of Christian practice, the task of theology, tries to pinpoint the peculiarity, the difference, of this practice by "making it strange," finding a new language for this difference less tainted with the over-familiarity of too many Christian words which tend to obscure Christian

singularity. The idea that this practice is essentially "music" would be an example of this "making strange." And as a second example, this music implies "community" in a very particular sense. For Christianity, true community means the freedom of people and groups to be different, not just to be functions of a fixed consensus, yet at the same time it totally refuses *indifference*; a peaceful, united, secure community implies *absolute* consensus, and yet, where difference is acknowledged, this is no agreement in an idea, or something once and for all achieved, but a consensus that is only in and through the interrelations of community itself, and a consensus that moves and "changes": a *concentus musicus*. Christianity (and not even Judaism, which postpones universality to the eschaton, a final chord) uniquely has this idea of community: this is what "Church" should be all about.

11. Unless it reflects upon the singularity of Christian norms of community, theology has really nothing to think about. For Christian practice, like every practice, is all external, a matter of signs and actions interpellating "persons." The tradition already insisted that "God" is only spoken about with reference to certain historical happenings and memories; a postmodern emphasis will underscore the traditional view that God is never directly seen, never looked at. The response to God is response to the pressure of the unknown, and if Christians ask what is God like, then they can only point to our "response" to God in the formation of community. God's self-disclousre does not precede liturgy. The community partially shows what God is like, and he is even more like the ideal, the goal of community implicit in its practices. Hence he is also unlike the community, and it is this inexpressible reality that the community continues to try to respond to.

12. If God can only be given some content forms through the mediation of community, then speaking of God is not just a matter of words, but also of images, and bodily actions. These all articulate "God."

13. The community as substantive peace, as musical difference, is actually performed, ideally imagined, and in both these aspects, contemplated.

14. Augustine already put the idea of the peaceful community at the center of his theology; thought of God, of revelation from God, was for him inseparable from the thought of heaven, of words and "musical laws" coming down from heaven. The heavenly city meant for Augustine a substantial

peace; but this peace could also be imperfectly present in the fallen world, in the sequences of time, and time redeemed through memory.

15. One way to try to secure peace is to draw boundaries around "the same," and exclude "the other"; to promote some practices and disallow alternatives. Most polities, and most religions, characteristically do this. But the Church has misunderstood itself when it does likewise. For the point of the supersession of the law is that nothing really positive is excluded—no difference, whatsoever—but only the negative, that which denies and takes away from Being: in other words, the violent. It is true, however, that Christians perceive a violence that might not normally be recognized, namely any stunting of persons' capacity to love and conceive of the divine beauty; this inhibition is seen as having its soul in arbitrariness. But there is no real exclusion here; Christianity should not draw boundaries, and the Church is that paradox: a nomad city.

16. The religions and polities that exclude characteristically seek to identify one thing that must be removed: a scapegoat, which can become in some ambiguous fashion "sacred," because of the efficacious effect of its expulsion, bearing away all that is undesirable, together with all the guilt of the community. At the same time, the relationship of the community to the transcendently divine often demands further acts of distinction in the form of "sacrifice." The divine demands an offering, the violent separation, by fire or knife, of spirit from body, a purging off, to send up to heaven. This could include the lives of those fallen in holy wars, or else the sacrifice of a pure ascetic spirit that has become indifferent to disturbing emotions.

17. Instead of multiple difference, there is dualism here; the banished, the purged-off, over against the included, the subsumed. The law of this dualism implies an ever-renewed conflict both within and without the city-gates. This is the *traditional* mode of violence, whose existence must certainly be noted, though it is different in kind to modern/postmodern regulated and "indifferent" conflict. Of course, legal monotheism, and Christianity when it has failed to escape this mode, remains half-trapped by this dualism. But a Christianity true to itself should oppose all modes of arbitrary or unjustifiable violence: the pre-modern violence of law, the modern violence of norms of subjective "rights," the postmodern violence of total lack of norms. Yet the rejection of dualistic violence grows throughout the Bible: monotheism and creation out of nothing eschew

the idea of a "chaotic" realm over against the divine, in eternal conflict with it. And the Jewish idea of law aspires to the idea of a law at one with life, with Being. But there is still some exclusion of the positive, some attempt to secure in a code the harmony of Being, and no complete recognition that perfect, divine rule is beyond all coercion. In a sense, this is a failure to have a perfect monotheism, and exhibits residues of dualism; in another sense mere monotheism is inadequate, as it cannot think of God as primarily the openness of love to the other.

18. Where there is a positing of a sacred over against a chaotic other, then the supremacy of the sacred can always be deconstructed, for it appears that there is something more ultimate that includes both the sacred and chaos, which governs the passage between them. Is not this passage itself chaotic? Hence there is a hidden connection between pre-modern pagan dualism and postmodern dualism. The latter's self-proclaimed paganism is a kind of deconstructed paganism, for the real pagans were always hoping to subordinate the admitted conflictual diversity of the gods to a harmonious order; an open celebration of the finality of the *agon* was only latent. But Christianity, which is not dualistic in this fashion, and already admits the flux of difference, is therefore outside the reach of deconstruction.

19. If pre-modern religions and postmodern nihilism are secretly akin, indeed different moments of a "dialectic" (postmodernism claims to refuse dialectic, but this is the instance of its failure to do so; it is right to make the effort), then, by contrast, one can trace in the Bible the slow emergence of opposition to the common factor of violence in all human norms. For it gradually takes the part of the scapegoat, and starts to place a ban on revenge against those who first violently excluded their brethren (the protection of Cain by God). The Hebrews were originally nomads, and chance and prophecy constantly recalled them to their nomad status (Girard).

20. In the course of this nomadic history, sacrifice is also commuted. Finally, in Christianity, God is thought of as asking only for the offering of our free-will, in a return of love to him. This is no longer in any sense a self-destruction, or self-division, but rather a self-fulfillment, an offering that is at the same time our reception of the fullness of Being. It is receiving God: "deification."

21. In a world dominated by evil and violence, self-offering to God and others inevitably involves suffering. This is why there is suffering at the heart of Christ's perfect self-offering to God.

22. This is not, of course the offering of a blood-sacrifice to God. Before the cross comes the preaching of the kingdom. The kingdom is really offered by Christ to humanity, and the cross is the result of a rejection of this offer. However, this very rejection tends to suggest the "original" character of human sin; to sin, theology has speculated, is to refuse the love of God, and so to render oneself incapable of recognizing God, by substituting the goals of human pride in his place The putting to death of God shows what evil is: its nihilistic pointlessness, its incomprehensibility (Schwäger).

23. This speculation continues: evil cannot fully see itself as evil; therefore only the uncontaminated good, God himself, can fully suffer evil—not in eternity, which is beyond suffering, but in the human creation: hence the necessity for the *Deus Homo*. Such a speculation is an important part of Christianity, a theoretical component which a postmodern approach can recognize as actually "taking off" from the narrative sources, as not *fully* grounded in them, and yet as validated by the profundity of the picture of God which results, merely by the pleasing shape of the conceits which it generates. However, at the same time a postmodern approach must do more justice to the narrative, practical, social level than in the past. For if Jesus's perfect suffering belonged to his "interiority," then how can it make any difference to us, how would we know about it? Much past theology has seemed to suggest that there is a change, consequent upon the atonement, in the divine attitude towards us, a change to which we are just "extrinsically" related, and which is just "positively" revealed to us. However, if the perfect character of Jesus's suffering is recognized by us, then this can only mean that it is present "on the outside," in his deeds, and words, and even in the words used by others which compose the record of Christ; for it is only the recorded, interpreted Christ who saves us, and this mediation does not conceal some more original, "self-present" Christ—that would be a mere asocial phantom. The speculation about atonement is grounded in a narrative relation to which we must constantly return: the Church considers that in all its actions it can learn to suffer truly (and thereby perceive our previous original sin of unperceived egotism) from the story of Jesus, so that

its plot can be fulfilled universally. Does this practical situation imply the finality of Jesus, his identity with the divine word? The more subtle reply is, not quite, for practice cannot claim to "know" the finality of what it treats as final. Even a theoretical, speculative discourse conceived as having a second order, "regulative" function is finally excessive (in a positive sense), and makes its own peculiar contribution to the content of Christianity, thereby insinuating itself back into first-order discourse from which it is only relatively distinguished (as all speech both orders and regulates, and regulates only in giving new orders). Thus, in the New Testament itself, speculative considerations about the atonement are celebrated in poetic, devotional terms. Already the metaphors and mythical "metanarratives" implying incarnation and atonement are "somewhat in excess"; they not only secure the first-order level of "historical" narrative recitation, they also go speculatively beyond this to suggest a particular "mythical" picture of God as becoming incarnate, suffering in our stead. Nothing entirely justifies this speculation except itself, and the way it illuminates and enriches the stories told, and re-doubles the perceived significance of Christian practices. Nevertheless the speculative truth is accorded a full metaphysical reality.

24. For the traditional speculation, God cannot endure the contradiction of sin; creation must offer itself back to God; evil prevents it from doing so; therefore God must offer creation back to God, through the incarnation of the *Logos*, who includes all things. Yet for early Christianity, it is clear that God suffers a contradiction until all make for themselves the offering already made by Christ. The "incarnation" has no meaning, therefore, except as "the beginning," the foundation of the Church, a new sort of community of charity and forgiveness, as a space for the possibility of this offering. For Augustine, it is the *Church* that is the adequate sacrifice to God; in other words the realization of perfect community. The centrality of incarnation and the cross in no way contradicts the truth that the central aspect of salvation is the creation of perfect community between humans and between humans and God.

25. Christianity is primarily about this hope for community. But it offers more than hope: it also remembers perfect community as once instantiated by the shores of Lake Galilee; this is a memory compounded only of words and images. But there should be no pathos here, and Christianity has too often been sunk in this pathos. It is not that we have

a few fragments of memory in lieu of the "real presence" of the resurrected Christ, but that these fragments are the real saving presence; they provide us—within the whole network of tradition within which they belong—with a new language of community. The Christian claim is that the narratives about Christ show what love—a difficult and demanding practice requiring more subtlety, style, and correct idiom than mere "well-meaning"—is. That here is the *logos*, the lost harmonic pattern of genuine human life, which can now be re-appropriated.

26. What are we to make of the fact that a "resurrection" forms a part of this memory? Resurrection is no proof of divinity, nor a kind of vindication of Jesus's mission. And no very good "evidence" survives, only the record of some strongly insisted-upon personal testimonies. What we have is the memory of communion, of "ordinary" conversation, of eating and drinking, continuing beyond death. Without this element, there could not really be a memory of a moment of "perfect" community, for this is normally inhibited by the forces of nature as we know them, and by death, especially.

27. To remember the resurrection, to hope for the universal resurrection, is a "political" act: for it is the ultimate refusal of all denials of community. The return of all the dead in reconciliation—the innocent, the guilty, the oppressed, and the oppressors—is looked for (Peukert).

28. The resurrection is about the persistence of the ordinary, and the doctrine of the Incarnation locates God in the ordinary, even if this is an ordinariness "transfigured." Although this doctrine is a radical speculation, which was only gradually articulated, it is also a rebuke to attempts to formulate metaphysically the divine perfection; one can make groping attempts, but finally God's perfection is most like this particular life, historically obscure, almost lost to view.

29. God is most to be found in this life recognizably like our own, yet also recognized as uniquely "other," because we take it as judging all other lives.

30. The doctrine of the Incarnation—of Jesus's "identity" with the divine *Logos*—secures this practical relation of the Church to Jesus, yet also goes beyond and reinforces it in the way suggested above. Its real validation is in allowing us to imagine a peaceful, totally charitable God, who cannot force us, and yet cannot let us go. Also, by returning us to the

narrative, by tying us to contingency, it suggests that divine goodness is no generalized intention, but always takes a very particular "form." That it is inseparable from aesthetic harmony.

31. Yet in the memory of Christ we are given the language of salvation and not formulas for how to use this language. For the universal offering to be made, the Church must creatively construct her own response to Christ. This is why there is a work of the Spirit that can be distinguished from that of Christ, even though this response itself is ideally and infinitely fulfilled within the Godhead.

32. For if evil is truly overcome in the perfect harmony of Christ's life in community with his followers, and in the language of this community that we remember, this still does not mean that here we possess a *gnosis*, in the sense of a given formulaic wisdom that we must just recite or magically invoke. Instead, this language allows us to *escape* from the dominating effects of human discourses that totally subsume all differences, new occurrences, under existing categories. Atonement means that the flux is permitted to flow again, that the *Logos* only really speaks with its real intent in the ever-different articulation of our responses. The Holy Spirit is associated with this diversity of answers. But they all form the continuous unity of the body of Christ.

33. The doctrine of the Trinity is a statement of faith that God is, "in himself," even though he also negatively *exceeds* this, in continuity with how he has been imagined by us to relate to human history. Here we imagine him to speak once as a Word that unifies all other words, and as continuously achieving that final unification of all other words by articulating a manifold response to the one Word. So God involves not just the first difference of expressive articulation of content (inseparable from content), but also the second difference of interpretation of expression (inseparable from expression, making expression always already conversation). Without this second difference, we would be tempted to think that the expression just carried us back to a pre-formed content, or else that God was but a single ratio, which would be little better than seeing him as but a single person With this second difference, one truly has a moment of response to expression in God, which goes beyond, is "excessive" in relation to, the expression. Hence the love that subsists between Father and Son is communicated as a further difference that always escapes, or, as Stanislas Breton put it, "an *infinite* relation."

34. God as Trinity is therefore himself community, and even a "community in process," infinitely realized, beyond any conceivable opposition between "perfect act" and "perfect potential." A Trinitarian ontology can therefore be a differential ontology surpassing the Aristotelian *actus purus*.

35. "In the image of the Trinity" means that "human beings" are moments of particularly intense and adaptive "recollection" within the temporal process, although such recollection is constitutive of the temporal process itself. For a present moment "is" in its repetitive holding of the past, yet in this "remembering" it escapes at one level the temporal continuum and arrives as a "meaning" which has a free capacity for adaptation and expansion (Augustine, *Confessions*; Deleuze).

36. The human mind does not "correspond" to reality, but arises within a process which gives rise to "effects of meaning." It is a particularly intense network of such effects. Our bodily energies and drives (for Augustine in *Civitas Dei*, the *ingenium* which images the power of the divine Father) are made "present" and articulate (so alone constituted and sustained) through the happening of linguistic "meaning," which is also the event of a "truth" which cannot "correspond." For Augustine this second moment is the cultural training of the artist's *ingenium*; it is also that active memory by which we constantly learn through repeating our individual and collective biographies. Knowledge "surfaces" as the process of learning, which is true if divinely "illumined"—it is not a knowledge of an object outside that process. (God being this process, in its infinite plenitude.)

37. The mind is only illumined by the divine *Logos*, if also our "preceding" energies, and our "emergent" desires, correspond to the Father and the Spirit, respectively. We know what we want to know, and although all desiring is an "informed" desiring, desire shapes truth beyond the imminent implications of any logical order, so rendering the Christian *logos* a continuous product as well as a process of "art." Moreover, if all that "is" is good and true, then no positive reality can be false as a "mistake," or as "non-correspondence," but only false as deficient presence, embodying the short-fall of an inadequate desire. Now true desire mediates to us reality.

38. All desire is good so long as it is a genuinely restless yet serene desire (a more-desiring desire), which is moved in part by persistent lack,

the pull of the "goal" as well as by a foretaste of consummation. Such desire is nonviolent, for it could only be content with the unrestricted openness, non-possessiveness and self-offering of resurrected bodies. Yet this is not the cold "detachment" (both in relation to creatures and away from creatures) of a "disinterested" *agape* sundered from *eros*. This would imply that finite reality, by always lacking, always being unworthy of erotic attachment, must always be evil. For Augustine, Christianity goes beyond this by conjoining to "the goal" also "the way," which means a constant historical determining that desire is well-ordered, not just through its deference to infinite fruition, but also by a particular selective pattern of finite use. The *appropriate* preferences of *eros*, the "right harmonies" with a musical sequence, alone ensure that this sequence "progresses" towards the infinite goal. For every new act, every new word, may be either enabling or inhibiting, and although inhibition is mere negation, this can only be registered by the "fine judgment" which recognizes an aesthetic distortion (*De Trinitate*).

39. "The way" is not theoretically known, but must be constituted through judgment in the repeated construction and recognition of "examples," which cannot be literally copied if they are to be genuinely "repeated." The first example, Christ, by being first, inevitably defines the way, because this way is considered to be a single way (if not single we are back in agonistics: this is the reason its singularity matters). Because Christ is remembered as a *founder*, whose character is by definition not representable in terms of prior cultural orders, it is inevitable that his character will *entirely coincide* in its representation with the new categories of the new ecclesial society. Hence as founder, Christ is also the total realized collective character of the Church which is yet to come, and will itself include all cosmic reality. It follows that the *topos* Christ-founder surprisingly bears in itself the elements of a high Christology. The correspondence of Christ to God, or the identity of the entire "pattern" of his life (which is what *persona* really implies, not any substantive "element") with the *Logos*, only makes sense within the broad context of the correspondence of the ecclesial "way" to God. For the "pattern" of Jesus's life is only provisionally and canonically complete; as the "context" for the new society it cannot "belong" to one human individual, and this is one reason why one should re-affirm the Chalcedonian insight that Jesus possessed no human *hypostasis*. For the "patterns" or "coherencies" of our lives, never

belong to us, are not "completed" at our deaths, and can be repeated, or even more fully realized, by others: this is supremely true of a pattern that is taken to be canonically normative, as eschatalogically coinciding with the identities of all of us, as omnirepeatable because it is "divine."

40. Furthermore, "the way" is not defined solely as such a repetition. Were this the case, then we would be remaining within the logic of parts and wholes which characterized Greek thinking both about the individual and society, and tended to exile individual awareness and expression to the asocial realm of *theoria*. By contrast, as Augustine saw, the primacy (or equiprimacy) of desire, implies that "individuality" arises only through the constant rupturing and "externalization" of the subject. To contemplate is now to desire the other, to enter further into relation both with God and with human beings and angels. And the way is a community, not just christological supplementation, but from the outset the inclusion of interpretative response in the relations of Mary, of John the Baptist, and the disciples to Christ. This is why there is a historical happening of Christ not *just* as the image of the Father, but also as the relation to the Father, which as invisible, and indeed only "imagined" in language, can only be made present as the inner-relatedness of the Church, including its "initial" relation to Jesus in his own relatedness to the traditional imagining of a Father-God. Desire exceeds even the Christian *logos*, and yet fulfills it and therefore does not after all exceed it (according to the logic of "substantive relations"), because the *usus* of the cultural product, understood "aesthetically" as a work of art, is not exhausted even by a sympathetic judgmental attentiveness to its "perfect" specificity. Desire, through re-application, both respects this perfection and undoes it through joining the work to the continuous musical series. Hence the way is Christ, but equally the Church as the work of the Spirit. And both are "real" as the cultural happening of "meaning."

41. "The way," which is redemptive, is only the proper occurrence of creation. This is why Augustine is right to think that the "economic" Trinitarian series of Paternal voice–Christ–Ecclesia discloses to us a Trinitarian ontology which allows us to describe the universal happening of humanity in and through time. In this account of participation in the Trinity (presented as "Trinitarian vestiges" in the soul) the historical mediation of the Trinity is upheld by Augustine *more* than by others, precisely because he makes this process the metahistorical context for all

historical reality, and so wisely and necessarily obscures its singularity: it is not just one revelatory event within an order that is quite otherwise (*De Trinitate*).

42. Creation is always found as a given, but developing "order." As the gift of God, creation also belongs to God, it is within God (together with the infinity of all articulations that there may be) as the *Logos*. But existing harmonies, existing "extensions" of time and space, constantly give rise to new "intentions," to movements of the Spirit to further creative expression, new temporal unraveling of creation *ex nihilo*, in which human beings most consciously participate. Yet even this movement, the vehicle of human autonomy, is fully from God, is nothing *in addition* to the divine act-potential, and not equivocally different in relation to him. The latter conception would be "pagan," "gnostic," "Cabbalistic," whereas it is God himself who is differentiation, ensuring that this process is "music," not the ceaseless rupture and self-destruction of a differentiation poised "univocally" (Deleuze) between an "indifferent" transcendence and an anarchic finitude. The trust that in our linguistic and figurative creations we can constantly recognize, when it arises, the aesthetically "right" addition, which is, in its specific content, a criterion of self-validation, is now the mode of recognition of a transcendental/ontological possibility of "participation." And so translates for us, "faith in the triune God."

17

THE TRANSCENDALITY OF THE GIFT

A Summary

The gift, according to ancient Seneca and modern Mauss, is supposed to form the primary social bond. Here, especially for Mauss, generosity precedes contract. The latter may be necessary in order to protect, but it is not fundamental. Gift, rather, is what connects and unites.

And yet it has come to be that which we most disagree about, beginning with the question of:

1. Gift and contract.

Is gift always gift-exchange? In order to give, must one already be in a relationship, and if gift is socially fundamental, does that mean that gifts have always already been exchanged? But if gift in this way begins as a return gift and itself expects in return a counter-gift, then is not gift itself an exotic mode of contract? But can that be a true gift? Already Seneca asked whether there can be an aristocratic, pure, disinterested gift, given for the sake of giving. For this "proto-modern" Stoic perspective, gift has more to do with absolute duty than with social bonds, with absolute ethical respect for the other, rather than with practices sustaining a specific community.

And so one gets the contrast between the pure, disinterested, unilateral gift on the one hand and the idea that any gift is always involved in the complex reciprocity of gift-exchange on the other. But then it has come to be asked:

2. Is the gift purely a social matter, or is it also ontological?

In the case of the unilateral imperative to give freely and disinterestedly, this has been grounded ever since Kant in an absolute divine imperative, a command to be good more fundamental than the divine bringing about of being and the human modification of the same. Equally, the perennial adepts of gift-exchange—most of humanity hitherto—have understood this exchange not to be merely social or cultural at all, but to be an aspect of a cosmic ecology: a vast circulation encompassing natural beings, the gods, and the ancestors.

A circumstance still perhaps reflected in our language, in which we speak of "the given" to refer to the inertly factual, and yet with a language that paradoxically conveys the notion of a personal transfer. When theorists, in turn, have reflected in the twentieth century on this circumstance, one gets:

3. The debate about the given and the gift.

All of modern philosophy, analytic and continental, sought to evade metaphysics by confining itself to the given, beginning with the given and remaining with the given, whether as the logical and grammatical parameters of possible sense, or as the noetic processes within which we receive and actively constitute a meaningful world.

But nothing, it turned out, was given in this inert fashion. There was no inviolable empirical data uncontaminated by synthesis or interpretation or evaluation. To find anything uncontestably given, one had rather to turn to our entire existential circumstance. Here "it is given" that we are beings able to reflect on the fact that there is being at all. Here our specific existence in time and space is also "given" to us. Finally, things are only "there" for us because they are able to appear to us in diverse and never exhaustive aspects, both across space and through time. Things arrive to us via spatial journeyings and temporal advents. This may be the crucial reason why we can speak of the factual as the "given"—in excess of ancestral habit. What is there arrives and is in this sense "donated"—we naturally greet the budding tree and the new dawn with grateful welcome.

But what can this mean? Here:

4. The analytic and the phenomenological approaches part company.

For analysis, once the given has become a "myth" and this is fully admitted, only the inanity of practice in order to be practical remains ("pragmatism"). For phenomenology on the other hand, it may be that we can salvage the anti-metaphysics of remaining with the given by re-interpreting the given literally as gift.[1] But does that mean that one turns at first to the rising dawn? No, because the phenomenological presumption of confinement to the given is that one remains with what appears within the realm of the thinking subject. If what is given within this appearance is fundamentally a gift, then this cannot be guaranteed by the off-limits "transcendence" of thought-independent being, but only in terms of this subjective space itself, even if this be a space where the primary subjectivity is that of "the other."

Therefore, it must be this space as such and not what appears to it, that is a gift. The gift of the thinking subject to itself? But how could such self-reference be a gift, or indeed fully proven as given even to itself? Instead, the subject must be given to itself before itself by an other in a "history" always older than itself.[2] No representation of an ineluctable given is required here, since the other is registered by my inescapable ethical response to her needy demand—a response which first of all ensures that I am "there" at all.

But how can we know such an imperative without characterizing the suffering other? Otherwise her demands upon me might be the inhuman and monstrous demands of a will to power, and not those of a passively suffering subjectivity at all. Moreover, if this subject does not, as an ethical subject, "appear" to me (as Levinas insists) how can I characterize her except by projecting my own experience of what it is to exist, to feel, and to know onto the other. Is not the "given" Cartesian subject still secretly prior in this *schema* after all? But this sort of givenness is supposed to have lapsed, along with all the other mythical "givens."

Therefore the priority of the ethical does not clearly work, and one is left with the question:

---

1. Levinas, *Otherwise Than Being*; Derrida, *Given Time*; Blanchot, "Relation of the Third Kind"; Marion, *God Without Being*.

2. Levinas, *Otherwise Than Being*.

5. Is the gift/given first enacted ethically, or first known about theoretically?

Instead of trying to save givenness as gift, could one not instead admit (now that the anti-metaphysical twentieth century is over) that one has always already speculatively ("metaphysically") transgressed the boundary between the immanently appearing and the excess of non-appearing in the real? If, as Marion says, the typical phenomenon is "saturated" in terms of an appearing that exceeds our full conceptual grasp, then does not this mean (beyond Marion) that we receive such an appearing also with the supplement of our poetic, constructive speculation concerning the hidden—else the non-appearing excess will be merely a sublime hyper-presence without character, neatly segmented from that which does definably appear? And an uncharacterizable hyper-presence might be menace as much as it is gift.

This consideration, of course, tends to return us to the issue of language and interpretation. But it also brings us back to the arriving dawn and the budding tree. For now it is possible that things as well as persons can be initially conceived as gifts. Already, Heidegger suggested that *es gibt* was the deeper name for being. So:

6. Can one substitute the gift for the given in ontological terms, instead of reading the given as the gift in phenomenological terms?

Yet to read being as time necessarily but tragically interrupted by presence[3] is to ensure that the gift is still an impersonal given and, moreover, that it is perpetual mutual sacrifice (of Being to beings and vice-versa) rather than gift-exchange. In addition, to claim that this is a true phenomenological reduction is still, after all, to locate the gift in the supposedly given.

Is another strategy possible? Supposing that I am myself, really, ontologically a gift? Then one does not immediately need to invoke the other in order to grant oneself this status. If mind or spirit is more than an illusory epiphenomenon, then it cannot derive purely from matter, which is, at least as far as natural science is concerned, completely describable without invoking any such reality. Therefore it must be in consequence a mysterious and fundamental gift from the unknown, superfluous to the

3. Heidegger, *On Being and Time*.

apparent needs of objective being as known to science.[4] If I am myself a gift, then what lurks in me from before myself is more than the human, horizontal other. It is rather the trace of a vertical donor. And it seems appropriate that this donor, "God," who gives gifts to nothing, and so gives gifts to themselves in order to establish gifts, should create first of all a creature able reflexively to exist by giving this gift to herself in turn. Is this not what it means to think?[5] Then gratitude for the gift of self spills later over into generosity towards the neighbour in imitation of that generosity that has first constituted us in being at all.

But if spirit is appropriately the first given, is it absolutely the first given? Is this not rather being in general, and does not this then allow that "I" am first co-given along with others? And what of the role after all of merely material things? Are they not also first given, with a contingency applying to the "whole" of material reality in a way that the restrictedly relative concerns of natural science can never in principle fathom? And do they not ensure that there can be between people a concrete shared community, rather than mere mutual sympathy and respect at a safe distance?

This raises:

7. The question of whether our approach to the gift should be primarily philosophical or else primarily ethnographical?

Or in other terms, can we define the gift most securely as an eidetic possibility (within phenomenology) or else as an ontological precondition of finite existence (Bruaire's metaphysics) or must we rather discover it from the complex actuality of historical practice? A phenomenology combined with an ontology of the gift[6] might perhaps conclude that gift is interpersonal, that to give one must already be responding and must already be in a relation of exchange to the proposed recipient. Moreover, it might also conclude that a gift, if it is to be accounted a gift at all, must be an appropriate gift—therefore the complex business of combining thing with person ("finding the right gift") is essential and not dispensable. Such a perspective suggests that gift is always a moment within gift-exchange.

4. Bruaire, *L'Être et l'esprit*.

5. Ibid.

6. Merleau-Ponty, "The Intertwining—the Chiasm."

But can there be an exchange that is not pure formal contract? That deconstructs our modern divisions between private freedom (of donation) and public duty (of binding prior word)? This would have to be in terms of timings and spacings judged equivalent, even though not measurable as such. Non-identical repetition. Asymmetrical reciprocity. Plus the appropriateness of the gift combined with a surprisingness that exceeds the "just what I have always wanted" which can derisorily suggest that the recipient was about to obtain the article for herself in any case. The difficult question then of the appropriate surprise—which judged wrongly could even be a violent intrusion. And since the horizon invoked here depends upon the reality of objective value, the possibility arises that a real but difficult gift might be wrongly received as a curse.

One can see then, in abstract formal terms, the possibility of an exchange that still sustains gift. It would be less a circle than an ongoing, never foreclosed spiral.[7] But to know if this apparent possibility can really be instantiated, one has to regard and judge historical actions—both on a micro and a macro scale. At this stage, historical ethnography becomes essential. But within ethnography as much as within philosophy, the question has been asked:

8. Is the gift unilateral or is it reciprocal?

Many anthropologists have seen in gift only disguised contract, and have assumed in effect the modern division between reciprocal contract and unilateral gift. Especially they have suggested that a gift is only a kind of loan secured by capitalized, ungivable items (Wiener, Godelier). But could it be that the ungivable and that which must be given are two halves of the same unmodern picture? Namely that, anciently, objects were not yet commodities, and so were seen as specific things with specific "reserved" characteristics liable to achieve specific but not quite predictable effects? Able, in fact, to move the human plot almost as much as persons do? In which case we have the issue:

9. Of the Spirit of the gift.

If the gift is also an actor and not simply an object, then the ungivable belongs to the person it defines (his inalienable name or property, etc.), while its surrogates must return as themselves or return in some sort of

7. See Godbout and Caillé, *World of the Gift*.

equivalent mode, because they must always *remain him* in some sense. Gift-exchange is possible in part because of a certain belief in the animation of objects.[8] But beyond this discussion one can ask:

10. Is the unilateral/reciprocal contrast absolute?

Perhaps both paradigms assume that a situation of equality between social parties is the norm. But is there not rather usually hierarchy? Or always at least temporary hierarchy in that one person talks—gives orders, reports, etc.—and is so superior for the moment, or else one person listens—and judges—and is so likewise thereby superior? The person who talks both gives in a one-way sense and creates the theme and space of a subsequent conversation. In a sense he (somewhat) unilaterally gives the space of future reciprocity. Thus unilaterality and reciprocity can operate simultaneously, yet at different levels of causality. Supremely, one could note, God unilaterally gives a creature whose whole existence must be response to him. It is indeed this interaction of two causal levels that helps to sustain the never-foreclosed spiral of gift-exchange.

But to speak of spoken sign as gift—what does this mean? If a gift is a signifying convention then is it at bottom a fiction? Is the impossibility of the pure gift according to Derrida (because we award ourselves economically even in telling ourselves that we have been generous) coterminous with the endless deferral of meaning by the sign, such that to speak is to endlessly project the arrival of meaning, while to act ethically is endlessly to strive towards a generosity that cannot be enacted? This implies however, as Derrida was aware, that postponement of meaning nonetheless remains "truer" than a foreclosed presence of truth, while equally the impossible gift remains "the good" in a way that economic and contractual self-assurance cannot be. So:

11. What is the co-implication between gift and fiction?

Is meaning just postponed? Or can it be in some measure anticipated? And if not, then is the gift basically a sign, a promise of special attention that can never be realized? But a sign has always a material vehicle, like the person speaking, the medium in which it is inscribed, the actions, place, and time that accompany it. This vehicle itself supplements the import of the sign, and not just the next sign to which it gives rise. This ensures

8. Godbout and Caillé, *World of the Gift.*

that *some* meaning is already realized. Is this meaning a suppression of indeterminacy, or does it of itself open up a specific but open horizon of meaning? If it does not, then the significance of the material for meaning seems to be suppressed by arbitrary *fiat*.

But a sign proffered by a material someone deploying a material vehicle is not just a sign, it is also a gift. Inversely, a material thing handed over must be also a sign in order to be a gift. So gift is the exact point of intersection between the real and the signifying. It thereby exceeds the contrast between history and fiction, just as, at the instance where we receive joyfully a gift, our lives have become saturated with meaning, like novels, as if we were truly living out a dream. Thus the instance of the gift is the instance of the closing of the gulf between the fictional and the desired on the one hand, and the real and the tedious on the other.

And yet this instance only reminds us that such closure is more fundamental than the rift, since, originally, no material thing appears to us before it has been interpreted as in some way significant; nor, on the other hand, can any signified meaning ever entirely float free of material actuality. Where this cultural presupposition is seen as itself a response to a prior gift (sign/reality) then one has "religion." Where the latter is absent, then the unavoidable presupposition of original gift—the givenness of gift, both historically and ontologically, for human existence—is placed, with a constant effort, in ironic brackets. Then the gift is seen as only a fantasy in order to escape the givennness of an endless drift, rising up without generosity from a fundamental void. All then unravels: there can be really no gift, unilateral or reciprocal, but only the assertive gestures of power and their self-interested mutual contracting.

So finally:

12. Is the gift the echo of divine creation and of divine grace?
    And otherwise, does it lose all reality?

It would seem from what I have already said that the answer to both questions must be "yes." But then the possibility arises that we can construe Christianity as the attempt to erect a cosmopolis on the basis of a universal gift-exchange. The *ecclesia* is nothing other than this enterprise. We could say, following Mauss, that the gift is the social transcendental; that the social process as such is gift-exchange, but add to this that it includes also an exchange with the divine. As Marcel Hénaff has argued, gift is older than sacrifice, because the latter only arises within pastoral economies that already see agriculture as an essentially human productive work which displaces hunting and gathering as an exchange with the sacred other. Sacrifice either expresses a sense of reserve about this secularization or else a new recognition that human power also is a divine gift: one could say that the Eucharist, where we give all and all returns to us without partition of an animal, is the perfect consummation of this sensibility.

However, localized gift-exchange was lacking in equity, in principles of just distribution, and in ability to meet contingent, individual needs. A money-based market compensates for these deficiencies. At the same time, Aristotelian notions of just distribution rely upon a continuing sense of the reciprocity of social roles and of the founding of society in friendship. In this way contract is still bent back within the bounds of reciprocity. Nor is it the case, as Hénaff argues, that gift-exchange was always basically a ritual function of mutual recognition, once explicitly foregrounded, now more obscure. He can only claim this by ignoring clear instances of a gift-exchange *economy* in the case of tribal societies without any central government, besides the more general case of the exchange of women and finally the case of the medieval feudal and ecclesiastical economies which are often better understood in terms of the exchange of gifts rather than those of contract.

In a sense, the Christian project searches for the "middle" between gift-exchange on the one hand, and distributive justice with market exchange on the other. Yet the latter are essential to ensure a true appropriateness of the gift, which is essential to the gift as such. A global gift-exchange, as inaugurated by Christianity, ceases to be one of fetishized items, but becomes one of all that is truly valuable from the perspective of love and universal harmony. This requires, of course, a continuous task of judgment and discernment as to what is valuable and when and where. But if Aristotle retained the context of reciprocity, Christianity stresses this still more by seeing justice as fulfilled in charity—an unlimited concern to fulfil the real potential of all, and of all in harmony with all.

In this way, one could say that gift-exchange as the social transcendental is like a natural anticipation in all human societies of the society of supernatural grace. Judaism, with the city and the state, moves away from the tribal, by embracing money and the written law. Yet unlike every city and state Christianity cycles back to the primitive by seeing the gift and the oral as lying once more beyond commerce and writing. In this way it poses a counter-universal to the universality of the abstract. Gift-exchange happened primitively between familiar neighbors; then more commercial transactions of barter between adjacent tribes. Finally, as Seneca stressed, total strangers must once more open negotiations with gift-exchanges. But with cosmopolitan, de-fetishized gift-exchange, one might say, the neighborly and the remote mode of exchange collide or endlessly oscillate. To live in one world-city is to live all the time with neighbours who turn out to be strange and to meet strangers who turn out to be oddly familiar. All this is always mediated by variously judged gifts—of things, words, and gestures.

Christendom, therefore, the sphere of *ecclesia* as necessarily both personal and material, is the fulfilment of gift-exchange as the social transcendental which is also a metaphysical and theological transcendental: indeed nothing less than the Holy Spirit as gift, or the bond of reciprocal loving union between Father and Son.

However, this means also that the true metahistory is at once the history of the gift and the history of the Church. And here there are two massive problems. First of all, if gift-exchange is the social transcendental, how today do we live in denial of this by splitting gift-exchange between private unilateral gift on the one hand, and ungenerous, purely self-interested contract on the other? Secondly, how has Christianity been complicit in this formation of a kind of anti-society?

To take the second question first. Transcendental gift-exchange was theologically undone. From the late Middle Ages onwards, theologians started to set divine and human activity over against each other. This meant that they could no longer see that all of human activity derived from God, such that to receive all from God is also to return all to God sacrificially in a gesture of active gratitude. Grace and merit were not earlier in competition with each other, and charitable exchanges between the living and the living, and the living and the dead, could be seen as contributing to the salvific process. But now the divine act of grace was seen as more emphatically unilateral. With the Reformers this starts to mean that it is less an act of divine friendship than one of arbitrary election, in the face of which gratitude is in a sense irrelevant. A meritorious response is then of no salvific merit and so the salvific economy gets entirely divorced from the material one. There can no longer be any symbolic, ritual good works establishing mutual bonds of human friendship; only one-way deeds of charity which demonstrate an individual's state of grace. In imitation of divine absolute arbitrary sovereignty, human rule starts to get construed in terms of formal entitlement rather than intrinsic justice, while the market is handed over entirely to contractual calculation, free of any reciprocal obligations. Following the diverse work of Hénaff and Robert Brenner, it is now possible to re-work the Weber and Tawney theses: in England alone, the reduction of the peasantry to the status of wage-laborers, and the massive boost given to agrarian capitalism by both the dissolution of the monasteries (whose property was quickly transferred from the crown to the gentry, as Hilaire Belloc pointed out[9]) and the rise of a Calvinist theology of grace and commerce allowed a fully-fledged capitalism to emerge in contingent circumstances that render capitalism itself a contingent accident of Western history.

Hence the loss of transcendental gift-exchange is the result of a heterodox Christian development. This answers the second question. As to the first—how, if gift-exchange is transcendental, do we manage today to live in an "impossible" society?—one has to re-affirm that society and the network of reciprocal friendship are coterminous. Society is the "society of friends," as the Quakers appropriately call the Church. (Even if they fail to understand what this really involves.) Yet it *is* possible to have a simulacrum of this such as we have to day. The simulacrum unites us all only by bonds of contract which seek to make one egoistic desire match with another—without friendship, generosity, or concern for the whole social organism. But this requires ever more draconian state policing in order that contractual freedom be not abused—for nothing in this system *can* ever explain to the individual why he or she should not abuse it. Indeed it rather suggests that it *ought* to be abused, if the individual can get away with it. In this way, the system tends to increasing delirium: increasing innovation for the sake of it; increasing attempts by individuals or groups to gain arbitrary power over each other and at the same time increasing attempts to counteract anarchy with iron discipline. Deviant forms of Christianity themselves underwrite this ride to an earthly Tartarus.

However, no rational argument can ensure that the simulacrum is a contradictory reality that must one day unravel. We cannot declare

9. Belloc, *Servile State.*

any theoretical limit to delirium nor to the downward spiral of pointless lateral macro and micro expansion. Instead, the transcendental norm of universal gift-exchange can only be recognized by a combination of moral commonsense and Christian faith. For only love can desire that there *should be* unlimited association in the true sense: a society of unlimited reciprocation, a society of friends.

18

THE FUTURE OF LOVE

A Reading of Benedict XVI's Encyclical Deus Caritas Est

Pope Benedict's choice of love as the topic of his first encyclical exhibited an unswerving boldness combined with a calm judgment. Love is the proper topic for the early twenty-first century because in the personal field there is a crisis over its meaning; in the religious field there is an increasing substitution of violence for loving persuasion; and finally in the world at large the global tightening of human bonds is not accompanied by an equivalent increase of solidarity secured through the exercise of charity.

At the same time, love is the most perennial human need; Christianity is the religion which most places love at its heart; and the Catholic Church is the corporate body which has attempted the largest systematic organisation of human love in response to the gift of divine grace.

By bringing together the immediately pressing with the perennial, Pope Benedict contrived to convey with both simplicity and subtlety just how the Catholic faith is able to offer a surprising fulfillment of universal human aspirations towards a loving peace and harmony. His thoughts are in continuity with those of his predecessor, yet they are marked by the fact that he is a theologian before he is a philosopher and a theologian in the lineage of the *nouvelle théologie* who tends to stress the implicit yearning of reason towards faith and the completion of reason by faith, even within its own proper sphere of human understanding.

In consequence, this encyclical exhibited a strong stress upon the priority of the spiritual and the mystically theological over practical details, ecclesial programs, and theoretical controversies. At the same time, the religious is linked, from the outset of the document, to a warm humanism, readily comprehensible by all. Nor is there any sign of a backing away from John Paul II's commitment to a thinking through of the moral and political issues of our day. One glimpses instead something like an accentuation of an insistence upon the relevance of the specific perspectives of faith to these issues, rather than just a reliance upon sound reason and natural law, although the fundamental importance and non-constrained character of human reasoning is not, of course, denied.

Correspondingly, there seems to be here an increased stress on the Church itself as an agency of justice and charity and on the Church itself as the final site of true human society. For this reason the encyclical moves from a general consideration of love in the first part to a consideration of the role of the diaconate in the second. This is the driest part of the document, but also, perhaps, the part which most invites interpretation. It would conceivably be possible to read it in a "neoconservative" fashion, and yet there are ample indications that such a reading would be totally mistaken. I shall return to this presently.

A correct reading of the second part of the document requires one, I think, to bear in mind the full implications of the analysis of love in the first. Here again, somewhat more than his predecessor, Benedict shows that he is very aware of recent debates in theology and philosophy about the nature of love, giving and friendship. Broadly speaking these hover (as we have already seen at various points in this book) about the issue of whether love is primarily an agapeic self-oblation, or whether, to the contrary, it is an erotic reciprocity and mutual fulfilling of desire. Here Benedict adroitly holds a balance between both emphases, and in doing so also undermines completely the claims of those who see Christianity as the enemy of erotic love.

In the face of the commodification of sex, and an illogical exaltation of homosexual relations to equal exemplarity with heterosexual ones, Benedict here makes heterosexual faithful union the central paradigm of love for human beings in a way that would surely have startled his nineteenth-century forebears. Indeed, he says that unless *agape* is instanced in this mode of love and in other, less acute instances of *eros*, it would be something merely abstract and without effect. For while, indeed, *agape* is the descending love of God that is totally self-giving and self-abandoning, it is still also a preferential erotic sort of love. God has elected all of humanity for his love; more specifically he has elected Israel and then Mary and the Church. The latter is the Bride of God the Son: hence the gospels are precisely, as Benedict says, a "love story," the story of God's seeking out of his lost love, the highest possible romance.

But even within his own Trinitarian life, God is not just a free-giving; he is equally a constant receiving. Thus Benedict insists that insofar as the Bible qualifies a Greek metaphysical presentation of the absolute with a personalist emphasis, it accentuates and purifies, rather than abandoning the Greek concern with *eros*. As personal, God himself not only exhibits preference but also receptivity.

Likewise, the Pope cunningly turns the conventional tables in the case of human *agape* also. To be sure, this concerns a love for the neighbor that must be self-sacrificial and include love for enemies and even the unknown. Yet how is such a superhuman and heroic love possible for us? Not because it is commanded. Rather, because its possibility is *given* to us insofar as it arrives along with our *agape* for God. But this love of God is overwhelmingly receptive and therefore has an erotic dimension: to love God is obviously not to meet his needs but rather to encounter him in personal union that issues in a merging of will and purpose.

At the heart of the gospels, moving a subtle degree beyond the Old Testament in this respect, lies the *absolute merging* of the commands to love God and the neighbour, without priority given to one or the other. The source of inspiration for unstinting love of the neighbor lies in mystical union with God: yet Benedict insists (in keeping with the *nouvelle théologie* perspective) that the only true mysticism is Eucharistic. Hence we encounter God only within the social body, only insofar as we also encounter the neighbor—and in a context of celebratory foretaste of the heavenly banquet rather than in a context of benefaction. Therefore, one might say, in an "erotic" context. Nevertheless, Benedict also insists that worship and ethics are entirely at one: it is part of the movement of Eucharistic worship itself for the body of the faithful to turn to active agapeic works of mercy.

These, however, insofar as they concern "love of the neighbor," are not to do with a merely sacrifical devotion to "humanity in general." Although the parable of the Good Samaritan insists that the far-one can be also the near-one, this (as we saw the Middle Ages realized in chapter 9) is no abandonment of the importance of proximity, but rather the paradoxical insistence that proximity can abolish alien distance while conserving the distance of respect.

So *agape* is also *eros*. But for Benedict the inverse equally applies. In pagan religion (he does not really discuss the role of *eros* in pagan philosophy) *eros* was ecstasy, in the mere sense of self-intoxication which often involved the gross exploitation of women. But in the Hebraic *Song of Songs* by contrast, the physically erotic is poetically intensified *precisely because* the erotic is now linked to preference for a single one, to fidelity and to commitment unto sacrificial death. Romance, one might say, is born here and not with the Greeks. Nor (and here Benedict is very acute) is this any abandonment of ecstasy: rather the truly ecstatic is discovered in terms of a self-abandoning movement towards the other that is also a paradoxical self-realization. Far from this being a banning of pleasure, it is rather the first discovery of real pleasure—including, one could add, in a physical sense.

To put it bluntly: Benedict here boldly declares that not only is the Catholic Church not opposed to sexual love—to the contrary, it alone truly understands it and fully promotes it. In an epoch-making fashion, a Pope now declares that the literal sense of the *Song of Songs,* in other words its first intention of meaning, is indeed what the naïve reader would take it to be. The mystical meaning arises now only through a proper acceptance of the worth of this literal meaning, while at the same time the depth of the latter is lost if it is not read also allegorically: that is as pointing to the mystical marriage between Christ and the Church.

Now difficult questions certainly follow here about the relative worth of celibate and married commitments and about the plight of those who appear to have an unalterable homosexual orientation—a plight that the Church now seems somewhat to concede. And these questions are linked to a deeper one: how to hold together such a rightly strong affirmation of the sacramental centrality of married heterosexual love to a continuing challenge to the ways of this world such as was upheld by celibate vocations in the past.

But perhaps the second part of the encyclical is in part a response to such a concern. Benedict here quite strikingly puts a new stress upon the exercise of *diakonia* as constituting one third of the Church's mission alongside the sacramental and teaching vocations. Clearly, this diaconate is today increasingly exercised by the Catholic laity within a huge range of voluntary charitable organizations. Quite rightly the Pope is concerned that this function, as much as clerical ones, be exercised as part of the Church's specific ethos, rule, and pedagogy, and do not occupy some sort of uneasy limbo between theological justification and secular ideology. He desires, then, one might interpolate, that a married Catholic laity carrying out ecclesial vocations should be able to stand outside the world while being immersed wholly within the world. Obviously this is the sort of challenge that organizations like *Communione e Liberazione* have tried to meet: whatever one's opinions about their success, their concern is unavoidable.

But it is this part of the encyclical that may most invite controversy. The Pope strongly insists that the offering of welfare is a proper aspect of the Church's own life and cannot be altogether handed over to the state. He also affirms that this offering must not be directed by worldly ideologies and continues to excoriate Marxism for suggesting that the giving of charity might inhibit the demand for justice. (While of course one agrees with Benedict, there is a slight sense here of flogging a dead horse—a rare moment of lack of relevance in a document whose sense of the global present is in general admirable.)

One can imagine, then, that certain neoconservative supporters of Bush, Blair, or Marcello Pera (the lay Catholic leader of the Italian Senate) would read into this an encouragement for the privatization of all welfare functions. And one might reiterate that the temptation offered by the Grand Inquisitor to the Church in our time (a temptation to which all too many Catholics have already succumbed) is the following: accept extreme free-market liberalism in return for increased Church power in the spheres of welfare, education, and medicine.

Yet it is very clear from previous publications as well as the present one, that Benedict wholly refuses such a temptation, in accordance with a general political orientation which includes a commitment to world peace, opposition to the Iraq war, nuclear weapons, and the armaments trade, plus a determination to end global economic injustice and an insistence that the market must be regulated—though not wholly controlled—in terms of a hierarchy of truly human ends, while profits must be shared by producers (stances which implicitly condemns most modern "economics"). As the American Catholic neoconservative Jody Bottum not quite accurately laments, he is essentially a German "social democrat," if anything to the left of his predecessor. His famed criticisms of Liberation Theology arose in part from a perfectly correct perception that it failed to derive its Catholic social radicalism from the heart of the gospel (rather than secular "scientific" diagnosis) and so in consequence distorted it.

Accordingly, Pope Benedict is no ideological dogmatist of the Right about welfare. He advocates collaboration with state and international agencies pursuing the genuine human good in every respect. So his insistence on the diaconate is not to be read as lining up with a privatization of welfare, but rather as a new and typically *nouvelle théologie* stress on the Church itself as the fulfilment of human society: with and yet beyond justice the Church is the place of the exercise of charity. State agencies can never displace ecclesial ones, because what the human person needs is direct attention and appreciation of his uniqueness beyond the mere just granting of him his due—and in the *Catechism* of the Church, which Benedict prior to becoming Pope oversaw, it is insisted that charity cannot *displace* the demands of the poor for justice. Moreover, Benedict suggests that even secular projects of justice will only reach fruition if they are infused by a grace-given sense of charity—by that sense that through the Eucharist, and in Christ, we are becoming at one with an infinite and all-powerful love. In practical terms this implies an increased role for "civil society" as opposed to either the sheerly profit-seeking market or the bureaucratic state.

In this way we can begin to see that the inseparability of *agape* and *eros* in the first part is the hermeneutic key for reading the lessons on the diaconate in the second. The ecclesial society of love exceeds the secular society of justice in part because it involves infinite concern for others beyond what is merely due to them; or rather this *is* what is due to them— perfect justice is charity. But it also exceeds just society in terms of a kind of extended *eros*: the true giver of charity, says Benedict, also *receives* love from the one he cares for. Such an arising of a personal bond cannot be planned for, nor commanded: it rather arises by divine gift, by grace.

It is, I suggest, for this theological reason and not for politically conservative ones, that Benedict opposes all secular "plans" for the improvement of the world. Of course, as he says, we should be trying to improve the world. However, this should never involve the sacrifice of present people to the future, in part because this is wrong anyway, but also because a perfected harmonization of people in truth and love cannot be planned, precisely because it is composed of a myriad of "erotic" as well as agapeic events of coming to a complex consent that blends differences into an analogical unity. A truly radical politics would therefore involve a hoping for such a future, and a kind of blind-but-trusting working towards such a future through many particularities. But to suppose one had a blueprint for such a future would be, as Benedict says, to suppress the most specifically personal dimension of human life.

In this way, more successfully than secular ideologies, the Pope is here able to link the personal with the political. What humans yearn for is inter-personal love. But the extension of this through tempered measures of organization committed to social justice and fraternity is the key to the arrival of a global loving community.

BIBLIOGRAPHY

Aarsleff, Hans. "Woodsworth, Language and Romanticism." In *From Locke to Saussure: Essays on the Study of Language and Intellectual History*, 372–81. London: Athlone, 1982.

Aers, David. "Coleridge and the Egg that Burke Laid." *Literature and History* 9:2 (1983) 152–63.

———, Jonathan Cook, and David Punter, editors. *Romanticism and Ideology: Studies in English Writing 1765–1830*. London: Routledge, 1981.

Agamben, Giorgio. *State of Exception*. Translated by Kevin Attell. Chicago: University of Chicago Press, 2005.

Alféri, Pierre. *Guillaume d'Ockham: Le Singulier*. Paris: Minuit, 1989.

Alliez, Eric. *Capital Times: Tales for the Conquest of Time*. Translated by George van den Abbeele. Foreword by Gilles Deleuze. Theory Out of Bounds 6. Minneapolis: Minnesota University Press, 1996.

Arnold, Matthew. *Culture and Anarchy*. Edited by J. Dover Wilson. Landmarks in the History of Education. Cambridge: Cambridge University Press, 1960.

Asad, Talal. *Genealogies of Religion: Discipline and Reasons of Power in Christianity and Islam*. Baltimore: Johns Hopkins University Press, 1997.

Barfield, Owen. *What Coleridge Thought*. San Rafael, CA: Barfield: 1971.

Barth, Karl. *Dogmatics in Outline*. Translated by G. T. Thomson. London: SCM, 1966.

Baudrillard, Jean. "L'Esprit du Terrorisme." Translated by Donovan Hohn. *Harpers*, February 2002, 13–18.

———. *The Mirror of Production*. Translated by Mark Foster. St. Louis: Telos, 1975.

Baum, Gregory. *Religion and Alienation: A Theological Reading of Sociology*. New York: Paulist, 1975.

Belloc, Hilaire. *The Servile State*. New York: Cosimo, 2007.

Benedict XVI, Pope. *God is Love: Deus Caritas Est, Encyclical Letter*. San Francisco: Ignatius, 2006.

Benjamin, Walter. *Illuminations*. New York: Harcourt, Brace, & World, 1968.

Berkeley, George. *Alciphron, or the Minute Philosopher*. The Works of George Berkeley 3. London: Nelson, 1964.

The Bhagavad-Gita. Translated by R. C. Zaehner. Oxford: Oxford University Press, 1979.

Birch, Dinah. "Ruskin's Womanly Mind." In *Ruskin and Gender*, edited by Dinah Birch and Francis O'Gorman, 107–20. Basingstoke: Palgrave. 2002.

Blanchot, Maurice. "The Relation of the Third Kind." In *The Infinite Conversation*, translated by Susan Hanson, 66–74. Minneapolis: Minnesota University Press, 1993.

Bibliography

Blumenfeld, Bruno. *The Political Paul: Justice, Democracy and Kingship in a Hellenistic Framework*. London: Continuum, 2001.

Booth, Edward. *Aristotelian Aporetic Ontology in Islamic and Christian Thinkers*. Cambridge Studies in Medieval Life and Thought 3:20. Cambridge: Cambridge University Press, 1988.

Boulnois, Olivier. *Être et representation: une généalogie dela métaphysique moderne à l'époque de Duns Scot*. Paris: Presses Universitaires de France, 1999.

———. *Au-delá l'image: une archélogie du visuel au Moyen Age (Ve-XVIe siècle)*. Paris: Seuil, 2008.

Boumediene-Thiery, Alima, Alain Krivine, and Giuseppe di Lello Finuoli. "Europe: vers l'état d'exception?" *Le Monde*, November 29, 2001.

Brenner, Robert. *Merchants and Revolution: Commercial Change, Political Conflict and London's Overseas Traders, 1550–1653*. London: Verso, 2003.

Brose, Olive J. *Frederick Denison Maurice: Rebellious Conformist*. Athens: Ohio University Press, 1971.

Brown, Callum. *The Death of Christian Britain: Understanding Secularisation, 1800–2000*. Christianity and Society in the Modern World. London: Routledge, 2000.

Bruaire, Claude. *L'Être et l'esprit*. Paris: Presses Universitaires de France, 1983.

Bruhat, Jean. "Le Socialisme Francais de 1815 à 1848." In *Histoire Général du Socialisme, Tome 1*, edited by Jacques Droz. Paris: Presses Universitaires de France, 1972.

Burrell, David B. *Faith and Freedom: An Interfaith Perspective*. Oxford: Blackwell, 2004.

———. *Freedom and Creation in Three Traditions*. Notre Dame: University Notre Dame Press, 1998.

———. *Knowing the Unknowable God: Ibn-Sina, Maimonides, Aquinas*. Notre Dame: University of Notre Dame Press, 1986.

Butler, Joseph. *The Analogy of Religion*. London: Routledge, 1885.

Castoriadis, Cornelius. *L'Institution Imaginaire de la Société*. Paris: Editions du Seuil, 1975.

Cavanaugh, William T. "'A Fire Strong Enough to Consume the House': The Wars of Religion and the Rise of the State." *Modern Theology* 2 (1995) 397–420.

———. *Torture and Eucharist: Theology, Politics, and the Body of Christ*. Challenges in Contemporary Theology. Malden, MA: Blackwell, 1998.

Chalmers, Thomas. *The Application of Christianity to the Commercial and Ordinary Affairs of Life*. Glasgow: Starke, 1832.

———. *On Political Economy, in Connexion with the Moral State & Moral Prospects of Society*. New York: Kelley, 1968.

Chaudhuri, Nirad C. *Hinduism*. London: Chatto and Windus, 1979.

Chesterton, G. K. *Orthodoxy*. London: Bodley Head, 1957.

Clarke, Simon. *Marx, Marginalism, and Modern Sociology*. London: Macmillan, 1982.

Cole, G. D. H. *Socialist Thought: The Forerunners 1789–1850*. London: Macmillan, 1965.

Coleridge, Samuel Taylor. *Aids to Reflection and The Confessions of an Inquiring Spirit*. London: G. Bell, 1893.

———. *Biographia Literaria*. Everyman's Library. London: Dent, 1934.

———. *Confessions of an Inquiring Spirit*. Edited by H. StJ. Hart. London: Black, 1956.

———. *The Friend*. The Collected Works of Samuel Taylor Coleridge. Volume 4. Edited by Barbara E. Rhodes. Princeton: Princeton University Press, 1969.

———. *Lectures on Revealed Religion*. The Collected Works of Samuel Taylor Coleridge. Volume 1. Edited by L. Patton and P. Mann. Princeton: Princeton University Press, 1971.

———. *On the Constitution of the Church and the Sate According to the Idea of Each*. The Collected Works of Samuel Taylor Coleridge. Volume 10. Edited by John Colmer. Princeton: Princeton University Press, 1976.

———. *Opus Maximum*. The Collected Works of Samuel Taylor Coleridge 15. Edited by Thomas McFarland. Princeton: Princeton University Press, 2002.

———. *The Philosophical Lectures (1818–1819) Hitherto Unpublished*. Edited by Kathleen Coburn. London: Pilot, 1949.

———. *The Poetical Works of Samuel Taylor Coleridge*. Edited by T. Ashe. Whitefish, MT: Kessinger, 2004.

———. *S. T. Coleridge's Treatise on Method, As Published in the Encyclopaedia Metropolitana*. Edited by Alice. D. Snyder. London: Constable, 1934.

———. "The Statesman's Manual." In *Lay Sermons*. The Collected Works of Samuel Taylor Coleridge 6. Edited by R. J. White. Princeton: Princeton University Press, 1972.

Colletti, Lucio. *Marxism and Hegel*. Translated by Lawrence Garner. London: NLB, 1973.

Cooley, Mike. *Architect or Bee?: The Human/Technology Relationship*. Slough: Langely Technical Services, 1980.

Corbin, Henri. *Alone with the Alone: Creative Imagination in the Sufism of Ibn'Arabi*. Princeton: Princeton University Press, 1997.

Courtine. Jean-Francois. *Suarez et le Problème de la Métsaphysique*. Paris: Presses Universitaires de France, 1990.

Cowling, Maurice. *Religion and Public Doctrine in Modern England: Volumes I-III*. Cambridge: Cambridge University Press, 1980, 1985, 2001.

Craig, David M. "Naves and Nukes: John Ruskin as 'Augustinian' Social Theorist?" *Journal of Religious Ethics* 32 (2004) 325–56.

Cray, Graham, editor. *The Mission-Shaped Church*. London: Church House, 2004.

Culverwell, Nathaniel. *An Elegant and Learned Discourse into the Light of Nature*. Edited by Robert A. Greene and Hugh MacCallum. Toronto: Toronto University Press, 1971.

Cunningham, Angela. "Shall Work set us Free." *New Blackfriars* 62 (1981) 63–77.

Cunningham, Conor. *Genealogy of Nihilism: Philosophies of Nothing and the Difference of Theology*. Radical Orthodoxy. London: Routledge. 2002.

Cuvillier, Armand. *P.-J.-B. Buchez et les Origines du Socialisme Chrétien*. Paris: Presses Universitaires de France, 1948.

Davidson, Donald. "The Structure and Content of Truth." *Journal of Philosophy* 87 (1990) 279–328.

Davies, Norman. *The Isles: A History*. Oxford: Clarendon, 1999.

Davis, Natalie Zemon. *The Gift in Sixteenth-Century France*. Madison: Wisconsin University Press, 2000.

Dawson, Christopher. *The Age of the Gods: A Study in the Origins of Culture in Prehistoric Europe*. London: Murray, 1928.

Deleuze, Gilles. *Différence et Répépitition*. Paris: Presses Universitaires de France, 1968.

———. *Logique du Sens*. Paris: Minuit, 1969.

Deleuze, Gilles, and Felix Guattari. *Anti-Oedipus: Capitalism and Schizophrenia*. Translated by Robert Hurley et al. London: Athlone. 1984.

————. *A Thousand Plateaus.* Translated by Brian Massumi. London: Athlone, 1988.

Demant, V. C. *Religion and the Decline of Capitalism.* London: Scribner, 1952.

Derrida, Jacques. *Given Time. 1, Counterfeit Money.* Translated by Peggy Kamuf. Chicago: University of Chicago Press, 1992.

————. *Of Grammatology.* Translated by G. G. Spivak. Baltimore: Johns Hopkins University Press, 1982.

————, and Pierre-Jean Labarriére. *Alterités.* Paris: Osins, 1986.

Desmond, William. *Being and the Between.* SUNY Series in Philosophy. New York: State University of New York Press, 1995.

Duffy, Eamon. *The Stripping of the Altars: Traditional Religion in England, c.1400–c.1580.* New Haven: Yale University Press, 1992.

Dulles, Avery. *The Assurance of Things Hoped For: A Theology of Christian Faith.* Oxford: Oxford University Press, 1994.

Dumézil, Georges. *Mitra-Varuna.* Paris: Gallimard, 1948.

Dumont, Louis. *From Mandeville to Marx.* Chicago: University of Chicago Press, 1977.

Eagleton, Terry. *Criticism and Ideology: A Study in Marxist Literary Theory.* London: NLB, 1976.

————. "Marxists and Christians: Answers for Brian Wicker," *New Blackfriars* 56 (1975) 465–70.

Eco, Umberto. *The Role of the Reader: Explorations in the Semiotics of Texts.* London: Hutchinson, 1981.

Edwards, Stewart, editor. *Selected Writings of Pierre-Joseph Proudhon.* London: Macmillan, 1969.

Everest, Kelvin. *Coleridge's Secret Ministry.* New York: Barnes and Noble, 1979.

Fierro, Alfredo. *The Militant Gospel.* London: SCM, 1977.

Findlay, J. N. *Kant and the Transcendental Object.* Oxford: Oxford University Press, 1981.

Fine, Arthur. *The Shaky Game.* Chicago: University of Chicago Press, 1986.

Finnis. *Natural Law and Natural Rights.* Clarendon Law Series. New York: Oxford University Press, 1980.

Foucault, Michael. *The Order of Things: An Archeology of the Human Sciences.* London: Travistock, 1970.

————. "Theatrum Philosophicum." In *Language, Counter-Memory, Practice,* 164–96. Oxford: Basil Blackwell, 1983.

Frazer, Elizabeth, editor. *Selected Writings of Pierre-Joseph Proudhon.* London: Macmillan, 1969.

Frédéric Nef, *Qu'est-ce que la métaphysique.* Paris: Gallimard, 2004.

Gill, Eric. *Art-Nonsense and Other Essays.* First edition. London: Cassell, 1929.

Girard René. *Things Hidden Since the Foundation of the World.* Translated by Stephen Bann and Michael Metteer. London: Athlone, 1987.

Godbout, Jacques T., and Alain Caillé. *The World of the Gift.* Translated by Donald Winkler. Montreal: McGill/Queen's University Press, 1998.

Godelier, Maurice *The Enigma of the Gift.* Translated by Nora Scott. Chicago: University of Chicago Press, 1999.

Godwin, William. *Enquiry Concerning Political Justice and its Influence on Morals and Happiness.* Edited by F. E. L. Priestly. Toronto: University of Toronto Press, 1946.

Gordon, Barry. *Economic Analysis before Adam Smith.* London: Macmillan, 1975.

Goux, Jean-Joseph. "Seneca against Derrida: Gift and Alterity." In *The Enigma of Gift and Sacrifice*, edited by Edith Wyschogrod et al., 148–60. New York: Fordham University Press, 2002.

Green, T. H. "Essays on Christian Dogma." In *Works*, edited by R. L. Nettleship. New York: AMS, 1891.

Greimas, A. J. *Sémiotique et Sciences Sociales*. Paris: Seuil, 1976.

Guardiola-Rivera, Oscar. *Being Against the World: Rebellion and Constitution*. London: Birkbeck Law, 2008.

Gutierrez, Gustavo. *A Theology of Liberation*. London: SCM, 1983.

Habermas, Jürgen. *Theorie des Kommunikativen Handelns*. 3rd edition. Frankfurt am Main: Suhrkamp, 1985.

Hacking, Ian. *The Emergence of Probability*. London: Cambridge University Press, 1975.

Halbfass, Wilhelm. *Indien und Europa*. Basel: Schwabe, 1981.

Harrison, Peter. *'Religion' and the Religions in the English Enlightenment*. Cambridge: Cambridge University Press, 1990.

Hart, David Bentley. "Christ or Nothing." *First Things* 136 (2003) 47–57.

———. "The Offering of Names: Metaphysics, Nihilism, and Analogy." In *Reason and the Reasons of Faith*, edited by Reinhard Hütter and Paul J. Griffiths, 55–76. London: T. & T. Clark, 2005.

Hauerwas, Stanley. "Some Theological Reflections on Gutierrez's use of 'Liberation' as a Theological Concept." *Modern Theology* 3 (1986) 67–76.

Hegel, G. W. F. *Phenomenology of Spirit*. Translated by A. V. Miller. Oxford: Oxford University Press, 1977.

Heidegger, Martin. *On Being and Time*. New York: Harper, 1972.

Hénaff, Marcel. *Le Prix de la Vérité: le don, l'argent, la philosophie*. Paris: Seuil, 2002.

Herdt, Jennifer. "The Endless Construction of Charity: On Milbank's Critique of Political Economy." *Journal of Religious Ethics* 32 (2004) 301–24.

———. *Religion and Faction in Hume's Moral Philosophy*. Cambridge: Cambridge University Press, 1997.

Hick, John, and Paul Knitter, editors. *The Myth of Christian Uniqueness: Towards a Pluralist Theology of Religions*. Maryknoll: Orbis, 1987.

Hill, Claire Ortiz. *Rethinking Identity and Metaphysics: On the Foundations of Analytic Philosophy*. New Haven: Yale University Press, 1997.

Hill, Geoffrey. *The Triumph of Love*. Boston: Houghton Mifflin, 1998.

Hilton, Boyd. *The Age of Atonement: The Influence of Evangelicalism on Social and Economic Thought 1795–1865*. Oxford: Oxford University Press, 1988.

Hirschman, Albert O. *The Passions and the Interests*. Princeton: Princeton University Press, 1977.

Holland, Henry Scott. "The Meekness of God." In *Logic and Life: With Other Sermons*, 227–39. London: Scribner, 1894.

Honnefelder, Ludger. *La Métaphysique comme science transcendentale*. Translated by Isabelle Mandrella. Paris: Presses Universitaires Frances, 2002.

Hume, David. *A Treatise of Human Nature: Being an Attempt to Introduce the Experimental Method of Reasoning into Moral Subjects; and Dialogues Concerning Natural Religion*. Aalen, Germany: Scientia, 1964.

Hunter, Michael. *The Occult Laboratory: Magic, Science and Second Sight in Late Seventeenth-Century Scotland*. Woodbridge: Boydell, 2001.

Husserl, Edmund. *Cartesian Meditations.* Translated by Dorion Cairns. Dordrecht, Holland: Kluwer, 1999.

Hyde, Lewis. *The Gift: Imagination and the Erotic Life of Property.* New York: Vintage, 1983.

Jacob Schmutz. "La doctrine médiévale des causes et la théologie de la nature pure." *Revue Thomiste* (2001) 217–64.

Janicaud, Dominique, Jean-Luc Marion, and Paul Ricoeur. *Phenomenology and the "Theological Turn": The French Debate.* Translated by Bernard G. Prusak. New York: Fordham University Press, 2000.

Johns, Alessa. *Women's Utopias of the Eighteenth Century.* Urbana/Chicago: Illinois University Press, 2003.

Jones, Gareth Stedman. *Languages of Class: Studies in English Working Class History, 1832–1982.* Cambridge: Cambridge University Press, 1983.

Kant, Immanuel. "Concerning the Ultimate Grounds of the Differentiation of Directions in Space (1768)." In *Theoretical Philosophy, 1755–1770,* edited and translated by D. Wolford and R. Meerbote, 361–73. Cambridge: Cambridge University Press, 1992.

———. "The Conflict of the Faculties." In *Religion and Rational Theology,* translated by Allen W. Wood and George Di Giovanni, 233–328. Cambridge: Cambridge University Press, 1996.

———. *Critique of Judgment.* Translated by Werner S. Pluhar. Indianapolis: Hackett, 1987.

———. "Dreams of a Spirit-Seer Elucidated by Dreams of Metaphysics (1766)." In *Theoretical Philosophy, 1755–1770,* edited and translated by D. Wolford and R. Meerbote, 301–61. Cambridge: Cambridge University Press, 1992.

———. "What Does It Mean to Orient Oneself in Thinking?" In *Religion and Rational Theology,* translated by Allen W. Wood and George Di Giovanni, 1–19. Cambridge: Cambridge University Press, 1996.

Kenny, Terence. *The Political Thought of John Henry Newman.* London: Longmans, 1957.

Kerr, Fergus. *Theology after Wittgenstein.* Oxford: Blackwell, 1986.

———, and David Nicholls, editors. *John Henry Newman: Reason, Rhetoric, and Romanticism.* Bristol: Bristol Classical, 1990.

Keynes, John Maynard. *Essays in Biography.* London: Hart-Davis, 1951.

Lash, Nicholas. *Easter in Ordinary.* London: SCM, 1989.

Latour, Bruno. *Politics of Nature: How to Bring the Sciences into Democracy.* Translated by Catherine Porter. Cambridge Mass: Harvard University Press, 2004.

Latourelle, René. *Theology of Revelation.* New York: Staten Island, 1987.

Lepew, David J., and Bruce H. Weber. "Genetic Darwinism and the Probability Revolution." In *Darwinism Evolving: Systems Dynamics and the Geneology of Natural Selection,* 167–335. Cambridge, MA: MIT Press, 1997.

Lévi-Strauss, Claude. *Introduction to the Work of Marcel Mauss.* Translated by Felicity Baker. London: Routeldge and Kegan Paul, 1987.

Levinas, Emmanuel. *Otherwise Than Being, Or Beyond Essence.* Translated by Alphonso Lingis. The Hague: Martinus Nijhoff, 1981.

Lowman, Moses. *A Dissertation on the Civil Government of the Hebrews.* London: Noon, 1974.

Libera, Alain de. *Le Problème de l'Être chez Maître Eckhart: Logique et Métaphysique de l'Analogie.* Geneva: Cahiers de la Revue de Théologie et de Philosophie 4, 1980.

Lubac, Henri de. *The Un-Marxian Socialist.* Translated by R. E. Scantlebury. London: Sheed and Ward, 1948.

Ludlow, J. M. "Prevailing Idolatries or Hints for political Economists." *Tracts on Christian Socialism* 6 (1851).

————. "The Working Associations of Paris." *Tracts on Christian Socialism* 4 (1851).

Lyotard, Jean-François. *The Differend.* Translated by Georges van den Abbeele. Manchester: Manchester University Press, 1988.

Lyotard, Jean-François, and Jean-Loup Thébaud. *Just Gaming.* Translated by Wlad Godzich. Minneapolis: University of Minnesota Press, 1985.

MacIntyre, Alasdair. *After Virtue: A Study in Moral Theory.* London: Duckworth, 1983.

————. *Whose Justice, Which Rationality?* Notre Dame: University of Notre Dame Press, 1988.

MacKinnon, Donald M. "Coleridge and Kant." In *Coleridge's Variety: Bicentenary Studies,* edited by John Beer, 183–203. Pittsburg: University of Pittsburg Press, 1974.

Macmurray, John. *The Clue to History.* London: SCM, 1938.

Malthus, Thomas. *An Essay on the Principle of Population.* First edition. London, 1798.

Mandel, Ernest. *Late Capitalism.* Translated by Joris De Bres. London: NLB, 1975.

————. *Long Waves of Capitalist Development.* Cambridge: Cambridge University Press, 1980.

Manent, Pierre. *An Intellectual History of Liberalism.* Translated by Rebecca Balinski. Princeton: Princeton University Press, 1995.

Marion, Jean-Luc. *Being Given: Toward a Phenomenology of Givenness.* Translated by Jeffrey L. Kosky. Stanford: Stanford University Press, 2002.

————. *God Without Being.* Translated by Thomas A. Carlson. Chicago: University of Chicago Press, 1991.

————. *Le Phénomène Erotique.* Paris: Grasset 2003.

Marshall, Bruce D. "'We shall bear the image of the Man of Heaven': Theology and the Concept of Truth." In *Rethinking Metaphysics,* edited by C. L. Jones and S. E. Rowl, 93–117. Oxford: Blackwell, 1995.

Marx, Karl. *Capital: A Critique of Political Economy.* 3 vols. Edited by Friedrich Engels and translated by Samuel Moore and Edward Aveling. London: Lawence and Wishart, 1949.

————. *Early Writings.* Translated by Rodney Livingstone and Gregor Benton. New York: Vintage, 1975.

————. *Grundrisse: Foundations of the Critique of Political Economy.* Translated by Martin Nicolaus. London: Allen Lane, 1973.

Marx, Karl, and Friederich Engels. *The Communist Manifesto.* London: Penguin, 1967.

————. *The German Ideology.* London: Lawrence and Wishart, 1974.

Massingham, H. J. *The Tree of Life.* Charlbury: Jon Carpenter, 2003.

Maurice, Frederick Dennison. *The Kingdom of Christ.* London: Darton and Clark, 1838.

————. *Social Morality: Twenty-one Lectures Delivered in the University of Cambridge.* London: Macmillan, 1869.

————. *The Life of Frederick Dennison Maurice.* London: Macmillan, 1884.

Mauss, Marcel. *The Gift: The Form and Reason for Exchange in Archaic Societies.* Translated by W. D. Halls. London: Routledge, 1990.

Maximus the Confessor. "The Church's Mystagogy." In *Selected Writings,* translated by George C. Berthold, 181–225. New York: Paulist, 1985.

McDowell, John. *Mind and World.* Cambridge, MA: Harvard University Press, 1994.

Bibliography

Meillassoux, Quentin. *Après la Finitude: Essai sur la nécessité de la contingence.* Paris: Seuil, 2006.

Merleau-Ponty, Maurice "The Intertwining—the Chiasm." In *The Visible and the Invisible,* translated by Alphonso Lingis, 130–56. Evanston, IL: Northwestern University Press, 1968.

Metz, Johann Baptist. *Faith in History and Society: Toward a Practical Fundamental Theology.* London: Burns and Oates, 1980.

———. *Theology of the World.* Translated by William Glen-Doepel. London: Burns and Oates, 1969.

Michalson, Gordon E. "Re-reading the Post-Kantian Tradition with Milbank." *Journal of Religious Ethics* 32 (2004) 357–83.

Milbank, John. *Being Reconciled: Ontology and Pardon.* London: Routledge, 2002.

———. "Can a Gift be Given?" *Modern Theology* 11 (1995) 119–61.

———. "Choreography: The Evasion of Kierkegaard?"

———. "An Essay Against Secular Order," *Journal of Religious Ethics* 15 (1987) 199–24.

———. "History of the One God." *The Heythrop Journal* 88 (1997) 371–400.

———. "Knowledge: The Theological Critique of Philosophy in Hamann and Jacobi." In *Radical Orthodoxy,* ed. John Milbank et al., 21–38. London: Routledge, 1999.

———. "The Linguistic Turn as a Theological Turn." In *The Word Made Strange,* 84–122. Cambridge, MA: Blackwell, 1997.

———. "The Name of Jesus: Incarnation, Atonement and Ecclesiology." *Modern Theology* 7 (1991) 311–33.

———. "Problematizing the Secular: The Post-Postmodern Problematic," In *The Shadow of Spirit,* edited by Phillippa Berry and Andrew Wernick, 30–44. London: Routledge, 1992.

———. "Sacred Triads: Augustine and the Indo-European Soul." In *Modern Theology* 13 (1997) 451–74.

———. "The Soul of Reciprocity." *Modern Theology* 17:3 (2001) 335–91 and 17:4 (2001) 485–507.

———. "The Sublime in Kierkegaard." In *Post-secular Philosophy: Between Philosophy and Theology,* edited by Philip Blond, 68–81. New York: Routledge, 1998.

———. "Sublimity: The Modern Transcendent." In *Religion, Modernity and Postmodernity,* edited by P. Heelas and P. Morris, 258–84. Oxford: Blackwell, 1998.

———. *The Suspended Middle: Henri de Lubac and the Debate concerning the Supernatural.* Grand Rapids: Eerdmans, 2005.

———. *Theology and Social Theory: Beyond Secular Reason.* 2nd edition. Malden, MA: Blackwell, 2006.

———. "The Thomistic Telescope: Truth and Identity" *American Catholic Philosophical Quarterly* 80 (2006) 193–226.

———. "William Warburton: An Eighteenth-Century Bishop Fallen among Post-Structuralists." *New Blackfriars* (July/August 1983) 315–25 and (September 1983) 374–84.

———. *The Word Made Strange: Theology, Language, Culture.* Cambridge, MA: Blackwell, 1997.

Milbank, John, and Catherine Pickstock. *Truth in Aquinas.* London: Routledge, 2001.

Milbank, John, et al. *Radical Orthodoxy: A New Theology.* London: Routledge, 1999.

Mileur, Jean-Pierre. *Vision and Revision: Coleridge's Art of Immanence.* Berkeley: University of California Press, 1982.

Bibliography

Mill, John Stuart. *Three Essays*. London: Oxford University Press, 1975.

Morgain, Stéphane-Marie. *La Théologie Politique de Pierre de Bérulle (1598–1629)*. Paris: Publisud, 2001.

Morris, Thomas V. *The Logic of God Incarnate*. Ithaca, NY: Cornell University Press, 1986.

Mulhall, Stephen. *On Being in the World: Wittgenstein and Heidegger on Seeing Aspects*. London: Routledge, 1990.

Mullin, Robert Bruce. *Miracles and the Modern Religious Imagination*. New Haven: Yale University Press 1996.

Muralt, André de. *L'unité de la Philosphie Politique: de Scot, Occam et Suarez au Libéralisme Contemporain*. Paris: Vrin, 2002.

Nancy, Jean-Luc. *The Inoperative Community*. Edited and translated by Peter Connor. Minneapolis: University of Minnesota Press, 1991.

Natarajan, Uttara. *Hazlitt and the Reach of Sense*. Oxford: Clarendon, 1998.

Nef, Frédéric. *Qu'est-ce que la métaphysique*. Paris: Gallimard, 2004.

Newman, John Henry. *Apologia pro Vita Sua*. Edited by Ian Kerr. London: Penguin, 1994.

———. *Arians of the Fourth Century*. London: Pickering, 1883.

———. *An Essay in Aid of a Grammar of Assent*. Introduction by Nicholas Lash. Notre Dame: Notre Dame University Press, 1979.

———. *Lectures on the Doctrine of Justification*. London: Rivingtons, 1874.

———. *Two Essays on Biblical and Ecclesiastical Miracles*. London: Longmans and Green, 1890.

Nietzsche, Friedrich. *Thus Spoke Zarathustra*. Translated by R. J. Hollingdule. Harmondsworth: Penguin, 1971.

Nockles, Peter B. *The Oxford Movement in Context*. Cambridge: Cambridge University Press, 1994.

Norman, Edward. *The Victorian Christian Socialists*. New York: Cambridge University Press, 1987.

Paley, William. *The Principles of Moral and Political Philosophy*. London, 1796.

Parfit, Derek. *Reasons and Persons*. Oxford: Oxford University Press, 1984.

Péguy, Charles. "Clio I," In *Temporal and Eternal*, translated by Alexander Dru, 101–8. London: Harvill, 1958.

Perrier, Emmanuel. "Duns Scotus Facing Reality: Between Absolute Contingency and Unquestionable Consistency." *Modern Theology* 21 (2005) 619–43.

Peterson, Linda H. "The Feminist Origin of 'Of Queens' Gardens.'" In *Ruskin and Gender*, edited by Dinah Birch and Francis O'Gorman, 86–107. Basingstoke: Palgrave, 2002.

Peukert, Helmut. *Science, Action and Fundamental Theology*. Cambridge, MA: MIT Press, 1986.

Pickstock, Catherine. *After Writing: On The Liturgical Consummation of Philosophy*. Oxford: Blackwell, 1998.

———. "Duns Scotus: His Historical and Contemporary Significance." *Modern Theology* 21 (2005) 543–75.

Pieper, Josef. *Leisure the Basis of Culture*. London: Faber and Baber, 1952.

Pocock, J. G. A. *The Machiavellian Moment*. Princeton: Princeton University Press, 1975.

Pollard, A. J. *Imagining Robin Hood: The Late-Medieval Stories in Historical Context*. London: Routledge, 2004.

Potter, Karl H. *Presuppositions of India's Philosophies*. Westport, CT: Greenwood, 1963.

Bibliography

Prickett, Stephen. *Romanticism and Religion: The Tradition of Coleridge and Wordsworth in the Victorian Church*. New York: Cambridge University Press, 1976.

Priest, Graham. *Beyond the Limits of Thought*. Cambridge: Cambridge University Press, 1995.

Putnam, Hilary. *Pragmatism: An Open Question*. Oxford: Blackwell, 1995.

Reid, Thomas. *Essays on the Intellectual Powers of Man*. Cambridge, MA: MIT Press, 1969.

———. *An Inquiry into the Human Mind on the Principles of Common Sense*. University Park: Pennsylvania State University Press, 1997.

Rorty, Richard. *Philosophy and the Mirror of Nature*. Princeton: Princeton University Press, 1979.

———. "Pragmatism, Davidson and Truth." In *Truth and Interpretation*, edited by Ernest LePore, 333–55. Oxford: Blackwell, 1986.

Rosemann, Philipp W. *Omne ens est aliquid*. Louvain-Paris: Peeters, 1996.

Rousselot, Pierre. *The Problem of Love in the Middle Ages: A Historical Contribution*. Translated by Alan Vincelette. Milwaukee: Marquette University Press, 2001.

Rowland, Tracy. *Culture and the Thomist Tradition after Vatican II*. London: Routledge, 2003.

Ruskin, John. "Fors Clavigera." In *The Works of John Ruskin*, edited by E. T. Cook and Alexander Wedderburn, 18:283–86. London: Allen, 1903–12.

———. *Modern Painters*. London: Allen, 1909.

———. "Of Queens' Gardens." In *Sesame and Lilies*, 105–46. London: Cassell, 1907.

———. "Of Kings' Treasuries." In *Sesame and Lilies*, 41–104. London: Cassell, 1907.

———. *Praeterita*. London: Rupert Hart-Davies, 1949.

———. *The Seven Lamps of Architecture*, London: Allen, 1894.

———. *Time and Tide by Wear and Tyne*. London: Allen, 1874.

———. "*Unto This Last*": *Four Essays on the First Principles of Political Economy*. New York: Wiley, 1881.

Sahlins, Marshall "The Spirit of the Gift." In *The Logic of the Gift*, edited by Alan D. Schrift, 70–100. London: Routledge, 1997.

Schiller, Friedrich. *Der Geisterseher: Aus dem memoires des Grafen von O*. Edited by E. S. Joynes. Boston: D.C. Heath, 1891.

Schmutz, Jacob. "La doctrine medievale des causes et la theologie de la nature pure (xiii^e–xvii^e)." *Revue Thomiste* (2001) 217–64.

Schopenhauer, Arthur. "Essay on Spirit Seeing and Everything Connected Therewith." In *Parerga und Paralipomena*, translated by E. F. J. Payne, 1:225–311. Oxford: Clarendon, 1974.

Schwäger, Raymund. *Der Wunderbare Tausch: Zur Geschichte und Deutu ng der Erlosu*. Munich: Kösel, 1986.

Schwartz, Regina M. *The Curse of Cain: The Violent Legacy of Monotheism*. Chicago: University of Chicago Press, 1997.

Schwarz, Jesse, editor. *The Subtle Anatomy of Capitalism*. Santa Monica: Goodyear, 1977.

Seabrook, Jeremy. *What Went Wrong? Working Peoples and the Ideals of the Labor Movement*. London: Gollancz, 1978.

Segundo, Juan Luis. *The Liberation of Theology*. Maryknoll, NY: Orbis, 1975.

Seneca "On Benefits" In *Seneca: Moral Essays*, vol. 3, translated by J. Basore. Loeb Classical Library. Cambridge: Harvard University Press, 1989.

Serres, Michel. *L'Incandescent*. Paris: Le Pommier, 2003.

Bibliography

Shaikh, Anwar. "The Poverty of Albegra." In *The Value Controversy*, edited by Ian Steadman and Paul Sweezy. London: NLB, 1980.

Shakespeare, William. *King Lear*. Edited by R. A. Foakes. London: Thompson, 2001.

Sharma, I. C. *Ethical Philosophies of India*. London: Allen and Unwin, 1965.

Sheehy, Maurice. *When the Normans Came to Ireland*. Cork: Mercier, 1998.

Smart, Ninian. "The Principles and Meaning of the Study of Religion." In *Concept and Empathy: Essays in the Study of Religion*, Ninian Smart, edited by Donald Wiebe, 194–206. New York: New York University Press, 1986.

Smith, Adam. *The Theory of Moral Sentiments*. New York: Kelley, 1966.

Spear, Jeffrey L. *Dreams of an English Eden: Ruskin and his Tradition in Social Criticism*. New York: Columbia, 1984.

Surin, Kenneth. "A Certain 'Politics of Speech': Religious Pluralism in the Age of the McDonald's Hamburger." In *Christian Uniqueness Reconsidered: The Myth of Pluralist Theology of Religions*, edited by Gavin d'Costa, 192–212. Maryknoll, NY: Orbis, 1990.

———. "September 11th and the Ethics of Violence." In *Strike Terror No More*, edited by Jon L. Berquist. St. Louis: Chalice, 2002.

———. *The Turnings of Darkness and Light*. Cambridge: Cambridge University Press, 1989.

Swedenborg, Emmanuel. *The Universal Human/Soul-Body Interaction*. Edited and translated by George F. Dole. London: Paulist, 1984.

Swinburne, Richard. *The Coherence of Theism*. Oxford: Oxford University Press, 1977.

Tawney, R. H. *The Acquisitive Society*. London, 1982.

———. *Religion and the Rise of Capitalism*. London: Murray, 1966.

Thompson, John B. *Studies in the Theory of Ideology*. Cambridge: Polity, 1984.

Trouillard, Jean. *La Mystagogie de Proclus*. Paris: "Les Belles Lettres," 1982.

Tuck, Richard. *Natural Rights Theories: Their Origin and Development*. New York: Cambridge University Press, 1979.

Tucker, Abraham. *The Light of Nature Pursued*. Cambridge: Cambridge University Press, 1831.

Tully, James. *A Discourse on Property: John Locke and His Adversaries*. New York: Cambridge University Press, 1980.

Turner, Bryan S. *Religion and Social Theory*. London: Hutchinson, 1982.

Van Dijk, S. J. P., and J. Halzelden Walker. *The Origins of the Modern Roman Liturgy: The Liturgy of the Papal Court and the Franciscan Order in the Thirteenth Century*. London: Darton Longman & Todd, 1960.

Vincent, K. Steven. *Pierre Joseph Proudhon and the Rise of French Republican Socialism*. London: Oxford University Press, 1984.

Weber, Max. "Politics as a Vocation," In *From Max Weber*, translated by H. H. Gerth and C. Wright Mills, 77–128. London: RKP, 1948.

———. "Science as a Vocation," In *From Max Weber*, translated by H. H. Gerth and C. Wright Mills, 129–58. London: RKP, 1948.

Webster, Richard. *Why Freud Was Wrong: Sin, Science, and Psychoanalysis*. London: HarperCollins, 1996.

Weiner, Annette. *Inalienable Possessions: The Paradox of Keeping-while-Giving*. Berkeley: University of California Press, 1992.

Wetzel, James. "Splendid Vices and Secular Virtues: Variations on Milbank's Augustine." *Journal of Religious Ethics* 32 (2004) 271–300.

Whately, Richard. *Introductory Lectures on Political Economy.* London: Fellowes, 1935.

Wheeler, Michael. *Ruskin's God.* Cambridge: Cambridge University Press, 1999.

Wiener, M. J. *English Culture and the Decline of the Industrial Spirit: 1850–1980.* Cambridge: Cambridge University Press, 1981.

Williams, Raymond. *Culture and Society: 1780–1950.* London, 1965.

———. *Towards 2000.* London: Chatto & Windus, 1983.

Williams, Rowan. "Liberation Theology and the Anglican Tradition." In *Politics and Theological Identity,* edited by Rowan Williams and David Nicholls. London: Jubilee Group, 1984. (Pamphlet).

———. "Newman's *Arians* and the Question of Method in Doctrinal History." In *Newman After a Hundred Years,* ed. Ian Kerr and Alan G. Hill, 263–85. Oxford: Oxford University Press, 1990.

———. *Writing in the Dust: After September 11.* Grand Rapids: Eerdmans, 2002.

Williamson, Tom. *The Origins of Norfolk.* Manchester: Manchester University Press, 1993.